Communal Identity in India

OXFORD IN INDIA READINGS
Debates in Indian History and Society

GENERAL EDITORS
- Sabyasachi Bhattacharya
- B.D. Chattopadhyaya
- Richard M. Eaton

Communal Identity in India

Its Construction and Articulation in the Twentieth Century

Edited by

BIDYUT CHAKRABARTY

UNIVERSITY PRESS

OXFORD

UNIVERSITY PRESS

YMCA Library Building, Jai Singh Road, New Delhi 110 001

Oxford University Press is a department of the University of Oxford. It furthers the
University's objective of excellence in research, scholarship, and education
by publishing worldwide in

Oxford New York
Auckland Cape Town Dar es Salaam Hong Kong Karachi Kuala Lumpur
Madrid Melbourne Mexico City Nairobi New Delhi Shanghai Taipei Toronto

With offices in

Argentina Austria Brazil Chile Czech Republic France Greece Guatemala
Hungary Italy Japan South Korea Poland Portugal Singapore Switzerland
Thailand Turkey Ukraine Vietnam

Oxford is a registered trade mark of Oxford University Press
in the UK and in certain other countries

Published in India
By Oxford University Press, New Delhi

© Oxford University Press, 2003

The moral rights of the author have been asserted
Database right Oxford University Press (maker)

First published 2003
Oxford India Paperbacks 2005

ISBN 019 567341 7

Typeset in Palm Springs 10/12 by Jojy Philip
Printed by Roopak Printers, Delhi 110 032
Published by Manzar Khan, Oxford University Press
YMCA Library Building, Jai Singh Road, New Delhi 110 001

To
Rimpi, Mini, Tinku, Barbie and Pavlo

Contents

General Editors' Preface

The DEBATES IN INDIAN HISTORY AND SOCIETY series is an exploration in the discourse of history to focus upon the diversity of interpretations. The series is intended to address widely debated issues in South Asian history (including contemporary history) through volumes edited by experts in the concerned area of study. The editor of each such volume is asked by the General Editors to select writings by various scholars focusing upon a debated theme and to write an introductory essay. This approach encourages the interrogation of history, as distinct from the common tendency to present history as a collection of 'given' facts. It brings to the reader the research base upon which scholars have founded their interpretative framework. And it opens up to the students bridge-heads into the terrain of research.

In this volume, the third in this series, a political scientist addresses the much debated issue of community identities as they evolved historically in course of the twentieth century in India. Bidyut Chakrabarty describes it as a 'contested terrain' and examines the debates inherent in the discourse concerning community identity with two objectives—to identify the conceptual and theoretical inputs, as well as the historical circumstances which moulded the discourse in the subcontinent in the last century. He demonstrates how the notion of syncretic nationalism was challenged, not only in ideological terms but also in the domain of praxis. Through representative pieces of writing selected by him, Chakrabarty explores the axis along which proponents of community identities conceptually articulated identity and deployed such constructions for purposes of aggregation and political mobilization. Since the number of such selected pieces is necessarily limited, the Introduction to the book offers an analytical survey of the vast literature on the subject to provide guidance for further readings.

Editor's Preface to the Paperback Edition

The volume is by no means an exhaustive study of the construction and articulation of communal identity in India. The primary aim is to provide a general introduction to the theme by incorporating excerpts/articles that will set the debate on identity in perspective. Given the limited number of essays that could be fitted into a single volume, several important writings have had to be left out.

Communal identity is a matter of serious debate and discussion in contemporary India. Not only is the definition of community controversial, the processes of its formation are equally debatable. Since modern era brings a multiplicity of influences that hinges on nation, region, gender, language, and citizenship, identity is always negotiated within a flow of multiple influences. While conceptualizing identities in such complex unfolding of circumstances one has to take into account the volatile context in which they are articulated and defined. In this respect, the volume is significant in setting both the circumstances and also the forms in which identity, communal identity in particular, is recast. Underlining the complex process of identity formation in a post-colonial society like India the volume has dwelled on various dimensions of debates concerning the articulation of identity and its manifestation in reality. The volume is unique not only for its focus on the sub-continent, but also for having raised issues which are relevant to similar situations elsewhere on the globe. By drawing attention to the debates on communal identity over a historical period, the volume is certain to contribute to an interesting debate on the nature identity and the processes of its formation in transitional societies.

The volume has three distinct parts. In the first part, the focus is on certain definitive texts articulating the contrasting viewpoints of Gandhi, Jinnah and Savarkar. The importance of this section lies in the fact that not only does it draw our attention to the specific view-points of India's nationalist phase it also identifies the distinct logic—whether 'sectarian' or otherwise—endorsing an identity that can either be exclusive or eclectic. Part II deals with both the particularis-tic and universalistic identities and also the tension in such a conceptualization. With remarkably varied contributions from re-nowned authors, the basic argument revolves around the complexity of identity formation in specific socio-economic and cultural con-texts. Dwelling on the gender question, the section also covers a relatively under-focused but very significant dimension of debates concerning identity. Instead of conceptualizing identity in mere black and white terms, this section has brought out the 'fuzzy-ness' of identity regardless of social, political, and cultural circumstances. The final part is about identity politics of the socio-politically mar-ginal sections of society. All these contributions in this section dwell on selected religious and ethnic groups. For obvious reasons, identity formation among the Indian tribes is always interesting to probe. Similarly, here ample focus was given to the relatively under-studied 'dalit' issues in articulating a specific dalit identity in contradiction with that of the caste Hindus. Despite the significance of assertive politics in contemporary India, the fact remains that identity always remains fluid and is thus constantly transformed due to internal socio-economic churning or outside thrusts or contestations. The principal argument that this volume makes draws on this fluid nature of communal identity in India and elsewhere with similar kinds of socio-economic and cultural milieu.

Acknowledgments

I am thankful to the series editors, especially Professor Sabyasachi Bhattacharya, for having chosen me for this volume. I owe a great deal to Ashok and Minu and Professor VS Parmar, my friends in a non-Social Science department for having sustained my creativity by innovative distractions as and when required. As usual, Professor Mohit Bhattacharya remains my inspiration. My children—Urna and Pablo—always provided emotional resources by shifting my attention away when I was stuck while articulating my thoughts. By descending at regular intervals, my best critic made me realize the importance of a family ambience in creativity. It would not be improper to record my appreciation for my mother who managed the children when I was struggling to meet the dateline. I fondly remember Bhuwan, Rajinder and Prakash for their assistance. Finally, I thank Oxford University Press for its support to the project.

Introduction

Bidyut Chakrabarty

Communal identity is a constructed category because communities continually recreate themselves. Its extent is however limited. The fluidity of communal identities is 'not completely free-floating but relates to conceptions of time and space, and the relationships between histories, cultures and biographies'.[1] That communal identity is open to change also confirms that identity is 'no more than relatively stable construction in an ongoing process of social activity'.[2] The act of redefinition is not a matter of accident. By highlighting some aspects of their distinctive character, setting themselves new goals, and redefining themselves in certain ways, communities articulate themselves differently. Yet, the redefinition of communal identity that they can effect is constrained by the past they inherit. In other words, the process of self-creation does not occur in a historical vacuum. A community's identity is therefore 'neither unalterable and fixed, nor a voluntarist project to be executed as it pleases, but a matter of slow self-recreation within the limits set by its past'.[3]

In the context of India's changed socio-economic and political environment, communal identity is a subject of agonized debate.[4] This is however not to suggest that there was complete unanimity regarding an individual's identity in the past. It is simply that it has become more difficult for us to establish who we are, given the plurality of identities that modernity has to offer.[5] Due to compulsions arising out of the struggle against the British for freedom, a concerted attempt was made to evolve a minimum set of shared identities for self-recognition along with the recognition of 'others'. This was certainly never quite as simple or stable. What is suggested here is that a limited range of acceptable rhetoric evolved in the context of the freedom struggle to fashion and sustain the anti-British political campaign as effectively as possible. The situation has however radically changed, and no longer can we consider the categories of identities to be sacrosanct. The primary aim of this volume is twofold: first, a brief account of the major theoretical inputs will acquaint readers with the issues that are relevant in meaningfully articulating the debates on the formation/construction of communal identity. As the process of recreation does not occur in a vacuum, the second equally important aim of the volume is, to link the debate with India's historical circumstances as far as possible.

Key Issues

As the modern era brings a multiplicity of identities that hinges on nation, region, class, gender, language, citizenship, identity is always negotiated within a flow of multiple influences. Our identity has therefore two dimensions, 'ontological' and 'epistemological', the former referring to who we are and the latter to who we think we are. The two necessarily shape each other and 'our identity is a constant and dialectical interplay between them'.[6] The modern subject is thus defined 'by its insertion into a series of separate value spheres, each of which tends to exclude or attempts to assert its priority over rest'.[7] Therefore, individual identity can never be permanently fixed, but is in constant flux due to socio-cultural and political reasons. One of the instances of a radical shift in identity was certainly the outcome of the divisive politics, articulated in the 1947 partition of the subcontinent of India. People's identities as Indians, as Asians or as members of the human race, writes Amartya Sen,

seemed to give way—quite suddenly—to sectarian identification with Hindu, Muslim or Sikh communities. The broadly Indian of January was rapidly and unquestioningly transformed into the narrowly Hindu or finely Muslim of March. The carnage that followed had much to do with unreasoned herd behaviour by which people, as it were, 'discovered' their new divisive and belligerent identities and failed to subject the process to critical examination. The same people were suddenly different.[8]

The contemporary debate on communal identity revolves around concerns in two complementary directions: first, as a community,

Indians 'lack' or have lost identity or that it has become diluted, eroded, corrupted, or confused. As a corollary to the first, the obvious concern is therefore how to retain, preserve, or strengthen the sense of identity. What is thus emphasized is a 'belief' that identity consists in being different from others and is invariably diluted by inter-cultural borrowing, that an identity is historically fixed, that it is the sole source of political legitimacy; that the state's primary task is to maintain it and that national identity defines the limits of permissible diversity.

The above argument does not appear to hold good as communal identity is not a substance but a cluster of tendencies and values that is neither fixed nor alterable at will, and needs to be periodically redefined in the light of historically inherited characteristics, present needs, and future aspirations. Identity is not something that 'we have'; rather, it is 'what we are'; It is not a 'property' but 'a mode of being'. Therefore, to talk of preserving, maintaining, safeguarding, or losing one's identity is to use misleading metaphors. By its very nature, a community's identity needs to be constantly reconstituted in response to broader historical dynamics, and it thus can never be an abstract, sterile, and essentialized category.[9] For instance, the contact with the West was a crucial factor in the transformation of modern Indian sensibilities. The contact 'was a catalyst: it triggered off responses and reactions which acquired life of their own'. The results, manifest in new ways of thinking, feeling, and action, 'were very different from their counterparts in the Indian past or the con-temporary western experience'.[10] It would therefore be self-defeating to view the Indian sensibilities in a stereotypical way. In the Indian context, both the appeal to shared experiences and the drawing of boundaries have, for instance, led frequently to fatal contradictions, probably because the appeal to shared experiences, though often meant as a device for inclusion, usually invoked the experiences of one particular group—upper castes, Hindus, the political élite—which was then made an authoritative marker of identity.[11] This obsession with boundaries has created divisions and often led to exclusions of significant communities and individuals that are as much a part of the cultural and historical fabric of India as anyone else.

Although, currently the term 'communal' usually refers to divi-sion on the basis of religion, particularly to the division between Hindus and Muslims, it had however different shades of meaning in north and south India in the pre-1947 period. For instance, in the south, the same term, in such phrases as 'Communal Award' or

'Communal G(overnment) O(rder)' referred to divisions between castes or groups of castes, particularly that between Brahmins and non-Brahmins. The caste quotas, codified in the 1927 Communal G.O., which laid down a scheme of reservation that lasted till 1947 when it was revised.[12] The Constituent Assembly sought to establish a polity in which individual and nation would prevail over caste and community though it concerned itself only with ascriptive social identities. Hence, caste, religion, and language were the only three distinct categories of communities that figured prominently in its deliberations.[13] Religion, caste, and language continue to remain probably the most effective in political mobilization in India even after decades of successful experiment with electoral democracy.

The Perspective

First of all, the construction of communal identity needs to be contextualized in the larger social processes in the nineteenth and twentieth centuries. The two most obvious ones are nationalism and democratization. In the context of the first, the question that deserves careful attention is why communities seek to redefine themselves as nations. What mark of distinctiveness does being a nation carry, and as a corollary what is denied to a community and its members if they do not claim their status as a nation? After all, the obsessive desire of communities to claim the status of nations or to define India as a nation is historically conditioned and textured. Simply expressed, after the late nineteenth century the claim to any form of self-government was shelved so long as it was not articulated as a claim to a nation. Colonial sovereignty in part rested upon denying that India was a nation. The nationalist project was not simply something that élites dreamt up to define others in their image, it also sought to identify and highlight the distinctive features of a population to justify its claim to nationhood.[14]

The belief in an Indian nationhood as a historical fact was based on Western models. However, it was also an emotionally charged reply to the rulers' allegation that India never was and never could be a nation.[15] The construction of even a vaguely defined Indian nationhood was a daunting task simply because India lacked the basic ingredients of a conventionally conceptualized notion of nation. There was therefore a selective appeal to history to recover those elements, transcending the internal schism among those who were marginalized under colonialism. Hence, a concerted and continuing effort was made to underline 'the unifying elements of the Indian religious traditions, medieval syscretism and the strand of tolerance and impartiality in the policies of Muslim rulers'.[16] Therefore the colonial milieu was an important dimension of the processes that led to a particular way of imagining a nation in a multi-ethnic context such as that of India which is so different from the perceptions based on Western experience. The political sensibilities of Indian nationalism 'were deeply involved in this highly atypical act of imagining'.[17]

Apart from colonialism, the major factor that contributed to the formation of a political entity that was India was the freedom movement. It is therefore no exaggeration to suggest that the Indian consciousness, as we understand it today 'crystallized during the national liberation movement', so national 'is a political and not a cultural referent in India'.[18] This perhaps led the nationalist leaders to recognize that it would be difficult to forge the multi-layered Indian society into a unified nation state in the European sense.[19] Accepting the basic premise about the essentially 'invented' nature of national identities and the importance of such factors as 'print capitalism' in their spread and consolidation, Partha Chatterjee challenges the very idea of 'modular forms', as articulated by Benedict Anderson[20] as it ignores the point that if modular forms are made available, nothing is left to be imagined.[21] It is true that the non-Western leaders involved in the struggle for liberation were deeply influenced by European nationalist ideas. They were also aware of the limitations of these ideas in the non-European socio-economic context due to their alien origin. Therefore, while mobilizing the imagined community for an essentially political cause they began, by the early twentieth century, to speak in a 'native' vocabulary. Although they drew upon the ideas of European nationalism, they indigenized them substantially by discovering or inventing indigenous equivalents and investing these with additional meanings and nuances. This is probably why Gandhi and his colleagues in the anti-British campaign in India preferred *swadeshi*[22] to nationalism. Gandhi avoided the language of nationalism primarily because he was aware that the Congress flirtation with nationalist ideas in the first quarter of twentieth century frightened away not only the Muslims and other minorities but also some of the Hindu lower castes. This seems the most pragmatic approach that could possibly be adopted in a country like India that was not united in terms of religion, race, culture and common historical memories of oppression and struggle. Underlying this lies the reason why Gandhi and his Congress colleagues preferred 'the relaxed and chaotic plurality of the traditional Indian life to the order and homogeneity of the European nation state [because they realized] that the open, plural and relatively heterogeneous traditional Indian civilization would best unite Indians'.[23] Drawing upon values meaningful to the Indian masses, the Indian freedom struggle developed its own modular forms that are characteristically different from that of the West. Although the 1947 Great Divide of the subcontinent of India was articulated in terms of religion,[24] the nationalist language drawing upon the exclusivity of Islam appeared inadequate in sustaining Pakistan following the creation of Bangladesh in 1971.

The second broader context that appears to have decisively shaped the quest for identity is democratization. What sort of 'unity' does democracy require. After all, it was a staple of liberal discourse (J.S. Mill, for instance) that democracy could not flourish in multi-ethnic societies. The important thing about Jinnah and Savarkar is that they were deploying precisely the liberal argument about why a unitary nationhood is necessary for a modern polity, providing too their own interpretations of how this was to be attained. Second, democracy complicates the problem of 'representation'. Who is being represented and on what terms? After all, the divisions between the Congress and Muslim League turned on issues of representation. This is however not to suggest that the state created two monolithic communities and that these came into being through 'the politics of representation' since the relationship between identity and democracy is far deeper and more complex than is generally construed in contemporary discourses on south Asia. Identity politics is about expressing one's agency and creating new forms of collective agency. In this sense, they are part of the democratic ferment, where people seek to fashion identities for themselves. This process will happen at all levels with a complicated relationship between the levels.

Furthermore, democratization is both inclusive and also exclusive. Inclusive because it unleashes a process to include people, at least theoretically, regardless of class, clan, and creed; it is essentially a participatory project seeking to link different layers of socio-political and economic life. Thus, as a movement, democracy, writes Charles Taylor, 'obliges us to show much more solidarity and commitment to one another in our joint political project than was demanded by the hierarchical and authoritarian societies of yesteryears'.[25] This is also why democratization tends towards exclusion that itself is a by-product of the need for a high degree of cohesion. Excluded are those who are different in so many ways. We are introduced to a situation where a communal identity can be formed or malformed in contact with significant 'others', generally projected with 'an inferior or demeaning image'.[26] For Charles Taylor, the politics of exclusion is a totally modern phenomenon as in the past

social recognition was built in to the socially derived identity from the very fact that it was based on social categories everyone took for granted. The thing about inwardly derived, personal, original identity is that it doesn't enjoy this recognition a priori. It has to Win it through exchange. What has come about with the modern age is not the need for recognition but the conditions in which this can fail. And that is why the need is now *acknowledged* for the first time. In pre-modern times, people didn't speak of 'identity' and 'recognition' not because people didn't have (what we call) identities or because these didn't depend on recognition, but rather because these were too unproblematic to be thematized as such.[27]

The 1919–21 Non Cooperation–Khilafat Movement is illustrative here. By a single stroke, both Hindus and Muslims were brought under a single political platform submerging, at one level, their distinct, separate identities. At another level, this movement is a watershed in the sense that these two communities remained separate as they collaborated as separate communities for an essentially political project.[28] Therefore, the politics of inclusion also led to exclusion of the communities that identified different political agenda to mobilize people.

In the imagination of communal identity, both these forces of nationalism and democratization appeared to have played decisive roles. Nationalism, as a concerted effort, was not merely unifying, it was also expansive in the sense that it gradually brought together apparent disparate socio-political groups in opposition to an Imperial power.[29] The character of the anti-British political campaign gradually underwent radical changes by involving people of various strata, region, and linguistic groups. The definition of nation also changed. No longer was the nation confined to cities and small towns, comprising innumerable villages which had thus far remained peripheral to the political activities generated by the feted struggle. Whatever the manifestations, the basic point relates to the increasing awareness of those involved in nation-building both during the anti-imperial struggle and its aftermath.

The construction of communal identity has thus to be viewed in the context of a search for nationhood and/or a distinct place within the nation by those who apparently felt threatened under the prevalent socio-economic configurations. For instance, one of the first serious attempts to establish Indian Muslims as a separate community was made by Rahmat Ali and others in 1933 on the ground that

our religion, culture, history, tradition, economic system, laws of inheritance, succession and marriage are basically and fundamentally different from those of the people living in the rest of India. The differences are not confined to the broad basic principles—far from it. They extend to the minutest details of our lives. We do not inter-dine; we do not inter-marry. Our national customs and calendars, even our diet and dress are different. [As] we possess a separate and distinct nationality from the rest of India where the Hindu nation lives and has every right to live. ..[w]e, therefore, deserve and must demand the recognition of a separate national status by the grant of a separate Federal Constitution from the rest of India.[30]

Although Rahmat Ali clearly articulated the demand for 'a separate national status' for the Muslims,[31] the 1916 Lucknow Pact appears to be the first well-defined attempt in this direction. In his earlier incarnation as the member of the Congress, Jinnah, underlining the distinctiveness of Muslims as a community, defended separate electorates for them as 'the only mechanism' to defuse inter-community tension. In an address to the Bombay Provincial Conference at Ahmedabad in October 1916, he thus warned his fellow Congressmen,

rightly or wrongly, the Muslim community is absolutely determined for the present to insist upon separate electorates. ... I would, therefore, appeal to my Hindu brethren that in the present state of [the] position they should try to win confidence and the trust of Muslims. ... If they are determined to have separate electorates, no resistance should be shown to their demands.[32]

Such Muslim leaders were clearly in favour of separate electorates for Muslims for the protection of their distinct identity vis-à-vis Hindus. It was therefore easier for the British to pursue a policy that culminated in the 1932 Communal Award. Underlining the distinct characteristics separating the two communities, the British premier Ramsay Macdonald, the architect of the Award, thus argued,

the contrast between these intermingled population[s] extends far beyond a difference in religious faith: differences of race and of history, a different system of law, widely opposed social observances and absence of intermarriage, set up barriers which have no analogy in the distinctions that may exist between religious denominations in any other existing state. It is not therefore altogether surprising that ... separate representation, namely the grouping of a particular category of voters in territorial constituencies by themselves, so as to assure to them an adequate number of members of their faith and race has been favoured.[33]

Not only was the Communal Award an institutional device to split the Indian communities on grounds of religion, but also an obvious choice for the British given the fact that 'Indian society ... is essentially a congeries of widely separated ... communities with divergencies of interests and hereditary sentiments which for ages have precluded common action or local unanimity'.[34] The 1932 scheme was the culmination of a series of efforts, undertaken by the Muslim leadership to ascertain both the distinctiveness of the community and thus the extent to which it was separate from Hindus. In the context of the new political arrangement following the adoption of the 1935 Government of India Act, the communal equations appeared to have significantly influenced the course of India's freedom struggle. A.K. Ghuznavi, a prominent Bengali Muslim leader, in his memorandum to the Simon Commission, 1927, emphasized that as the Muslim community was educationally, economically, and politically behind the Hindus of the province, 'further extensions of parliamentary institutions without proper and definite safeguards would place the Muslims permanently in a position subservient to the Hindus'.[35] Jinnah's Fourteen Points Programme was the formulation of the above in concrete terms. These points, inter alia, demanded that 'all legislatures in the country and other elected bodies should be reconstituted on the definite [principle] of adequate and effective representation of minorities in every province without reducing the majority of any province to a minority ... the representation of communal groups shall continue to be by means of separate electorate'.[36] Thus, what was articulated in the 1932 Communal Award was nothing other than a well-prepared design to strengthen the argument that as Muslims constituted a separate community with a distinct identity their claim for a separate status within British India appeared most logical.

Communal Identity and the Historical Context

Communal identity is multi-layered and diversely textured. However if one looks at the British perception of communal identity, as codified in the Communal Award, one is struck by its simplistic nature as it was defined exclusively in terms of religion. Hindus, Muslims and other religious groups were thus placed in neat compartments. The colonial rulers, by according equal status to all religions, placed these identities in competition with each other.[37] Recognizing that Hindus and Muslims were communities with completely different identities, the dominant political group, the Congress, devised a strategy of absorbing dissent in the form of the 1923 Bengal Pact[38] which sought to accommodate educated Muslims in the Hindu-dominated white collar world. What added a new dimension to the debate was the Poona Pact of 1932 which, for the first time, placed the backward classes, later classified as the scheduled castes in the 1935 Government of India Act, on the centre stage of Indian politics with a separate identity.[39] From now on, the scheduled castes invariably figured in any discussion on national identity. Although in Ambedkar, the scheduled castes found a powerful leader, they continued to remain a politically significant 'minority' with narrow social, economic', and political goals. As a dissenter bent on dismantling an oppressive caste system, Ambedkar therefore 'fulfilled the historical role of dissent not only to question hateful religious dogma but also unbuckle the consolidating ambitions of the secular state within which former religious orthodoxies are subsumed'.[40] What is striking is that despite having opposed Hindu orthodoxy, manifested in caste rigidity of which he was a victim, Babasaheb 'attempted to steer a steady course between a separatist, sectarian stance and unconditional citizenship function in which identity of untouchables would be subsumed within Hinduism'.[41]

The 1932 Poona Pact is the first well-articulated arrangement in which the scheduled castes were identified as a separate group within Hinduism; their emergence with a distinct political identity significantly influenced the provincial elections that followed the 1935 Government of India Act. Apart from the Muslims, who had already asserted their existence as a significant community, the ascendancy of the scheduled castes clearly indicated the complexity of the future course of Indian history, which had thus far glossed over the well-entrenched fragmented identities within both the Hindu and Muslim communities. Indeed, the Pakistan demand that drew upon Jinnah's 'two nation theory' hinges on the exclusive identities of both the principal communities, Hindus and Muslims, despite their shared socio-economic and politico-cultural milieu. For the nationalists, the idea of separate Hindu and Muslim identities had no natural basis and also the two communities were politically separated through the manoeuvres of communal forces and imperial *divide et impera*.[42] For Jinnah and the Muslim League, the demand for a sovereign and independent Muslim state was logical as Muslims constituted a separate nation with a different religious philosophy, social customs, and literature. Hindus and Muslims belong to two completely different civilizations which drew on conflicting ideas and conception.[43] The Hindu counterpart of this logic was articulated by V.D. Savarkar who argued strongly for a separate Hindu identity because of distinctive features separating Hindus from Muslims though its root can be traced back to the eighteenth century when English writing on India clearly provided the Hindus with a distinct identity 'in racial, religious and linguistic terms'.[44] One of the earliest attempts to organize the Hindus as a community was the Hindu Sabha that flourished in Punjab 'to protect the interests of the Hindus by stimulating in them the feelings of self respect, self help and mutual cooperation so that by a combined effort there would be some chance of promoting the moral, social and material welfare of the individuals of which the nation is composed'.[45]

Drawing upon the cultural differences vis-à-vis Hindus, Jinnah defended his argument for a separate identity for Muslims. Savarkar too sought to construct the Hindu identity by underlining the well-entrenched cultural distinctiveness of the Hindus. Defining a Hindu as a person 'who regards his land of Bharatvarsha from the Indus to the Seas as his fatherland as well as his holyland', Savarkar identified the following four specific features that distinguish them from Muslims,

(a) all those sects and panths, whether Vedic or non Vedic in their origin who consider 'Aa Sindhu' Hindustan [i.e. the Indian subcontinent from the river Sindhu to the Indian Ocean] as their fatherland and motherland; (b) all Hindus who belong to the same racial stock; (c) they all share a common cultural heritage; (d) those who regard *Bharat* as their *punyabhumi*, the sacredland (or, holyland in the sense Christianity uses the term holy).[46]

Thus, Savarkar's construction of Hindu identity is secular in that it is territorial (the land between the Indus to the Indian Ocean), genealogical (fatherland), and religious (holy land). The Hindu *Rashtra* was therefore more a territorial than religious nationalism because Hindus represented a cultural and civilizational synthesis which is more 'a secular–rationalist than an religio–fundamentalist construction'.[47] Notwithstanding its clarity, the formulation has elements that could be used for other purposes given the attempt at cultural homogenization of a multifaceted country like India. Furthermore, this particular conceptualization was also the outcome of a specific politico–ideological debate that unfolded with the propagation of the two nation theory by the Muslim League in the wake of the struggle for the freedom of India. Therefore, by highlighting the cultural aspect of Hindu *rashtra*, Savarkar, the ideologue of Hindu nationalism strove to provide an alternative to the construction of Hindus and Muslims as two separate nations.

In his formulation, Savarkar underlined the importance of a specific territory that he conceptualized through the notion of *pitribhumi* in the construction of a Hindu nation. He had then shifted his emphasis towards Hindu 'sentiments' or 'culture' by arguing that only among Hindus could *pitribhumi* and *punyabhumi* be identical. It was M.S. Golwalkar who sought to construct 'a Hindu society' on the basis of this argument, highlighting the cultural uniqueness of Hindus who 'have set up standards ... prescribed duties and rights [and] shed their blood in defence of the sanctity and integrity of the Motherland'.[48] While articulating the relationship between Hindus and non-Hindus in Hindustan, Golwalkar argued against the ideal of composite nationalism by saying that:

the non-Hindu people must either adopt the Hindu culture and language, must learn to respect and revere Hindu religion, must entertain no idea but the glorification of the Hindu nation, i.e. they must not only give up their attitude of intolerance and ingratitude towards this land and age-long traditions, but must also cultivate the positive attitude of love and devotion instead; in one word, they must cease to be foreigners or *may stay in the country wholly subordinated to the Hindu nation claiming nothing, deserving no privileges, far less any preferential treatment, not even citizen's rights* [emphasis added].[49]

What is unique in the exercise, undertaken by Golwalkar and those espousing the cause of Hindu nationalism is the consistent effort to pose Hindus as a community against its binary opposite, Muslims.[50] Projecting Muslims as 'traitors', Golwalkar thus proclaimed,

they have developed a feeling of identification with the enemies of this land. They look to some foreign lands as holy places. They call themselves Sheikhs and Syeds ... They still think they have come here to conquer and establish their kingdoms. So we see that it is not merely a case of change of faith, but a change in national identity. *What else is it if not treason, to join camp of the enemy leaving the mother nation in the lurch?* [emphasis added][51]

The Great Divide and After

The idea that Hindus and Muslims are completely different and hence the genesis of the 1947 Great Divide being located in Hindu–Muslim chasm, figured prominently in the debate on partition immediately after the transfer of power.[52] The importance of ascriptive identity was further reiterated in the Constituent Assembly which concerned itself only with ascriptive communities. Hence, religion, caste and language were the distinct categories of communities that were considered.[53] Within this perspective, the Constitution sought to protect the rights of those groups which are distinct in terms of socio-cultural characteristics.[54] The Indian nation state at Independence was therefore said to have been confronted with the task of evolving a 'unified' national and political society out of a formidable diversity of regional, religious, linguistic, and caste identities.

Although religious identity was the primary basis of aggregating people and identifying Minorities, the demand to demarcate regions on the basis of a shared language significantly influenced the process of identity formation since the 1905–8 Swadeshi movement in Bengal. The 1928 All Parties' Conference laid down the principles for the redistribution of provinces on a linguistic basis.[55] As an idea, the linguistic regrouping of Indian provinces was greatly appreciated[56] though its application was likely to complicate the scenario by creating a new majority and minority within a province. For instance, in those Oriya towns adjacent to Andhra Pradesh, Oriya and Telugu are both spoken though Oriya-speaking people constitute about sixty per cent of the population and hence the Telugus are reduced to the status of a minority. There are areas where the religious majority and minorities came to be redefined in the context of these regions.[57] Linguistic reorganization thus blurred the distinction between the majority and minority as people accustomed to seeing themselves as a majority could, in a different location, be reduced to a minority. Simultaneously with the movements for linguistic divisions of provinces, there began what is defined as 'the nativist movements' championing the demands of the 'sons of the soil'. Articulated by the Shiv Sena in Maharashtra and Asom Gana Parishad in Assam, these movements were swept to the top on a staggering wave of popular sympathy within a short period.[58] These movements also captured the aspirations for regional identity[59] that drew upon the linguistic, religious, and ethnic sentiments of the people concerned. In the movement to create greater internal cohesion and to more effectively press ethnic demands against rival groups, 'ethnic élites', argues Paul Brass, 'increasingly stress the variety of ways in which the members of the group are similar to each other and collectively different from others'.[60] By asserting the distinctive characteristics in relation to 'the other', the search for identity has led to a process of what S.J. Tambiah calls, 'the politicization of ethnicity', a contemporary phenomenon, associated mostly with 'politics of elections'. This political equation, Tambiah argues, 'combined with the capabilities of the mass media, radio, television, and print capitalism, so effectively deployed in our time, makes present day ethnic riot crowds very different from the crowds of pre-industrial Europe'.[61]

The gradual consolidation of the Sikh identity during the last two decades of the twentieth century underlines the significance of 'ethnicity' as a factor in the formation of a 'community' that transcends national boundaries. Several studies have firmly established that ethnicity is a broader concept as it accommodates within itself the unifying characteristics of both 'religious' and 'linguistic' distinctiveness.[62] Significance of ethnicity as a powerful determinant of identity is undoubtedly refreshing in the sense that it is a break with the past in which the basic thrust of the debate revolved around caste as the only ascriptive denomination of human existence in India. This is not to belittle the significance of caste as an important marker of one's identity, but to expand its viability as an explanatory tool in association with other factors.[63] Although caste continues to be significant in Indian politics, the centre of gravity appears to have shifted from the upper castes to those characterized as the Other Backward Castes (OBCs). Drawing upon the ascriptive identity, the 1980 *Mandal Commission Report* identifies 3,743 OBCs in India.[64] Apart from underlining the complexity of the caste system, the report is an eye-opener in its depiction of the intimate link between social backwardness and poverty that remained probably the most important issue in Indian politics following the acceptance of the reservation scheme enunciated by the Mandal Commission.

As the discussion so far has shown, the context appears to be a significant variable in the construction of both individual and communal identity. The formulation brings out the complexity of tribal identity in the subcontinent that clearly defies the stereotypical understanding of the phenomenon. As tribal identity is integrally linked to various other, and yet distant, 'external' influences, it is extremely difficult to capture the so-called general characteristics, applicable to different tribal groups, scattered all over the subcontinent. Moreover, the changing nature of tribal identity also captures the varied impact of the external world. In other words, an explanation for the different nature of tribal population in India has to be located in the socio-cultural milieu which they confront in their day-to-day interaction. Here lies a possible answer as to why the Jharkhandis prefer to be accommodated in the nation state while some of their north-eastern counterparts resort to armed struggle for an autonomous existence.[65] Therefore, rather than identifying the so-called 'fundamental' features of tribal identity, the process that is articulated in its shaping has to be contextualized to grasp the obvious impact of the prevalent socio-economic and political forces on identity.

Articulation of Debates

Communal identity is a contested terrain. There are, therefore, formulations and counter-formulations and thus , for historical reasons, there is no unanimity among those striving to grapple with the complex processes of identity formation in an absolutely volatile socioeconomic formation. What is significant here is the perception that there are two inter-related, though different, processes that need to be understood in any endeavour to understand identity and its manifestation in post-colonial societies: first, to begin with, identity in a semi-modern society, like the subcontinent of India, is essentially ascriptive as one's identity is permanently determined at birth. The ascriptive identity is, at best, a rough indicator of one's socio-economic status in a hierarchy-ridden structure of human existence. The second process is, therefore, equally crucial in grasping the metamorphosis in one's identity due to influences from within as well as outside the society in question. As the modern state is both totalizing and individualizing it contributes to a collective identity without however undermining one's ascriptive identity. Therefore the project that the state undertakes creates a totality, whether of Indians, Pakistanis, or Bangladeshis, at one level and nurturing, if not strengthening, religious, linguistic, ethnic, or caste identities of those constituting the totality at another.

Broadly speaking, there are the following major trends, articulated in the form of debates, in the conceptualization of communal identity in the subcontinent. Inspired by Gandhian and later Nehruvian notion of syncretic nationalism, the nationalist historians—R.C. Mazumdar, Bisheshwar Prasad, Amales Tripathi, B.R. Nanda among others[66]—grappled with the question of identity somewhat uncritically. Not only did they underplay the division between Hindus and Muslims, they also appeared to have totally ignored the internal schism within these communities. They were, it seems, swayed by the Nehruvian slogan of 'unity in diversity' and thus argued for the espoused cause of constructing a homogeneous nation, deliberately glossing over diversities, internal to the socio-cultural texture of the subcontinent. The goal was to 'set up a homogeneous, democratic, secular state ... [and] those devices which were hitherto employed to keep different sections of society apart have to be scrapped'.[67] Committed to the creation of a nation more or less in the European sense, evidently Nehru would argue for 'a national philosophy/national ideology [for] a new country like India whose people were divided on religious, ethnic, linguistic, and other grounds, economically undeveloped, socially static and politically inexperienced'.[68] The idea was to evolve a shared philosophy or ideology to unite 'the people' and provide them with a set of clearly defined 'goals' and `objectives'. A conservative thinker like Morris-Jones, who attributed the rise of India as a nation in the aftermath of freedom to Nehru's syncretic nationalism, thus argued that 'a shared citizen identity was perhaps best bonding principle for the nation that made its appearance following the trauma of partition'.[69]

Historically speaking, the debate highlighting the so-called nationalist version on collective identity in the subcontinent has two broad directions: on the one hand, were the communitarian nationalists in the Hindu Mahasabha and Muslim League, for whom the nation should be a political codification of a single cultural community. Hence, Partition in 1947 was most significant as it was instrumental in lending that critical variable without which the modern nation state was inconceivable, namely, the popular sacralization of territory.[70] There was, on the other, Gandhi and Nehru's syncretic nationalism that apparently drew upon the orientalist idea of India as series of discrete communities united under a larger, spiritual idea of the nation as a unifying whole. Nation was thus a supra-entity in which caste and community appeared peripheral. In the nationalist mode of conceptualization, the question of communal identity, as shown above, was discussed in a fairly simple form. Both Hindus and Muslims were generally considered as homogenous communities with those horizontal divisions, based on well-entrenched rituals and practices. The national movement, therefore, represented the interests of the people or the nation as a whole which also rendered the well-entrenched socio-economic and cultural divisions among those communities constituting the nation irrelevant.

Both the versions of the nationalist angle converged on one point, namely the assumption of nationhood, unproblematized, and uninterrogated, inherited from the Western experience and crystalized through the national movement. This idea of nationhood saw 'the nation as a homogenizing and unifying force, a linear narrative of universalization, as it were'[71] and hence it refused or failed to see nationhood itself as an extremely fragile and negotiated image.

The Marxist intervention in the debate has two broad directions. On the one hand, some of the leading Marxists[72] argued that India was not a nation because it had neither a common language nor a common culture. What India represented was in reality a combination of nationalities with different languages and cultures of their own.[73] Characterizing the nationalist movement as a bourgeois movement in which the bourgeoisie played a crucial role, they tended to equate or conflate the nationalist leadership with the bourgeoisie or capitalist class. The so-called classical position on identity does not appear to be conclusive as the argument is structured around categories that had no organic links with the complexity of a colonial state, like India. While explaining the nationality question in India, the later Marxists,[74] however, took into account the growth of the national movement and a historical process through which Indian people got formed into a nation or a people. During the freedom struggle, the nation remained a singular unit and was never counterposed to the diverse regional, linguistic, and ethnic identities in India. Therefore, the opposition to an imperial power led to national solidarity; a consciousness that glossed over other identities, such as caste, religion and region under specific circumstances in which the principal contradiction was between nationalism and imperialism.[75] For the Marxists, communalism also contributed to social cohesion and hence an identity, based on the appeals to the forms of oppression internal to Indian society or imaginary oppression, built around 'a culture' transmitting a specific kind of historical consciousness. It was therefore easier for both Gandhi and Jinnah to construct absolutely secluded Hindu and Muslim identities by drawing upon 'a past' selectively in the light of contemporary needs. Gandhi sought to build 'a patchwork alliance of existing communities, classes, and religious groups by basing himself on their existing states of consciousness.[76] Communal identity was thus historical and organically linked with the processes that also contributed to national identity. Thus, as Javeed Alam argues '[t]he inheritance of cultural givenness and intellectual preoccupations, in multiple ways of reconstruction, became an important ingredient in the making of ... Indian nation state. The freedom struggle, particularly in its later stages, with masses on the move had a great contribution to make in the refraction of the idea of India as a Nation'.[77]

The debate on communal identity has acquired a new dimension with the neo-traditionalist intervention. While pursuing the neo-traditionalist logic, John Broomfield, was probably the first to have identified the limitation of an approach that drew upon ethnic and religious homogenization in a multicultural society like India. In his study of Bengal, he demonstrates the extent to which the Hindus in Bengal were a fractured community though the élites (or *bhadralok* in his conceptualization) are an apparently homogenous group drawing primarily from the upper castes with an exclusive background in terms of both social and economic status.[78] While accepting *bhadralok* as a viable category of identity in colonial India, Anil Seal further defended the argument that despite well-defined divisions among the two major communities, the élites remained more or less a unified group presumably because of a uniform social and educational background. What is unique in Seal's study is the attempt to apply the formulation to India as a whole.[79] Following Seal's initiative, the leading members of the so-called Cambridge School, like Chris Bayly, David Washbrook, and Rajat Ray among others, elaborated the argument with evidence from Allahabad, Tamil Nadu, and Bengal respectively. As a conceptual notion, *bhadralok* underlines the peculiarity of the colonial élite that had a hegemonic role in the late nineteenth and early twentieth centuries when 'politics' was narrowly conceived with Calcutta, Bombay, and Madras as focal points. With the expansion of boundaries of politics especially following the rise of Gandhi, the conceptualization of identity based on *bhadralok* appeared hollow,[80] primarily because of the failure to articulate the anti-colonial movements at the grassroots that brought in several individuals, and later groups, with a completely different socio-economic background and also a different political perspective to the centre stage. Notwithstanding its limitations, the Cambridge School introduced a new dimension to the debate on identity by shifting our attention away from monolithic categories like Hindus and Muslims.

The debate, articulated in culturological terms, is a step forward in the discourses on communal identity. Instead of focusing on the stereotypical categories, like Hindus and Muslims, as the denominator of individual/collective identity, the 'cultural' argument is usually structured around those influences, real and imaginary, which play decisive roles in its actual construction.[81] Rafiuddin Ahmed's study of the Bengal Muslims is a well argued demonstration of the extent to which the contextualized Muslim identity was substantially different from that of the rest of South Asia. In his analysis of the nature of Muslims in Bengal, he has drawn our attention to those regional peculiarities, manifested in language and culture, that are crucial in the articulation of identity in colonial Bengal. Underlining the unique cultural ethos that drew largely on 'the Bengali way of life', Ahmad has critically explained the process that led to differentiating popular Islam in Bengal from the local cultural tradition, much of which came to be identified with Hinduism and polytheism and thus as anti-Islamic.[82] Thus the Bengali Muslims were a completely different socio-cultural entity that was neither purely Islamic nor pan-Indian. Similarly, caste identity for the scheduled castes of Bengal was devoid of those stereotypical characteristics as it coexisted with broader—religious, class, and national identities. At a particular historical juncture, one might take precedence over others, but this does not imply that competing identities were completely displaced or eliminated. The notion of community and its boundaries were constantly shifting, depending on their varying responses to changing historical circumstances and ideological influences. For instance, the involvement of the scheduled caste peasants, once swayed also by the Hindu Mahasabha for greater Hindu militancy and its demand for a separate Hindu homeland in the more class-oriented tenants and sharecroppers' movement under the Communist leadership 'clearly showed that it was not caste identity alone that determined their worldview and that their identity could at times become subservient to other overlapping identities of nation, religion or class'.[83]

The same process appeared to have influenced the construction of Sikh identity in the late nineteenth century in which the role of religion was marginal. While exploring the process, Harjot Oberoi emphatically argues that Sikhism in its 'pure' form had nothing to do with the way people experienced reality, their mode of imagination, and the vehicle through which knowledge was represented in the Sikh tradition. He further elaborates that for the greater part of the last century, Sikh identity was not simply an extension of the religious tradition but embedded in a complex idiom of kinship, patron–client relationships and asymmetrical reciprocity. Therefore, he concludes that universal religious communities, as has often been the case in Europe, do not appear to be significant in grasping identity in a society that confronted a completely alien civilization in the wake of colonialism.[84] This has been corroborated in a recent study on the Jat identity demonstrating the extent to which the Jats have succeeded in negotiating with a variety of options arising out of a heterogeneous society like that in India. When confronted with colonial

modernization, they 'discarded some aspects of their existing popular culture and at the same time, readily refashion certain other
idioms, symbols and traditions that were rooted in the peasant–
pastoral culture'.[85] Also as the process that was underway brought
about a radical shift in the articulation of *kaum* (the community), the
Jat identity was not entirely an invention.

Colonialism separated Hindus and Muslims by its strategy of
divide and rule. What accounts for the gradual consolidation of these
two rival blocs was probably the logic internal to these communities
which, of course, had its root in the larger socio-economic and political environment. For instance, the rise and consolidation of Hindu
blocs in the 1920s in Bengal drew largely upon the 'communal common sense of dying Hindu'. The Hindu demographic strength was
certain to decline, runs the argument, in view of the proliferation of
Muslims for reasons connected with their social system. The fear of
being outnumbered by Muslims appeared to be an effective instrument for those 'engaged in the mobilization for an exclusive Hindu
constituency'.[86] Equally important was the process that led to the
construction of a Muslim bloc and consequently the othering of Hindus. With their economic prosperity at the grassroots through jute
cultivation, Muslims gradually emerged as key players in 'high politics' and demands were placed for reservation of seats for the community in educational institutions and government employment. As
the progress of a people is evidenced 'by the increase of wealth and
knowledge',[87] several leading Muslim intellectuals of various districts constantly underpinned the necessity of material improvement
for their community. Islam had a role to play and thus Usman, the
model farmer in *Adarsha Krishak* 'calls out the *azan* when he goes to
work in his fields',[88] indicating the commitment to community imperatives along with dedication to profession.

The subaltern school articulates the most recent intervention in the
debate on communal identity. Challenging the stereotypical description of Hindus as a majority and the Muslims as a minority, the
subaltern school argues that they are historically constituted and
thus subject to change. For instance, Muslims were not a minority in
prepartition Bengal, Punjab, Sindh, or Malabar. Moreover, Muslims
were a majority in these areas only in the minimal, numerical sense in
which Hindus were a majority in all-India statistics. Muslims were a
minority politically only on those issues that separated Muslims as a
whole from Hindus as a whole, and such issues were few and far
between. For the rest, they were peasants, artisans, and labourers,

Bengalees, Punjabis, and Malayalees, men and women, and the like. On many political issues, then, Muslims could think and act as Hindu/ Sikh/or even Christians could think and act, as parts of other communities: those of region, caste, sect, occupation, or gender. Underlining the communitarian logic, these writers with a subaltern perspective, insist that each of us, as an individual, develops an identity, talents, and pursuits in life only in the context of a community. In other words, the identity of an individual is invariably connected with the community as the community is what determines and shapes individuals' nature. Hence, in their writings, the focus is primarily on the fragments of Indian society:[89] the smaller religious and caste communities, tribals, industrial workers, and activist women's groups, all of which might be said to represent a different world-view which is invariably at variance with that of the mainstream (Brahminical) tradition.[90]

So overwhelming is its presence that community consciousness always prevails over communal consciousness. As Dipesh Chakrabarty has shown, poverty gave the jute mill workers a sense of identity that was so well-entrenched that '[e]ven when issues like religion divided them, there still remained, in their own minds, a fundamental distinction between themselves as "poor people" and others who seemed well-off'.[91] For the jute workers, religion may have been a cementing factor, as was evident in riots in jute mill areas, but its influence in structuring the mentality was marginal. What is perhaps crucial was their identity as a part of the community, which drew its sustenance from 'an anti-employer and hence potentially uniting mentality' as against 'a religious and potentially divisive outlook'.[92] Therefore the community survived without serious distortions in its texture not because of 'primordial ties' among the jute workers but because of the peculiar circumstances of the labour market in Bengal, especially in the aftermath of the great depression. The pattern is evident in Benaras where, argues Nita Kumar, the existential experiences of the Hindus and Muslims, based on their culture of everyday life, was what constituted their identity. '[i]dentity in Benaras has not [therefore] been communal in the past, nor is it progressively becoming so. It is based rather on occupation, social class and a city's tradition'.[93] Similarly while describing the weavers in Benaras, Abdul Bismillah in his novel, *Jhini Jhini Bini Chadaria*, focused on the underlying thread linking the weavers regardless of religion as a community which 'is, in many different ways, different from other communities in the world'.[94]

The same argument is advanced by subaltern historians while explaining the peasant movements. Partha Chatterjee has, for instance, shown that peasantry in Bengal always rose against an external authority—be it the zamindars or the state—as a community, primarily because it was rooted in an agrarian economy which clearly demarcated the boundary between the oppressor and the oppressed. Therefore, whatever the variation in the specific social constitution of a peasant community and also the symbols and beliefs governing the relations of the community with the 'outside' authority, when a community acts, argues Chatterjee, 'collectively the fundamental characteristics are the same everywhere'.[95] What is common to both Chakrabarty and Chatterjee is the conceptualization of community which itself is a significant marker of a collective identity without submerging its distinctive characteristics in the amorphous structure, called nation. What distinguishes Chatterjee from Chakrabarty is the formulation that peasant–communal consciousness undergoes radical changes in view of the linkage with the organized world of politics which designates one movement as 'Gandhian', the other 'terrorist', and yet another 'communalist'.[96] It would therefore be wrong to conceive identity as permanently fixed given the well-defined characteristics of the community in question as its texture is certain to undergo metamorphosis in response to what structures the organized world of politics.[97]

The communitarian logic is further reinforced in the subaltern approach to gender identity. In the 'fragmented' nation, women are said to constitute its 'inner' or 'spiritual' domain, different from the 'outer or material' domain which is constituted in the economy, science, technology, and statecraft in which the West proved its superiority and the East succumbed. The world is external, the domain of the material, while the home represents one's inner spiritual self, one's true identity. The world is the domain for the pursuit of material interests and is typically the domain of the male. The home, in its essence, 'must remain affected by the profane activities of the material world—and woman is its representation'. Therefore one gets 'an identification of social roles by gender to correspond with the separation of the social space of *ghar*[home] and the *bahir*[world]'.[98] The argument is further extended by pointing out that as the European power was superior in the material domain 'the subjugated must learn the modern sciences and arts of the material world from the West in order to match their strength and ultimately overthrow the colonizer'.[99] In the inner domain however, no encroachment by the colonizer must be allowed as this would be 'tantamount to anni-hilation of one's very identity'.[100] Thus it is not surprising that one of the recurring themes in the contemporary literature was 'the threat-ened westernisation of women'. Besides, the nation was always most reluctant to accept the role of the colonial state in reforming women's lives. Such a stance, the argument follows, is logical and the reason is located 'in the refusal of nationalism to make the women's question an issue of political negotiation with the colonial state'.[101] Therefore the women's identity was largely defined in relation to a new patriar-chy that drew upon the selective interpretation of 'cultural tradition' of an imagined nation.[102] The subaltern 'resolution' of the women's question appears to be too narrow to actually comprehend the dra-matic changes in the so-called inner domain, presumably because of its overemphasis on an 'entrenching' religio–cultural essence in which gender is conceptualized. By constructing the 'spiritual' as abso-lutely insulated from the economy and society, the formulation tends to impute a fixed, an unchanging and fundamental character to this domain which is difficult to accept given its constantly changing nature due to obvious political engagement in, what is defined as, the material world. The argument is thus theoretically 'myopic' and ideologically 'restricting' as the subalternity of women 'is rendered invisible or unimportant, while their patriarchal, brahminical and male oppressors take on a "subaltern" hue and the domination of indigenous women becomes a blueprint of hegemonic success'.[103] As a critical change is equated to colonial discourse, 'the credo of Hindu revivalists becomes the political unconscious of the nation and naturalises misogyny propelled by its own cultural and political logic'.[104]

Whatever the assessment of the critics, the subaltern intervention in the debate is refreshing and intellectually stimulating for having placed women as a community in juxtaposition with other compet-ing communities within the framework of a loosely defined nation which itself had a doubtful existence. That women were invisible and their identities were negatively portrayed through a vast silence[105] provide an adequately informed insight regarding their existence or otherwise in the nationalist discourse. The debate in India over a uniform civil code that began in the early 1980s has however posed the gender question more sharply than ever.[106] It has brought into sharp focus the contradiction between the claims of community iden-tity of Muslims and claims to other kinds of identity, namely, gender. The Muslim collective identity was therefore counterposed to the

gender identities of Muslim women. The legal guarantee of a separate civil code for the Muslims is a clear refutation of rights of Muslim
women who are equally entitled to basic citizen's rights, as protected
by the constitution of India, and thus the Muslim woman's community identity is privileged over her identity as a citizen. Therefore,
romanticizing the community is bound to undermine the sovereignty
of its individual constituents as self-defining and self-determining
subjects. The other related significant issue concerns the nature of the
Muslim women community which is not as homogeneous as it appears.[107] There is a sharp contradiction between their religious and
gender identity and assertion of one identity is a clear violation of the
other. Both as a member of a community and as a woman, the Muslim
female citizen 'is [thus] doubly disadvantaged'. The source of her
oppression, material and ideological, may also be, argues Niraja
Gopal Jayal, 'mutually reinforcing, as [and] when the state and patriarchy act in tandem'.[108]

Similarly, with direct participation of women in movements championing *Hindutva*,[109] the feminist discourse has to take into account
the broader socio-political and economic environment that obviously
provides a different perspective in which gender issues are likely to
be perceived differently. Whatever the underlying assumptions, these
endeavours, by privileging the identity of women over all other
identities, have, in effect, brought important socio-political institutions from the family to the state into question.

Given the multiplicity of identity schemes that emerged in India in
the form of the so-called 'modern' influences, unleashed by the onset
of colonialism, communities generally became 'fuzzy' in nature.[110]
The Census had, therefore, provided 'a disciplinary role in the
formation and freezing of identities along the lines of caste and
religion',[111] an exercise that intended to make 'objective to the Indians
themselves their culture and society',[112] became crucial in segregating the communities in terms of their distinctive socio-economic and
cultural characteristics. This is what contributed to 'the deadly politics of community', argues, Arjun Appadurai, although he recognizes the extent to which 'the idea of essentialized and enumerated
communities ... must have varied according to various dimensions of
the colonial subjects in India: her gender, her closeness to or distance
from the colonial gaze, her involvement with or detachment from
colonial politics, her participation in or distance from the bureaucratic apparatus'.[113] In their critique of the nation state, the leading
exponents of the communitarian school draw heavily upon the

homogenizing character of the nation state that attempts to homogenize people in terms of the identity of equal citizenship, thus not allowing for the possibility of cultural identities developing outside the problematic of nationalism.[114] The communitarian perspective has also provoked severe criticism from among those who hold nation as the basic unit of analysis in which communities are not as important as they are projected to be. A nation's history is an adequate mode of understanding the communities even without privileging community and class over nation. The technique, as fine-tuned by the subaltern historians, 'is [as much] an attack on the focus on the history of nation' as on the study of communities simply because it glosses over the dialectics of communities and nation in the context of a given socio-economic and cultural milieu.[115]

The discussion, pursued so far, has clearly shown that essentializing 'socio–cultural' identity is not only theoretically misleading but also historically flawed. Identity is constructed and reconstructed through a complex process of contestation. Religion is, for instance, a powerful ideological force that may, under specific circumstances, contribute to the construction of a political community. Its capacity of binding people, divided on various other counts, however, appears ephemeral as soon as identity is sought to be crystallized in terms of markers other than religion. Not only is this evident in India, but has also been clearly demonstrated in the socio-economic evolution of Pakistan and Bangladesh. However, at the outset the debate on communal identity in Pakistan drew on the religious chasm in the subcontinent, and other obvious socio-economic and cultural cleavages separating people from one another even while endorsing the same religious faith, were thus conveniently ignored. In other words, there was no scope in such a debate, articulated in a somewhat unilinear fashion for obvious political compulsion, to even underline the prevalence, leave alone conceptualization, of cultural communities as against an hegemonic and hegemonizing political community.

The orthodox version simply endorsed the two nation theory. As late as 1972, E.L. Hamza characterized the Muslims as 'a homogeneous national individuality [which was possible because] the Muslims developed their culture in an Islamic way and preserved their racial identity by a complete avoidance of intermarriage with their non-Muslim neighbours'.[116] Attributing the homogeneous Muslim identity to 'the cultural uniformity', the argument appears to be derived from a deliberate 'misconception' of Pakistan's socio-cultural reality which was as fragmented as India's. Even the meanings attached to Islam in religious and cultural practices at the locality level differed in essentials from its state-sponsored monolithic version. That Muslims are homogeneous has further been defended from a rather 'conservative' interpretation of Islam where the factual heterogeneity of the community[117] is underscored. Thus, it is argued that,

[p]lacing emphasis upon people and their homogeneity, Islam has oriented Muslims to give first consideration to the Muslimness of a person, rather than the country of his origin, and this especially because Islam recognises no bar of colour, birth or race. The moment a person becomes a Muslim he joins the community of the faithful.[118]

Based on the official discourse of inclusionary nationalism, the above argument is too simplistic to articulate the complexity of identity formation in Pakistan that was equally in ferment due to contestations drawing upon regionally based cultural beliefs and practices or economic and political interests even within 'an Islamic nation'. Ayesha Jalal therefore argues that

the relative autonomy of culture at the level of local and regional social formations has not only contested a reductionist state ideology based exclusively on religion but sought to affirm difference and distinctiveness in the politics of linguistic regionalism or sub-regionalism, the highest possible common denominator available in a state that has been federal in form but unitary and undemocratic in spirit.[119]

Apart from the Shia–Sunni and Muhajir–non-Muhajir identities, Pakistan is a community of communities, as Jinnah himself was reported to have stated in a speech delivered to the Pakistan Constituent Assembly in 1947.[120] Islam can, therefore, no longer be treated as a static point of reference. Constructed across 'different, intersecting and antagonistic sites, discourses and practices',[121] Pakistani identities are constantly in the process of making and unmaking. The fluidity of identity is what constitutes the basic direction of debates.[122] No longer can we assume the existence of a single and inalienable Muslim identity, argues Akbar S. Zaidi.[123] What Islam failed to do in the North-Western Frontier Province, for instance, was accomplished by Pashtu, the shared language of the Pakhtuns or Pathan tribes which now makes for a stronger sense of regional–cultural identity despite internal differentiation along lines of clan. Here language, certainly a powerful cementing factor, has never become an ideology against the centre probably because of 'the absence of immediate threat from a rival linguistic community'.[124] The situation was totally different in the erstwhile east Pakistan which, comments Badruddin Omar, declined to submerge its distinctive cultural identity within the national discourse when an attempt was made to impose Urdu there.[125] The Muslim identity was relegated to irrelevance and was replaced by a well-crafted Bengali identity drawing upon the distinctive cultural and regional characteristics of which language was perhaps the most important aspect. It is not therefore surprising that during the freedom struggle the issue of cultural alienation was what galvanized the masses into action despite adverse consequences. Conveying the long-standing cultural alienation, the Bengalees suffered under the Pakistani *junta*, Shamsur Rahaman, the renowned poet of Bangladesh, wrote:

> Freedom:
> you are Tagore's ageless poetry
> his immortal songs.
> Freedom:
> you are Kazi Nazrul, wild-haired sage
> trembling with the thrill of creation,
> Freedom:
> you are that meeting at the martys's monument
> on the eternal twenty-first of February*.[126]

* On 21 February 1952, students of Dhaka University protesting the language policy of the government of Pakistan were gunned down by the police.

The argument, structured around language-inspired sentiments, has counterposed Bengali identity to Urdu-dominated west Pakistan Muslim identity. The Bengali identity was sought to be privileged over other ethnic identities following the emergence of Bangladesh as an independent nation that was considered a threat to those socio-economic groups with distinct languages, histories and culture. Therefore, the present debate on identity in Bangladesh is clustered around issues arising out of the concern for sustaining the identities of various ethnic communities as against the homogenizing Bengali identity. The major intervention is by Amena Mohsin[127] who has shown, while seeking to explain the identity of the Chittagong Hill people or *Chakmas*, the significance of *jhum* cultivation in constructing a counter identity where *jhum* constitutes not only a mode of cultivation but also a way of life. Based on *jhum*, the Chakmas are being united under what they define as 'Jumma nationalism' that has 'infused the Chittagong Hill people with a sense of pride in their past, their system and values which have been the objects of repeated onslaughts by outsiders'.[128] The construction of a powerful 'other' is

what sustains as well as strengthens the emotional boundary between the 'homogenic' and 'marginal' socio-economic identities. It is
not therefore surprising that the unique socio-cultural features of the
Chakmas are usually shown to have been undermined and occasionally rendered extinct primarily due to the state-sponsored
hegemonizing Bengali identity, as the following poem by Kavita
Chakma unambiguously articulates:

> Why shall I not resist !
> Can they do whatever they please ...
> Turn settlements into barren land
> dense forests into deserts
> mornings into evenings
> turn fertile into barren.
> Why shall I not resist!
> Can they do whatever they please...
> Estrange us from the land of our birth
> enslave our women
> blind our vision
> put an end to creation.
> Neglect and humiliation cause anger
> the blood surges through my veins
> breaking barriers at every stroke
> the fury of youth pierces the sea of consciousness
> I become my whole self ... why shall I not resist.[129]

As the debates on the subject, in their various articulated forms, have
clearly demonstrated, communal identity in the subcontinent is constructed through a complex process of contestation in which the local
context is extremely significant. Drawing upon the debates in Pakistan and Bangladesh, it can thus be safely argued that an apparent
religious homogeneity does not necessarily preclude the importance
of other factors in shaping other competing socio-cultural identities
downplaying, if not undermining, 'monolithic' Islam. Examination
of 'identity narratives'[130] also reveals that they are instruments of
transformation. Behind the projected homogeneity and permanence
of communal identity, there are processes seeking to articulate competing identities largely on the basis of 'fear' and 'anxiety' of being
swallowed by the dominant/majority community. The existence of a
'feared' 'other' emerges as an additional justification for the con-
tinual assertion of uniqueness. The process of constructing identity
by 'othering' 'encourages', as Parekh maintains, 'the community to

pay far more attention to how and how much it differs from the others than to whether or not it is true to itself'.[131] Underlying this 'tension' are the values and moral aspirations, which sustain distinct socio-cultural identity of the community. Narratives thus bring about changes—in the individuals, in their cultures, in the groups they form and in the way, they act. Identity narratives—produced through a dialectics of communal affectivity and the specific socio-economic and cultural context—introduce new interpretations of the world in order to transform it.

Concluding Remarks

A thorough scan of the debates reveals two fundamental points: first, the communal identity is imagined and constructed. But that does not mean that it is unreal or it can be constructed without constraint and contestation. On the contrary, the 'constructionist' view clearly suggests the role of several socio-political and cultural elements—language, past history, tradition, landscape, monument, and so on—in articulating identity in a particular way. Identity grows out of a constant dialogue between the past and the present in which each interrogates and illuminates the other. Communal identity is therefore both given and constantly reconstituted. Secondly, the survey of the debates also underlines the theoretical limitation of an 'essentialistic' invocation of identity. By critically interrogating the 'totalising' dimension of the nationalist project—where a single entity, called nation, always prevails over other forms of identity, the discussion has also shown the importance of underlying cognitive and ethical claims which are invariably lodged in and emanate from contradictory social locations. In other words, identities are not singular but multiple and thus difficult to capture on a single axis.

So, communal identity is neither monolithic nor totalising. Rabindranath Tagore was perhaps the first to emphatically argue against this view that identity in the subcontinent was uni-dimensional. Challenging the concept of 'nation' as it undermines the multi-layered Indian identity, Tagore reminds us of the combined role of the 'little' and 'great' traditions in shaping what he loosely defined as the Indian nation.[132] India's diversity, Tagore felt, was her 'nature [and] you can never coerce nature into your narrow limits of convenience without paying one day very dearly for it'.[133] Not only 'have religious beliefs cut up society into warring sections ... social antagonisms [between Hindus and Muslims] have set up impassable barriers every few miles—barriers which are guarded night and day by forces wearing the badge of religion'.[134] For Tagore, the gulf between the communities was largely due to 'the cultural forces', released by British colonialism that 'fractured the personality of every sensitive exposed Indian and set up the West as a crucial vector within the Indian self'.[135] As India's social system got distorted, '[l]ife departed', argued Tagore, 'from her social system and in its place she is worshipping with all ceremony the magnificent cage of countless compartments that she has manufactured'.[136] While Tagore was critical of artificial division among the communities, created and consolidated by forces supporting colonialism, he was equally alarmed by the drive to gloss over India's diversity for the sake of creating a nation-state as in Europe since it would strike at the very foundation of a civilizational society that flourished in India over the centuries.[137]

Manifested in an ideological design, described as Hindutva, the recent endeavour to redefine and restructure identity in India in order to construct a new homogeneous monolithic Hindu identity has posed the issue of communal identity in a manner that bears considerable resemblance to that in Germany and Canada. The construction of such an overarching homogeneous identity not only debunks the historical and civilizational complexities but also reduces the entire diversity of sects and cults within and other distinctive multifaceted aspects of India's plural social personality into 'straitjacketed monolithic Hinduism'.[138] Hindutva is thus a deliberate ideological construction to erase multiple identities within the category of caste, sect, region, gender, class, or belief. The idea itself is a contradiction of the pluralistic personality of a country like India 'that has had millennia of flourishing diversity in the form of nurturing different religious—what is important to emphasize—diverse non-religious beliefs'.[139] In other words, the redefinition of Hinduism as a monolithic and uniform religion is conceptually indefensible because it is essentially a mosaic of distinct cults, deities, sect, and ideas ranging from animistic spirits, cults to others based on subtle philosophical concepts.[140] Furthermore, given the increasing proliferation of many other revivalist ascriptive identities around language, caste, tribe, and region, the drive for the construction of a Hindu identity drawing solely on religion seems merely to be a ripple of history that was formed to inevitably disappear.

Notes

1. W.A. Radcliffe and A. J. Westwood, *Remaking the Nation: Place, Identity and Politics in Latin America*, Macmillan, London, 1999, p. 24.

2. Craig Calhoun, *The Question of Class Struggle: Social Foundations of Popular Protest in Industrializing England*, Chicago University Press, Chicago, 1982, p. 14.

3. Bhikhu Parekh, 'The Concept of National Identity', *New Community*, vol. 21, no. 2, 1995, p. 264.

4. Indian democracy, writes a commentator, seems inexorably to be moving 'towards the politics of identity which represent and uphold the interests of specific groups based on religious, ethnic, caste, linguistic and minority identities. This appears to be the almost natural outcome of a democratic process. As people belonging to different groups become conscious of their identities and of their rights and aspirations, they form political parties and try to influence the political process to serve their group interests'. Arjun Sengupta, 'Identity Politics: Narrow Interests to Grand Causes', *The Times of India*, Delhi, 1 April 2000.

5. As the individual in pre-modern states had limited access to a range of identities in comparison to modern world traditional ideologies could provide an all-encompassing range of identities, where individuals were 'fixed' in a particular position. The ideology of Hinduism through ages, for instance, offered such an all encompassing ideology. Castes were consecrated through access or denial of access to privileges and rituals, and this was recognized by a variety of authoritative others. What we need to recognize is that this was politically contextualized and facilitated by the power arrangements of the pre-modern state. Neera Chandhoke advances and elaborates this argument in her, *Beyond Secularism: The Rights of Religious Minorities*, Oxford University Press, Delhi, 1999, pp. 29–33.

6. Bhikhu Parekh, 'National Identity in a Multicultural Society', in Mohmmad Anwar and Ranjit Sondhi (eds), *From Legislation to Imagination*, Macmillan, London, 1999, p. 197.

7. A.J. Cascardi, *The Subject of Modernity*, Cambridge University Press, New York, 1992, p. 3. For Cascardi, the tension and incommensurability among various spheres of values at the extreme where they claim autonomy appear not as external difficulty for the individuals but as a series of contradictions within the subject self. It is therefore obvious that in circumstances where individuals had little access to the wider political arena and even less access to other identities, the situation appears less complicated than those in which individuals constantly confront separate, if not conflicting, spheres of values.

8. Amartya Sen, *Reasons Before Identity*, OUP, New Delhi, 1999, p. 20.

9. Critical of the orientalist discourse seeking to essentialize the so-called fundamental characteristics of Indian society, Ronald Inden argues that

European subjugation of India was facilitated by European-trained writers who successfully defined Indian society in terms of various essences that kept India essentially ancient and passive. Inden, speaking of the cognitive categories which the tradition of Indology has generated, gestures towards the political flaws of that particular intellectual vision which freezes the temporal and the spatial dimension of Indian society. It is true that the contributions of the Indologists who exercised a powerful hold on the socio-logical imagination have done much to capture and freeze Indian society in terms of her essences such as caste, Hinduism, villages, and sacred kingship. Ronald Inden, *Imagining India*, Basil Blackwell, Oxford, 1990.

10. Tapan Raychaudhuri, *Perceptions, Emotions, Sensibilties: Essays on India's Colonial and Post-Colonial Experiences*, OUP, New Delhi, 1999, p. 4.

11. This is what made the basis of Indian nationalism so fragile. G. Aloysius thus argues that '[i]n the absence of actual change within society, in our case, the destruction of the Brahminic social order, nationalism's relation to the potential nation becomes ambiguous at best. Here the process of *invention* is displaced by one of *prevention*: when imagination is limited to a minority of the elite, it turns out be an illusion to the masses—the nation' [emphasis added]. G. Aloysius, *Nationalism Without a Nation in India*, OUP, Delhi, 1997, p. 225.

12. The following reservation scheme was provided in the Communal G(overnment) O(rder) of 1927:

Non-brahmin Hindus 5 out of 12 posts	42%
Brahmins 2 of 12 posts	17%
Muslims 2 of 12 posts	17%
Anglo-Indians 2 of 12 posts	17%
Depressed classes 1 of 12 posts	8%

Source: The Report of the Backward Classes Commission (pt 2), vol. III to IV, Government of India, 1980, p. 147.

Underlining the importance of caste identity in south India because of peculiar historical circumstances, André Béteille sought to explain the continuity of caste quotas in public employment in terms of what began in the form of opposition to the brahmin hegemony. André Béteille, 'Resistance to Reservations: Some North-South Differences', in his, *The Backward Classes in Contemporary India*, OUP, New Delhi, 1992 (rpt), pp. 100–6.

13. For details, see Shibanikinkar Chaube, *Constituent Assembly of India: Springboard of Revolution*, Manohar, Delhi, 2000 (2nd edn), pp. 146–55; Gurpreet Mahajan, *Identities and Rights: Aspects of Liberal Democracy in India*, OUP, New Delhi, 1998, pp. 149–58.

14. The notion of identity therefore involves both negation and difference. Post-structuralists such as Derrida, argues Eli Zaretsky, 'problematized

identity for example by arguing that identity presupposes difference, that it involves the suppression of difference or that it entailed an endless process of deferral of meaning'. Post-structuralists therefore contributed to identity politics 'by introducing what is sometimes termed a politics of difference, a politics aimed less at establishing a viable variety for its constituency than at destabilizing identities, a politics that eschews such terms as groups, rights, value and society in favour of such terms as places, spaces, alterity and subject positions, a politics that aims to decenter or subvert than to conquer or assert'. Eli Zaretsky, 'Identity Theory, Identity Politics: Psychoanalysis, Marxism and Poststructuralism', in Craig Calhoun, *Social Theory and the Politics of Identity*, Blackwell, Oxford, 1995, p. 200.

15. Tapan Raychaudhuri, *Perceptions, Emotions, Sensibilities: Essays on India's Colonial and Post-colonial Experiences*, OUP, Delhi, 1999, p. 18.

16. Ibid., P. 19.

17: Ibid., p. 19.

18. T.K. Oommen, *State and Society in India: Studies in Nation-Building*, Sage, New Delhi, 1990, p. 39.

19. Ravinder Kumar thus argues, 'any nationalist transformation of Indian civilization, which rested upon a dozen and more well articulated regional and linguistic cultures, could not be easily compared to the emergence of the European Nation-States, which grew out of the consolidation of disaggregated polities, or a breakdown of composite empires'. Ravinder Kumar, 'India: A "Nation-State" or a "Civilization State"?', *Occasional Paper on Perspectives in Indian Development*, Nehru Memorial Museum and Library, no. VIII, New Delhi, 1989, p. 22.

20. For Benedict Anderson, historical experience of nationalism in Western Europe, America and Russia had supplied for all subsequent nationalisms a set of modular forms from which nationalist élites of Afro-Asian countries chose those they liked. Benedict Anderson, *Imagined Communities: Reflections on the Origin and Spread of Nationalism*, Verso, London, 1983.

21. Partha Chatterjee, *The Nation and its Fragments: Colonial and Post-colonial Histories*, OUP, Delhi, 1994, p. 5.

22. Swadeshi is an Indian expression, popularized with loaded meaning in the course of freedom struggle which meant (a) collective pride, (b) ancestral loyalty, and (c) communal integrity or amity.

23. Bhikhu Parekh, 'Ethnocentricity of the Nationalist Discourse', *Nations and Nationalism*, 1, 1, p. 39.

24. This is particularly true of the Muslims engaged in redefining their religiously informed cultural identity in the face of modernity underwritten by the fact of British sovereignty. Ayesha Jalal thus argues, '[c]ontinued recourse to the colonial privileging of religious distinctions thwarted many well-meaning attempts at accommodating differences within a broad framework of Indian nationalism'. Ayesha Jalal, 'Nation, Reason and Religion: Punjab's Role in the Partition of India', *Economic and Political Weekly (EPW)*, 8 Aug. 1998, p. 183.

25. Charles Taylor, 'The Dynamics of Democratic Exclusion', *Journal of Democracy*, vol. 9, 4, Oct. 1998, p. 144.

26. Charles Taylor, *The Ethics of Authencity*, Harvard University Press, Cambridge, 1991, p. 48.

27. Ibid.

28. Gail Minault argues that although the 1919–21 Non Cooperation–Khilafat Movement did not succeed in forging a permanent Hindu–Muslim nationalist alliance, it certainly created 'a self-conscious and unified Indian Muslim political constituency'. Gail Minault, *The Khilafat Movement: Religious Symbolism and Political Mobilization in India*, OUP, New Delhi, 1999 (rpt).

29. One of the major constraints of the Gandhi-led freedom struggle, writes M.N. Roy, is due to the fact that 'it rests on the reaction against a common oppression. This negative basis, however, renders the national liberation movement inherently weak [because it failed to combat] the dividing forces, generated and nurtured by nationalism itself. M.N. Roy, *India in Transition*, Nachiketa Publications, Bombay, 1971, p. 150.

30. India Office Library and Records, London (IOL) L/P & 1/8/689, Rahmat Ali, Md. Aslam Khan, Sk. Mohammad Sadiq and InaYat Ullah Khan, 'Now or never: are we to live or perish for ever?' Although this proposal was not placed before the second Round Table Conference, it wascirculated among some of its participants.

31. One of the concerns that appeared to have haunted Rahmat Ali was perhaps the fear that Muslims were likely to be marginalized, if not assimilated, by Hindus through sheer demographic preponderance. That probably accounts for the high value he placed on orthodoxy because it maintains the identity of a community as against other communities and prevents an assimilation that could lead to the community disintegrating and being absorbed by others. See India Office Records, London, L/P&J/8/689, Rahamat Ali to the Secretary of State, 8 July 1935. By 1935, it was more or less accepted by the government that the difference between Hindus and Muslims, as the report of the Joint Select Committee on Indian Constitutional Reforms (1934) shows, 'is not only one of religion in the stricter sense, but also of law and culture. They may be said indeed to represent two distinct and separate civilizations'. India Office Records, London, *Report of the Joint Select Committee on Indian Constitutional Reform, 1934*, vol. 1, p. 1.

32. Quoted in M.H. Saiyid, *Mohammad Ali Jinnah: A Political Study*, Ashraf, Lahore, 1953, p. 67.

33. IOL, L/PO/78(I). The prime minister's statement for release on Tuesday, 16 August, afternoon in time for publication in the morning newspapers in India and UK of Wednesday, 17 August 1932.

34. IOL, L/P0/49 (ii), John, Lothian (The Chairman of the Franchise Committee, 1932), to the Viceroy, Government of India, 8 Aug. 1932.

35. CMD 2360, vol. xvi, memorandum by A. K. Ghuznavi, p. 188.

36. IOL, L/P0/48 (ii), Muslim demands, including Jinnah's Fourteen Points Programme were placed before the open meeting of the All India Muslim League in Delhi in March 1929.

37. The Lucknow pact, 1916 is the first political arrangement at the all India level dividing the two principal communities, Hindus and Muslims. In his study of the Lucknow Pact, Hugh Owen has shown that even the two bodies, the Congress and Muslim League, who made the Pact, 'were quite fundamentally arrayed against each other in their notions of their own identity. The Congress claimed to speak for all Indians, including Muslims, whereas the Muslim League claimed to speak for Indian Muslims, and had in fact spoken with some success for them in the years preceding the Pact. In terms of the objects of these two organizations, Congress, under the moderate leadership, had worked for a secular India and had repeatedly deplored recognition of communal or religious distinctions in political matters, whereas the Muslim League asserted that Indian Muslims must work as members of the Muslim community for representation and safeguards for that community as such'. Hugh Owen, 'Negotiating the Lucknow Pact', *Journal of Asian Studies*, vol. 31, 3, May 1972, p. 561.

38. Ujjwalkanti Das 'The Bengal Hindu–Muslim Pact', *Bengal Past and Present*, 99, 188 (Jan.–June, 1980). The idea of composite culture that informed the Bengal pact was not novel for Bipin Chandra Pal had visualized a federal India in which the units were to be the religious communities: Hindu, Muslim, Christian, and aborginal. Rabindranath Tagore had wanted a *swadeshi samaj* under the joint control of a Hindu and a Muslim. *Bangabasi* suggested in 1908 that the adherents of different religions should each form a party of their own and then cooperate among themselves. Sumit Sarkar, *The Swadeshi Movement in Bengal, 1903–1908*, People's Publishing House, New Delhi, 1973, pp. 422–4.

39. Mahatma Gandhi, for instance, insisted that the scheduled castes were a part of Hindu society and separating the two would be detrimental to the interests of the nation. He therefore, opposed the plea for separate electorates for scheduled castes, accepting however the idea of reservations through a system of joint electorates. One of the best literary works on both the socio-political background and the consequences thereof is Mulk Raj Anand's *Untouchable*, a novel that defended Gandhi as against Ambedkar who, according to the novelist, sought to undermine the manifesto of political freedom on which the Indian nationalist movement was based. See *Untouchable* (preface by E.M. Foster), Penguin Books, London, 1940 (rpt). In her *Children of God*, Shanta Rameshwar Rao dealt with the Gandhi–Ambedkar controversy on the issues raised in the Poona Pact. See *Children of God*, Orient Longman, Calcutta, 1992 (rpt). The occlusion of Ambedkar in both these novels is consistent with a certain tradition of writing about 'untouchability' that has its root in the antagonistic rhetoric of the Indian National

Congress which responded to Ambedkar's threat of splitting the leadership with disdain and fear. Apart from literary works, the Poona Pact appears to be an under-researched subject. However, the following two articles are indicative of 'the mindset' that appeared to have significantly influenced the Pact and its critic. (a) Ravinder Kumar, 'Ambedkar, Gandhi and the Poona Pact', Occasional Paper on Society and History, no. 20, Nehru Memorial Museum and Library, New Delhi, 1985; and (b) Valerian Rodrigues, '*Between Tradition and Modernity*: The Gandhi–Ambedkar Debate', in A.K. Narain and D.C. Ahir (eds), *Dr. Ambedkar, Buddhism and Social Change*, B.R. Publishing, Delhi, 1994, pp. 129–45.

40. Gauri Viswanathan, *Outside the Fold: Conversion, Modernity and Belief*, OUP, New Delhi, 1998, p. 213.

41. For an elaboration of this argument, see Gauri Viswnathan, op cit., ch. 7, pp. 211–39.

42. In his 1940 Ramgarh presidential address, Abul Kalam Azad argues, that '[f]or a hundred and fifty years, British imperialism has pursued the policy of divide and rule, and, by emphasizing internal differences, sought to use various groups, for the consolidation of its own power. That was the inevitable result of India's political subjection, and its folly for us to complain and grow bitter. A foreign government can never encourage internal unity in the subject country, for disunity is the surest guarantee for the continuance of its own domination'. Azad's presidential address at Ramgarh, 1940 in A.M. Zaidi and S.G. Zaidi (eds), *The Encyclopedia of the Indian National Congress*, vol. 12, p. 355–6.

43. Reiterating the famous 1940 Lahore resolution of the All India Muslim League demanding an independent state for the Muslims as they constituted a separate nation, Jinnah always insisted that 'there are two major nations [in India]. This is the root cause and essence of our troubles. When there are two major nations how can you talk of democracy which means that one nation majority will decide everything for the other nation although it may be unanimous in its opposition. ... these two nations cannot be judged by western democracy. But they should each be treated equals and attempts should be made to solve the difficulties by acknowledging the fact'. Jinnah's press statement on 31 July 1946; *Dawn*, 1 Aug. 1946. It is however debatable whether the highly publicized conflicting ideas and conception lay at the root of Hindu–Muslim chasm at the grassroots as it has been amply demonstrated that 'explicit rivalries between the [principal] communities tended to exist [during the period preceding partition] at ... the level of organized politics at the top where Hindu and Muslim élites were rivals for influence with government and eventually for the control of government itself'. Ayesha Jalal and Anil Seal, 'Alternative to Partition: Muslim Politics Between the Wars', *Modern Asian Studies*, Cambridge, 15.3.1984, p. 415.

44. Sushil Srivastava, 'Constructing the Hindu Identity: European Moral and Intellectual Adventurism in 18th Century India', *EPW*, 16–22, 1998,

p. 1186. According to Srivastava, 'English writing on India that appeared after 1780 was preoccupied with the obligation [sic] to expound and glorify the literary and other achievements of the ancient past of the Hindoos. In this process, the Brahminical system and practices were naturally glorified and the newly discovered Sanskrit language was said to be the only source that could open the unknown mystifying world of brahmans. Sanskrit literature was alone distinguished as the sole source of knowledge that could unravel the mysteries of the glory that was India.'

45. *The Tribune*, Lahore, 24 Aug. 1906, quoted in John Zavos, 'Searching for Hindu Nationalism in Modern Indian History: Analysis of Some Early Ideological Developments', *EPW*, 7 Aug. 1999, p. 2272. According to Zavos, '[t]he representation of the community of Hindus, an idea which under-pinned the Sabha movement at the outset, was related to struggles within the Congress over how precisely the Indian nation was to be represented. It is this notion of representation, indeed, which dominated the politics of [the first ten years of the twentieth century] and in a sense, provided the space for the articulation of the community of Hindu.'

46. V.D. Savarkar, *Who is a Hindu? Hindutva*, S.P. Gokhale, Poona, 1949. According to Ashis Nandy, Savarkar appeared to have borrowed this defini-tion from those thinkers of the nineteenth century Bengal who advanced more or less this definition. Ashis Nandy et al., *Creating a Nationality: The Ramajanmabhumi Movement and Fear of the Self*, OUP, Delhi, 1995, p. 67.

47. D.H. Dhanagare, 'Three Constraints of Hinduism', *Seminar*, no. 411, Nov. 1993, p. 25.

48. M.S. Golwalkar, *Bunch of Thoughts*, Jagarana Prakashan, Bangalore, 1980 (rpt), pp. 123-4. For a detailed analysis of the evolution of the concept of Hindu community, see Tapan Basu et al., *Khaki Shorts and Saffron Flags: A Critique of the Hindu Right*, Orient Longman, Delhi, 1993, pp. 12–55. and Pralaya Ranjan Kanungo, *Politics and Ideology of the Rashtriya Swayam Sevak Sangh*, 1973–90, Ph.D. dissertation, University of Delhi, 1997, pp. 98–153.

49. M.S. Golwalkar, *Bunch of Thoughts*, p. 52.

50. Not only were Hindu men sought to be organized, a concerted effort was also made to bring Hindu women under a platform to champion the cause of Hindus. Tanika Sarkar has shown that in 1936, eleven years after the formation of the RSS, a women organization, Rashtrasevika Samiti, was founded with daily *shakhas* that provided physical, martial arts as well as ideological or *'boudhik'* training. Tanika Sarkar, 'Pragmatics of the Hindu Right: Politics of Women's Organizations', *EPW*, 31 July 1999, pp. 2159-67.

51. M.S. Golwalkar, *Bunch of Thoughts*, p. 128.

52. Penderel Moon, *Divide and Quit: An Eyewitness Account of the Partition of India*, OUP, Delhi, 1998 (rpt), ch. 1, pp. 11–28.

53. In the Constituent Assembly, the speeches of representatives belong-ing to most religious communities reflected concerns regarding the

submergence of a distinct cultural identity in independent India. Considerations of cultural autonomy were sought to be rendered compatible with the nationalist élite's concerns regarding national unity. It was emphasized that only through the retention of their own distinct culture could members of these communities contribute effectively to the nation. Their arguments drew on early nationalist conceptions that regarded communities, defined in religious, caste, and linguistic terms, rather than individual citizens as the building blocks of the nation. The anxiety for a strongly centralized identity is comprehensible in a newly fledged nation that had absorbed the trauma of Partition. For a critical analysis of the debates on the minorities in the Constituent Assembly, see Rochana Bajpai, 'Constituent Assembly Debates and Minority Rights', *EPW*, vol. 35 (21, 22), 27 May 2000, pp. 1837-45.

54. The dominant opinion during this period regarded 'socio–economic backwardness' as constituting legitimate basis for claims for special provision, and this criterion was applicable only to the lower castes and tribal groups and not to the religious minorities. Opposing an amendment initiated by Sikh representatives that all minorities receive considerations in the matter of appointments to the public service, Vallabhbhai Patel argued, after all, what is the Sikh community backward in? Is it backward in industry, or commerce or anything? *Constituent Assembly Debates: Official Reports*, Government of India, New Delhi, 1949, vol. 10, pp. 247-9.

55. As the Conference resolved, 'if a province has to educate itself and do its daily work through the medium of its own language, it must necessarily be a linguistic area. ... Hence it becomes most desirable for provinces to be regrouped on a linguistic basis.' *The Report of the All Parties Conference*, All Parties Conference, All India Congress Committee, Allahabad, 1928, p. 62.

56. For a critical analysis of the arguments and counter-arguments of Jawaharlal Nehru and his colleagues in the Congress party on the linguistic regrouping of the provinces, see Robert D. King, *Nehru and the Language Politics of India*, OUP, New Delhi, 1997.

57. *The Report of the State Reorganization Commission*, 1955 is instructive and even-handed both in its exposition of the history of the movement towards linguistic provinces and in explaining its recommendations on where to draw the state boundaries, whether one agrees with either the logic or reasoning of the Commission or its recommendations. One of the first and also finest study of the linguistic identity that surfaced before and after Independence is Jyotirindra Dasgupta, *Language Conflict and National Development*, University of California Press, Berkeley, 1970; Prakash Karat, *Language and Nationality Politics in India*, Orient Longman, New Delhi, 1973; Paul Brass, *Language, Religion and Politics*, University of California Press, Berkeley, 1974; and Robert D. King, *Nehru and the Language Politics of India*, OUP, New Delhi, 1997, esp. ch. 3, pp. 52–96.

58. Dipankar Gupta, *Nativism in a Metropolis: The Shiv Sena in Bombay*, Manohar, Delhi, 1982; Myron Weiner, *Sons of the Soil, the Assam Movement*,

Orient Longman, New Delhi; and also Sanjib Baruah, *India Against Itself: Assam and the Politics of Nationality*, University of Pennsylvania Press, Philadelphia, 1999.

59. The search for a separate regional identity and its articulation in the form of movements led to the rise of the Akali Dal, DMK, and Telugu Desam which succeeded in infusing the identity aspirations of the concerned communities with a political content in Punjab, Tamil Nadu, and Andhra Pradesh. The reasons attributed to a search for regional identity are generally, (a) influx of migrants, (b) cultural differences between the migrants and local people, (c) restricted job opportunities for the indigenous middle class, (d) immobility of the local population, (e) rapid growth of education among the lower middle class, (f) a competitive labour market, and (g) language domination or a sense of insecurity of language-culture-religion. Robert Hardgrave's analysis of the Dravidian movement that led to the emergence of the DMK in Tamil Nadu is an evenly balanced study of the factors contributing to the consolidation of regional identity in the post-1947 era. Robert L. Hardgrave, *The Dravidian Movement*, Popular Prakashan, Bombay, 1965; and Sajal Basu, *Regional Movements: Politics of Language, Ethnicity-Identity*, Manohar, New Delhi, 1992, ch. 3, (pp. 46–70): Baldev Raj Nayer, *Minority Politics in the Punjab*, Princeton University Press, 1966, ch. II (the chapter seeks to identify those factors shaping the nature of regional aspiration, as witnessed in Punjab in the early 1960s).

60. Paul Brass, *Ethnicity and Nationalism: Theory and Comparison*, Sage, New Delhi, 1991, p. 21.

61. J. Tambiah, *Levelling Crowds: Ethnonationalist Conflict and Collective Violence in South Asia*, University of California Press, Berkeley, 1996, p. 217.

62. Dipankar Gupta, The Politics of Ethnicity: Sikh Identity in a Comparative Perspective, OUP, New Delhi, 1996, pp. 102-15.

63. There are quite a number of studies focusing exclusively on caste as a factor in ascriptive identity. André Béteille's work on Tamil Nadu however stands apart for having lucidly dealt with the question in the context of a somewhat conservative society that had experienced several violent movements successfully challenging upper caste hegemony. André Béteille, Society and Politics in India: Essays in a Comparative Perspective, OUP, Delhi, 1991, pp. 89–121.

64. *The Mandal Commission Report* is certainly an expansion of the 1955 *Kelkar Commission Report* which identified 2399 castes as OBCs. The report of the Mandal Commission is an in-depth analysis of the caste configuration in India that goes beyond the stereotypical division of the ascriptive identity in terms of four major castes.

65. Susana B.C. Devalle dwells on the tribal perception in the Jharkhand areas in her ch. 6, 'the culture of protest', (pp. 210–27), in *Discourses of Ethnicity: Culture and Protest in Jharkand*, Sage, New Delhi. 1992, while S.K.

Chaube deals with the complexity of identity formation in the context of north-east India where the ramifications were altogether different. See his, 'Tribal Societies and Nation Building in North East India', in B. Pakem (ed.), *Nationality, Ethnicity and Cultural Identity in North East India*, Omsons, Guwahati, 1990, pp. 15–26.

66. (a) R.C. Mazumdar, *History of Freedom Movement*, 3 vols, Calcutta, 1962–3; (b) Bisheshwar Prasad, *Changing Modes of Indian National Movement*, New Delhi, 1966; (c) Amales Tripathy, *Swadhinata Sangrame Bharater Jatiya Congress, 1885–1947*(Bengali), Ananda, Calcutta, 1990; (d) B.R. Nanda, *Mahatma Gandhi: A Biography*, George Allen & Unwin Ltd, 1958.

67. S. Radhakrishnan's speech in the Constituent Assembly. *Constituent Assembly Debates*, vol. IV, pp. 283–4.

68. Bhikhu Parekh, 'Nehru and the National Philosophy of India', *EPW*, vol. 26, nos 1 & 2, 5 Jan. 1991, p. 35.

69. W.H. Morris-Jones, 'Shaping the Post-imperial State; Nehru's Letters to Chief Ministers' in Michael Twaddle (ed.), *Imperialism, the State and the Third World*, British Academic Press, London, 1992, p. 222

70. Underlining the significance of territory in the formation of a modern nation state, Hobsbawn thus argued, '[t]he equation nation = state = people, and especially sovereign people, undoubtedly linked nation to territory, since structure and definition of states were essentially territorial'. E.J. Hobsbawm, *Nations and Nationalism: Programme, Myth, Reality*, Canto, Cambridge, 1992 (2nd edn), p. 19.

71. Aditya Nigam, 'India after the 1996 Elections: Nation, Locality and Representation', *Asian Survey*, vol. 36, no. 12, Dec. 1996, p. 1169.

72. (a) R.P. Dutt, *India Today*, Manisha, Calcutta, 1970 (rpt); (b) M.N. Roy, *India in Transition*, Nachiketa Publications, Bombay, 1971 (rpt); (c) A.R. Desai, *Social Background of Indian Nationalism*, Allied, Bombay, 1966.

73. Irfan Habib, 'Emergence of Nationalities in India, *Social Scientist*, vol. 4(1), Special no., Aug. 1975.

74. For instance, Bipan Chandra forcefully articulated this point of view in *India's Struggle for Independence*. See Bipan Chandra et al:, *India's Struggle for Independence*, 1857–1947, Penguin, New Delhi, 1989 (rpt), pp. 21–3.

75. Hence a commentator argued that '[t]he given totality of existing identities, such as caste, religion, language or region, is sucked into the melting pot of the formation of a new identity of national consciousness as a result of transformation of these earlier identities, embodying the various threads of the accumulated subjective experience under a colonial environment. This consciousness which infuses this identity with its dynamic content, implies a necessary opposition to all forms of imperialism'. Bhagwan Josh, *The Colonial State, the Left and the National Movement, 1934–41*, vol. II, Sage, New Delhi, 1992, p. 60. The argument seems derivative of a 1946 circular of the Communist Party of India that declared, '... in India, nationalists like Sindhis, Pathan, Bengalis, Maratha, Gujeratis, Tamils, Oriyas,

Andhras, Kannadigas etc., are growing, while, at the same time, the common bonds of the people of all these nationalities are also growing in *the common struggle against imperialism for independence, freedom and democracy* (emphasis added). The Communist Party of India circular to members, issued in March 1946.

76. Achin Vanaik, *The Painful Transition: Bourgeois Democracy in India*, Verso, London, 1990, p. 142.

77. Javeed Alam, 'Behind the Verdict: What Kind of Nation Are We?', *EPW*, vol. 31 (25), 22 June, 1996 p. 1616. Alam also distanced himself from those highlighting India's multinational identity. According to him, '[t]he discourse about India as a nation seems to have seeped down into popular consciousness over a large geographical space from the north to the west whereas it has failed to do so in an unqualified way in the east, north-east and south, an equally large geographical expanse. In an extended belt comprising many regions, the discourse and process correspond while in the other belt the 'discourse' and the process sharply diverge. When, therefore, it is viewed from the one side it is clearly not multinational but the same country viewed from another side has indeed many features including the perpetual ones to consider it as multi-national. [In other words], the specificities of the refraction of the idea of India in different regions/belts is so different that in spite of a strong common denominator it cannot be the same discursive entity'. See Javeed Alam, 'Behind the Verdict ...', pp. 1617 and 1619.

78. John H. Broomfield, *Élite Conflict in a Plural Society*, University of California Press, Berkeley, 1968, ch. 1.

79. Anil Seal, *The Emergence of Indian Nationalism: Competition and Collaboration in the Later Nineteenth Century*, Cambridge University Press, 1968, ch. 2 (pp. 25–113).

80. Underlining the unavoidable and semantic problems with the term *bhadralok*, Sumit Sarkar thus argues that '[t]he trouble about this term in fact is that it seems much too broad, ranging presumably from Maharaja of Mymensingh to the East Indian Railway clerk; it consequently offers little or no real guide in any study of socio-economic compulsions behind political action. ... The tacit identification between *bhadralok* and certain Hindu upper castes (*brahmin, vaidya* and *kayastha*) is also not quite tenable—how are we to categorize, for example, a brahmin cook or a village priest?' Sumit Sarkar, *The Swadeshi Movement in Bengal, 1903–8*, People's Publishing House, New Delhi, 1973, pp. 509–10.

81. Based on the anthropological tools for the study of community, culturological history provides an explanatory model to understand the construction of a community both in terms of its internal dynamics and the external socio-economic and political milieu in which it is placed. The use of religious symbols, for instance, argues Dipankar Gupta, 'is not what distinguishes one class from another, but it is the use to which they are put; that is to say it is the manner in which cultural symbols are employed to express

42 COMMUNAL IDENTITY IN INDIA

existential problems, that separates one class from another. So, it is not 'mentality' nor even the 'habit of thinking', but the contingent and real conditions which distinguish one form of ideological articulation from another. The dense richness of symbols pre-empt a fixed horizontal alignment of symbols, and that is why symbolic usage should be read vertically in the context of not another symbol but something outside it, namely the contradictions of life or, perhaps, life itself.' Dipankar Gupta, *Rivalry and Brotherhood: Politics in the Life of Farmers in Northern India*, OUP, New Delhi, 1981, ch. IV, pp. 106–32.

82. Rafiuddin Ahmad, *The Bengal Muslims: The Quest for Identity*, OUP, New Delhi, 1981, ch. IV, pp. 106–32.

83. Sekhar Bandyopadhyay, 'From Alienation to Integration: Changes in the Politics of Caste in Bengal, 1937–47', *Indian Economic and Social History Review*, 31.3.1994, p. 350-1. Bandyopadhyay develops this argument further in his 'Transfer of Power and the Crisis of Dalit Politics in India, 1945–47' *Modern Asian Studies*, vol. 34, no. 4, 2000, pp. 893–942.

84. Harjot Oberoi, *The Construction of Religious Boundaries: Culture, Identity and Diversity in the Sikh Tradition*, OUP, New Delhi, 1994, ch. 6 (pp. 306–27 & 351–5).

85. Nonica Datta, *Forming an Identity: A Social History of the Jats*, OUP, New Delhi, 1999, p. 190.

86. P.K. Datta, *Carving Blocs: Communal Ideology in Early Twentieth Century Bengal*, OUP, New Delhi, 1999, p. 22.

87. Ibid., p. 71.

88. Ibid., p. 73.

89. Defending the communitarian logic, Gyan Pandey argues, '[p]art of the "fragmentary" point of view lies in this, that it resists the drive for a shallow homogenization and struggles for other, potentially richer definitions of the "nation" and the future political community'. Gyanendra Pandey, 'In Defense of the Fragment: Writing about Hindu-Muslim Riots in India Today' (pp. 1–33), in Ranajit Guha (ed.), *A Subaltern Studies Reader, 1986–1995*, OUP, New Delhi, 1998, p. 1.

90. Partha Chatterjee, *The Nation and its Fragments* (OUP, New Delhi, 1994) is probably a powerful intervention in the debate within the communitartian perspective. While ch. 11 (pp. 220–40) reiterates the communitarian argument with supporting evidence from colonial India, chs 6 (pp. 116–34), 8 (pp. 158–72), and 9 (pp. 173–99) dwell on the questions concerning women, peasants, and outcasts respectively.

91. Dipesh Chakrabarty, *Rethinking Working-Class History: Bengal, 1890–1940*, OUP, New Delhi, 1989, p. 86.

92. Ibid., p. 194.

93. Nita Kumar, *The Artisans of Benaras: Popular Culture and Identity, 1880–1996*, Princeton University Press, Princeton, 1988, p. 227.

94. Cited in Sudhir Kumar, 'Reconstructing the Nation: Image of the

Nation in the Fiction of Muslim Writers', in *Studies in Humanities and Social Sciences*, Shimla, vol. 1, Nov. 1994, p. 125.

95. Partha Chatterjee, 'Agrarian Relations and Communalism in Bengal, 1926–1935', in Ranajit Guha (ed.), *Subaltern Studies: Writings on South Asian History and Society*, vol. 1, OUP, New Delhi, 1986 (rpt), p. 35.

96. Ibid., pp. 34–7.

97. There is an interesting similarity between Ashis Nandy's subaltern perspective, holding the 'community' as a viable theoretical construct in explaining the organic structure of Indian society. Defending the communatarian viewpoints, Nandy thus argues that traditional community structures have more effective civilizational resources than the institutions of the modern state to resolve disputes, tolerate difference, and allow for the development of a better adjusted and accommodative personality. The crucial institutions here are those belonging to the 'little or folk' traditions of local community life which are transmitted from one generation to another over the ages. See Ashis Nandy, *The Intimate Enemy: Loss and Recovery of Self under Colonialism*, OUP, New Delhi, 1989, (rpt).

98. Partha Chatterjee, 'The Nation and its Women', in Ranajit Guha (ed.), *A Subaltern Studies Reader, 1986–1995*, OUP, New Delhi, 2000, p. 245.

99. Partha Chatterjee, *The Nation and its Fragments: Colonial and Post-Colonial Histories*, OUP, New Delhi, 1994, p. 21.

100. Ibid., p. 121. The demarcation between the inner and outer domains is, not as compartmentalized as it appears to suggest. In her study of the participation of women in national politics and the Self Respect Movement in Tamil Nadu, C.S. Lakshmi has shown that in everyday life and dealings, the two domains constantly run into each other, blurring the boundaries though the separateness is always maintained. Therefore women's functioning in the outside world was always 'accommodated into a certain logic of what is termed feminine to make it seem like a continuation of her historical and cultural role'. Such a notion of separateness also 'created a mental image of women "coming out" for a specific purpose and then "going back:' to where they belonged.'. See C.S. Lakshmi, 'Bodies called Women: Some Thoughts on Gender: Ethnicity and Nation, *EPW*, vol. 32 (46), 15 Nov. 1997.

101. Ibld., p. 132.

102. It would however be wrong to argue that the inner domain was absolutely free from the influences of the external domain because the changes in man–woman relationships were inconceivable without reference to the colonial encounter. Contrary to the stereotypical perception of the husband–wife relationship in which the wife unconditionally surrender to the husband's will, Dwarkanath Tagore's wife, as Tapan Raychaudhuri has shown, 're-fused to even touch him but continued to perform her other duties as a wife [because] ... her husband had broken the taboos regarding comensality by dining with Englishmen'. Tapan Raychaudhuri, *Perceptions, Emotions, Sensibilities: Essays on India's Colonial and Post-colonial Experiences*, OUP, New Delhi, 1999, p. 74.

103. Himani Bannerje, 'Project of Hegemony: Toward a Critique of Subaltern Studies' Resolution of the Women's Question', *EPW,* vol. 35 (11),11 March 2000, p. 916.

104. Ibid. p. 916.

105. The Congress leadership, including Gandhi, effectively mediated women discontent so that they remained targeted exclusively at imperialism. The women however gained from the alliance with the freedom struggle in the sense that nationalist political activities radicalized them into expressing their own grievances and defused male opposition to the cause, but the nationalists also limited the women's movement inasmuch as they maintained control over women's activity and could not be relied upon to support women's demands when male privileges were under threat. For details of this argument, see Joana Liddle and Roma Joshi, *Daughters of Independence: Gender, Caste and Class in India,* Kali for Women, New Delhi, 1986. Furthermore, in her study of women jute workers in Bengal in the 1920s and 1930s, Samita Sen has graphically illustrated how the women workers organized themselves in trade unions championing principally issues other than those concerning gender though women constituted a bulk of the working force. Notwithstanding their reputation for militancy, women workers articulated their protest more in the form of 'confrontation' than 'organized resistance' on economic and gender issues. See her *Women Workers in the Bengal Jute Industry, 1890–1940: Migration, Motherhood and Militancy,* PhD thesis, Cambridge University, 1992, ch. 6 (pp. 218–61).

106. Nivedita Menon, 'Women and Citizenship', in Partha Chatterjee (ed.), *Wages of Freedom,* OUP, New Delhi, 1998, pp. 241–66.

107. This argument has been pursued by Omar Khalidi in his 'Muslims in Indian Political Process: Group Goals and Alternative Strategies', *EPW,* vol. 28 (1, 2), 2–9 Jan. 1993.

108. Niraja Gopal Jayal, Democracy and the State: Welfare, Secularism and Development in Contemporary India, OUP, New Delhi, 1999, p. 150.

109. Tanika Sarkar, 'The Women as Communal Subject: Rashtrasevika Samiti and Ram Janmabhoomi Movement', *EPW,* 31 Aug. 1991.

110. Sudipta Kaviraj, 'The Imaginary Institutions of India', in Partha Chatterjee and Gyanendra Pandey (eds), *Subaltern Studies,* vol. VII, OUP, New Delhi, pp. 20–33.

111. Nandini Sunder, 'The Indian Census, Identity and Inequality', in Ramchandra Guha and Jonathan P. Parry, *Institutions and Inequalities: Essays in Honour of André Béteille,* OUP, New Delhi, 1999, p. 104.

112. Bernard S. Cohn, *An Anthropologist Among the Historians and Other Essays,* OUP, New Delhi, 1990, p. 250.

113. Arjun Appadurai, 'Number in the Colonial Imagination' in C.A. Breckenridge and P. van der Veer (eds), *Orientalism and Postcolonial Predicament,* University of Pennsylvania Press, Philadelphia, 1993, pp. 334–5, 336.

114. Though refreshing, the communitarian approach has provoked critiques for having completely undermined individuals for the community. Sarah Joseph identifies some of the major weaknesses in the communitarian writings that essentially flow from the distinctive individual identity as against community. See her, 'Politics of Contemporary Communitarianism', *EPW*, 4 Oct 1997, pp. 2517–23.

115. Sucheta Mahajan, *Independence and Partition: The Erosion of Colonial Power in India*, Sage, New Delhi, 2000, pp. 17- 24.

116. E.L. Hamza, *Pakistan: A Nation*, S.H. Muhammad Ashraf, Kashmiri Bazar, Lahore, 1972, p. 98.

117. For a detailed discussion of the heterogeneity of the Muslim community in the subcontinent, see Imtiaz Ahmad (ed.), *Modernization and Social Change Among Muslims in India*, Manohar, New Delhi, 1983.

118. Saleem M.M. Qureshi, *Jinnah and the Making of Pakistan*, Council for Pakistan Studies, Karachi, 1969.

119. Ayesha Jalal, *Democracy and Authoritarianism in South Asia: A Comparative and Historical Perspective*, Cambridge University Press, 1995, p. 223.

120. Wali Khan reconfirmed this in his memoirs. See Wali Khan, *Facts are Facts: The Untold Story of India's Partition*, Vikas Publishing House, New Delhi, 1987, p. 160.

121. Mushirul Hasan (ed.), Inventing Boundaries: Gender, Politics and the Partition of India, OUP, New Delhi, 2000, p. 11.

122. According to Feroz Ahmed, ethnic boundaries and ethnic identities in Pakistan are too fluid to be addressed by a preordained framework. He further argues that [d]ue to the increasing ethnic heterogeneity of Pakistan's provinces, the growing economic and political interdependence, and increasing cultural homogenization, it has become imperative and even possible to seek solutions to the regional and ethnic problems in a multi-ethnic framework. Feroz Ahmed, 'Ethnicity, Class and State in Pakistan', *EPW*, 23 November, 1996, p. 3053.

123. Akbar S. Zaidi (ed.), *Regional Imbalances and the National Quest in Pakistan*, Vanguard, Lahore, 1992, pp. 7–9.

124. Ayesha Jalal, *Democracy and Authoritarianism ...*, p. 231.

125. Badruddin Omar, *Bangladesher Madhyabitta O Sanskritik Paristhithi* (Bengali), Pallav Publisher, Dhaka, 1988, pp. 60–4.

126. Cited in Ayesha Jalal, 'Exploding Communalism: The Politics of Muslim Identity in South Asia', in Sugata Bose and Ayesha Jalal (eds), *Nationalism, Democracy and Development: State and Politics in India*, OUP, New Delhi, 1997, p. 98.

127. Amena Mohsin, *The Politics of Nationalism: The Case of CHT [Chittagong Hill Tracts]*, Bangladesh, UPL, Dhaka, 1997.

128. Idem, 'Identity, Politics and Hegemony: The Chittagong Hill Tracts,

Bangladesh', in *Identity Culture and Politics: An Afro-Asian Dialogue*, vol. 1(1), Jan. 2000, p. 80.

129. Kabita Chakma, *Joli no Uddim Kiteye*, Nari Grontho Prabartana, Chattagram, 1997, cited in ibid., pp. 81–2.

130. The expression is borrowed from Denis-Constant Martin. According to Martin, identity narratives, as articulated by those involved in defending an identity in contrast with others, are powerful methodological tools to explain the conditions in which political competitions unfold, in particular when they develop into violent conflict. See Denis-Constant Martin, 'The Choices of Identity', *Social Identities*, vol. 1 (1) 1995, pp. 1–20.

131. Bhikhu Parekh, 'Discourses on National Identity', *Political Studies*, Sept. 1994, p. 503. According to Parekh, identity, drawn upon difference, 'fetishises difference and discourages inter-communal borrowing. It also leads to stress only those aspects in which [the community] differs from others and to distort and falsify its way of life'. Identity, conceptualized in this way, dominated, as Parekh further argues, most of the debates on the subject. For example, 'many Germans continue to be obsessed with *Sonderweg* and feel deeply worried that their post-war democratic institutions will assimilate them to the West and undermine their identity. Many Canadians ask how they differ from the Americans and how best they can preserve their differences. Quebec nationalists ask the same questions about themselves and the rest of Canada. In Japan the preoccupation with national distinctiveness has generated an extensive literature known as *nihonjinon*, and in Russia anything inconsistent with the "Russian Idea" is dismissed as anti-national. This is just as true of Algeria, Iran, and most developing countries'.

132. With remarkable clarity of vision, Rabindranath Tagore succinctly wrote about his views on nation in a rather small piece, entitled *Nation Ki* (Bengali). During his lecture tour in America, 1916–17, he elaborated some of these points, including his views on nationalism in India, See *Nationalism*, Rupa, Delhi, 1994 (rpt of the collection, originally published in 1917), pp. 77–99.

133. See ibid., p. 89.

134. Rabindranath Tagore to Amiya Chakraborty, no date, in Sabyasachi Bhattacharyya (compiled and edited), *The Mahatma and the Poet: Letters and Debates Between Gandhi and Tagore*, 1915–1941, National Book Trust, New Delhi, 1997, p. 172.

135. Ashis Nandy, *The Illegitimacy of Nationalism*, OUP, New Delhi, 1994, p. 89.

136. Rabindranath Tagore, *Nationalism*, p. 90.

137. Ashis Nandy thus aptly comments that Jana Gana Mana 'could only be the anthem of a state rooted in the Indian civilization [and] not of the Indian nation-state trying to be the heir to British-Indian empire'. Ashis Nandy, *The Illegitimacy of Nationalism*, OUP, New Delhi, 1994, p. 88.

138. Susan Bayly's thorough study of caste, society, and politics in India

since the eighteenth century confirms that 'India is not and never has been a "monolithic" caste society'. Susan Bayly, *Caste, Society and Politics: From the Eighteenth Century to the Modern Age*, Cambridge University Press, Cambridge, 1999, p. 382.

139. Amartya Sen, 'India's pluralism', *India International Quarterly*, 20, 3, 1993, p. 37.

140. The distinctiveness of India as socio-cultural conglomeration lies, as Yogesh Atal argues, in 'plurality of people and multiplicity of identities [that] characterize the conglomerate Indian culture'. India's emergent composite culture, he further asserts, 'allowed for the survival of diversities— insiders of the composite culture of India simultaneously enjoy outsider and insider statuses through their membership of 'the various subcultures and groups within the broader society', *EPW*, vol. 36, no. 36, 8 Sep. 2001, p. 3460.

Some Definitive Texts

1

Extracts from *The Collected Works of Mahatma Gandhi*[*]

M.K. Gandhi

A Baffling Situation

A question has been put to me:

Do you intend to start general civil disobedience although Quaid-e-Azam Jinnah has declared war against Hindus and has got the Muslim League to pass a resolution favouring vivisection of India into two? If you do, what becomes of your formula that there is no swaraj without communal unity?

I admit that the step taken by the Muslim League at Lahore[1] creates a baffling situation. But I do not regard it so baffling as to make civil disobedience an impossibility. Supposing that the Congress is reduced to a hopeless minority, it will still be open to it, indeed it may be its duty, to resort to civil disobedience. The struggle will not be against the majority, it will be against the foreign ruler. If the struggle succeeds, the fruits thereof will be reaped as well by the Congress as by the opposing majority. Let me, however, say in parenthesis that, until the condition I have mentioned for starting civil disobedience are fulfilled, civil disobedience cannot be started in any case. In the present instance there is nothing to prevent the imperial rulers from declaring their will in unequivocal terms that henceforth India will

[*] *The Collected Works of Mahatma Gandhi,* vol. 71, Publications Division, Ministry of Information, Government of India, New Delhi, 1978 (hereafter, *CWMG*).

govern herself according to her own will, not that of the rulers as has happened hitherto. Neither the Muslim League nor any other party can oppose such a declaration. For the Muslims will be entitled to dictate their own terms. Unless the rest of India wishes to engage in internal fratricide, the others will have to submit to Muslim dictation if the Muslims will resort to it. I know no non-violent method of compelling the obedience of eight crores of Muslims to the will of the rest of India, however powerful a majority the rest may represent.

The Muslims must have the same right of self-determination that the rest of India has. We are at present a joint family. Any member may claim a division.

Thus, so far as I am concerned, my proposition that there is no swaraj without communal unity holds as good today as when I first enunciated it in 1919.

But civil disobedience stands on a different footing. It is open even to one single person to offer it, if he feels the call. It will not be offered for the Congress alone or for any particular group. Whatever benefit accrues from it will belong to the whole of India. The injury, if there is any, will belong only to the civil disobedience party.

But I do not believe that Muslims, when it comes to a matter of actual decision, will ever want vivisection. Their good sense will prevent them. Their self-interest will deter them. Their religion will forbid the obvious suicide which the partition would mean. The 'two nations' theory is an untruth. The vast majority of Muslims of India are converts to Islam or are descendants of converts. They did not become a separate nation as soon as they became converts. A Bengali Muslim speaks the same tongue that a Bengali Hindu does, eats the same food, has the same amusements as his Hindu neighbour. They dress alike. I have often found it difficult to distinguish by outward sign between a Bengali Hindu and a Bengali Muslim. The same phenomenon is observable more or less in the South among the poor who constitute the masses of India. When I first met the late Sir Ali Imam I did not know that he was not a Hindu. His speech, his dress, his manners, his food were the same as of the majority of the Hindus in whose midst I found him. His name alone betrayed him. Not even that with Quaid-e-Azam Jinnah. For his name could be that of any Hindu. When I first met him, I did not know that he was a Muslim. I came to know his religion when I had his full name given to me. His nationality was written in his face and manner. The reader will be surprised to know that for days, if not months, I used to think of the late Vithalbhai Patel as a Muslim as he used to sport a beard and a Turkish cap. The Hindu law of inheritance governs many Muslim groups. Sir Mahommed Iqbal used to speak with pride of his Brahmanical descent. Iqbal and Kitchlew are names common to Hindus and Muslims. Hindus and Muslims of India are not two nations. Those whom God has made one, man will never be able to divide.

And is Islam such an exclusive religion as Quaid-e-Azam would have it? Is there nothing in common between Islam and Hinduism or any other religion? Or is Islam merely an enemy of Hinduism? Were, the Ali Brothers and their associates wrong when they hugged Hindus as blood brothers and saw so much in common between the two? I am not now thinking of individual Hindus who may have disillusioned the Muslim friends. Quaid-e-Azam has, however, raised a fundamental issue. This is his thesis.[2]

It is extremely difficult to appreciate why our Hindu friends fail to understand the real nature of Islam and Hinduism. They are not religions in the strict sense of the word, but are, in fact, different and distinct social orders, and it is a dream that the Hindus and Muslims can ever evolve a common nationality. This misconception of one Indian nation has gone far beyond the limits and is the cause of most of our troubles and will lead India to destruction if we fail to revise our notions in time.

The Hindus and Muslims have two different religious philosophies, social customs, literatures. They neither intermarry, nor dine together, and indeed, they belong to two different civilizations which are based mainly on conflicting ideas and conceptions. Their aspects on life and of life are different. It is quite clear that Hindus and Mussalmans derive their inspiration from different sources of history. They have different epics, their heroes are different, and they have different episodes. Very often the hero of one is a foe of the other and, likewise, their victories and defeats overlap. To yoke together two such nations under a single State, one as a numerical minority and the other as majority, must lead to growing discontent and final destruction of any fabric that may be so built up for the government of such a State.

He does not say some Hindus are bad; he says Hindus as such have nothing in common with Muslims. I make bold to say that he and those who think like him are rendering no service to Islam; they are misinterpreting the message inherent in the very word Islam. I say this because I feel deeply hurt over what is now going on in the name of the Muslim League. I should be failing in my duty, if I did not warn the Muslims of India against the untruth that is being propagated amongst them. This warning is a duty because I have faithfully served them in their hour of need and because Hindu-Muslim unity has been and is my life's mission.

Sevagram, 1 April 1940.
Harijan, 6.4.1940

Hindu–Muslim Tangle

The partition proposal[3] has altered the face of the Hindu–Muslim problem. I have called it an untruth. There can be no compromise with it. At the same time I have said that, if the eight crores of Muslims desire it no power on earth can prevent it, notwithstanding opposition, violent or non-violent. It cannot come by honourable agreement.

That is the political aspect of it. But what about the religious and the moral which are greater than the political? For at the bottom of the cry for Partition is the belief that Islam is an exclusive brotherhood, and anti-Hindu. Whether it is against other religions it is not stated. The newspaper cuttings in which Partition is preached describe Hindus as practically untouchables. Nothing good, can come out of Hindus or Hinduism. To live under Hindu rule is a sin. Even joint Hindu–Muslim rule is not to be thought of. The cuttings show that Hindus and Muslims are already at war with one another and that they must prepare for the final tussle.

Time was when Hindus thought that Muslims were the natural enemies of Hindus. But as is the case with Hinduism, ultimately it comes to terms with the enemy and makes friends with him. The process had not been completed. As if nemesis had overtaken Hinduism, the Muslim League started the same game and taught that there could be no blending of the two cultures. In this connection I have just read a booklet by Shri Atulanand Chakrabarti which shows that ever since the contact of Islam with Hinduism there has been an attempt on the part of the best minds of both to see the good points of each other, and to emphasize inherent similarities rather than seeming dissimilarities. The author has shown Islamic history in India in a favourable light. If he has stated the truth and nothing but the truth, it is a revealing booklet which all Hindus and Muslims may read with profit. He has secured a very favourable and reasoned preface from Sir Shafaat Ahmed Khan and several other Muslim testimonials. If the evidence collected there reflects the true evolution of Islam in India, then the Partition propaganda is anti-Islamic.

Religion binds man to God and man to man. Does Islam bind Muslim only to Muslim and antagonize the Hindu? Was the message of the Prophet peace only for and between Muslims and war against Hindus or non-Muslims? Are eight crores of Muslims to be fed with this which I can only describe as poison? Those who are instilling this poison into the Muslim mind are rendering the greatest disservice to Islam, I know that it is not Islam, I have lived with and among Muslims not for one day but closely and almost uninterruptedly for twenty years. Not one Muslim taught me that Islam was an anti-Hindu religion.

Sevagram, 29 April 1940
Harijan, 6.4.1940

Notes

1. At its Lahore Session in March.
2. As expounded in his Presidential address at Lahore.
3. *CWMG*, vol. 72
4. The all India Muslim League meeting at Lahore passed a resolution on March 23, recording the view that no constitutional plan would be workable unless it was based on territorial readjustment and the creation of independent Muslim States.

2

Presidential Address of M.A. Jinnah, Lahore, March 1940*

M.A. Jinnah

The Hindu-Muslim Situation

Ladies and gentlemen, that is where we stand after the war and up to the 3rd of February. As far as our internal position is concerned, we have also been examining it; and, you know, there are several schemes which have been sent by various well-informed constitutionalists and others who take interest in the problem of India's future Constitution, and we have also appointed a subcommittee to examine the details of the schemes that have come in so far. But one thing is quite clear. It has always been taken for granted mistakenly that the Musalmans are a minority and of course we have got used to it for such a long time that these settled notions sometimes are very difficult to remove. The Musalmans are not a minority. The Musalmans are a nation by any definition.

The British and particularly the Congress proceed on the basis. 'Well, you are a minority after all, what do you want? What else do the minorities want? Just as Babu Rajendra Prasad said. But surely

* S.S. Pirzada (ed.), *Foundations of Pakistan, All Indian Muslim League Documents, 1906–1947,* vol. 2, National Publishing House Ltd., Karachi, 1970.

the Musalmans are not a minority.' We find that even according to the British map of India, we occupy large parts of this country where the Musalmans are in a majority—such as Bengal, Punjab, NWFP, Sind, and Baluchistan.

Now the question is, what is the best solution of this problem between the Hindus and the Musalmans? We have been considering—and as I have already said, a committee has been appointed to consider the various proposals. But Whatever the final scheme for a Constitution, I will present to you my views and I will just read to you, in conformation of what I am going to put before you, a letter from Lala Lajpat Rai to Mr. C.R. Das. It was written I believe, about 12 or 15 years ago, and the letter has been produced in a book by one Indra Prakash, recently published, and that is how this letter has come to light. This is what Lala Lajpat Rai, a very astute politician and a staunch Hindu Mahasabhite said—but before I read his letter, it is plain that you cannot get away from being a Hindu if you are Hindu. The word 'Nationalist' has now become the play of conjurers in politics. This is what he says:

There is one point more which has been troubling me very much of late and one which I want you to think (about) carefully, and that is the question of Hindu–Mohammedan unity. I have devoted most of my time during the last six months to the study of Muslim history and Muslim law, and I am inclined to think it is neither possible nor practicable. Assuming and admitting the sincerity of Mohammedan leaders in the non-cooperation movement, I think their religion provides an effective bar to anything of the kind.

You remember the conversation I reported to you in Calcutta which I had with Hakim Ajmal Khan and Dr Kitchlew. There is no finer Mohammedan in Hindustan than Hakim Ajmal Khan, but can any Muslim leader override the Quran? I can only hope that my reading of Islamic law is incorrect.

I think his reading is quite incorrect.

And nothing would relieve me more than to be convinced that it is so. But if it is right, then it comes to this, that although we can unite against the British, we cannot do so to rule Hindustan on British lines. We cannot do so to rule Hindustan on democratic lines.

Ladies and Gentlemen, when Lala Lajpat Rai said that we cannot rule this country on democratic lines it was all right, but when I had the temerity to speak the same truth about 18 months ago, there was a shower of attacks and criticism. But Lala Lajpat Rai said 15 years ago that we cannot do so, viz. rule Hindustan on democratic lines. What is the remedy? The remedy according to the Congress is to keep us the minority and under the majority. Lala Lajpat Rai proceeds further:

What is then the remedy? I am not afraid of the seven crores of Musalmans. But I think the seven crores in Hindustan plus the armed hosts of Afghanistan, Central Asia, Arabia, Mesopotamia and Turkey will be irresistible.

I do honestly and sincerely believe in the necessity or desirability of Hind–Muslim unity. I am also fully prepared to trust the Muslim leaders. But what about the injunctions of the Quran and the Hadis? The leaders cannot override them. Are we then doomed? I hope that your learned mind and wise head will find some way out of this difficulty.

Now, ladies and gentlemen, that is merely a letter written by one great Hindu leader to another great Hindu leader 15 years ago. Now, I should like to put before you my views on the subject, as it strikes me, taking everything into consideration at the present moment. The British Government and Parliament, and more so the British nation, have been, for many decades past, brought up and nurtured with settled notions about India's future, based on developments in their own country which have built up the British constitution, functioning now through the Houses of Parliament and the Cabinet system. Their concept of party-government, functioning on Political planes, has become the ideal with them as the best form of government for every country; and the one-sided and powerful propaganda which naturally appeals to the British has led them into a serious blunder, in producing a constitution envisaged in the Government of India Act of 1935. We find that the leading statesmen of Great Britain, saturated with these notions, have in their pronouncements seriously asserted and expressed a hope that the passage of time will harmonize the inconsistent elements in India.

A leading journal like the London *Times,* commenting on the Government of India Act of 1935, wrote:

Undoubtedly the difference between the Hindus and Muslims is not of religion in the strict sense of the word, but also of law and culture, that they may be said indeed to represent two entirely distinct and separate civilizations. However, in the course of time the superstitions will die out, and India will be moulded into a single nation.

So, according to the London *Times,* the only difficulties are superstitions. These fundamental and deep-rooted difference, spiritual, economic, cultural, social and political, have been euphemized as mere 'superstitions'. But surely, it is a flagrant disregard of the past history of the subcontinent of India, as well as the fundamental

Islamic conception of society, vis-à-vis that of Hinduisim, to characterize them as mere 'superstitions'. Notwithstanding a thousand years of close contact, nationalities which are as divergent today as ever cannot at any time be expected to transform themselves into a one nation merely by means of subjecting them to a democratic constitution and holding them forcibly together by unnatural and artificial methods of British Parliamentary Statutes. What the unitary Government of India for 150 years had failed to achieve cannot be realized by the imposition of a central federal government. It is inconceivable that the fiat or the writ of a government so constituted can ever command a willing and loyal obedience, throughout the Subcontinent from various nationalities except by means of armed force behind it.

Autonomous National States

The problem in India is not of an inter-communal but manifestly of an international character, and it must be treated as such, So long as this basic and fundamental truth is not realized, any constitution that may be built will result in disaster and will prove destructive and harmful not only to the Musalmans, but also to the British and Hindus. If the British Government are really in earnest and sincere to secure the peace and happiness of the people of this subcontinent, the only course open to us all is to allow the major nations separate homelands, by dividing India into 'autonomous national States'. There is no reason why these States should be antagonistic to each other. On the other hand, the rivalry and the natural desire and efforts on the part of the one (community) to dominate the social order and establish political supremacy over the other in the government of the country will disappear. It will lead more towards natural goodwill by international pacts between them (the states) and they can live in complete harmony with their neighbours. This will lead further to a friendly settlement all the more easily with regard to minorities by reciprocal arrangements and adjustment between the Muslim India and the Hindu India, which will far more adequately and effectively safeguard the rights and interests of Muslims and various other minorities.

It is extremely difficult to appreciate why our Hindu friends fail to understand the real nature of Islam and Hinduism. They are not religions in the strict sense of the word, but are, in fact, different and distinct social orders. It is a dream that the Hindus and Muslims can ever evolve a common nationality, and this misconception of one Indian nation has gone far beyond the limits, and is the cause of most of our troubles, and will lead India to destruction if we fail to revise our notions in time. The Hindus and the Muslims belong to two different religious philosophies, social customs, and literature. They neither intermarry, nor interdine together, and indeed they belong to two different civilizations which are based mainly on conflicting ideas and conceptions. Their aspects on life and of life are different. It is quite clear that Hindus and Musalmans derive their inspiration from different sources of history. They have different epics, their heroes are different, and they have different episodes. Very often the hero of one is a foe of the other, and likewise, their victories and defeats overlap. To yoke together two such nations under a single State, one as a numerical minority and the other as a majority, must lead to growing discontent and the final destruction of any fabric that may be so built up for the government of such a State.

History has presented to us many examples, such as the Union of Great Britain and Ireland, of Czechoslovakia and Poland. History has also shown to us many geographical tracts, much smaller than the Subcontinent of India, which otherwise might have been called one country, but which have been divided into as many states as there are nations inhabiting them. The Balkan Peninsula comprises as many as seven or eight sovereign States. Likewise, the Portuguese and the Spanish stand divided in the Iberian Peninsula. Whereas under the plea of the unity of India and one nation, which does not exist, it is sought to pursue here the line of one Central Government, when we know that the history of the last 12 hundred years has failed to achieve unity and has witnessed, during the ages, India being always divided into Hindu India and Muslim India. The present artificial unity of India dates back only to the British conquest and is maintained by the British bayonet; but the termination of the British regime, which is implicit in the recent declaration of His Majesty's Government, will be the herald of an entire break-up, with worse disaster than has ever taken place during the last one thousand years under the Muslims. Surely that is not the legacy which Britain would bequeath to India after 150 years of her rule, nor would the Hindu and Muslim India risk such a sure catastrophe.

Muslim India cannot accept any Constitution which must necessarily result in a Hindu majority Government. Hindu and Muslim brought together under a democratic system forced upon the minorities can only mean Hindu Raj. Democracy of the kind with which the

Congress High Command is enamoured would mean the complete destruction of what is most precious in Islam. We have had ample experience of the working of the provincial Constitutions during the last two and a half years; and any repetition of such a Government must lead to civil war and raising private armies, as recommended by Mr Gandhi to Hindus of Sukkur, when he said that they must defend themselves violently or non-violently, blow for blow; and if they could not, they must emigrate.

Musalmans are not a minority, as it is commonly known, and understood. One has only got to look round. Even today, according to the British map of India, 4 out of 11 provinces, where the Muslims more or less dominate, are functioning notwithstanding the decision of the Hindu Congress High Command to non-cooporate and prepare for civil disobedience. Musalmans are a nation according to any definition of a nation, and they must have their homelands, their territory and their State. We wish to live in peace and harmony with our neighbours as a free and independent people. We wish our people to develop to the fullest our spiritual, cultural, economic, social, and political life in a way that we think best, and in consonance with our own ideals and according to the genius of our people. Honesty demands—and the vital interests of millions of our people impose a sacred duty upon us to find—an honourable and peaceful solution which would be just and fair to all. But at the same time, we cannot be moved or diverted from our purpose and objective by threats or intimidations. We must be prepared to face all difficulties and consequences, make all the sacrifices that may be required of us to achieve the goal we have set in front of us.

Conclusion

Ladies and gentlemen, that is the task before us. I fear I have gone beyond my time limit. There are many things that I should like to tell you; but I have already published a little pamphlet containing most of the things that I have been saying, and I think you can easily get that publication, both in English and in Urdu, from the League Office. It might give you a clearer idea of our aims. It contains very important resolutions of the Muslim League and various other statements.

Anyhow, I have placed before you the task that lies ahead of us. Do you realize how big and stupendous it is? Do you realize that you cannot get freedom or independence by mere arguments? I should appeal to the intelligentsia. The intelligentsia in all countries in the world have been the pioneers of any movements for freedom. What does the Muslim intelligentsia propose to do? I may tell you that unless you get this into your blood, unless you are prepared to take off your coats and are willing to sacrifice all that you can, and work selflessly, earnestly and sincerely for your people, you will never realize your aim. Friends, I therefore want you to make up your minds definitely, and then think of devices, and organize your people, strengthen your organization and consolidate the Musalmans all over India. I think that the masses are wide awake. They only want your guidance and lead. Come forward as servants of Islam, organize the people economically, socially, educationally, and politically, and I am sure that you will be a power that will be accepted by everybody.

3

Excerpts from *Hindutva* *

V.D. Savarkar

Who is a Hindu?

The words Hindutva and Hinduism, both of them being derived from the word Hindu, must necessarily be understood to refer to the whole of the Hindu people. Any definition of Hinduism that leaves out any important section of our people and forces them either to play false to their convictions or to go outside the pale of Hindutva stands self-condemned. Hinduism means the system of religious beliefs found common amongst the Hindu people. And the only way to find out what those religious beliefs of the Hindus are, i.e. what constitutes Hinduism, you must first define a Hindu. But forgetting this chief implication of the word, Hinduism, which clearly presupposes an independent conception of a Hindu, many people go about to determine the essentials of Hinduism and finding none so satisfactory as to include, without overlapping all our Hindu communities, come to the desperate conclusion—which does not satisfy them either—that therefore those communities are not Hindus at all; not because the definition they had framed is open to the fault of exclusion but because those communities do not subject themselves to the required tenets which these gentlemen have thought it fit to label as 'Hinduism'. This way of answering the question 'who is a Hindu' is really preposterous and has given rise to so much of bitterness amongst some of our brethren of [the] Avaidik school of thought, the Sikh, the

* V.D. Savarkar, Hindutva, 6th edn, Savarkar Prakashan, Sarvarkar Sadan, 1989, Mumbai.

Jain, the Devsamaji and even our patriotic and progressive Aryasamajis.

'Who is a Hindu?'—he who is subject to the tenets of Hinduism. Very well. What is Hinduism?—those tenets to which the Hindus are subjected. This is very nearly arguing in a circle and can never lead to a satisfactory solution. Many of our friends who have been on this wrong track have come back to tell us 'there are no such people as Hindus at all!' If some Indian, as gifted as that Englishman who first coined the word Hinduism, coins a parallel word 'Englishism' and proceeds to find out the underlying unity of beliefs amongst the English people, gets disgusted with thousands of sects and societies from Jews to the Jacobins, from Trinity to Utility, and comes out to announce that 'there are no such people as the English at all', he would not make himself more ridiculous than those who declare in cold print 'there is nothing as a Hindu people'. Anyone who wants to see what a confusion of thought prevails on the point and how the failure to analyse separately the two terms Hindutva and Hinduism, renders that confusion worst confounded may do well to go through the booklet 'Essentials of Hinduism' published by the enterprising 'Natesan and Co.'

Hinduism means the 'ism' of the Hindu; and as the word Hindu has been derived from the word Sindhu, the Indus, meaning primarily all the people who reside in the land that extends from Sindhu to Sindhu, Hinduism must necessarily mean the religion or the religions that are peculiar and native to this land and these people. If we are unable to reduce the different tenets and beliefs to a single system or religion, then the only way would be to cease to maintain that Hinduism is a system and to say that it is a set of systems consistent with, or if you like, contradictory or even conflicting with, each other. But in no case can you advance this, your failure to determine the meaning of Hinduism as a ground to doubt the existence of the Hindu nation itself, of worse still to commit a sacrilege in hurting the feelings of our Avaidik brethren and Vaidik Hindu brethren alike, by relegating any of them to the non-Hindu pale.

The limits of this essay do not permit us to determine the nature of the essentials of Hinduism or to try to discuss it at any great length. As we have shown above, the enquiry into what is Hinduism can only begin after the question 'who is a Hindu'? is rightly answered, determining the essentials of Hindutva; and as it is only with these essentials of Hindutva, which enable us to know who is a Hindu, that this our present enquiry is concerned, the discussion of Hinduism falls necessarily outside of our scope. We have to take cognizance of it only so far us it trespasses on the field of our special charge. Hinduism is a word that, properly speaking, should be applied to all the religious beliefs that the different communities of the Hindu people hold. But it is generally applied to that system of religion which the majority of the Hindu people follow. It is natural that a religion or a country or community should derive its name from the characteristic feature which is common to an overwhelming majority that constitutes or contributes to it. It is also convenient for easy reference or parlance. But a convenient term that is not only delusive but harmful and positively misleading should not any longer be allowed to blind our judgement. The majority of the Hindus sub-scribes to that system or religion which could fitly be described by the attribute that constitutes its special feature, as told by Shruti, Smriti and Puranas, or Sanatan Dharma. They would not object if it even be called Vaidik Dharma. But besides these there are other Hindus who reject either partly or wholly, the authority—some of the Puranas, some of the Smritis, and some of the Shrutis themselves. But if you identify the religion of the Hindus with the religion of the majority only and call it orthodox Hinduism, then the different heterodox communities, being Hindus themselves, rightly resent this usurpa-tion of Hindutva by the majority as well as their unjustifiable exclu-sion. The religion of the minorities also requires a name. But if you call the So-called orthodox religion alone as Hinduism then naturally it follows that the religion of the so-called heterodox is not Hinduism. The next most fatal step being that, therefore, those sections are not Hindus at all. But this inference seems as staggering even to those who had unwillingly given wholehearted support to the premises which have made it logically inevitable that while hating to own it they hardly know to avoid arriving at it. And thus we find that while millions of our Sikhs, Jains, Lingayats, several Samajis and others would deeply resent to be told that they—whose fathers' fathers up to the tenth generation had the blood of Hindus in their veins—had suddenly ceased to be Hindu!—yet a section amongst them takes it most emphatically for granted that they had been faced with a choice that either they should consent to be a party to those customs and beliefs which they had in their puritanic or progressive zeal rejected as superstitions, or they should cease to belong to that race to which their forefathers belonged.

All this bitterness is mostly due to the wrong use of the word Hinduism to denote the religion of the majority only. Either the word should be restored to its proper significance to denote the religions of all Hindus or if you fail to do that it should be dropped altogether. The religion of the majority of the Hindus could be best denoted by the ancient accepted appellation, the Sanatan Dharma or the Shruti-Smriti-Puranokta Dharma or the Vaidik-Dharma; while the religion of the remaining Hindus would continue to be denoted by their respective and accepted names, Sikha Dharma or Arya Dharma or Jain Dharma or Buddha Dharma. Whenever the necessity of denoting these Dharmas as a whole arises then alone we may be justified in denoting them by the generic term Hindu Dharma or Hinduism. Thus, there would be no loss either in clearness or in conciseness but on the other hand a gain both in precision and unambiguity which, by removing the cause of suspicion in our minor communities and resentment in the major one, would once more unite us all Hindus under our ancient banner representing a common race and a common civilization.

The earliest records that we have got of the religious beliefs of any Indian community—not to speak of mankind itself—are the Vedas. The Vedic nation of the Saptasindhus was subdivided into many a tribe and class. But although the majority then held a faith that we for simplicity call Vedic religion, yet it was not contributed to by an important minority of the Sindhus themselves. The Panees, the Dasas, the Vratyas, and many others from time to time seem to have either seceded from or never belonged to the orthodox church and yet racially and nationally they were conscious of being a people by themselves. There was such a thing as Vedic religion, but it could not even be identified with Sindhu Dharma; for the latter term, had it been coined, would have naturally meant the set of religions prevailing in Saptasindhu, orthodox as well as heterodox. By a process of elimination and assimilation, the race of the Sindhus at last grew into the race of Hindus, and the land of the Sindhus, that is, Sindhustan, into the land of the Hindus, i.e. Hindusthan. While their orthodox and the heterodox schools of religions have—having tested much, dared much and known much-having subjected to the most searching examination possible till then, all that lay between the grandest and the tiniest, from the atom to the Atman—from the Paramanu to the Parabrahma—having sounded the deepest secrets of thoughts and having soared to the highest altitudes of ecstasy—given birth to a synthesis that sympathizes with all aspirants towards truth from the monist to the atheist. Truth was its goal, realization its method. It is neither Vedic nor non-Vedic, it is both. It is the veritable science of religion applied. This is Hindudharma—the conclusion of the conclusions arrived at by harmonizing the detailed experience of all the schools of religious thought: Vaidik, Sanatani, Jain, Baudda, Sikha, or Devasamaji. Each one and everyone of those systems or sects which are the direct descendants and developments of the religious beliefs Vaidik and non-Vaidik, that obtained in the land of the Saptasindhus or in the other unrecorded communities in other parts of India in the Vedic period, belongs to and is an integral part of Hindudharma.

Therefore the Vaidik, or the Sanatan Dharma itself, is merely a sect of Hinduism or Hindu Dharma, however overwhelming be the majority that contributes to its tenets. It was a definition of this Sanatan Dharma which the late Lokamanya Tilak framed in the famous verse:

प्रामाण्यवुद्धिर्वेदेषु साधनानामनेकता ।
उपास्यानामनियम एतद्धर्मस्य लक्षणम् ॥

Belief in the Vedas, many means, no strict rule for worship—these are the features of the Hindu religion.

In a learned article that he had contributed to the *Chitramaya jagat,* which bears the mark of his deep erudition and insight, Lokmanya in an attempt to develop this more or less negative definition into a positive one, had clearly suggested that he had an eye not on Hindutva as such but only on what was popularly called Hindudharma, and had also admitted that it could hardly include in its sweep the Aryasamajis and other sects which nevertheless are racially and nationally Hindus. That definition, excellent so far as it goes, is in fact not a definition of Hindudharma, much less of Hindutva, but of Sanatan Dharma—the Shruti-Smriti-Puranokta sect, which being the most popular of all sects of Hindu Dharma was naturally but loosely mistaken for Hindu Dharma itself.

Thus Hindu Dharma being etymologically as well as actually and in its religious aspects only (for Dharma is not merely religion), the religion or the Hindus, it necessarily partakes of all the essentials that characterize a Hindu. We have found that the first important essential qualification of a Hindu is that to him the land that extends from Sindhu to Sindhu is the Fatherland (Pitribhu), the Motherland (Matribhu) the land of his patriarchs and forefathers. The system or set of religions which we call Hindu Dharma—Vaidik and non-Vaidik—is as truly the offspring of this soil as the men whose thoughts they are or who 'saw' the Truth revealed in them. To Hindu Dharma, with all its sects and systems, this land, Sindhusthan, is the land of its revelation, the land of its birth on this human plane. As the Ganges, though flowing from the lotus feet of Vishnu himself, is even to the most orthodox devotee and mystic so far as [the] human plane is concerned the daughter of the Himalayas, even so, this land is the birth place—the Matribhu (motherland) and the Pitribhu (father-land)—of that Tatvajnana (philosophy) which in its religious aspect is signified as Hindu Dharma. The second most important essential of Hindutva is that a Hindu is a descendant of Hindu parents, claims to have the blood of the ancient Sindhu and the race that sprang from them in his veins. This also is true of the different schools of religion of the Hindus; for they too being either founded by or revealed to the Hindu sages and seers are the moral and cultural and spiritual descendants and development of the Thought of Saptasindhus through the process of assimilation and elimination, as we are of their seed. Not only is Hindu Dharma the growth of the natural environments and of the thought of the Indus, but also of the Sanskrit or culture of the Hindus. The environmental frames in which its scenes, whether of the Vaidik period or of Bauddha, Jain, or any extremely modern ones or Chaitanya, Chakradhar, Basava, Nanak, Dayanda, or Raja Rammohan, are set, the technical terms and the language that furnished expression to its highest revelation and ecstasies, its mythology and its philosophy, the conceptions it controverted and the conceptions it adopted, have the indelible stamp of Hindu culture, of Hindu Sanskriti, impressed upon them. Hindu Dharma of all shades and schools lives and grows and has its being in the atmosphere or Hindu culture, and the Dharma of a Hindu being so completely identified with the land of the Hindus, this land to him is not only a Pitribhu but a Punyabhu, not only a fatherland but a holyland

Yet, this Bharatbhumi, this Sindusthan, this land of ours that stretches from Sindhu to Sindhu is our Punyabhumi, for it was in this land that the Founders of our faith and the Seers to whom 'Veda', the Knowledge, was revealed, from Vaidik seers to Dayananda, from Jina to Mahavir, from Buddha to Nagasen, from Nanak to Govind, from Banda to Basava, from Chakradhar to Chaitanya, from Ramdas to Rammohan, our Gurus and Godmen were born and bred. The very dust of its paths echoes the footfalls of our Prophets and Gurus. Sacred are its rivers, hallowed its groves, for it was either on their moonlit ghats or under their eventide long shadows, that the deepest problems of life, of man, soul, and God, of Brahma and Maya, were

debated and discussed by a Buddha or a Shankar. Ah! every hill and
dell is instinct with memories of a Kapil or a Vyas, Shankar or Ramdas.
Here Bhagirath rules, there Kurukshetra lies. Here Ramchandra made
his first halt of an exile, there Janaki saw the golden deer and fondly
pressed her lover to kill it. Here the divine cowherd played on his
flute that made every heart in Gokul dance in harmony as if in a
hypnotized sleep. Here is Bodhi Vriksha, here the deer-park, here
Mahavir entered Nirvana. Here stood crowds of worshippers amongst
whom Nanak sat and sang the Arati 'the sun and the moon are the
lights in the plate of the sky?' Here Gopichand the king took on vows
of Gopichand the Jogi and with a bowl in his hand knocked at his
sister's door for a handful of alms! Here the son of Bandabahadur was
hacked to pieces before the eyes of his father and the young bleeding
heart of the son thrust in the father's mouth for the fault of dying as a
Hindu! Every stone here has a story of martyrdom to tell! Every inch
of thy soil, O Mother! has been a Sacrificial ground! Not only 'where
the Krishnasar is found' but from Kasmir to Sinhar it is 'Land of
sacrifice', sanctified with a Jnana Yajna or an Atmaajna (self sacrifice). So to every Hindu, from the Santal to the Sadhu this Bharata
bhumi this Sindhusthan is at once a Pitribhu and a Punyabhu—
fatherland and a holy land.

That is why in the case of some of our Mohammedan or Christian
countrymen who had originally been forcibly converted to a non-
Hindu religion and who consequently have inherited along with
Hindus, a common Fatherland and a greater part of the wealth of a
common culture—language, law, customs, folklore, and history—
are not and cannot be recognized as Hindus. For though Hindusthan
to them is Fatherland as to any other Hindu yet it is not to them a
Holyland too. Their holyland is far off in Arabia or Palestine. Their
mythology and Godmen, ideas and heroes are not the children of this
soil. Consequently their names and their outlook smack of a foreign
origin. Their love is divided. Nay, if some of them be really believing
what they profess to do, then there can be no choice—they must, to a
man, set their Holy land above their Fatherland in their love and
allegiance. That is but natural. We are not condemning nor are we
lamenting. We are simply telling facts as they stand. We have tried to
determine the essentials of Hindutva and in doing so we have discovered that the Bohras and such other Mohammedan or Christian communities possess the essential qualifications of Hindutva but one and
that is that they do not look upon India as their Holyland.

It is not a question of embracing any doctrine propounding any new theory of the interpretation of God, Soul and Man, for we honestly, believe that the Hindu Thought—we are not speaking of any religion which is dogma—has exhausted the very possibilities of human speculation as to the nature of the unknown—if not the Unknowable, or the nature of the relation between *that* and *thou*. Are you a monist—monotheist—a pantheist—an atheist—an agonostic? Here is ample room, O soul! whatever thou art, to love and grow to thy fullest height and satisfaction in this Temple of temples, that stands on no personal foundation but on the broad and deep and strong foundation of Truth. Why goest [thou] then to fill thy little pitcher to wells far off, when though standest on the banks of the crystal-streamed Ganges hereself? Does not the blood in your veins, O brother, of our common forefathers cry aloud with the recollections of the dear old scenes and ties from which they were so cruelly snatched away at the point of the sword? Then come ye back to the fold of your brothers and sisters who with arms extended are standing at the open gate to welcome you—their long lost kith and kin. Where can you find more freedom of worship than in this land where a Charvak could preach atheism from the steps of the temple of Mahakal—more freedom or social organization than in the Hindu society where from the Pandas of Orissa to the Pandits of Benares, from the Santalas to the Sadhus, each can develop a distinct social type of polity or organize a new one? Verily whatever, could be found in the world is found here too. And if anything is not found here it could be found nowhere. Ye, who by race, by blood, by culture, by nationality possess almost all the essentials of Hindutva and had been forcibly snatched out of our ancestral home by the hand of violence—ye have only to render wholehearted love to our common Mother and recognize her not only as Fatherland (Pitribhu) but even as a Holyland (punyabhu); and ye would be most welcome to the Hindu fold.

This a choice which our countrymen and our old kith and kin, the Bohras, Khojas, Memons, and other Mohammedan and Christian communities are free to make—a choice again which must be a choice of love. But as long as they are not minded thus, so long they cannot be recognized as Hindus. We are, it must be remembered, trying to analyse and determine the essentials of Hindutva as that word is actually understood to signify and would not be justified in straining it in its application to suit any preconceived notions or party convenience.

A Hindu, therefore, to sum up, the conclusions arrived at, is he who looks upon the land that extends from Sindu to Sindu—from the

Indus to the Seas as the land of his forefathers—his Fatherland (Pitribhu), who inherits the blood of that race whose first discernible source could be traced to the Vedic Saptasindhus and which on its onward march, assimilating much that was incorporated and ennobling much that was assimilated, has come to be known as the Hindu people, who has inherited and claims as his own the culture of that race as expressed chiefly in their common classical language Sanskrit and represented by a common history, a common literature, art, and architecture, law and jurisprudence, rites and rituals, ceremonies and sacraments, fairs and festivals; and who above all, addresses this land, this Sindhusthan as his Holyland (punyabhu), as the land of his prophets and seers, of his godmen and gurus, the land of piety and pilgrimage. These are the essentials of Hindutva—a common nation (Rashtra) a common race (Jati), and a common civilization (Sanskriti). All these essentials could best be summed up by stating in brief that he is a Hindu to whom Sindhusthan is not only a Pitribhu but also a Punyabhu. For the first two essentials of Hindutva—nation and Jati—are clearly denoted and connoted by the word Pitrubbu while the third essential of Sanskriti is pre-eminently implied by the word Punyabhu, as it is precisely Sanskriti including *sanskaras* that is, rites and rituals, ceremonies, and sacraments, that makes a land a Holyland. To make the definition more handy, we may be allowed to compress it in a couplet—

आसिंधुसिंधुपर्यंता यस्य भारतभूमिका ।
पितृभुः पुण्यभूश्चैव स वै हिंदुरिति स्मृतः ।।

A Sindu Sindhu paryanta, Yasya Bharatbhumika
Pitribhuh Punyabhushchaiva sa vai Hinduriti smritah

Particularistic and Universalist Identity

4

Fluidity or Compartments
Hindus, Muslims, and Partition

Bidyut Chakrabarty

Partition is a story of renegotiation or reordering. It is also a resolution, at least politically, of 'a conundrum' involving Hindus and Muslims in the presence of 'a third party', namely the British. It is furthermore an unfolding of historical processes into which people were drawn spontaneously or under compulsion. They participated as significant actors in what was also 'a history of struggle' for survival in changed circumstances following the construction of a new political identity as Indians or Pakistanis. Independence came in 1947, but with it came Partition. The single most important event that interrogated the concept of 'nation' was Jinnah's success in creating a sovereign Muslim homeland.[1] While the idea of an Indian or Pakistani nation was largely constructed or imagined, it had acquired distinctive characteristics in the struggle against imperialism. The imagined nation was influenced by history, memory of the past, both constructed and real, as well as the philosophical inclinations of India as a socio-cultural identity. This story can be told in two ways: first, one may focus on institutional politics to map the unfolding of the events and processes that eventually led to Partition by linking the various levels of politics over a historical period. Undoubtedly significant, the importance of institutional politics, both in its 'high' and 'low' (sic) form, may look teleological unless it is linked with what had fashioned its articulation in a particular way. In other words, a critical engagement with the British political design to pursue the imperial goal is one of the ways of critically dealing with the outcome with reference to both its immediate and ultimate background. The other interesting way is to capture the multiple 'voices' of those who were directly or peripherally affected following the sudden changes in the political map of India. Some of them were passive but interested observers. Some represented the élites, but most were, argues Mushirul Hasan, 'ordinary folks whose fortunes and destinies were changed without taking into account their feelings and interests'. They spoke 'in different voices', expressed 'varying concern' and chose 'separate and distinct points of identification'.[2]

With the demarcation of boundaries, to those uprooted, the geographical space became a part of memory overnight. Partition is therefore a nodal point underlining a massive shift in conceptualizing 'the self' and 'the collectivity' in relation to the politically demarcated boundaries. How does one capture the 'shift', which was partly obvious given the changed complexion of the idea of nation that began transforming to advance a political goal ever since the articulation of Hindu-Muslim differences? Here, the creative writings of this phase are most crucial to capture and meaningfully explain the multifaceted voice of the people.

The immediate circumstances were a new social landscape in which communities were redefined in consonance with a political goal of the new states. Those who suffered in consequence were 'ordinary folks' who hardly had roles in the realm of 'high' politics. What figured prominently in the literary construction of the event is the break-up of an organic society and the resultant dislocation causing numerous cracks in both intra- and inter-communal relationships.[3] Critical in these narratives was not so much the event of Partition, but 'the impingement of its consequences on the consciousness of the individual: a defining moment that forces him/her to realize the pastness of the past and the presence of the here and now'.[4] The individual was torn between the lost past and an uncertain future. The individual found himself/herself rootless and homeless, a refugee 'who has to strive to relocate his/her identity in a radically different present, which, paradoxically enough, is shaped, influenced and conditioned by the very past which is irrecoverable'.[5]

There is no doubt that in articulating the history of Partition, these voices are very important. Their recovery is not however unproblematic because, (a) there are multiple voices and, (b) they are represented by authors who interrogated Partition from where they were located. In other words, the importance of the perspective is what invariably structured their sensibility and consequently the approach. What is critically imperative is to underline that the representation of the experiences of the creative authors are, after all, their representations, selectively highlighted by their concerns and priorities. The memory or the experience that informs them is a significant input while articulating the voice of the people that may not always correspond with the pattern elsewhere.[6]

What I propose to do now is to selectively draw upon creative writings, primarily from Bengal, to map out the people's voice. My concern is twofold: first, as history, written from archival sources is generally tilted in favour of the 'official' voice, the other side of the story representing different political discourses where people figured prominently remain peripheral, if not completely bypassed. Secondly, it is not my endeavour to place these voices against the 'conventional' and factual history of Partition. Rather, I would like to place them alongside the existing history. In other words, articulation of peoples' voice is complementary to and not contradictory to what has been incorporated in the official records and documents.[7] Underlying different voices lies a common note that informs nearly all the stories, novels, and poems written about Partition and its trauma. A note of utter bewilderment seems to be the basic theme that runs through these writings. Partition radically altered human life on both sides of the border and 'the memories of their collective rites and traditions, stories and songs, names of birds and trees were permanently tinged with the acrid smell of ash, smoke, and blood'.[8]

Hindu-Muslim Quotidian Life

The impact of Partition was enormous in Bengal because not only was it politically divided, but the province witnessed a completely different kind of tension, nurtured and aggravated by communal differences. This is not to suggest that the Hindu-Muslim chasm was articulated only during and after Partition. In the quotidian life, as the contemporary literature illustrates, Hindu-Muslim separation was articulated simultaneously by highlighting the humanitarian dimensions that figured prominently in interactions involving the Hindus and Muslims. One may not find this in the characters Bankim Chandra Chatterjee created to construct a Hindu nation in opposition to Muslim rule. As the old Hindu had suffered from the absence of a combination of physical prowess and desire for self-rule, the new

Hindu, argues Tanika Sarkar, 'will only have arrived when he proves himself in a final battle that will overwhelmingly establish his superiority over the Muslims who had in the past always defeated the Hindus'.[9] While Bankim had a goal for which a strong Hindu appeared to be the most important requirement, Rabindranath Tagore emphasized the egalitarian principles of Islam in contrast to the constrains and injustices, inherent in the caste system. In a short story, *The Tale of a Muslim Woman*,[10] Tagore narrated the plight of Kamala who had no alternative but to take shelter in a Muslim home when she was left behind by her husband and others during her journey to her in-law's house immediately after her wedding. Kamala here is a representative character articulating the agonies of those women who lost their parents and were imposed on relatives for survival. She had to agree to marry the son of a businessman who was 'a womanizer, involved in falcon-flying, gambling and bulbul fights'. On their way, 'the robber', Madhumuller and his gang, attacked the marriage party. Abandoned by her new-found relatives, Kamala was rescued by Habir Khan, a widely respected local Muslim, who brought her home. While describing Khan's house, Tagore sketched in those features, that are reflective of Hindu-Muslim composite culture, but forgotten in the course of untoward circumstances nurtured and created by 'people' with narrow socio-political goals. That Kamala was surprised 'to find a Shiva temple equipped with all the paraphernalia for performing Hindu rituals' is not perplexing. Once Kamala expressed a desire to return home, her decision was carried forward by Habir Khan with a cautionary warning that she would 'not to be taken back home, and will be dumped on the road' simply because she had lived in a Muslim household. This proved prophetic, and Kamala was hounded out of her old home by underlining that it was impossible for them to take her back because 'a fallen woman' who spent nights with Muslims had no place in 'a ritualistic pure caste society'. Kamala returned and arrangements were made for her to live like a Hindu along with Habir Khan's other children. Later in the story, Kamala converted to Islam on her own volition to marry Habir Khan's younger son whom she loved. She was now Meherjan who became an integral part of Khan's household. Tagore concluded the story by re-enacting the incident in which Kamala's uncle's daughter was involved. This time, Meherjan rescued her cousin from the Madhumullar gang when the wedding party was attacked. 'Have no fear, sister,' stated Meherjan. 'You'll be protected by one [Habir Khan] who does not make any distinction between religions.' She also ensured that nobody touched her sister to avoid the plight she had following her compulsion to live in Khan's family immediately after she was deserted by those who accompanied her during the journey for her 'new home'.

As the story suggests, Tagore challenged the stereotypical image of Muslims. For him, Habir Khan is the epitome of a composite culture where boundaries between the communities were created and therefore unreal. The voice that the poet sought to create was neither Hindu nor Muslim but humane—a voice crippled by those, swayed by narrow considerations of caste, clan, or religion. That Kamala became Meherjan is also indicative of the difficulty of an inter-communal marriage without conversion. Overall, this 1941 story, informed by Tagore's own concern for Hindu-Muslim amity, is a significant comment on Bengal's socio-cultural profile at a time when narrow religious considerations were continuously highlighted to advance the interests of one community at the cost of others.

The other example I have drawn upon to capture the neglected voice of history is *Mahesh*,[11] a short story written by Saratchandra Chattopadhyay, depicting the extent of deprivation of the landless peasant in Bengal. Gafoor in *Mahesh* could have been a Hindu or a Muslim. For those who flourished by exploiting the landless peasant, whether the peasant was a Hindu or a Muslim hardly mattered. The story of *Mahesh* is a comment on inter-communal relations in Bengal, woven around the day-to-day life of Gafoor, a Muslim weaver who lost his livelihood with the mechanization of weaving. He lived with his daughter, Amina and Mahesh, a cow that grew up in the family despite severe poverty. Apart from the social distance parting Hindus and Muslims, reflected in the behaviour of Tarkaratna, the 'village priest, the underlying theme of the story revolves around the authors' indictment of the Hindu priest–zamindar combination in rural Bengal that throve on the exploitation of the rural poor irrespective of religion. Gafoor was constantly abused and taunted by Tarkaratna for having christened a cow Mahesh, another name for Shiva of the Hindu pantheon. Tarkaratna also found Gafoor, at fault when he tied Mahesh to an old Acacia tree to prevent him from grazing in others' fields. Just like the other family members, Mahesh was starving to death, and, one day he had 'broken loose from the tether and strayed into the zamindar's garden trampling the flowers. Then Mahesh had spoiled the rice left to dry in the sun and when the gardener tried to catch him he had pushed the landlord's youngest daughter and escaped'. Gafoor was summoned and greatly humiliated by the zamindar. Gafoor went completely 'out of his mind and seizing the ploughshare that lay close by struck Mahesh violently on his bent head. ... His whole body shook twice and then, stretching his hind legs as far as they went, Mahesh breathed his last'. The story concludes with Gafoor leaving the village, along with Amina, in the darkness of the night to work in the Jute factory in Fulbere which he had earlier declined to do because 'there was no religion, no honour and no privacy for women. Although Gafoor had no complaints about his miseries, he however implored Allah to punish those 'who robbed Mahesh of the grass and [which] are your gifts to all creatures'.

Set in twentieth-century Bengal, these stories are clearly indicative of a milieu in which Hind–Muslim relations were constructed. Underlying them lies a common theme that binds the exploiter and the exploited in a common frame regardless of whether they are Hindus or Muslims. What is significant in these two stories is the fact that since Hindus and Muslims were differently placed in socio-cultural terms, it was easier for those with selfish motives to exploit the inter-communal differences to their benefit. Challenging the stereotype description of Hindu-Muslim relations, *Mahesh* and *The Tale of a Muslim Woman* are illustrative of multiple voices of people bound together by a reality where caste and religious prejudices determined inter-communal relations.

Woven around a four-poster bed, Narendra Nath Mitra's *Palanka* (The Four Poster)[12] is a powerful portrayal of Hindu-Muslim quotidian life in east Pakistan immediately after Partition. What is emphasized here is the human bond that held the communities together even when most Hindus left for West Bengal. There was also a noticeable behavioural change amongst Muslims who realized how vulnerable Hindus were in the changed circumstances. Once, when Rajmohan was heckled by Muslims when he demanded that Makbul should return the bed as he had not paid enough, local Hindus persuaded him not to pursue the matter because 'these Moslems are all one.

They have their secret support, or how could Makbul have the cheek to defy [Hindus]? You have to swallow it, there is no other way. The times are not good. You have lost a single bed. So many have given away their houses and lands practically for nothing. What does it matter really? ... You are not going to die for the loss of that bed'.

Rajmohan seemed persuaded because 'it was now Pakistan and it would serve no purpose except to infuriate the big guns of the Moslem community'. Hindus had lost their pre-eminence and the fate of the poor Muslims had not changed either. Hence Fatima, Makbul's wife, failed to understand why in 'Pakistan with a government of the Moslems', Muslims should starve. In response, Makbul philosophically and evocatively says, 'the poor like us have no Pakistan or Hindustan. The grave is the only place we have any right to claim'.

Thus far, the story is woven around the familiar voice of communities that were socio-culturally demarcated. What finally triumphed was the human bond that matured and crystallized by being together even in circumstances when inter-communal relations were not at their best. When Makbul agreed to part with the bed for sheer survival, he asked Rajmohan to take it back before it was resold. Rajmohan declined after having seen the children sleeping peacefully on the bed. For him, 'the bed was, [so far], just an empty pedestal. Today [he saw his] Radha and Govinda on it. My god has returned,' he exclaimed. What is most revealing is the fact that despite fractured voices, perhaps a product of the prevalent socio-cultural differences, highlighted conveniently to further separate the communities, the human bond continued to bind Hindus and Muslims together even when the political map of the subcontinent had entirely changed.

The Pangs of Separation

The Partition stories are more direct, depicting the agony and pain of those who underwent the trauma for no fault of theirs. Based on their experiences of the trauma of the period, the creative writers have evoked the critical voice of the people who had to suffer simply because of the accident of birth by which they were identified as belonging to one particular religion. A new nation was born; antagonistic communities were constructed and justified by exclusionist interpretation of Hinduism or Islam. The outcome was suffering of human beings, classified as Hindus and Muslims. Samaresh Basu's *Adab*[13] is a powerful portrayal of the agony human beings undergo, be they Hindus or Muslims, when caught in a riot. In *Adab*, a Hindu weaver and a Muslim boatman met, not as deadly enemies, but as neighbours in suffering. The poor Muslim sees the poor Hindu as a friend, fleeing a common enemy, the riot. Set in riot-torn Dhaka, to escape from police firing a Hindu worker took shelter in a dustbin where a Muslim boatman had also hidden for safety. What merges from their conversation is a clear note of how 'ordinary folks' endure the trauma when riots strike. I don't understand all this,' remarked the boatman, sharply underlining this by adding:

I am only asking as what will come about from so much killing. Some men from your side will die and some from mine. How will the country gain? You might die or I, our wives and kids will have to beg. .... Who will think of us? Amidst all this rioting how will I earn who will give me food? Will I get my boat back? We are not human beings. We are like vicious dogs.

What is remarkable here is the articulation of a powerful human voice that cuts through artificially created divisions along religious lines. Not only did the boatman or the weaver lose their sources of livelihood but were also the victims of circumstances that did not discriminate between people on the basis of religion. The boatman, identified by the police as 'a dacoit' was shot dead as he was running away when asked to stop. Evoking the sufferings of the innocent, the story articulates a common theme underlying the experiences of people in similar circumstances where religion or community emblem hardly matters.

Salil Choudhary's *The Dressing Table*[14] is a short story based on four letters Rahim wrote to his wife Amina of Howrah when he had gone to Khulna after Partition to search for a job there. These letters were found in a dressing table by Nanda for whom it had been brought by her husband. Replete with references to Hindu-Muslim tensions in Khulna, Rahim was however confident that 'these days cannot last long. We must have faith in our hearts and continue to hope that one day humanity will win'.[15] He failed to understand why Amal, a college teacher in Khulna, decided to leave because Khulna belonged to Pakistan and ceased to be his country. The incident that appeared to have led to Hind–Muslim skirmishes involved primarily 'scheduled caste farmers and fisherman, united to fight the injustice and brutality of the Muslim zamindars'. The police came to arrest the 'leaders of the rebellious villagers—one of whom was a Hindu and the other Muslim'. With the villagers' refusal to hand over the leaders, the police retreated but retaliated by setting fire to several houses in the village. Taking advantage of the situation, a few goondas in the town looted and burnt the shops owned by the Hindus amidst slogans like 'throw the Hindus out'. Not only was this incident presented in the local newspapers in a distorted form but it was also reported that 'not a single Muslim has been left alive in Calcutta', More and more people, wrote Rahim, 'are becoming suspicious of each other, losing faith in each other's integrity. ...People seem to have lost even the last drop of humanity. Bestiality, in its most terrifying form, has been unleashed upon the town'.

In the first part of *The Dressing Table*, the author has portrayed the agony of those poor Hindus who had no option but to continue to live in what later became Pakistan. Once the story shifted to Ujainpura, Howrah, the scene was no different. Poor Muslims, including Rahim's family, were brutally burnt to death. In the words of the author, 'one day, at midnight, the house was locked from outside and set on fire. There was a lot of firing, bullets were flying all around and it was impossible to step outside.' Amina, Rahim's wife, was presumed dead. This is one level of human agony when those who failed to comprehend the sudden changes in their identity following Partition experienced the highest form of brutality, including death. The other form was articulated by those who became *udvastu* (uprooted from home) or *sharanarthi* (shelter-seeker) as soon as the drive to identify aliens began.[16] Muslims poured into Dhaka as they apprehended trouble in Calcutta while Hindus came in groups to Calcutta leaving their homes in east Bengal. In a dilapidated house, the author describes, 'there were at least twenty people inside. Some of them were sitting with their babies, and some lay on the floor. The conditions of the women seemed to be worse than that of the building. They were refugees from East Bengal.' Thus, Partition was a story of displacement of people who neither articulated its form nor contributed to its devastating consequences and yet became its innocent victims.

This theme has been portrayed more sharply by Homen Borgohain in his *Search of Ismail Sheikh*.[17] The story, woven around a search for a character called Ismail, narrates the plight of the refugees who were evicted from east Bengal by force. The first part of the story is a graphic illustration of how a Brahmin father and his daughter lost everything, including their dignity, once they arrived in Calcutta as refugees. The father became a destitute in Sealdah railway station eating the left over food while his daughter 'descended from the sacred height of a Brahmin's house to the depth of a prostitute's room'. Why did they leave East Bengal? 'It is because of the Muslim *goondas* who ruined our life. It is because of them that the daughter of a scholarly Brahmin is a prostitute'. So bitter was the woman that even a Muslim name rattled her as she herself was brutally tortured by the Muslim goondas. The second part of the story revolves around Ismail Sheikh, a Muslim immigrant who left East Bengal in search of better opportunities in Assam. He came to Assam with the hope that he would own land as he had heard of millions of acres of land lying fallow'. He was soon disillusioned and became a virtual slave of the landowners. Later, he 'set up settlements in the dense Assam forests where life was a constant struggle with nature'. In course of time, the

Brahmaputra, the mighty Assamese river, swallowed the settlement which Ismail and his 'comrades' had built up by hard physical labour. They applied to the government for land but were turned down. They therefore encroached upon the government land for sheer survival. In order to reclaim the land, the government ordered that their huts be pulled down by elephants. In the process, Ismail lost two of his children who could not move out of the hut as they were down with smallpox.

The story had a very poignant end with a message that is universal. The victims, whether of Partition or poverty, have no nationalities. The tears one sheds in the face of pain and suffering have no religion. They are neither Hindu nor Muslim. Similarly, the colour of blood is red, be the victim a Hindu or Muslim. Whether in Dhaka or in Delhi, the colour remains unchanged. What comes out of this story is a familiar theme of human suffering in a particular location. How is it possible? 'It is a conspiracy of history,' the author argues, 'in which a handful of landlords and capitalists play crucial roles in fomenting communal frenzy or dividing people in religious terms simply to sustain the rule of the few.' The Muslims in east Bengal, as the story concludes, stained their hands with Hindu blood in the name of religion. The fact is that the leaders had made them drunk on the wine of religion. If not dead-drunk, how could one rape a woman about to give birth to a baby?'

The silent majority continues to suffer. In a metaphorical way, Jayanta De, in *The Pendulum*,[18] links the pangs of Partition with the agony of the people who had confronted the demolition of the Babri Masjid in 1992. In the name of respecting a faith, innocent people suffered in an event that they had neither desired nor to whose articulation they had contributed. In the form of a dialogue between a father and his son, the story portrays the pernicious impact of such political actions on those who simply become the victim of circumstances, be it Partition or the Babri Masjid demolition. During the 1946 Partition riot in Calcutta, communal frenzy was at its peak with Hindus and Muslims pitted as adversaries. We also decided, as the story continues, that 'for every Hindu killed we shall kill ten Muslims'. What had provoked the Hindus was the desire to retaliate against the Muslim leadership for having created a situation in which Hindus and Muslims simply became enemies. This is also a story portraying the emergence of Hindus as a bloc despite obvious internal schisms. Under those circumstances, the Hindu voice was remarkably singular. What brought them together against Muslims

was the slogan, Bande Mataram, apart from 'vengeance for the killing of Hindus'. Decades have passed and the pendulum continues to
swing in the same way probably to indicate that inter-communal
communication has not improved to the extent expected. In 1946 it
was Partition and in 1992 it was the Babri Masjid demolition that
substantiates the point beyond doubt that Hindus and Muslims continue to remain adversaries notwithstanding a long experience with
democratic values.

The White House[19] is an absorbing story of how a horse became a
prey in the bloodbath of the 1946 Calcutta riot. This is not merely a
story of an animal; through a symbolical representation of a horse,
Ramesh Chandra Sen wove in the feelings of those who simply
became victims in an environment, that was not of their creation.
Who suffered most? Innocent people, both Hindus and Muslims,
bore the brunt of the political decisions, taken by the leaders without
taking their views into account. The white horse is perhaps a symbol
bringing together people from both communities. When alive, the
white animal 'brings a fresh whiff of life into the riot torn locality. The
boys are totally absorbed in the horse. The small ones are delighted at
its sight. The bigger one come close and caress its body'. When dead,
Shorab, the horse, brought Hindus and Muslims together to ponder
over who caused his death. Were the soldiers who fired responsible,
or the crowd who provoked the army to resort to firing or the coachman who allowed Shorab to roam freely? The alternatives were many
but the answer remained elusive.

There are two clear voices in this story. The one that is quite
familiar delves into the stereotypical description of Hindus and Muslims at loggerheads as a consequence of religious schism. A riot was
inevitable as the culmination of Hindu-Muslim animosity. This was
evident when the crowd was intent on killing the Muslim coachman
who came to Hindu locality in search of Shorab as vengeance for
brutal murder of Hindus in Metiabruz. Opposed to this was the other
critical voice, which, spoke in a language without rancour. When a
number of people advanced from the crowd to kill the coachman,
Jamuna, Nontey, Habul, and other boys formed a cordon around the
old man to resist the attackers though 'the old man does not seem to
find reassurance in the hundreds of cruel eyes turned in his direction'. What caused them to protect the coachman was a concern for
humanity, which becomes the first casualty in communal frenzy.
Articulating both the mutually exclusive voices, The White Horse
also reiterates the difficulty in conceptualizing Partition as the

inevitable, and possibly the best, outcome merely of circumstances when Hindus and Muslims became permanent adversaries.

Confusion Over Boundaries

Two new nation states were born and the boundaries demarcated in just seven weeks. Those affected, Hindus, Muslims and Sikhs, had no perception of national borders, and yet it was they who were drawn into new nations with completely different labels of identification. Some became Indians and some Pakistanis: new labels of identity which, they had neither created nor easily accepted. There were uncertainties and no one seemed aware of the fate of the place in which they were located. As the novelist Bapsi Sidhwa graphically describes

Hysteria mounted when the fertile, hot lands of Punjab were suddenly ripped into two territories—Hindu and Muslim, India and Pakistan. Until the last moment no one was sure how the land would be divided. Lahore, which everyone expected to go to India because so many wealthy Hindus lived in it, went instead to Pakistan. Jullundur, a Sikh stronghold, was allocated to India.[20]

This is probably the most apt description of how the 'the shadow lines', to borrow the expression from the novelist Amitav Ghosh, was contextualized in contemporary articulation. People simply failed to comprehend the implications that the Radcliffe exercise would have for them. Totally unaware of the plan, they expressed shock and utter bewilderment at the way boundaries were drawn separating people on both sides who had a long history of cultural and social contact. This was most vividly expressed in Satinath Bhaduri's *The Champion of the People*[21] (sic). Located in Aruakhoa, a small village situated between the districts of Purnea and Dinajpur, the story graphically illustrates the predicament of those who did not know whether their village belonged to Pakistan or India. The village had a mixed population of Hindus and Muslims, and had been affected by the 1946 Calcutta and Noakhali riots. Within a year, the scars had healed and 'the compulsion of habit and livelihood once again pulled their patchwork lives together'. This was the context when the Boundary Commission was involved in the demarcation of boundaries.

The story is told through a character called Munimji, the local agent of Johurlal Dokania who owned Sudhani depot. The story began with Munimji's disclosure that Dinajpur and Malda had already become part of Pakistan. The information spread like wildfire and people gathered in the market to collect as much rice as possible to survive this hour of crisis. In view of the sudden demand, Saoji, the local trader immediately raised the price to take advantage of the situation despite the protests of Haji Sahib who appeared to have lost the moral authority he had held just a week prior to Munimj's revelation.

'The panic in the air could make even the strongest of minds unsure of himself. The narrow eyes of the Rajbanshis, the local dwellers, dilate with terror'. Now, Arukhoa wears a changed look. It used to host a market only once a week; now there is miserable crowd of terrified men and women at all hours of the day and night. Cart after cart trundles across the bridge from the direction of Sripur, another village nearby. Droves of women, children, cattle and goats come on foot. Even a little boy carries a pile of pots and pans on his head. A man struck by *kala-zar*[sic] staggers along, gasping for air, a cat held in his scraggy arms. An asthmatic crone goes wheezing past, about to cough up her life, it seems, in her desperation to escape Pakistan. All this time the world of these people was small. Today, however, some of them will move like hunted deer to an uncertain address, after a brief halt at the market place.[22]

Located in two independent nations, India and Pakistan, the people celebrated, Independence Day on 15 August with great enthusiasm. The bridge separating Aruakhoa and Sripur had suddenly become 'unreal', apart from its importance in dividing two nations. This was a poignant moment for those who left Sripur to escape Pakistan. To Darpan Singh of Sripur, the bridge was not merely a physical link between India and Pakistan and also 'the only link between his soul and body'. 'It was because of the bridge that he could escape in time; he might go back to his own country, God willing. Or, is it the will of the [Radcliffe] Commission? Could the Commission be mightier than God', he exclaims.[23]

What radically altered the sombre scene was Munimji's announcement that the Commission had incorporated the district of Malda, including Sripur, in Hindustan. It electrified the atmosphere. Darpan Singh who had left his estate in Sripur 'flings his arms round the Munim'. His father 'bows low to God and the Commission'. He was happy now because 'he will be cremated in the land of Hindus'. Pora Gossain, the religious man, had reasons to curse God as Titlia thana of Jalpaiguri where he lived was included in Pakistan. 'Oh God, did you have to do this? Now I am going to be buried when I die. The Mussalmans won't even let me go to the temple.' In contrast to Hindus who were forced to leave home because their villages were reported to have been integrated with Pakistan, Muslims were relieved when Haripur and Mirpur were included in Pakistan. The experience of those Muslims who stayed back in Mirpur is illustrative here. On hearing that Mirpur formed part of Pakistan, 'Achhimaddi starts to cry. We were running towards Haripur. Mirpur has been Hindustan for the last two days. The Hindus say [that] they will be forced to pray facing east, that they won't let us kill chicken. So, we cleared out everything behind.'

The voice that emerges is unambiguous. Hindus were scared because of possible Muslim atrocities once the Muslim administration took over, while their Muslim counterparts feared the same in areas that became part of Hindustan. The contrasting examples also demonstrate the extent to which the stereotypical Hindu/Muslim perception governed the expression of those affected. What had upset Hindus most was the possibility that they would be buried, not cremated, while to Muslims the possibility of having to pray facing east was most un-Islamic. The impact of the verdict of the Commission was therefore well-anticipated. Here, the boundary between the communities seemed to be clear and not fuzzy, as was the case elsewhere in Bengal presumably due to the 1946 riot that adversely affected the inter-communal socio-cultural contact. Muslims were scared because the 1946 Bihar riot had shown the ugly face of Hindu communalism while the Hindus apprehended Muslim revenge once Partition formally recognized a Muslim state.

People suffered, as the story clearly shows. Who had gained? The rural élite, whether Hindu or Muslim, took full advantage of the confusion created by the Munim himself when he informed the villagers of the eventual contour of the area. Saoji raised the price of rice once villagers apprehended a crisis following the reported verdict of the Commission. Munimji and the local élite made money by re-selling the respective national flags of India and Pakistan to both the Muslims and Hindus, made possible due to the prevalent uncertainty in which he played a role, regarding the status of these villages. As Satinath Bhaduri eloquently puts it:

The Pakistani flags he had sold are handed back to him. Tomorrow, these need to be taken to Titlia, Munimji tells himself. ... These flags will have to be sold there, and the Hindustani flags taken back. The same goods are to be sold twice. He tries to reckon what his profits will add up to. The Commission has given a lot to some people; from others, it has taken a great deal. But it has not failed him; he has extracted his fair share from its verdict. He got the Commission right; there was no mistake.[24]

While Satinath Bhaduri depicted the complexity of life of both communities brought about by the uncertainty of the Boundary Commission verdict Jibananda Das, in a 1948 novel, *Jalpaihati*,[25] dwells on the Hindus predicament pending decision on the fate of Jalpaihati.[26] The principal characters are Nishith, a professor of English in a local college, and his son, Harit, who was inclined toward communism. Nishith came to Calcutta in search of a job in a college that had been set up by Joynath, a rich man who made money by providing admission to students from east Bengal who thronged the city apprehending massive Muslim retaliation after Partition. Harit's purpose was different. 'Although nation is free, its true freedom requires a major revolution indeed,' Harit felt. Both Nishith and Harit were disillusioned because neither was Nishith absorbed in the college nor did Harit meet anybody in Calcutta to appreciate his revolutionary zeal. They were in a limbo. 'They can't go back to Jalpaihati because as Hindus they would hardly be welcomed there.' Although they realized that Jalpaihati was a better alternative, the uncertainty that prevailed over the village pushed them to decide otherwise. Calcutta was equally distressed. 'There are no houses, no jobs or food in Calcutta. Death certainly lies waiting—yet like deformed children they came, only to fall flat on their faces in the alleys, corners and footpaths of this un-welcoming city.'

Once the the story shifted back to Jalpaihati, the scene was familiar. Hindus were leaving the village notwithstanding the request of the Congress leader, Abani Khastagir, not to desert in panic. What disturbed the Hindu sensibilities most adversely was the free movemnt of Muslims in Hindu households, asking for bidis and seeking matrimonial alliances with Hindus. Hitherto unknown of, this dimension of the emergence of Muslims as equal in social interactions was probably most serious socio-cultural affront to the Hindus. It is this attack on the Hindus and a reversal of rituals of deference that 'becomes the moment of realization of the inevitability of migration for the bhadralok families'.[27]

Both, *The Champion of the People* and *Jalpaihati* have one common voice; that of the deeply hurt Hindus. Apprehending that he would not be cremated when he died, Pora Gossain of Titlia was terribly upset once he was told that that his village had been included in Pakistan. This was a serious affront to a Hindu for whom 'cremation was the only way of relief from the mundane human existence'. Similarly, the free access of Muslims to a Hindu household and their expressed desire to marry Hindu girls in Jalpaihati were equally disturbing to the Hindus who preferred migration to Calcutta to avoid their imminent cultural degradation. Despite hardships in a new city, which was not at all friendly, the option to return home was not even suggested once by Nishith or Harit. They confronted the present as unavoidable for a new beginning in the near future.

As in the novels and short stories, the predicament of the refugees constitutes an important theme in contemporary Bengali plays.[28] Of these plays, Salil Sen's *Natun Ehudi* (The New Jews), published in 1950, is probably most subtle in elaborating the text of Partition and the subtext that followed in the aftermath of the division of Bengal. The play is about a refugee family who became the quintessential outsider in Bengal, just like the Jews, in what traditionally belonged to them. This is also an extensive comment on the city of Calcutta that continued to remain alien to this family from East Pakistan. Manmohan Bhattacharya, a Sanskrit teacher in a village school, lost his job once the Muslim-dominated school committee declined to continue with certain practices that were evidently Hindu. Sanskrit was first target as it was 'a sacred language' of Hindus. The playwright has depicted the historical context because the Muslim ministry undertook specific steps to increase Muslim membership of various school boards to purge schools of Hindu influences. In order to tune the school curriculum to Islamic teachings, the syllabi were also radically altered.

Partition made his decision to migrate to Calcutta easier. He had some money which he got by selling his house. Along with his wife and three children, Manmohan spent several days in Sealdah station. He was hopeful that the city, his new home, would without delay provide an appropriate source of livelihood. He was soon disillusioned. For sheer survival, Manmohan accepts the offer to serve as an assistant to the cook in marriage feasts. This was most degrading for a Hindu *bhadralok* who also felt humiliated by the habitual insolent behaviour of his employer. Manmohan found this impossible to bear and soon died after a brief illness. Dukhia, his son, involved in petty criminal activities after Manmohan's demise, was killed in a road accident, and his daughter, Pari, was lured into prostitution. That was the end of the family that had remained alien to the city due to the unfolding historical circumstances they had neither created or played any part in designing.

Concentrating on the agony of the refugees, Metaphorically called *Natun Ehudi*, the play has captured one particular voice: that of the refugees. It is therefore a commentary on the subtext of Partition, dwelling on how the refugee confronted the new status and at what cost. Interestingly, the basic theme, the plight of the refugees, that runs through the play is in clear correspondence with that of *In Search of Ismail Sheikh*, though revolved around the Bengali immigrants in Assam. Sharing the same profession, teaching Sanskrit in village school, Anandacharan Mukhopadhyay in the latter and Manmohan Bhattacharya in the former had to accept jobs not befitting their caste and status. Interestingly, their daughters shared the same fate, both being forced into the flesh trade. The voice in both these creative works is subtle than is expressed. In the story of Ismail Sheikh, the daughter of Anandamohan attributed her becoming a prostitute to Muslims who forced her family out of their home during the Partition riot, while Pari, Manmohan's daughter had to accept prostitution as a profession just for sheer survival in Calcutta. Juxtaposed with the plight of Ismail Sheikh, Homen Borgohain, the author, voices a significant facet of history, of these families suffering and succumbing not because of Partion but because of 'a conspiracy of history' that was articulated in different forms with Partition as one of them. Ismail Sheikh was unable to save his family, including his two severely ill children who were crushed to death when the government officer ordered an elephant to pull down his thatched house which he viewed as an encroachment on government land. Partition was remotely linked to Ismail Sheikh who came to Assam from east Bengal for survival, and yet he experienced the same fate as the victims of Partition. *Natun Ehudi* is more explicit and spells out what was described as 'the conspiracy of history' at the end of the play when Mohan, the only son of Manmohan who survived, exhorted,

[b]ut the causes that led to the death of his father and brother still persist, and they have left us to demand an explanation. ... So be one with the oppressed and take a vow that you will punish the selfish and the greedy and those who are playing with the lives of all of you. Take a vow that you will end the exploitation of the cruel oppressors.[29]

The Multifaceted or Fabricated Public Face(s)?

Childishness[30] is a sarcastic comment by Manik Bandyopadhyay on those adults who by magnifying the Hindu-Muslim divide articulated and defended Partition. The story is told at two levels. At a somewhat mundane level, the author believes that the communal divide was temporary and it was therefore childish to attempt a serious discourse; at a more philosophical level, the author was persuaded to accept that the Hindu-Muslim schism was deep-rooted with well-entrenched prejudices and distrust of each other. That Hindus killed Muslims and vice-versa in riots clearly reveal that the inter-cultural penetration was largely superficial rather than organic.

The story is woven around two families, one Hindu and the other Muslim, located in the bylanes of Calcutta. Although they lived in two separate areas of the same building, the wall dividing them was too small to actually detach the families. Both the families were faced with a common predicament and compulsion. Tarapada and Nasiruddin both went out to work in the morning and returned home exhausted at the end of the day. 'The same blighted dreams and eager imaginings piled up day by day in both their hearts, the same anger against the same forces grew intenser everyday.' The wives, Indira and Halima, shared similar lifestyles as they lived in identical socio-economic circumstances. Nonetheless, there was hardly any communication between the families until children were born to them. Indira's daughter, Gita, and Halima's son Habib shattered the division 'with their denial of any unnatural man-made remoteness'. They drew the families closer.

Intimacy between the families developed. One day when Gita ate beef from Habib's plate, neither Tarapada nor his wife took notice as it was quite normal among the children. Indira, Tarapada's wife, justified this by saying 'if beef doesn't harm Habib why should it harm her daughter?' What does it matter if she's eaten some—a tiny girl like her'. It may not have affected their Hindu sensibility, but they were well aware that their acceptance might not go down well in the locality as beef-eating is a taboo for Hindus. Indira, therefore warned Halima 'don't tell anyone sister'. The incident clearly illustrates the predicament of familes which, despite their intimacy, are governed by deep-seated prejudices against each other. Not only did Indira take cognizance of the incident, but Halima felt bad that Gita ate beef from Habib's plate. Similarly, the fact that Habib offered flowers and partook of *prasad* at Saraswati Puja did not make any difference to Tarapada and his wife. It was however made to happen when 'there is no one in the room'. Again, this demonstrates that in the private sphere, this type of inter–communal exchange is perfectly in tune with Hindu sensibilities and is not at all vitiated by the campaign in the public domain. It is however difficult, if not impossible, to argue that the nature of public and private interaction between the communities is uniform simply because the pattern radically varies from one location to another and from one phase of history to another. For Gita and Habib, it was simply beyond their comprehension 'why there should be so much fighting and killing all around; why it [a riot] should suddenly rear its head in such ugly shape?' They were bewildered and terrified; their hearts quavered.

Apprehending a riot, the locality instituted a joint peace committee not because of 'idealistic outpouring of Hind–Muslim unity', but because of 'the simple material truth , that 'violence in this mixed area would be equally dangerous for all'. The idea of an impending riot became real in the public sphere. The families were drawn into it, but the riot provided the children with a specific type of sport in which they utilized knife and razor to give it an appearance of reality. In the process, one of them sustained a slight wound. This led to a situation when 'the two obstinate, unruly children began stabbing and lunging at each other with a blunt knife and a blunt razor, crazed by pain, rage and resentment'. What appears to have given this story a fantastic dimension was the involvement and counter-accusation of the families holding one or the other responsible for the incident. One thing led to another. Indira and Halima rushed like 'madwomen; their heads knock together; they look at each other with savage eyes, like two tigresses about to attack.' Tarapada and Nasiruddin were not left behind. Threatening each other with dire consequences, they appear to have been drawn to the public sphere drawing sustenance from the unbridgeable communal distinction between Hindus and Muslims. The situation worsened in the evening when neither Gita nor Habib was to be found in the rooms in which they slept. When the search yielded no results, both the families began accusing each other of having 'lured the children' as a matter of vengeance. The message spread like wildfire. Drawing upon the mutual distrust between the communities, an atmosphere was created which gained credibility in view of the tension-prone environment of the city. As Bandyopadhyay describes,

This time, there is no way to stem the tide: rumour and tension begin to spread like fire. All these days, for all their efforts, the provocations haven't been able to shown their fangs in the neighbourhood. They must have been waiting for just this chance, and now they spring. In trice, two bands of demented men gather in front of the two houses. This lot wants to attack that house, that lot this. But as there are two groups, neither can reach its target without first defeating the other in a street battle.[31]

The battle was about to commence when the children reappeared.

They had climbed unobserved to the roof of the house to play at some time of the day. This is the punch line of the story. Those who caused consternation among the families, so far living like a unit, were hardly affected by the growing separation between communities in the public domain. For many of those who 'had flocked there, out of their minds with homicidal rage, didn't even know [that] these two were the cause of the trouble'.

Appropriately entitled *Childishness*, the story brings out multiple voices, articulated at different levels. For Gita and Habib, a riot was a frightening but at the same time an amusing event because it became a game, different from those they were accustomed to. The families were split despite extended social and cultural contact in various forms and ways. What it shows is the role of public sphere in clearly shaping a particular type of human response. The immediate environment had a role to play; what the story reiterates was the growing importance of a voice that loomed large under circumstances where narrow and parochial considerations were privileged to fulfill a specific socio-political goal. What is puzzling is why the individuals, not so much influenced by sectarian aims, merge their identities with those seeking to attain a goal in the name of a community. In *Childishness*, the inhabitants lived side by side, mixed together, and the communal divide never became a factor in their day-to-day interaction. Perhaps, as the author laments, 'they had not, at all, mixed intimately'. The story reveals aspects of Hindu-Muslim schism, and also the mutual distrust perpetuating the image and construction of the 'other'. Living side by side does not necessarily mean living with each other. Is interaction at festivals like Saraswati Puja, sufficient to banish the exclusivist mindset built into the collective psyche of the people? The story has no conclusive answer but simply underlines the structural ingredients of an environment in which the people's voice is fractured, foregrounding, on occasion, the human over parochial considerations.

The Other Side of Partition

Violence seems to be one of the important dimensions of stories from Punjab[32] while in Bengali creative writings, it has generally been underplayed, presumably to highlight the mutually inclusive existence of Hindus and Muslims over generations. One Bengali writer who dealt with this aspect of Partition is Saradindu Bandyopadhyay. In his writings, Partition violence constitutes an unavoidable aspect that suddenly became dominant in inter-communal interaction during those tumultuous days, particularly in Calcutta. There are five stories—two detective stories, *Adim Ripu* (Primeval Enemy), *Rakter Daag* (The Bloodstrain); a novel, *Rimjhim* (Pitter and Patter); two short stories, *Bisher Dhnoya* (The Poisonous Smoke), *Dui Dik* (Both Sides)[33]—in which the principal themes are violence and the resultant insecurity of the Bengali middle class. Of these, *Adim Ripu* is perhaps the most clearly documented narration of Partition violence where the underlying theme is the growing importance of the underworld in sustaining and fomenting communal violence in Calcutta. It is also there that the author confronted the most chaotic part of history which also saw the growing distance between the two communities. How was it possible in view of a long-term social and cultural contact between Hindus and Muslims over generations? The author appears to have attributed the gory Partition violence to the hegemonic role of the underworld. His voice is from both Hindus and Muslims who unquestionably suffered equally as the events unfolded.

The underworld came alive under the cover of communal violence. To the fear of the knife held in the hands of the violent 'other', was added 'the fear of the goondas who extracted his own charge for the continuing safety of the people in his locality'.[34] The author had to maintain a steady supply of cigarettes and tea to the goondas for the security of his family. There is no doubt that in the Partition violence, it was the goondas who benefited most. Also, whether they were Hindus or Muslims, goondas were similar in their behaviour and activities. In *Adim Ripu*, it was a Hindu, Bantul Sardar, who rose to prominence for having provided safety to the Hindus in the Bowbazar area during the riot. No dissent to his order was acceptable. Even the Hindus who provided protection to Muslims in the area were not spared. Bantul threatened Ajit, another character, who did not find any logic in killing Muslims because they were Muslims, with dire consequences if he continued to intervene in this struggle 'to finally settle the score with the Muslims'.

That goondas have no religion, no nationality finds further sharp restatement in *Dui Dik* where Noor Mian, a Muslim goonda, discharged similar responsibilities vis-à-vis Muslims in areas between Mechobazar and Badurbagan. The story is woven around a Hindu doctor who had a dispensary in this area. Once, when there was a rumour that Hindus killed Muslims in other areas of Calcutta, Noor Mian plunged into action by butchering Hindus indiscriminately.

From the outset, his familiar pattern of action was to knife the Hindus who unsuspectingly passed through his area or came to visit the doctor for treatment. Informed by his cronies, he could easily identify Hindus vis-à-vis Muslims. Later, Hindus, especially Marwaris, came as 'hunter, armed to the teeth' and the situation worsened.

Thus far, the story is confined to familiar terrain: Noor Mian's involvement in the riot is articulated in the binary opposition between Hindus and Muslims. The voice is undiluted and the explanation is mono-causal. Caught in a dilemma given his Hindu identity and profession, the doctor is probably the most significant character articulating the multiple voices of those who suffered equally whether they were Hindus or Muslims. As his dispensary was located in a Muslim majority area, he had, to the extent possible, submerged his Hindu identity. As a doctor who treated the wounded, Hindus or Muslims, he escaped Noor Mian's wrath. Under the circumstances, the doctor's dilemma was resolved by underplaying his Hindu identity and this suffused his mind with resentment. In other words, the voice that took precedence here was the deeply felt fear that engulfed him who fathomed the consequences of a riot but failed to comprehend how 'human beings' who grew up together in the same area could become so brutal.

There was another interesting twist when Noor Mian, fatally wounded by 'a *chotidhari* Hindustani' was brought to the doctor for treatment. The doctor was in a dilemma. He appeared to be happy because a Hindu had finally succeeded in showing his strength vis-à-vis Noor Mian, the architect of goonda raj in the area. 'I felt like letting the wretch lie there and die—as you sow, so shall you reap. Let him atone for his sins with his face grounded in mud,' felt the doctor. Apprehending that 'he will be poisoned by the Hindu doctors in Mitya College', he urged the doctor to treat him at his dispensary. Torn between his hate for Noor Mian and his professional duty to save an injured Muslim, the doctor himself was amazed at the way his conscious mind was clearly divided: 'when he wanted to give Noor Mian poison, he gave him fruit juice, and when the delirious man yelled out, *maro Hindu, maro Hindu* [kill Hindus], he pressed ice bags to his head'.[35] The doctor in him won, and the Hindu self was contained, or humanity prevailed over other parochial considerations. This was sharply delineated when Noor Mian insisted on paying the doctor a hefty sum for having saved his life. 'You can't repay me money, but you can repay me with something far more difficult than that', doctor said. Noor Mian pledged to do anything except abdicate his religion. The doctor sought an assurance that he would abdicate his career as a goonda and also forsake his cocaine habit. Noor Mian was astounded, and momentarily speechless, but after a while, said 'Malik, you have just robbed me of the only life I have ever known, but your demand, I will do my best to obey'.

The Partition riots are an occasion, as Bandyopadhyay chronicles, when the appearance of goondas as saviours tends to consolidate the separate Hindu-Muslim identities as contrasting, if not antagonistic, blocs. Also, when it comes to cruelty, neither Hindu nor Muslims differ from each other. How do they gain legitimacy? Hinting at the charged atmosphere due to brutal killings of Hindus by Muslims and vice versa, the author seeks a possible explanation. The city was not clearly bifurcated along religious lines. Even the doctor who saw Hindus being butchered by Noor Mian and his cronies at the doorstep of his dispensary faced a serious dilemma, as the Hindu in him was brutally hurt and would probably have welcomed a vengeance when Noor Mian was under his medication. In his reconstruction of the past the doctor clearly saw that it was not merely is professional ethics, but his faith in humanity that eventually determined his behaviour when Noor Mian was under his care. This is also evidenced in the doctor's inclination to forget those traumatic days as mere ripples in human history when he says 'I do not see the least necessity of describing the macabre sight in detail; you had all been in Calcutta in those days, you have all witnessed a little or much of that I have seen'. Forgetting the past creatively was probably the best way of remembering bygone days.

As the stories have shown, the voice of the people is clearly fractured though there is an underlying thread of unity based on the trauma of Partition. In other words, although clearly fractured, these multiple voices are nonetheless well-articulated, underling the most defining moment in South Asian history brought about by circumstances beyond their control. Munimji in *The Champion of the People* and, Noor Mian, in *Dui Dik* are, for instance, not peculiar to Partition, forever thriving in times of acute uncertainty and dislocation. That a Hindu doctor saved Noor Mian's life shows that even at the height of communal distance human identity, justified in terms of professional ethics, prevailed over other narrow and parochial considerations. This also emerges from the recorded views of a large number of Bengali Hindu women who became easy targets at the time of Partition.[36] They were certainly traumatized, but never held the entire Muslim community responsible for this event presumably

because several Muslims, individually as well collectively, both protected them and provided an escape route when troubles brewed in
the locality. While narrating her story, Pramila Das, who had to leave
east Bengal in the wake of the Partition riots in 1946, simply refused
to blame Muslims in general for the bloodbath. Once 'Muslims ma-
rauders attacked our house and butchered every member of my
family—male, female and child', she reminisced, 'I fled secretly
through a backdoor, ran breathlessly and reached a neighbouring
Muslim house. They were kind enough to hide and protect me as a
family member. It was they who informed my husband who rescued
and took me back to Shillong'.[37] Similarly, Anupama Deb too was
faced with a frightening situation during the height of a riot when a
student of her husband saved the family by moving them to his house
and later escorted them to Khulna that was relatively free from
communal skirmishes.

How do they explain the volcanic eruption-like violence in Bengal
where Hindus and Muslims had been symbiotically associated over
generations? The answer varied, though in their elaboration of the
circumstances two factors appear to have gained enormous significance. First, as the explanation is couched in socio-economic terms,
primacy is given to the precarious economic conditions of the Muslim peasants vis-à-vis the Hindus who were relatively well-placed.
This was compounded by the growing cultural differences that en-
gendered a deep sense of alienation between Muslims and their
Hindu neighbour. The second factor was the success of the local
mullahs in disseminating the view that the Hindu attitude stemmed
from their abhorrence of Islam. Once the questions of Islam was
raised several Muslim families who were otherwise not antagonistic
to their Hindu neighbours remained aloof. It was 'this indifferent
silent majority' that made a significant differences to those who took
full advantage of 'the chaos and uncertainty'.

Among the women, the impact of Partition varied depending on
their socio-economic status. Those who belonged to the rich or landed
class, the educated middle class, or the professional category were
undoubtedly caught up as victims of circumstances but survived
once they migrated to Calcutta. Their economic circumstances were
however far below what they had earlier been. The economic difficulties they faced was attributed to the dislocation from their 'homes'.
Severe mental trauma resulted from 'the sense of loss' after they were
forcibly uprooted 'from their birthplace, their home and hearth'. It
was further aggravated when, as refugees, they were often ridiculed,

as Prabharani recollected with agony, by 'their neighbours in Calcutta'. The standard charge was that 'the city has become filthy due to the flooding of the refugees [who] have distorted the city's image by their dialect, their dress and the way they live'. This is one part of the story. The other part dwelt on the experiences of the relatively poorer section of Hindus in east Bengal who migrated to Calcutta in the wake of communal attacks on them. They were petty traders, artisans, masons, carpenters, and fishermen. Illustrative of their life in the aftermath of migration in Calcutta are the stories of Kusum and Kamala. They led a comfortable life with the income provided by their husbands. Once in Calcutta, they took shelter on the railway platforms and in transit refugee camps. For them, Partition completely dislocated their lives and made them 'destitute'. There were hardly jobs to which their husbands could apply their skills. Calcutta thus became '*narak* [hell] for us after a week of arrival in the city [which] offered neither shelter nor allowed us opportunities to live in a respectful manner'. As there was no alternative, Kamala and Kusum were forced to take jobs as maidservants in a variety of households. Partition was thus not merely an event of August 1947 that had caused immense misery to Hindus of east Bengal but also a constant reminder to these families of their sudden loss of dignity and social status which they had to compromise for sheer survival.

Partition is also the story 'of displacement and dispossession, of large-scale and widespread violence, and of realignment of family, community and national identities'.[38] Juxtaposed with the creative writings, the oral testimony of these women reveals the human dimension of the 'event' that not only brought about radical cartographic changes in the subcontinent, but also transformed the mental map of those who overnight became 'alien citizens' due to circumstances beyond their control. Partition therefore lives, as the commentator argues; 'in family histories ... where tales of horror and brutality, the friendship and sharing, are told and retold between communities, families and individuals'.[39] Gendered oral narratives also underline that the brutal story cannot only be articulated in binary opposition between a vulnerable Hindu woman and the Muslim aggressor; there are innumerable instances of Muslims protecting and rescuing Hindu families. Not only have these instances challenged the 'cultural incompatibility' between the two communities, embodied in Jinnah's two nation theory, they have also foregrounded the human over other narrow and parochial considerations.

In contrast to the Bengal experiences, what emerges from the oral testimony of Hindu and Sikh women in Punjab is a mixed bag. On the one hand, Hindus and Muslims had lived together without large-scale friction for generations although culturally segregated in watertight compartments. As Urvashi Butalia argues, what alienated the Muslim was the way they were 'ill-treated' by the Hindus in their day-to-day interactions. For instance, 'if a Muslim guest comes to [a Hindu] house, he was asked to eat from the earmarked utensils and also wash them. While serving, *rotis* were thrown from such a distance to avoid being polluted by an accidental touch with the utensils'.[40] This is one side of the story; the oral narratives of Subhasani whose father was murdered by Muslims represents the other side. This event became a reference point for any discussion on Partition by her. She was happy when 'the Hindu community, imbued with the spirit of sacrifice and revenge ... wanted to take revenge for what was being done to our brethren in Punjab [though she felt bad] by the treatment meted out to Mussalman women and children. It was not a very pleasant experience', she underlined, 'to see Mussalman women and children being brutally killed'.[41]

The Un-fractured Bengali Sensibilities: The Other Side of Partition

Partition marks a breakdown of that community which had defined the individual and his/her identity. That is the common theme running through most east Pakistani creative writing seeking to articulate the voice of the people. There is however a significant difference: while in most of the stories in the context of Partition riots in Punjab, violence seems to be an important, if not overarching, dimension of the human experience, Bengali stories are relatively free from violence in its crudest form. As violence is peripheral in most of these Bengali stories, killings are usually shown as 'isolated' events with a distant backdrop of Partition riots. Even the death toll in Bengal was smaller than in the western part of India and there were no parallel massacres of people in the trains or in refugee camps. Stories are plenty though the theme is more or less similar, as Niaz Zaman has shown in *A Divided Legacy*.[42]

What is conspicuous in most of the stories is an articulation of Bengali cultural sensibilities that appear to have surpassed other parochial considerations, based on a narrow interpretation of religion. The Bengali identity appears to have, on occasion, surpassed the religious distinction of the communities. 'Here no one is a Hindu, no one is a Muslim. We are Bengalis. We are one,' proclaimed Shanti Muzumdar, the principal character in *The Mother of Dhirendu Muzumdar*.[43] She also warned that 'if the head and the body were separated, then like Rahu and Ketu they will play a very destructive game. Both the sun and the moon will come under total eclipse.' While this was clearly a voice of opposition, the sense of loss and agony appear to be conspicuous in most of the stories. Set in the height of communal animosity, Syed Waliullah's *The Story of the Tulsi Plant*,[44] for instance, captures the emotional predicament of a family of Muslim refugees when a tulsi plant, a Hindu religious symbol, was discovered in a house into which they trespassed for shelter. The inmates in the house, which was deserted, had no problem so long as its identity was not known. With the presence of a tulsi plant, it was different because 'this half dead, dried, insignificant Tulsi plant, caught unaware, had revealed the secrets of the house'. Therefore 'it has to be torn out because no Hindu symbols can be tolerated' as some members of the family maintained. The others thought of the woman who had nurtured the plant religiously as an integral part of the household.

They were not entirely familiar with Hindu customs; but they had heard that in a Hindu home, the mistress of the house lighted a lamp under the plant at dusk, and with the end of her *sari* wrapped her neck, made a *pranam*, bowing touch the earth with her head. Though it was overgrown with weeds now, someone had lighted a lamp every evening under this abandoned Tulsi plant too. When the evening star, solitary and bright, shone in the sky, a steady quiet flame had burned red, like the touch of crimson paint on the bowed forehead.

The plant survived, and even the staunch Hindu baiter in the family who wanted to destroy the plant at the outset began caring for it as the days passed: the human voice had prevailed. What it is relevant to note is the underlying theme, articulated in the pain and agony of the Hindu family that had vacated the house and that of those who had occupied it. Their plight was the same. Both the families are victims of circumstances beyond their control and became homeless refugees with an uncertain future in an unknown place. For the Hindu housewife, 'tending the plant might have been a religious duty', for the refugees, who took care of it despite initial reluctance, 'it was a reminder of their common humanity, of the need for roots, for the ordinary rhythms of life which the political events and upheavals [violently] disrupt'.[45] Once uprooted, the *udvastu* became vulnerable even when they were 'the government's people'.

With the requisitioning of the house by the state, the inmates were asked to vacate within twenty-four hours as 'they have illegally occupied the house'. A shadow of gloom descended upon the house. 'There was no end to anxious speculations. Where could they go, they wondered.' This is where Waliullah is at his best in focusing on the trauma of human beings who became the first victims of Partition. Just like the tulsi plant, which had a fresh lease of life due to the support of those who had occupied the house despite initial reluctance, the refugees, whether in Pakistan or India, were equally helpless in the radically altered circumstances. They were as 'vulnerable as the Tulsi plant [as] the life and well-being of the tulsi plant could not be insured by its own powers of self-protection'.

Abu Rushd's *Nongor* is another fine representation of the contrasting voices of the Muslims who also happened to be Bengalis. Two major themes recurred in the novel. The first is the enthusiasm with which Pakistan was conceptualized. Pakistan was 'necessary' for Kamal, the principal character in *Nongor*, 'to understand that the entire world is mine. In its paddy fields, I find my own fragrance. I revivify in the electric violence of storms. Its fruits and flowers sustain and refresh me. Its breezes will lull my child to sleep. There my being is different, secure and unique.'[46] Kamal was happy because Radcliffe 'has promised Nazimuddin that Calcutta, from Sealdah to Park Circus, where the wealthy Muslims live—would go to Pakistan. The second equally important concern of Rushd centres around the fate of those Muslims left behind. At least seven crores of Muslims 'will benefit', Kamal confidently claims. What will happen to those stuck in India? Kamal had no clue. This was true of the Hindus who stayed back in Pakistan even after the *batwara* (division)! So, 'the problem has not been solved', concluded Kamal.

In *Nongor*, Partition constitutes the background and there is scarcely any detailed comment on it. Kamal left Calcutta not because of communal strife but for a better life that was assured to him as it was 'a Muslim land'. There are however stray references to Partition that 'aroused suspicion and raised walls between the communities which till then had coexisted peacefully, if not happily'. What does stand out is the Bengali identity, nurtured and refined by both Hindu and Muslim cultural ethos over generations. Therefore Kamal, who most happily accepted Pakistan, did never compromise with his identity, rooted in 'composite Bengali culture' by saying that 'supporting Pakistan does not mean that I will cut myself off from my entire past. My unique identity is inseparably made up of my past, present and future. After I finish my life on earth perhaps I shall return as a lotus flower, or a cock to wake up people in the morning, or perhaps even a star to shine up above.'[47]

Concluding Observations

Partition is a watershed event in the construction of nation in the aftermath of British rule in India. Redefining Hindus, Muslims and Sikhs as Indians or Pakistanis, the 1947 division is a story of renegotiation and reordering of the identity of the individual or the community. It was not merely a history of violence, or victimhood, or of madness, but also 'a history of struggle of people fighting to cope, to survive and build anew'.[48] What appears to have emerged in the context of Partition were two mutually contrasting tendencies: on the one hand, the clamour for Partition, supported by both the Congress and League high command, clearly demarcated Hindus and Muslims at every level of their existence despite them having lived side by side over generations; in contrast there is another layer of existential experience where Hindus and Muslims remained organically linked with one another as human beings despite the well-designed attempts to segregate the two.[49] As shown, examples abound in the creative writings of the period from both sides of the border. By focusing on individuals, their agony, pain, and sorrow in particular historical circumstances, these stories become representative of the time and its predicament; they thus provide 'a mental map' of Partition. Because literature transcends time, these stories 'are relevant ... as they vividly portray the existential absurdity of the hatred [and also how they] negotiated the complexity and liminality of expression of people, caught in the competitive savagery of Partition'.[50]

The literature of Partition affirms that 'the subject of Partition was first the human being—not the Hindu human being nor the Muslim, nor the Sikh—[and] the experiences of each community distinctly mirror one another, indeed reach out to and clutch at one another'.[51] Sadat Hasan Manto's Toba Tek Singh was at a complete loss once the country was divided and people labelled Hindustani and Pakistani. '[A]ll the inmates in the asylum found themselves in a quandary; they could not figure out whether they were in Pakistan or India, and if they were in Pakistan then how was it possible that only a short while ago they had been in India when they had not moved from the asylum at all'.[52] Most of the characters are not reconciled to borders being drawn and people being uprooted from their familiar socio-cultural milieu. They remind us time and again, as Mushirul Hasan succinctly puts it, 'regardless of religious passions being heightened by the politics of hate and of the fragile nature of inter-community relations in the 1940s, most people had no clue whatsoever' of the nature of the forthcoming division.[53] Perhaps the most significant was how the boundaries arbitrarily dissolved older identities as towns, cities, and villagers mercilessly scattered right or left as the juggernaut of Partition etches its way across the face of the country'.[54] Nothing can be more explicit than the growing unease of Toba Tek Singh regarding the 'whereabouts' of his village.

He began asking people where Toba Tek Singh was, for that was his home town. But no one could answer that question for him. And if someone did make an attempt to figure out the present status of Toba Tek Singh, more confusion would follow. It had been rumoured that Sialkot, which was once Hindustan was now in Pakistan today; who can say where Lahore, which was in Pakistan today, would be tomorrow, and was there anyone who could guarantee that both Pakistan and Hindustan would not disappear someday?[55]

It is evident that the high politics of Partition constitutes the background of the majority of the stories. People affected in a variety of ways stand out even in the context of the acute uncertainty following the transfer of power. Dwelling on 'the affective experience of the events and their consequences for the ordinary people', these stories not only delineate 'the ways the partition felt', but also articulated 'the historical memory' of a phase in which human beings suffered, both physically and emotionally, for reasons beyond their control.[56] It was not only that 'the country was split into two—bodies and minds were also divided'. Ismat Chughtai, the creative Urdu writer, also notes,

Those whose bodies were whole had hearts that were splintered. Families were torn apart. One brother was allotted to Hindustan, the other to Pakistan; the mother was in Hindustan, her offsprings were in Pakistan; the husband was in Hindustan, his wife in Pakistan. The bonds of relationship were in tatters, and in the end many souls remained behind in Hindustan while their bodies started off for Pakistan.[57]

There is a familiar theme in all the stories, be they from the east or west. People suffered due to circumstances of which they were the victims. Arbitrary boundaries were drawn and two nations became sovereign after protracted struggle against colonialism. The colonial atmosphere created an imagined collectivity in response to a political campaign for separate nation-states. In other words, the collectivity that came into being was a political construct: the product of human interaction and human imaginations drawing upon particular historical circumstances. It would not be an exaggeration to argue therefore that movements for and against Partition had an adequate support base in certain quarters, including those who mattered at the level of high politics. As shown, both in Bengal and Assam, Partition emerged as the best possible solution to avoid an imminent bloodbath on a mass scale. This is an equally important part of the story of Partition that simply cannot be wished away while grappling with the 'events' and the subsequent consequences. The creative writings, which are powerful portrayals of a fragmented and wounded society, act as complementary sources to piece together the relatively unknown dimension of those tumultuous days when the religious description of the community appeared to have been privileged. The aftermath of Partition is what constituted the backdrop of most of the stories underlining the impact of displacement, uprootedness, and alienation of the inner self and the renegotiation of identity within a radically altered milieu. In this sense, they serve a useful historical purpose in grasping the processes, manifested in the articulation of a new identity both for the nation and its citizens—where the past, present, and future come together to mutually redefine themselves through an equally intricate process of contestation and adjustment.

Notes

1. There was a parallel attempt by the 'depressed classes' to construct an independent identity, as Urvashi Butalia informs us. According to her, 'a sense of separateness seemed to have become essential to establishing a sense of identity. Thus the fear of conversion at the hands of "others"—Muslims, Sikhs [and] Christians. Conversion was suspect because it was done, clearly with a view to increasing their number solely for political purpose. A demand for separate electorates, for proportional political representation, for a presence in the important decision-making bodies, these were some of the broader realities that underlay the sense of difference [and] of separateness. ... And lest this seem like a chimera, they had provided a rationale, and invented a name for this imaginary homeland: Achhutistan, the land of the untouchables.' Urvashi Butaiia, *The other Side of Silence: Voices from the Partition of India*, Viking, New Delhi, 1998, pp. 238–9.

2. Mushirul Hasan, *India Partitioned: The Other Face of Freedom*, vol. I, Roli Books, New Delhi, 1995. p. 26.

3. Mushirul Hasan thus argues, 'the intellectual resources made available

to us by such creative writings ... provide a foundation for developing an alternative discourse to current expositions of a general theory on inter-community relations'. Mushirul Hasan. 'Memories of a Fragmented Nation: Rewriting the Histories of India's Partition', in Mushirul Hasan (ed.), *Inventing Boundaries: Gender, Politics and the Partition of India*, OUP, New Delhi, 2000. pp. 39–40.

4. Bodh Prakash, 'Nation and Identity in the Narratives of Partition', in Vinita Damodaran and Maya Unnithan Kumar (eds), *Post Colonial India: History, Politics and Culture*, Manohar, New Delhi, 2001, p. 75.

5. Ibid.

6. There is great difficulty in articulating people's voice through these narratives. As Urvashi Butalia argues, there is invariably a gulf between, for instance, how people define their identity and how they are represented in accounts, written by others. The representation of experiences of women, children, and scheduled castes at Partition are, after all, her construction, selectively illuminated by her concerns and priorities. 'To me', she argues further. 'these make for another voice: a voice that reads into and interprets other voice', U. Butalia, *The Other Side of Silence*, p. 265.

7. This is more or less true. As evidenced in recent publications of short stories, novels, plays, and poems, the creative writers interrogating Partition were largely traumatized both by the suddenness of the event and its pernicious impact on the inter-communal relationships involving Hindus, Muslims, and Sikhs which was explicable but not acceptable given the historically-tested organic unity among the communities under normal circumstances. The most important and exhaustive collections are: Saros Cowasjee and Kartar Singh Duggal (eds), *When the British Left: Stories on the Partitioning of India, 1947*, Arnold–Heinemann, New Delhi, 1987; M. Hasan (ed.), *India Partitioned;* Mushirul Hasan and M. Asaduddin (eds), *Image and Representation: Stories of Muslim Lives in India*, OUP, New Delhi, 2000; Alok Bhalla (ed.), *Stories about the Partition of India*, vols 1, 2, & 3. Indus, New Delhi, 1994; Muhammad Umar Memon (ed.), *An Epic Unwritten: Penguin Book of Partition Stories in Urdu*, Penguin, New Delhi, 1998.

8. A. Bhalla (ed.), Ibid., vol. 1, p. ix.

9. Tanika Sarkar, 'Imagining Hindurashtra: The Hindu and the Muslim in Bankim Chandra's Writings', *in* David Ludden (ed.), *Making India Hindu: Religion, Community and the Politics of Democracy in India*, OUP, New Delhi, 1996, p. 163.

10. Rabindranath Tagore, *The Tale of a Muslim Woman*, translated by M. Asaduddin and reproduced in Mushirul Hasan and M. Asaduddin (eds), *Image and Representation: Stories of Muslim Lives in India*, OUP, New Delhi, 2000, pp. 48–52. All the following quotations are from this volume.

11. Saratchandra Chattapadhyay, *Mahesh*, translated by M. Asaduddin and reproduced in M. Hasan and M. Asaduddin *Image and Representation*, pp. 17–27.

12. Narendra Nath Mitra, *The Four Poster*, in S. Cowasjee and K.S. Duggal (eds), *When the British Left*, pp. 114–42. All the citations are from this volume unless otherwise stated.

13. Samaresh Basu, *Adab*, in A. Bhalla (ed.), *Stories About the Partition of India*, vol. III, pp. 21–8. All the citations are from this volume unless otherwise stated.

14. Salil Choudhary, *The Dressing Table*, in A. Bhalla (ed.), *Stories About the Partition of India*, vol. I, p. 33.

15. Ibid.

16. For a detailed and critical exposition of the refugee problem in West Bengal, see Ranabir Samaddar, *The Marginal Nation: Transborder Migration from Bangladesh to West Bengal*, Sage, New Delhi. 1999.

17. Homen Borgohain, *In Search of Ismail Sheikh*, trans. M. Asaduddin, and in M. Hasan and M. Asaduddin (eds), *Image and Representation*. All the following quotations are from this volume.

18. Jayanta De, *The Pendulum*, trans. Hiten Bhaya and reproduced in M. Hasan and M. Asaduddin (ed.), *Image and Representation*, pp. 156–68. All the following quotations are from this volume..

19. Ramesh Chandra Sen, *The White House* in A. Bhalla (ed.), *Stories About the Partition of India*, vol. 2, pp. 126–33.

20. Bapsi Sidhwa, *The Pakistan Bride*, Penguin, New Delhi, 1983, p. 4 quoted in M. Hassan (ed.), *Inventing Boundaries*,p. 15.

21. Satinath Bhaduri, *The Champion of the People*, in Bhalla (ed.), *Stories about the Partition of India*, vol. 1, pp. 209–28.

22. Satinath Bhaduri, *The Champion of the People*, in A. Bhalla (ed.), *Stories About the Partition of India*, vol. 1, p. 228.

23. Ibid., pp. 225–6.

24. Satinath Bhaduri, *The Champion of the People*, in Bhalla (ed.), *Stories About the Partition of India*, vol. 1, p. 216.

25. *Jalpaihati*, taken from *Jibananda Samagra*, Mitra Prakashan, Calcutta, 1985, All the citations are from this volume unless otherwise stated

26. Tapati Chakravarty very illuminatingly disucussed this novel with *Swaralipi* (1952) by Sabitri Roy and Pratibha Basu's *Samudra Hriday* (1959) in her 'The Paradox of Fleeting Presence: Partition and Bengali Literature', in S. Settar and Indira B. Gupta (eds), *Pangs of Partition: The Human Dimension*, Manohar, New Delhi, 2002, pp. 261–81.

27. Tapati Chakravarty, 'The Paradox of Fleeting Presence: Partition and Bengali Literture', in S. Settar and I.B. Gupta (eds), *Pangs of Partition*, p. 270.

28. Jayanti Chattapadhyay attempted a very useful content analysis of Salil Sen's *Nutun Ehudi* (The New Jews), 1950 and *Banglar Mati* (The Earth of Bengal), 1953 by Tulshidas Lahiri in her 'Representing the Holocaust: The Partition in Two Bengali Plays', in S. Settar and I.B. Gupta (eds) pp. 301–12.

29. Salil Sen, *Nutun Ehudi*, Sc. xvii quoted from Jayanti Chattopadhyay,

'Representing the Holocaust: The Partition in Two Bengali Plays', in S. Settar and B. Gupta (eds), *Pangs of Partition*, p. 305.

30. Manik Bandyopadhyay, *Childishness* in A. Bhalla (ed.), *Stories About the Partition of India*, vol. 1, pp. 127–36.

31. Ibid., p. 135

32. Of all the writings, Sadat Hasan Manto's *Siyah Hashye* [Black Margins] is perhaps the most revealing exposition of violence in the context of Partition and its aftermath. For this, see Hasan (ed.), *India Partitioned*, vol. 1, pp. 88–99.

33. *Saradindu Omnibus*, vols I–XII, Tuli Kalam, Calcutta, 1977. All the citations are from this collection, unless otherwise stated. *Adim Ripu* was published in 1955; *Rakter Daag, Rimjhim*, and *Bisher Dhnoya* in 1961; and *Dui Dik* in 1964.

34. Anindita Mukhopadhyay, 'Partition Relived in literature', in S. Settar and B. Gupta (eds), *Pangs of Partition*, p. 212.

35. Ibid., vol. II, p. 215.

36. One has to be careful about these oral testimonies, as Mushirul Hasan warns. Because they constituted memories across space and time by writers who have an agenda of their own, oral interviews cannot be a substitute for archival research. Therefore, gender narratives, personal and collective memories can at best enrich Partition debates and not constitute an alternative discourse to the existing ones. Mushirul Hasan (ed.), The *Partition Omnibus*, OUP, New Delhi, 2002, p. xxxix.

37. The interview with Pramila Das has been reproduced from Monmayee Basu, 'Unknown Victims of a Major Holocaust', in S. Settar and I.B. Gupta (eds), *Pangs of Partition*, vol. II, p. 153.

38. Ritu Menon and Kamla Bhasin, *Borders and Boundaries: Women in India's Partition*, Kali for Women, New Delhi, 1998, p. 9.

39. U. Butalia, *The Other Side of Silence*, p. 8.

40. Urvashi Butalia, 'Listening for a Change: Narratives of Partition', in S. Settar and I.B. Gupta (eds), *Pangs of Partition*, vol. II, p. 136.

41. Nonica Datta, 'Partition Memories: A Daghter's Testimony', in Mushirul Hasan and Nariaki Nakazato, *The Unfinished Agenda: Nation-building in South Asia*, Manohar, New Delhi, 2001, p. 43

42. Niaz Zaman, *A Divided Legacy: The Partition in Selected Novels of India, Pakistan and Bangladesh*, New Delhi, 2000. Perhaps the most exhaustive study of the Bengali novels, written by the Bengali writers located in East Pakistan. All the citations will be from this volume unless otherwise stated.

43. Lalithambika Antharjanam, 'The Mother of Dhirendu Muzumdar', in A. Bhalla (ed.), *Stories About the Partition of India*, vol. ii, p. 203. All citations are from this volume unless otherwise stated.

44. Syed Waliullah, 'The Story of the Tulsi Plant', in A. Bhalla (ed.), op cit., vol. II, pp. 191–8. All citations are from this volume unless otherwise stated.

45. N. Zaman, *A Divided Legacy*, pp. 132–3.

46. Abu Rushd, *Nongor*, Boi Ghar, Chittagong, 1967, p. 265.

47. Ibid., p. 265.

48. Gyanendra Pandey, *Remembering Partition: Violence, Nationalism and History in India*, Cambridge University Press, Cambridge, 2001, p. 187.

49. It has now been well-established that there has never been, despite the rhetoric of theologians and publicists, 'a single, inalienable Muslim identity and that identities are inclusive and often rooted in local cultures, languages, oral traditions, influenced by complex historical processes'. M. Hasan and M. Asaduddin, *Image and Representation*, p. 15.

50. M. Asaduddin, 'Fiction as History: Partition Stories', in S. Settar and I.B. Gupta (eds), *Pangs of Partition*, p. 329.

51. Jason Francisco, 'In the Heart of Fracticide: The Literature of India's Partition Burning Freshly', in M. Hasan (ed.), *Inventing Boundaries*, p. 392.

52. Sadat Hasan Manto, *Toba Tek Singh*, in A. Bhalla (ed.), *Stories About the Partition of India*, vol. III, Indus, New Delhi. 1994, p. 2. *Toba Tek Singh* is a story of loss of identity against the backdrop of the communal massacre and transfer of population during Partition. Viewing Partition from the perspective of a lunatic, Toba Tek Singh, the story is a powerful argument challenging the decision that finally led to the separation.

53. M. Hasan (ed.), *Inventing Boundaries*, p. 16.

54. Bodh Prakash,'Nation and Identity: Narratives of Partition', in V. Damodaran and M. Unnithan Kumar (eds), *Post Colonial India*, p. 77.

55. Sadat Hasan Manto, *Toba Tek Singh*, in A. Bhalla (ed.), *Stories About the Partition of India*, vol. III, pp. 3–4.

56. Jason Francisco, 'In the Heart of Fracticide: The Literature of India's Partition Burning Freshly', in M. Hasan (ed.), *Inventing Boundaries*, p. 382.

57. Ismat Chughtai, *My Friend, My Enemy: Essays, Reminiscences, Portraits*, New Delhi, 2001, p. 3, quoted in M. Hasan (ed.), *The Partition Omnibus*, p. xi.

5

Discourses on National Identity*

Bhikhu Parekh[1]

Every polity has a more or less coherent conception of the kind of collectivity it is, what it means to belong to it, who belongs to it or is an outsider, and how it differs from others. It is united and conducts its affairs in a specific manner, and displays singularity and individuality. In Western thought, systematic reflection on the nature and locus of national identity, that is, on the collective identity of a polity began with the emergence of the Greek *polis*, and has over the centuries given rise to different views, of which the following three are among the most influential.

Surrounded as they were by several polities, the Greek philosophers asked how each of them was held together and differed from others. For Plato the identity of the *polis* lay in the way it defined and organized itself for the pursuit of the good life. He distinguished several conceptions of the good life and classified politics accordingly. His view was broadly accepted by Aristotle and other Greek, Roman, and Christian thinkers, for almost all of whom a polity was united in terms of and distinguished from others by its collectively shared substantive conception of the good life.

A different view of national identity emerged in the seventeenth century. As Hobbes rejected the possibility of a collectively shared

* *Political Studies* (1994), vol. xlii, no. 42(3), Sept. 1994, 492–504.

conception of the good life and abstracted the state from society, he located the identity of a polity in its formal and autonomously constituted structure of authority. In his view, a polity was united in terms of, and constituted as, a specific kind of community by virtue of its shared conception of legitimacy and the structure of authority derived from it. Locke, Rousseau and many other writers shared Hobbes' view in varying degrees.

The rise of nationalist ideas in the nineteenth century marked the emergence of a very different view of national identity. For the nationalist writers, every polity was an organic whole, almost like a living organism, and distinguished by a unique spirit, genius, or soul which infused, ordered, and gave life to its legal, social, cultural, political, and other institutions. Its national soul or spirit made it the kind or polity it was, and both united and distinguished it from others.[2]

During the past few decades, the concept of national identity has once again become a subject of intense political and philosophical debate in many countries. Rather than analyse the concept abstractly with all its obvious disadvantages I shall locate it in the ongoing debates in different countries and explore how the participants define it, what they are debating in its name, and why they regard the debate as of utmost political importance. In the first section I offer brief sketch of some of these debates, and in the second comment on their confusions and limitations.

I

Britain began to undergo significant changes from the early 1960s onwards. As a result of the decolonization of most of the empire, its two centuries of imperial adventure came to an end, leading to a drastic shrinkage of its geographical expanse and political power. Thanks to the arrival of a large number of black and brown immigrants from the erstwhile colonies and to their concentration in the major cities British society was becoming recognizably different and faced with problems created by the presence of 'alien' cultures. The British economy was in a state of decline. Its industrial productivity low, its technology outdated the quality of its industrial management poor, and its balance of payment unfavourable. British political institutions were widely perceived to be ineffective and commanded only a limited popular support. The pressure from influential quarters to join the European Community generated widespread fears about the loss of its distinct political identity. The emergence of Scottish and to a lesser extent Welsh nationalism also aroused fears about Britain's territorial and political integrity. In short, almost all the traditional sources of pride in terms of which Britain had for several centuries constructed its collective identity, namely the empire, social cohesion, stable democratic institutions, the industrial leadership of the world, superiority to the rest of Europe, political unity, and the like, were proving problematic. The cumulative impact of these and related changes was considerable. Not surprisingly, they created a widespread sense of decline and disorientation, and provoked a debate on the causes and the best ways of arresting its decline.[3]

It was in this context that the New Right, which was finely tuned to the national mood, introduced the idea of national identity as an integral part of its programme of national regeneration.[4] In its view, Britain was steadily declining because, among other things, its national identity was being increasingly eroded, it had no clear conception of what it stood for and lacked a sense of national purpose. It was losing touch with its great past and becoming devoid of the qualities of character that had made that past possible. As a result, Britain was beginning to drift and falling prey to the fashionable but highly dubious ideas and practices imported from abroad. For the New Right the answer to Britain's predicament was obvious. It needed to return to its roots, reestablish contacts with its past, and revive its characteristic virtues. British national identity, a product of its long history, was already formed, and the British people only needed to know it. As the New Right defined it, the British national identity largely consisted in a specific body of virtues and values and a specific form of historical self-understanding.

Once the New Right put the question of national identity on the public agenda, it provoked considerable controversy. Some, mainly on the Left, dismissed it as an empty slogan devoid of explanatory and normative power, and designed only to give the emerging British, especially English nationalism a respectable disguise. Others accepted the legitimacy of the concept, and either gave a different, principally liberal account of British national identity, or argued that its identity was not static and immutable, and needed to be redefined by each generation in the light of its needs and circumstances. Partly because these critics failed to offer clearly worked out alternatives, and partly because the New Right has remained in power since the late 1970s, its conception of national identity enjoyed considerable popularity and prestige. The Thatcher government used it to power and legitimize its massive programme of producing British men and women possessed of the 'vigorous' virtues and self-confidence of their forbears, concentrating on the educational and economic policies as the central tools of cultural engineering.

Canada is another country where the question of national identity has dominated the public agenda since the early 1970s.[5] For long, Quebec was in no doubt that it was French and Catholic, and that the Catholic church was the custodian of that identity. Thanks to the cumulative effect of urbanization, social atomization, secularization, and the immigration of people of different races and religions, its social and political life underwent profound changes after the Second World War. This led to much anxious debate about what it once was and had since become, and how it was to define and preserve its traditional way of life. The task of defining its national identity that had hitherto been discharged by the clergy was now taken over by the intellectuals and the Quebec government replaced the church as its guardian. In the new definition of its national identity, Catholicism lost its earlier centrality to French language and culture which were now regarded as the essential components of Quebec's identity. The nature and content of the French culture were nowhere clearly defined, but that did not prevent the emergence of the widely shared view that Quebec was 'essentially' French, that its cultural identity was under grave threat, and that the newly formed alliance between its intellectuals and government had a vital role to play in defining, preserving, and propagating it.

On the basis of its redefinition of its identity, Quebec's leaders argued that it was not just a province of Canada or what was long called French Canada but a distinct nation and that correspondingly the rest of Canada did not consist of separate and distinct provinces but constituted a homogeneous English nation. Canada was a bi-national country, and the composition and functioning of its political institutions must reflect their equality. Quebec leaders also argued that it had a right to protect its identity, and hence to control immigration, to make English alone its official language, to require all immigrant children to go to French schools, and in general to do all that was necessary for that purpose. For its part, the Canadian state was asked to recognize Quebec as a 'distinct society' (a strikingly non-ethnic concept with a French form and an English content), regard its protection as one of its major national goals, and grant the latter rights not demanded or needed by other provinces. As Quebec's needs were different from theirs, there was nothing unfair about its enjoyment of special rights.

Quebec's demands, later taken over by the older original nations of Canada, raised several questions about the nature and identity of the Canadian state. The first question related to the historical self-understanding of Canada. Was it an essentially Anglo-Saxon country with several linguistic and cultural minorities, the French being only one of them? Or was it a bi-national country founded by two distinct nations, and thus endowed from the very beginning with a dual identity? Or was it a trinational country made up of these two and the original nations? Or perhaps a multi-ethnic country composed of several distinct communities including the three major ones and several others that had later made in their home? In short, was the Canadian identity essentially singular and homogeneous, two-in-one, three-in-one, or many-in-one? The answer to the question had profound constitutional and cultural implications.

The second question concerned the organizing principles of the Canadian state. Should it concede the demands of the original nations, and especially of Quebec, and create not just an asymmetrical and even unequal federation but also a hybrid state based on the principles of both liberal individualism and a recognition or collective rights? or should it refuse to compromise its much-cherished commitment to liberal individualism and reject all attempts to limit it in the name of cultural self-preservation? Many Anglophones thought that if Canada opted for the former, it could no longer call itself a liberal society, and that that represented such a grave erosion of its identity that they could not live with in. Some others were prepared to compromise their liberal identity in the interest of Canadian unity, but continued to feel deeply uneasy about it. A few saw no reason why a liberal society could not accommodate collective rights, and offered ingenious restatements of liberalism.[6]

The third question related to the nature of Canadian citizenship. Should Canada insist on equal and uniform citizenship and require that all its citizens belong to it in an identical manner? Or should it allow mediated and differentiated modes of citizenship such that some could belong to specific national groups, say, Quebec and through that to Canada, and thus become not Canadians *sans phrase* but Quebecquois-Canadians? This looks like, but is really quite different from, the hyphenated identities or the ethnic minorities in the United States. The Polish-Americans and the Irish-Americans are all Americans enjoying equal citizenship and identically relating to the

American state. Their ethnicity does not adjectivize or qualify their citizenship and has only a cultural significance. By contrast, the differential form of citizenship demanded by the French Canadians and the native peoples gives their ethnicity or nationhood a political significance, and ethnicizes and pluralizes the very structure of the Canadian state.

Finally, the Canadians asked how they differed from their powerful southern neighbour and where their distinctiveness lay. Most of them were convinced that they had different cultural traditions, values, modes of conducting their affairs, attitude to the government, and the like, in a word, a distinct national identity, and that they were finding it difficult to preserve it under the pressure of increasing American cultural domination. Some thought that the presence of Quebec provided them with a bulwark against the American threat. They were therefore keen to accommodate its demands *provided that* these did not weaken its unity or render its identity so diffused and vague as not to make it worth preserving. Much therefore depended on the kinds of demands Quebec made and the nature and degree of accommodation required from the rest of Canada.

In Germany also the question of national identity has been a subject of much anguished debate. The debate was initially provoked by the Nazi experience, especially the murder of six million Jews. The trauma was too acute for the Germans to raise disturbing questions soon after the Second World War, and many of those who could have raised them were too compromised or diffident to do so. Most Germans wanted a clean break with their recent past and set about giving themselves a new identity in the form of newly established democratic institutions. The study of history was replaced by social studies in many German schools, and systematic attempts were made to instil and nurture the new identity. As the latter took root, and as a new generation of Germans with sufficient self-confidence and detachment grew up, several important questions about national identity were raised.[7]

The first question related to what the Nazi experience revealed about the German national character and identity. German writers asked if the murder of six million Jews was 'singular' and historically unique, or whether it was like such other acts of genocide as the Turkish massacre of the Armenians and Stalin's liquidation of the Kulaks. If the former, it said something deeply disturbing about the dark and mysterious forces lurking in the German character. If the latter, it was capable of explanation in terms of the usual political and personal factors, although that did not diminish the enormity of the deed. In either case the question remained as to how the Germans could do such a thing. They were no more evil than human beings elsewhere, and the same nation that produced Hitler had also produced Kant and Herder. Was the holocaust then an aberration? or was the German national character deeply self-divided and schizophrenic? or were its outrageous propensities merely the obverse of its noble qualities?? Whatever the explanation, the Nazi atrocities had at least some roots in the German national character, raising disturbing questions about how the Germans were to come to terms with it and guard themselves against their recurrence.

The second question concerned the continuity of the German identity and the so-called 'historicization' of the Nazi period. Is German history to be seen as continuous or does it fall into three distinct phases, namely pre-1933, 1933 to 1945, and post-1945? If it is continuous, how is the second period to be integrated in its historical self-understanding? If it is discontinuous, how can the discontinuity be explained and the Germans arrive at a coherent conception of their history? Habermas stressed the continuity of German history. He located German identity in its way of life and argued that, as the latter had remained the same over time and persisted till today, there was no rupture in German identity. As he put it, 'our identity is permanently interwoven with it, from bodily gestures through the language to the rich interplay of intellectual customs'. This means that the present day Germans are concocted with Auschwitz 'not through contingent circumstances but internally'. His critics rejoined that he was wrong both to see the Nazi period as a necessary expression of the German way of life, and to suggest that the present German way of life remained substantially similar to that obtaining between 1933 and 1945.

The third question related to Germany's new post-war identity. The Germans had now given themselves a new national identity in the form of its democratic institutions, abandoned their traditional preoccupation with the Sonderweg (a special path of development that was neither Eastern or Western), and stressed their European roots as a way of guarding themselves against themselves. This raised the crucial question as to whether such a constitutional and Europeanized patriotism, or what Habermas called a 'post-conventional' identity, was enough to define their national identity. Habermas thought that it was not only sufficient but the only form of identity possible in the plural and globalized modern state. Others disagreed.[8]

In their view, a nation could not be held together by a largely formal constitutional patriotism alone and needed deeper emotional and cultural bonds. They also thought that so long as the Germans lived within the framework of the nation state, a post-national identity was both utopian and dangerous. Even they, however, appreciated that as interpretations of the German past were bound to differ, an attempt to ground the new national identity in a unified understanding of history could easily destroy the post-war consensus.[9] This left the Germans with two painful choices. Either they should eschew all attempts to give the new identity a historical basis, or they should give it one and endanger the identity by provoking a hitherto silent right wing reading of German history. The first alternative entailed a deliberate historical amnesia and was emotionally and intellectually difficult. The second was fraught with unacceptable political risks.

The post-war division of Germany also raised important questions about its identity. Were there now two German states, both equal and legitimate? Or was there only one Germany illegitimately divided into two states? If the latter, did its oneness consist in its pre-war territory, ethnicity or as was commonly argued—its nationhood? The overwhelming majority of West Germans and a large section of even the East Germans were in no doubt that West Germany was the 'real' Germany and true heir to the German past. Accordingly, the West Germans decided not to give themselves a constitution, for that implied an endorsement of the division, but a Basic Law (Grundegesetz), which was to remain effective only until such time as the country was united.[10] Not surprisingly, when the two halves were united, the Unification Treaty simply extended the Basic Law to and incorporated East Germany into West Germany. Acutely aware of the role of collective memory in the maintenance of national identity, the Treaty sought to wipe out the memory of East Germany by avoiding as far as possible any mention of it.[11] Like post-war Germany, post-unification Germany wanted a clean break with its recent past as the only way of giving itself a secure and undivided identity. As the unification was widely popularized in the name of the unity of the German nation, it gave the new German state a nationalist dimension which most of the post-war leaders were deeply anxious to avoid. The recent rise of the neo-Nazi and other racist movements based on the slogan of 'Germany for the Germans' seems to bear out their fears.

Among the developing countries, India was one of the first to embark on a debate on national identity. From the early decades of the nineteenth century onwards, Indian leaders began to ask why their country had repeatedly fallen prey to foreign invasions and rule. A large body of influential opinion concluded that the causes of India's predicament lay in its deeply flawed national character and social structure. The only way to regenerate India was to make a clean break with its past by giving it a wholly new and modern identity. The modernists appreciated that some aspects of its past, especially the classical past, were commendable. They were however afraid that any attempt to resuscitate these fragments would only open the door to revivalism and undermine the new identity. They also appreciated the need for a coherent conception of their history, but were aware that it was bound to run up against the periods of foreign rule, especially the Muslim, and disrupt its new identity. Like the Germans, the modernist Indian leaders thought it unwise to seek to give the new national identity a historical and cultural basis, and resisted the temptation to evoke historical memories and draw historical parallels. When the country became independent in 1947, its first prime minister Jawaharlal Nehru insisted that it must be based on a new liberal, democratic and secular 'national philosophy'. As he won successive elections, and claimed democratic legitimacy for the new national identity, he declared it the 'absolute' and 'unquestionable' foundation of the Indian state from which it could deviate only at its peril.[12]

In recent years India has thrown up a new debate on national identity, which bears considerable resemblance to that in Germany and Canada. Some Indian leaders mainly Hindu, have argued that the new post-Independence national identity remained abstract and fragile unless it was given historical roots. Some of them would like to ground it in a suitably reinterpreted conception of their past, whereas others would like to indigenize it and change it in parts. As the modernists had feared, these attempts revived garbled collective memories of the centuries of Muslim rule and stoked anti-Muslim prejudices, leading to the destruction of the Babri mosque in 1992 and the violence that followed. Indians, especially Hindus, would like to reclaim their past and arrive at a coherent understanding of their historical identity, but find that they cannot do so without endangering their future.

The kind of debate on national identity that has taken place in India is to be found in almost all developing countries. They want to modernize themselves, but they also want to retain much of their traditional way of life. As the two are not easy to reconcile, their deeply divided self-consciousness periodically triggers off intense debates about who they were and have become, where they are going and what kind of society they are creating. When the changes brought about by modernization affect their most cherished institution, especially religion, the structure of the family and the relations between the sexes, they draw such volatile groups as the petty bourgeoisie, the artisans, and the urban migrants into political life. The debate on their national identity then becomes polarized, fierce, and even violent.

At Independence, Algeria gave itself a modern and secular identity. A few years later the cry of 'depersonalization' and 'loss of national identity' was heard in many parts of the country, and demands were made to 'repersonalize' it by restoring its 'traditional Islamic identity'. As the movement gathered momentum and led to a fierce clash of the two conceptions of national identity, the Algerian republic faced its severest crisis in the early 1990s. Democratic elections gave the Islamicists a majority, which the frightened secularists subverted with the help of the army. Like Algeria, Iran under the Shah opted for a secular national identity. Unlike Algeria, India and the post-war Germany, the Shah sought to give himself and his modernist project historical legitimacy by linking up with the pre-Islamic classical past. The marginalized Islam, refusing to see itself as just one phase in Iran's long history, began to claim the monopoly of its 'soul'. As the modernist project bit deep into the traditional institutions and unsettled the social balance, the Islamicists under Khomeini won enough popular support to take over the country. Other countries in Asia and Africa have faced or are facing similar battles.[13]

They are now joined by countries recently liberated from Communist rule. The debates on national identity there, centre not only on the appropriate paths of economic development but also on the centrality of religion, the place of indigenous or 'imposed' minorities in the national life, and the best way to interpret and incorporate the years of communism in their conceptions of their character and history. In some cases, such as Bosnia, the stark contrast between the country's self-conception and the outsiders' view of it has internationalized and added a new poignancy to their search for national identity. Most Bosnian Muslims see themselves as European Muslims; as Europeans who only happen to be practising Islam, whereas most of their neighbours and even the West perceive them as Muslim Europeans; as Muslims who happen to be living in Europe. As the West tends to define Europe in predominantly Christian terms, its definition not only de-Europeanizes the Bosnian Muslims but also regards them as an alien and illegitimate presence.

I have so far sketched the different ways in which the concept of national identity entered political discourse in different countries and the kinds of debate it provoked, The countries concerned experienced a sense of decline. disorientation, discontinuity, or disunity. This led to critical self-reflection on their history, their characteristic strengths and weaknesses, the ways in which they needed to change, and their hopes for the future with a view of developing a coherent conception of themselves that could both give them the necessary self-confidence and guide and legitimize their choices.

As the debates about the nature and locus of national identity in different countries had a common origin in a sense of crisis, they shared several common features. Because the nature of the crisis varied from country to country, and because different countries have different histories, cultures, and political structures, the nature and content of their debates varied greatly. In Britain, the debate on national identity was triggered off by several interrelated factors, of which the general feeling of *economic and political* decline was the most important. Given the country's imperial and industrial history, the debate had an inescapable historical orientation, and was centred around the form of self-understanding and the qualities of character that had once stood it in good stead and which many thought could be revived.

In Germany, the debate on national identity had a largely *moral and political* origin. It was provoked not by a sense of decline but by a profound sense of discontinuity caused by the Nazi experience and by the anxiety about the stability of the post-war democratic institutions. Unlike Britain, Germany was not unified until the late nineteenth century and could not hope to revive a past historical period. Its debate on national identity was therefore largely future-orientated. The national identity was not to be revived or retrieved but reconstituted, and the past was to play only a limited role in it. Unlike Britain and Canada, the German debate also raised large questions about the country's sense of historical continuity and how it was to relate to its past. The questions bore remarkable resemblance to the familiar philosophical discussions about the nature of personal identity.

The Indian situation was not very different. A country that had been under foreign rule for centuries and which had never before been united, lacked a single and continuous past to turn to. Even the Hindu revivalists could only appeal to the great *Cultural* achievements of classical India, and knew that these could not provide the necessary *political* elements for their collective self-definition. The debate on national identity therefore centred around the *political and cultural* regeneration of India. In Canada, the debate on national identity was provoked not by a sense of decline or discontinuity, but by disorientation and disunity generated by Quebec nationalism and to a lesser extent by the fear of American domination. The debate therefore took a predominantly *constitutional* form and centred around redefining the structure of the Canadian state. In Iran, Algeria, and other countries debates on national identity raised religious issues that did not figure in their counterparts elsewhere, had to cope with the colonial rupture in their history, and were conducted in different idioms. In short, there is no single and homogeneous discourse on national identity, but a plurality of discourses sharing some features in common but differing in their logical structures and ways of defining, debating, and reconstituting national identities.

In different countries debates on national identity involve different kinds of perplexity and agonizing choices. In those with a continuous and not too shameful past, the present can be integrated with it, and the search for identity involves no discontinuity. In countries with a fragmented, discontinuous, or disastrous past, the search for identity involves at least a temporary break with it and some measure of historical discontinuity. Some of them can have either a future or a past but not both, at least for the present, and must rely on a deliberately induced historical amnesia to maintain their political stability. Furthermore, as they cannot always turn to their past for inspiration and guidance, they must either muddle through as best as they can or seek inspiration from only the partially relevant historical experiences of Western states. Not surprisingly they lurch from one extreme to another, promiscuously play with different alternatives, and find it difficult to evolve coherent identities.

II

In the previous section I outlined the kinds of debate on national identity that are taking place in different countries. The debates are clearly uneven and often marred by conceptual confusions. I might mention three by way of illustration. This is not intended to discredit but to clarify the debate, and to suggest how the profound issues it raises can be more fruitfully discussed.

First, the debates about national identity that we have sketched are all about the identity of a political community.[14] A political community is a territorially concentrated group of people bound together by their acceptance of a common mode of conducting their collective affairs, including a body of institutions and shared values. It is a public institution shared by its members collectively, as a community. It is not shared by them in a way that we might share a piece of cake, but in a way that we share streets, parks, the institutions of government, and the like. Also, it is common to them not in a way that having two eyes is common to all human beings, but in a way that a dining table is common to those seated around it. The identity of a political community lies in what all its members share not individually but collectively, not privately but publicly, and has an inescapable institutional focus.

Many discussions on national identity do not appreciate this distinction. These look for the identity of a political community in the traits of temperament, character, habits, customs, social practices, etc., in a word, in the cultural or ethno-cultural characteristics that are supposed to be common to all its members. These are all personal or individual characteristics, rarely shared by them all, and even then as individuals and not as a collectivity. They do not pertain to their public or political life and, at best, define and distinguish Germans or Canadians but not Germany or Canada. The tendency to locate the identity of a political community in the cultural characteristics of its members and to equate it with national character is evident in the German as well as the British New Right discussions of national identity mentioned earlier.

The confusion between the political and the cultural life of a community has unfortunate consequences. It equates the political community with the culture of the dominant ethnic or national group, and undermines its public, open, and shared character. This means that one cannot be a full citizen of, say, Britain unless one is culturally British or even English and shares the character and the cultural practices that are supposed to be common to the British people. Britain must then, like Germany, either deny citizenship or at least equal citizenship to those who are not ethnically or culturally British and do not belong to the British 'nation' even though they might have lived there for years, or vigorously assimilate them. In either case, it marginalizes a large body of men and women, treats them as second class citizens, and encourages much intolerance. Furthermore, as few, if any, cultural characteristics are common to all British people, and since these are complex and not easy to specify, the cultural definition of British national identity invariably leads to a biased and ideologically abridged definition of 'Britishness' and distorts the British way of life.

The second confusion in the discussion of national identity centres around the concept of *identity*. In most discussions of national identity, the term is used in one of two senses. First, it refers to the inner structure and the organizing or constitutive principles of a community; that is, to the way it is constituted and its different parts are integrated into a coherent whole. Secondly, the term national identity is used to refer to what is unique peculiar, or specific to a community and distinguishes it from others.[15]

Although the two senses are related, they have different thrusts and implications, in the first sense of national identity, the intention is to explore a community from within and to elucidate its constitutive characteristics. Whether these characteristics are unique to it and make it different from others is immaterial. Difference *is* important, but it is ontologically secondary and derivative. It is, of course, most likely that as every community has a unique history, geography, economic and political structure and the like, its constitutive characteristics would be different from others. However, even if they are not, that is not a matter of anxiety. And when they are different, it is not the difference *per se* but the fact that it springs from the kind of community it is that is important.

In the second sense of national identity the relationship is reversed. Difference is made the basis of the identity of the community, and the latter's constant concern, if it is not to erode or lose its identity, is to maintain its differences from others at all cost. When so defined, the preoccupation with national identity leads to paradoxes and is ultimately self-defeating. As difference from others constitutes the community's identity, others become its constant frame of reference. It measures itself against them lest it should become like them. It therefore becomes other-directed and preserves its identity at the expense of its autonomy. The second sense of identity also fetishizes difference and discourages inter-communal borrowing. It encourages the community to pay far more attention to how and how much it differs from the others than to whether or not it is true to itself. It also leads it to stress only those aspects of it in which it differs from others and to distort and falsify its way of life.

The second sense of national identity has dominated most of the debates in the subject. Many Germans continue to be obsessed with Sonderweg and feel deeply worried that their post-war democratic institutions will assimilate them to the West and undermine their identity. Many Canadians ask how they differ from the Americans and how best they can preserve these differences. Quebec nationalists ask the same question about themselves and the rest of Canada. In Japan, the preoccupation with national distinctiveness has generated an extensive literature known as *nihonjinon*, and in Russia anything inconsistent with the 'Russian Idea' is dismissed as antinational. This is just as true of Algeria, Iran, and most developing countries. In all these cases, similarity to others is perceived as a deep ontological threat, and differences from them are given undue importance. Hardly anyone asks why it is important and desirable to remain different, whether all differences or only those deemed to be worth preserving are to be retained, and if the latter, how they determine these.

The third confusion relates to the *nature* of national identity. For some it is historically determined; a brute and unalterable fact of life, and passively inherited by each generation.[16] All one can do is to acquire a more or less authentic understanding of it and conform to its imperatives. Some others take the opposite view that national identity is a matter of collective choice; a historical project to be executed by each generation in the light of its needs and circumstances. The inherited identity is a product of past choices and can be altered at will.[17] For yet others, national identity both is and is not a matter of collective choice. Every generation is free to define its national identity but not as it pleases. It is a product of and deeply shaped by its inherited identity and can only change the latter within limits.[18]

The first two views are deeply flawed. The first, which I might call a realist or substantialist view of national identity, is refuted by the historical experiences of every known community. As national identity is product of history, it can also be remade in history unless one naively assumes that history somehow came to an end at a particular point in time. The realist view also fails to appreciate that a community's identity is not a substance but a cluster of interrelated and relatively open-ended tendencies and impulses pulling in different directions and capable of being developed and balanced in different ways, The second, which I might call volitionalist view of national identity, fails to appreciate that a community is not a tabula rasa. Its historically evolved structures persist over time and restrict choices. To say that each generation is free to redefine its national identity in the light of its needs is to ignore the basic fact that the very definition of the needs and of what it considers acceptable ways of satisfying them are shaped by the inherited way of life.

The third, which I might call a constructivist view of national identity is the most satisfactory, provided that it is not interpreted mechanistically. The past is not a passive storehouse of material from which each generation chooses whatever it likes for the reconstruction of its national identity. Nor do inherited institutions limit its choices rigidly and mechanistically. The past never passes away; it lives on in the present. A coherent view of national identity must grow out of a constant dialogue between the past and the present in which each interrogates and illuminates the other. Neither the Germans nor the Indians nor any other community can for long insulate their self-given national identity against the impact of their past. As their past is divisive, painful, or humiliating, they may wisely keep it in a state of suspended animation, but they must, over time, find ways of grounding their new identity in their critically interpreted history and reconciling their past with their future.

In addition to these three confusions, there are also several others bedevilling the discussion of national identity. These include such untenable beliefs as that the national identity is a coherent whole; that it can be stated in a crisp formula; that it can and ought to be fostered by the state; that it can be insulated against change; that the state derives its legitimacy from its capacity to express and preserve the national identity; and that no society can last without a collectively shared thick identity.[19] Every political community, especially one as complex and atomized as ours needs a broadly shared and inescapably thin conception of itself, the search for such a conception can easily produce murderous consequences if not freed of the kinds of confusions mentioned earlier.

Notes

1. This chapter was first presented as a paper at the Jowett Society of the University of Oxford. I am grateful to the participants, especially Alan Montefiore, for their comments. I also thank Martin Burch for his valuable advice.

2. The nationalist literature abounds in metaphors of national genius, national soul, collective self, and national spirit, and locates national individuality or identity in them. See Anthony Smith, *National Identity*, Penguin, London, 1991, ch. 4.

3. For a good discussion, see Robert Skidelsky (ed.), Thatcherism, Blackwell,

Oxford, 1989. In 1978 the *Sunday Telegraph* ran a series of fifteen articles on the state of Britain. These were later collected in Patrick Hutber (ed.); *What is Wrong with Britain?* Sphere, London, 1978.

4. See Roy Lewis, *Enoch Powell*, Cassell, London, 1975, pp. 86f; Margaret Thatcher's Bruges Speech of 1988, Conservative Political Centre, London, 1988; John Casey, 'One Nation: The Politics of Race', *The Salisbury Review* 1 (1982), 23–8; Ian Crowther, 'Mrs Thatcher's Idea of Good Society', *The Salisbury Review* 2 (1983), 40–3; and Maurice Cowling (ed.), *Conservative Essays*, Cassell, London, 1978. For a critique of their views, see my 'National Identity and the Ontological Generation of Britain', in Paul Gilberrt and Paul Gregory (eds), *Nations, Culture and Markets*, Averbury, London, 1994.

5. For a good summary and discussion of the Canadian debate, see Charles Taylor, Reconciling the Solitudes: Essays on Canadian Federalism and Nationalism, McGill-Queen's University Press, Montreal, 1993; A. C. Cairns, *Charter versus Federalism: The Dilemmas of Constitutional Reform*, McGill-Queen's University Press, Montreal, 1992; and R.L. Watts and D.M. Brown (eds), *Options for a New Canada*, university of Toronto Press. Toronto, 1991. See also James Tully, 'Multirow Federalism and the Charter', in Phil Bryden, Stephen Douis and John Russell (eds), *The Charter—Ten Years after*, University of Toronto Press, Toronto, 1992: the two useful articles by Michael D. Levin and Paul-Andre Lintau in *Indian Journal of Canadian Studies*, 1 (1992); and William Kaplan (ed.), *Belonging: The Meaning and Future of Canadian Citizenship*, McGill-Queen's University Press, Montreal, 1991.

6. As liberalism is currently more severely tested and contested in Canada than in almost any other Western country, and as most Canadian writers on it are also politically engaged, the recent Canadian contribution to the development of liberalism displays unusual richness and depth. Indeed, a distinctly Canadian form of liberalism has now come of age.

7. The most useful place to follow the German debate: is the famous *Historikerstreit* debate, now helpfully collected in James Knowlton and Truett Cates (trans), *Forever in the Shadow of Hitler?* Humanities, New Jersey, 1993. See also Barbara Heimannsberg and Christopher J. Schmidt (eds), *The Collective Silence: German Identity and the Legacy of Shame*, Maxwell Macmillan, London, 1993. For obvious reasons trust between generations and the transmission of experience and views from one generation to another, without both of which a society cannot preserve its continuity, were effectively shattered in Germany. This created a disturbing void at the very heart of the young German's sense of personal and national identity.

8. Knowlton and Cates, *Forever in the Shadow of Hitler?*, p. 165.

9. Ibid., pp. 181f, 196f and 202ff.

10. For a useful discussion, see Elmar M. Hucku (ed.), *The Democratic Tradition: Four German Constitutions*, Berg, Leamington Spa, 1987.

11. The fear of the past was so deep that many west Germans hotly debated what to call their divided country. An influential group preferred

'Federation of German Länder'. Theodor Heub, the first federal president, thought that this implied an 'evasive action before one's own identity' *(ein Aüsweichen ror sich selbst)* and persuasively advocated the name of 'Federal Republic of Germany'. See Hucku, *The Democratic Tradition*, p. 69.

12. For a fuller discussion, see my 'Nehru and the National Philsophy of India' in *Economic and Political Weekly*, 26 (1991), 35, 48, and *Colonialism, Tradition and Reform*, Sage, Delhi, 1989, ch. 2. The appeal to a 'new national philosophy' is to be found in the rhetoric of almost all newly independent countries.

13. See Kemal H. Karpat (ed.), *Political and Social Thought in the Contemporary Middle East*, Praeger, New York, 1982. For a fuller exploration of why the search for identity often ends up in fundamentalist *cul-de-sac*, see my 'The Concept of Fundamentalism', in Aleksandras Shtromas (ed.), *The End of 'isms'?* Blackwell, Oxford, 1994.

14. The term 'national' refers to both the nation and the state. Hence the debate about national identity can be about the identity of the nation as well as that of the state. One can ask what constitutes the identity of a specific political community or a state, as also where lies its identity as a nation or a self-conscious and cohesive ethno-cultural community. As the various debates that I have sketched pertain to the state I concentrate on it.

15. The excessive preoccupation with difference vitiates the discussions of both personal and national identity. It is strikingly absent in many conservative writers. See, for example, the discussion of national identity in Michael Oakeshott. *Rationalism in Politics and Other Essays*, Methuen, London 1962, chs 5 and 7. The obsession with being different is largely a legacy of certain kinds of liberalism and, of course, romanticism. It is to be found in J.S. Mill's *On Liberty*, ch. 3, where individuality is sometimes but not always equated with being different. For references to the celebration of difference as the very basis of identity in Herder, Schleiermacher, and others. See Elie Kedourie, *Nationalism*, Hutchinson, London, 1960, ch. 4.

16. A recent clear statement of this view is to be found in Roger Scruton, *The Philosopher on Dover Beach*, Carcanet, London, 1990, ch. 28.

17. This view is common to Marxists and even some liberal writers. See Stuart Hall's article in Stuart Hall, David Held, and Tony McGrew (eds), *Modernity and its Future*, Polity, Cambridge, 1992.

18. See David Miller, 'In Defence of Nationality', *Journal of Applied Philosophy*, 10 (1993), 3–16.

19. For criticisms of some of these confusions, see the articles by Anthony Arblaster, David Marquand, David Miller, and myself in *New Community* 21 (1995). The entire issue is devoted to national identity. See also my 'politics of Nationhood', in K. von Benda-Beckman and Maykel Verkutyen (eds), *Cultural Identity and Development in Europe*, University College of London Press, London, 1994.

6

Race, Caste, and Ethnic Identity*

André Béteille[1]

The attempt to view race and caste within the same framework of understanding could take us in two different directions. In the first place, we might consider to what extent systems of stratification based on caste (as in India) and on colour (as in the south of the United States of America) can be regarded as analogous in structure; this is a problem in comparative sociology. In the second place, we might ask how far in India caste distinctions correspond to second place; we might ask how far in India caste distinctions correspond to differences in physical or racial type; this problem is of greater special interest to students of India society and history.[2]

When American social anthropologists, principally under the influence of Lloyd Warner, began to study the Deep South of the United States in the thirties, they found it useful to speak of a caste system in representing the cleavages between Negroes and whites in rural and urban communities there.[3] Gunnar Myrdal employed similar terms and categories in his classic study of the American Negro made at about the same time.[4] The metaphor of caste has since then been widely used in describing multiracial societies in other parts of the world, notably South Africa.[5]

* International Social Science Journal, vol. xxxiii, no. 4, 1971 (UNESCO): issue devoted to a discussion of the racial situation.

There are certain obvious parallels between the Indian caste system and the system of stratification based on colour, whether in the United States' South or in South Africa. In studying the United States' South both Warner and Myrdal were struck by the rigid distinctions maintained between Negroes and whites which seemed to them to be in marked contrast with the more flexible pattern of relations in a class system. Their purpose in labelling as 'caste' the system of stratification based on colour was not so much to explore its similarity with the Indian system as to emphasize its difference from the class system in America and other Western societies.

It might be useful to explore a little further the similarities between the Indian caste system and what I shall call for short the colour-caste system. In both systems the component units are differentiated from each other by clearly defined boundaries. Differences between castes are reinforced by a measure of homogeneity within the caste.

Caste systems may be described as systems of cumulative inequality. Advantages of status tend to be combined with advantages of wealth and power, and those who are socially under-privileged also tend to be at the bottom of the economic and political scales. There are many exceptions to this in the colour–caste system where poor whites coexist with well-to-do Negroes,[6] but exceptions of the same kind have existed in Indian society for a long time.[7]

In both systems the component units maintain their social identity through strict rules of endogamy. In a class system individuals tend to marry within their own class but there are no prescribed rules which require them to do so. In the United States' South marriages between Negroes and whites were strictly forbidden and this is still the case in South Africa. In India, the principle of endogamy was in certain areas mitigated by the practice of hypergamy (*anuloma*) by which a man from a higher caste could, under prescribed conditions, marry a girl from a lower casts. It must be emphasized that traditionally the practice of hypergamy was governed by strict rules which recognized the distinctions between castes as well as their hierarchical order; and, as Irawati Karve has pointed out, it 'is found in certain parts of India among only certain castes and is not a general practice in any region'.[8] Those who define systems of stratification in terms of the rigidity of marriage rules are bound to be struck by the similarity between the Indian and the colour–caste systems.

Closely associated with the rules regulating marriage are certain attitudes towards women, characteristic of both types of society. A very high value is placed on the purity of women belonging to the upper strata, and they are protected from sexual contamination by men of the lower strata by sanctions of the most stringent kind.[9] On the other hand, there is a strong element of 'sexual exploitation' in the relations between men of the upper strata and women of the lower. Berreman notes that the `sexual advantages', enjoyed by high caste men in an Indian village studied by him are similar even in their details, to those enjoyed by white men in the town studied by Dollard in the United States' South.[10]

We might at this stage sum up the characteristics of castes by saying that they are hierarchically ranked groups or categories based on hereditary membership which maintain their social identity by strict rules of endogamy. The fact of hereditary membership is of great importance. It fixes the social status of the individual at birth and prevents his movement from one group of category to another. Notwithstanding many exceptions, these factors combine to fit the social divisions in a caste society into an uncommonly rigid mould.

If I began by considering the similarities between the two types of social stratification, this was not to imply that I consider these to be in some sense more fundamental than their differences. Opinion is sharply divided on the significance to be attached to these similarities and differences,[11] and scholars like Dumont[12] and Leach[13] would consider it misleading to describe systems of stratification based on colour as caste. For them, the institution of caste in the true sense of the term is a unique feature of the pan-Indian civilization.

The differences between the two types of caste system, using the same term for convenience, are obvious enough but it has not proved easy to sum them up in a formula. Some would draw the distinction by saying that one represents a 'cultural model' and the other a 'biological model'.[14] The caste system in India is certainly a cultural phenomenon, but is it adequate to represent the colour–caste system in the United States' South (or in South Africa) simply in biological terms? Both Warner[15] and Myrdal[16] had first considered and then rejected the view that the groups they were studying be described as races. A quick look at their argument will throw some light on the complex relations between race, culture, and society, and help us to probe a little deeper into the subject of our study.

Warner insists that in the stratification system of the Deep South the categories Negro and white are socially and not biologically defined. Persons who are socially defined as Negroes might be bio-logically classified as white and people who are regarded as Negroes in one society might in another society be viewed as whites.[17] Myrdal's position is similar. He points out, first, that 'the "Negro race" is defined in America by the white people' and, secondly, that 'this definition of the Negro race in the United States is at variance with that held in the rest of the American continent'.[18] What is significant is not merely the presence of physical distinctions but also the manner in which they are socially recognized which is essentially conventional. Neither Negroes nor whites in the United States' South can be regarded as races in the strictly biological sense of the term.

Kingsley Davis sought to characterize the distinction which we are considering as being between 'racial' and 'non-racial' caste systems:

A non-racial caste system, such as the Hindu, is one in which the criterion of caste status is primarily descent symbolized in purely socio–economic terms; while a racial system is one in which the criterion is primarily physiognomic, usually chromatic, with socio–economic differences implied.[19]

We have just seen why it is not wholly satisfactory to describe the caste system in the United States as racial; and it is not entirely clear that the chromatic differences there are more fundamental than the socio–economic ones as Davis would seem to suggest. Nor is it wholly satisfactory in this context to view 'race' and 'descent' in opposition for in both cases we are concerned with the cultural definition of biological processes.

It is true, nonetheless, that visible differences are much more conspicuous in the colour–caste system than in the Indian system. An outsider in the United States' South will not have much difficulty in deciding in the majority of cases who belongs to which caste merely from appearance. In India he will find it difficult if not impossible to do this beyond a certain point. This in itself would not however establish the absence of more fundamental genetic differences between castes in Indian society. Indeed, their complete absence would be surprising in view of the fact that members of most castes are believed to have practised strict endogamy for countless generations.

Those who emphasize the differences between the Indian and the American systems would base their argument on the uniqueness of Hindu cultural values. In fact, one might distinguish between the 'structural' view of caste which draws attention to broad similarities and the 'cultural' view which regards the caste system in India as unique.[20] There is no doubt that in India caste is embedded in a system of religious values which has no counterpart either in the United States' South or in South Africa.

Western scholars have been struck by the importance of hierarchy in the Hindu scheme of values.[21] Central to this are the notions of dharma and karma.[22] These are both complex, philosophical notions and it is difficult to put them in a nutshell. Very briefly, dharma implies right conduct in accordance with one's station in life, defined largely by one's caste: karma explains, and justifies, one's birth in a particular station in terms of one's actions in a previous life. In other words, moral rules and standards of worth would differ from one caste to another. Most Western observers have been struck by the iniquity of the system, but scholars like Leach would point out that it ensured a measure of material and psychological security to all sections of society, particularly those at the bottom of the hierarchy.[23]

In contrast to the values of traditional India, the American creed has always placed the highest social value on the equality of men. Thus, the moral environment in which rigid social distinctions exist in America is quite different from the moral environment in India. One may say that the American system is disharmonic; inequalities exist in fact although rejected by the normative order. The traditional Indian system was, by contrast, harmonic; rigid social distinctions not only existed but were generally accepted as legitimate. If this argument is correct, then the two types of system would show very different patterns of tension and conflict.

The values of a society are not easy to describe in an objective way. They are often ambiguous and made up of conflicting elements. It is difficult to believe that hierarchical values were accepted in the same way by all strata of Indian society. Most of what we know about traditional Indian values is based on texts written by people who belonged to the top of the hierarchical system. Perhaps we will never know in quite the same detail how the order of caste was perceived by people at the bottom of the hierarchy.

Berreman, who, unlike most students of Indian society, has studied a village community by living with the lower castes, would contend that there are sharp differences of perspective between the lower and the upper strata.[24] Others too have noted the existence of tensions and conflicts between castes which would not be expected if everyone accepted without question the position assigned to him within the hierarchical order.[25] However, most of these tendencies have been recorded within the past twenty years and their emergence in contemporary India would not contradict the assertion that traditionally the Indian caste system approximated to the harmonic type.

Berreman also rejects the view that the American value system can be unambiguously defined in terms of its emphasis on equality.[26] He quotes Spiro's critique of Myrdal to support his argument:

The assumption of egalitarian culture norms is untenable unless one adopts an idealist conception of ideal norms which are irrelevant to human behaviour and aspirations. Actually discrimination against the Negro is not in violation of southern ideal norms; it is in conformity with them.[27]

There is also the question of the colour–caste system in South Africa. Can we say, perhaps, that here we have a normative order which accepts the existing structure of inequality between groups as legitimate?

Differences between the colour–caste system and the Indian system are not confined to the realm of values. There are important differences in the structure and composition of the groups that constitute the two types of system. In the United States' South there are only two principal castes, Negroes and whites; in South Africa there are four, Africans, whites, 'coloureds' and Asians.[28] In India the caste system comprises a large number of groups whose mutual relations are of an extremely complex nature.

In India it is not at all uncommon for a single village to have as many as twenty or thirty castes.[29] Each linguistic region in the country has between 200 and 300 castes. Many of these are divided into sub-castes which might in turn be further subdivided.[30] If we leave the village and take a larger territorial unit, it becomes impossible even to determine the exact number of castes in it. The distinctions between caste, sub-caste and sub-sub-caste become blurred. The same caste might be called by different names and different castes by the same name.

There is no single rank order for all the castes and sub-castes that applies to every region. Perhaps all that can be said very firmly for the country as a whole is that Brahmins rank at the top and Harijans at the bottom. There is a great deal of ambiguity in the middle region. The different cultivating castes make competing claims to superior status. The Brahmins (like the Harijans) are themselves divided into a number of castes and sub-castes whose mutual ranks are by no means easy to determine.[31] All this is not to deny that a certain measure of consensus in regard to caste ranking does exist within the local community.[32] This consensus was probably stronger in the past than it is today.

It can be argued that structurally there is a basic difference between a dichotomous system and a system of gradation in which there are many terms. Once again, the two types of systems are likely to display very different patterns of social conflict. Theories of social class and of conflict assign a crucial significance to the dichotomous division of society.[33] Where the contending parties are two in number, the conflict tends to be intense; where they are many, a shifting pattern of coalitions reduces the intensity of conflict. The same theory can be extended to caste. Where the community is divided into Negroes and whites, the conflict is likely to be sharp; where it is divided into twenty or thirty groups, no particular conflict is likely to absorb the energies of the community as a whole.

We shall now try to see if any relationship can be established between caste distinctions and physical differences in the Indian population. It might be said at the outset that if such a relationship exists it is not likely to be either simple or direct. Physical differences are not polarized in India but are spread over a continuum. The population cannot be readily divided into races or even into clearly recognizable physical types. The caste system in its turn is a system of great complexity. It is divided and subdivided into innumerable groups, and a consideration of these might provide a convenient point of departure.

The word 'caste' is used in India to refer to groups and categories of very different kinds. Two types of distinctions are particularly important. The first is between varna and jati, and the second between caste and sub-caste. The difference between varna and jati can be briefly described as the difference between a model or a conceptual scheme on the one hand, and a set of real social groups of categories on the other. There are only four which are arranged in a particular order, whereas jatis are many and their rank order is both more ambiguous and more flexible.[34] Jatis should not be viewed as having grown out of divisions and subdivisions within a set of four original varnas. Rather, as Irawati Karve has argued, varna and jati have coexisted as two different but related systems for at least two thousand years.[35]

The distinction between castes and sub-castes is of a different kind. Both are real social divisions, but one is more inclusive than the other. If we take potters or carpenters as examples of castes, we will find that in any given region there are two or three different kinds of potters or of carpenters, differentiated according to technique or provenance, or sect, or some other less tangible factor. These different divisions we might refer to as sub-castes. They are similar in structure to the more inclusive groupings and are generally endogamous.

Scholars like Ghurye would maintain that the different types of potters are sub-castes, being products of segmentation within the potter caste.[36] Irawati Karve, on the other hand, has argued that the different types of potters are often unrelated and that each should be called a caste and the potters as a whole a 'caste cluster'.[37] Her argument is important in this context because she has tried to support it with anthropometric data.[38]

Sometimes there are several levels of differentiation and not just two. Thus, the Tamil Brahmins are of three principal kinds: temple priests, domestic priests for the non-Brahmins, and scholars and landowners. The last are divided into Smartha and Shri Vaishnava, Smartha Brahmins are in turn, further subdivided into Vadama, Brihacharanam, Astasahashram, and Vattima. The Vadama, finally, are divided into Vadadesha and Chozhadesha Vadama.[39] This kind of differentiation makes it useful to view caste as a segmentary or structural system,[40] for even though each segment is endogamous, the social distance between segments is variable. Thus social distance between Vadama and Brihacharanam is smaller than that between a Vadama and Shri Vaishnava segment which in turn is smaller than that between any Brahmin segment and any non-Brahmin segment. This way of viewing the system leads us to ask if there is any relationship between social distance and racial distance.

Most anthropologists who have analysed caste from the biological point of view would concede that some physical differences do exist between castes, but they are sharply divided on the significance they attach to these differences. On the whole, earlier scholars emphasized the differences in physical type they observed between castes. Contemporary scholars are more inclined to stress the fact that most castes are more or less heterogeneous in their physical composition and that variations within a caste are sometime greater than variations between castes.

It is not enough to know that castes differ from one another in their biological make-up. We would like to know in addition whether the extent to which they differ in this regard is related to their social distance. Castes that are socially adjacent might be quite different in their biological composition while those which are at opposite ends of the social scale might show very little difference biologically. To answer this kind of question satisfactorily we will need a great deal of systematic empirical material. The evidence that we now have is scanty and does not all point in the same direction.

The first serious effort to study physical or racial differences between castes systematically was made towards the end of the century by Sir Herbert Risley.[41] Risley not only believed that such difference existed but argued that they were systematically related to differences of social rank between castes:

If we take a series of castes in Bengal, Bihar, the United Provinces of Agra and Oudh, or Madras, and arrange them in the order of the average nasal index so that the caste with the finest nose shall be at the top, and that with the coarsest at the bottom of the list, it will be found that this order substantially corresponds with the accepted order of social precedence.[42]

Risley was also struck by the fact that the upper castes were in general lighter skinned than the lower and drew attention to a number of local proverbs in which this distinction was given recognition.

Risley developed an elaborate theory to explain the social ranking of castes. He argued that the caste system was the outcome of the encounter between two distinct racial groups, one representing a light-skinned, narrow-nosed, 'Aryan' type, and the other, a dark-skinned, broad-nosed 'non-Aryan' type. The Aryans, according to the theory, were not only the dominant group but also adopted the practice of hypergamy. This practice led to the formation of a series of intermediate groups whose social rank varied directly with their amount of Aryan blood. Risley sought to support his arguments with anthropometric data. His conclusions were challenged by later scholars who found fault with both his data and his methods.[43]

Ghurye criticized Risley's work but did not reject his argument altogether. He emphasized the importance of regional variations and noted that a caste which ranked very high in one area might closely resemble in its physical features a caste which ranked very low in an adjacent area. He pointed out that in many parts of the country there was no clear relationship of the kind which Risley had sought to demonstrate:

Outside Hindustan in each of the linguistic areas we find that the physical type of the population is mixed, and does not conform in its gradation to the scale of social precedence of the various castes.[44]

Ghurye however agreed that in the Hindi-speaking area itself there was a close correspondence between the 'physical hierarchy' and the 'social hierarchy'.

Here the Brahmins were long-headed and narrow-nosed, and very low castes like the Chamar and the Pasi were broad-headed and broad-nosed. On the basis of such evidence, Ghurye was prepared to conclude that here, at least, 'restrictions on marriage of a fundamentally endogamous nature were thus racial in origin'.[45]

The most comprehensive single investigation so far carried out is the anthropometric study of Bengal undertaken jointly by an anthropologist, D.N. Majumdar and a statistician, C.R, Rao[46] The data were collected from a defined cultural region, Bengal, comprising both, West Bengal and East Pakistan. Sixty-seven groups were investigated, including Muslims, Christians, a few tribal groups, and a large number of Hindu castes. These groups were studied with regard to sixteen basic anthropometric characters and a number of indices derived from them. Some serological data were collected in addition. The anthropometric data were analysed by means of rigorous and sophisticated statistical tests.

Notwithstanding many qualifications, Majumdar concluded that there was some clustering of groups according to their social proximity. The tribal and semi-tribal groups tended to be clustered at one end and at the other end were the higher castes such as Brahmin, Baidya, and Kayastha,[47] Majumdar pointed out that these data confirmed the observations made by him in two other areas in India, Gujarat and Uttar Pradesh:

In all the three surveys, it has been found that some correlation exists between the order of social precedence in a state or region, and the ethnic constellations based on anthropometric data.[48]

It must be emphasized, however, that the relationships which emerge from the study by Majumdar and Rao are of a far more complex nature than those that Risley believed he had established.

Studies undertaken more recently do not all support Majumdar's conclusions. Karve and Malhotra have published the results of a detailed comparison between eight Brahmin 'sub-castes' in Maharashtra, taking anthropometric, somatoscopic, and serological data into account.[49] Their data show the existence of significant differences among some of the Brahmin 'sub-castes'. Comparing their findings with those of other scholars, they conclude that there is no necessary relationship between social distance and physical distance.

Thus there is no justification for assuming that the distance between the Brahmin 'castes' under investigation is less than the distance between a Brahmin 'caste' and a non-Brahmin 'caste', for some Brahmins are closer to members of other 'castes' than to each other.[50]

It would appear that the more closely we look at the system the less firm we can be about the linkage between caste and race.

The shift from morphological to genetical indicators would seem to confirm the view that the linkage between social and physical distance is tenuous and uncertain. As my last example I shall take a study by Sanghvi and Khanolkar which examines the distribution of seven genetical traits among six endogamous groups in Bombay.[51] Of the six groups, four are Brahmins; one is high non-Brahmin caste, Chandraseniya Kayashth Prabhu (CKP), ranking next only to the Brahmins; and the other is a cultivating caste, Maratha (MK), belonging to the middle level of the hierarchy. As the authors point out, all these groups have been regarded by earlier anthropologists as being of the same physical type. The results of the analysis show a rather complex pattern of variations. Some of the Brahmin groups are quite close to each other, and one of them is very similar in its genetical composition to the non-Brahmin Marathas. The Koknasth Brahman (KB) are, on the other hand, quite distinctive in their genetical composition as are also the CKP. Moreover, these two groups are markedly different from each other.

The magnitude of differences between the groups KD and CKP for each one of the seven genetical characters is more or less similar to that between American whites and American Negroes.[52]

Although the CKP are non-Brahmins, they rank very high and might be regarded as being socially proximate to the Koknasth Brahman.

This leads us to a consideration of the social significance of genotypical as opposed to phenotypical differences. Earlier anthropologists such as Risley sought to establish a relationship between the social rank of a caste and the physical appearance of its members. They were encouraged in their pursuit by beliefs widely held in Indian society about the existence of such a relationship.[53] Upper castes are universally believed to be light-skinned and narrow-nosed, and lower castes to be dark skinned and broad-nosed. It would now appear that two socially adjacent castes whose members are very similar in their physical appearance might nevertheless be quite different in their genetical composition.

Genetical differences are likely to acquire social significance only if their existence is widely known or if they are reflected in clear differences in physical type. As I have indicated, certain broad differences in appearance exist between castes at opposite end of the hierarchy in many parts of the country and equally significant are the beliefs and stereotypes regarding these differences which persist in spite of much evidence to the contrary. Beliefs that are technically wrong or inconsistent sometimes assume crucial significance in social life. As Passin has argued:

The relation of caste to race is not simply a question of whether the groups are in fact racially different, but rather that there seems to be some disposition to attribute racial difference, to even the most marginal cues in caste and caste-like situations.[54]

This is particularly true in the Indian context where in some languages the same word is used to denote both caste and race.[55]

What is important in social life is the sense of solidarity which people feel when they belong to the same community and the sense of distance which separate members who belong to different communities. The sense of community is often based on the feeling that its members have a common origin. The feeling may be vague or it may be consciously formulated in an ideology. It may be strengthened if the community is marked out by distinctive physical features, but this is not a necessary condition for its existence. Sometimes a strong sense of community can exist even in the absence of visible physical indicators. This leads us to a consideration of ethnic groups and identities.

The systematic use of the concept of ethnicity is of relatively recent origin in sociology and social anthropology although the presence of ethnic groups in the United States has been widely discussed for many years.

An ethnic group is a distinct category of the population in a larger society whose culture is usually different from its own. The members of such a group are, or feel themselves, or are thought to be bound together by common ties of race or nationality or culture.[56]

As this description suggests, there is no single criterion by which ethnic groups can be defined.

In the United States, the term 'ethnic group' came into use to describe immigrants from the different parts of the world. Examples of these would be the Irish, the Italians, and the Poles who settled in the country in successive waves of migration. These groups were not all differentiated by visible physical indicators. Initially there were major differences of language, culture, and religion among the groups. As some of these differences began to diminish among second- and third-generation immigrants, it was felt that a culturally homogeneous population would emerge out of the melting pot of American society. However, in spite of a high degree of mobility, both horizontal and vertical, and certain amount of intermarriage between groups, ethnic identities have proved to be remarkably persistent in American society.[57]

The presence of ethnic groups is of course not a unique feature of American society. They exist in all societies where cultural differences are given a particular meaning and are organized in a particular way. Ethnic differentiation has been a conspicuous feature of the so-called plural societies of South and South-East Asia.[58] Sometimes this differentiation is associated with the presence of large groups, such as the Chinese and the Indians in Malaysia, which differ markedly from each other in language, religion, and provenance. The coexistence of such disparate groups is likely to generate tensions and conflicts which might, in the extreme case, threaten the integrity of the very political framework.

Ethnic identities might persist even when ethnic groups are not visibly different or politically organized. In a recent collection of paper Barth and his colleagues have argued persuasively that ethnic identities do not depend for their survival on any particular aggregate of cultural traits.

It is important to recognize that although ethnic categories take cultural differences into account, we can assume no simple one-to-one relationship between ethnic units and cultural similarities and differences.[59]

Eidheim gives a graphic account of the manner in which an ethnic boundary is maintained between Lapps and Norwegians even in the absence of any readily visible physical or cultural difference between them.[60]

Ethnic groups are generally endogamous, and in that sense they tend to be biologically self-perpetuating.[61] Even in the complete absence of diacritical distinctions, endogamy could of course serve to keep ethnic boundaries intact. When all marriages do not take place within the group, ethnic boundaries might still be maintained if intermarriage is governed by the rule of hypergamy; the practice of hypergamy acts as an important boundary maintaining mechanism among certain sections of the hill Rajputs in India.[62] Far from dissolving ethnic boundaries altogether, intermarriage might, under certain conditions, serve to bring these boundaries into sharper relief.

Thus, the concept of ethnic group is somewhat broader in its scope than that of race. Ethnic differences might be based at least partly on race, as in the case of Malays, Chinese, and Indians in Malaysia or of Negroes, Indians, and whites in the Caribbean. They might also exist in a society which is racially more or less homogeneous as in the case of the Pathans in West Pakistan and Afghanistan or of some of the multi-tribal systems in East Africa.

The caste system may, in turn, be viewed as a particular case of ethnic differentiation. Whether or not 'racial' differences exist between castes, they are often differentiated from one another culturally, in their dress, diet, and rituals. Where even these distinctions are feeble or absent, the boundaries between castes are maintained by the rules of endogamy and hypergamy. However, even if we regard caste as system of ethnic groups, it is a system in which the different groups are all integrated within a hierarchical order. Ethnic groups are not necessarily arranged in a hierarchy and they are not always integrated within a unitary system.

We notice a close similarity between caste in India and ethnic groups in the United State when we examine the part they play in the political process.[63] In the United States, ethnic solidarities are widely used for mobilizing political support and ethnic rivalries have to be taken into account in formulating electoral strategies.[64] In India, caste enters into the political process in a number of ways.[65] Caste associations have not only acted as pressure groups but, in at least one area, have transformed themselves into political parties.[66] Rivalries between parties are sometimes heightened when they base their support on mutually antagonistic castes.[67] However, in both India and the United States the relationship between caste or ethnic identity and the political process is complex and ambigious. The political process brings out not only the cleavages between such groups but also the possibilities of coalitions among them.

The Harijans provide a particular example of solidarity based on caste or ethnic identity. In the past the barrier of pollution kept them segregated from many areas of social life. These barriers have now been legally abolished but the Harijans retain much of their traditional stigma and continue to be socially and economically underprivileged. However, they are now provided with opportunities to organize themselves politically.[68] This has enabled them to gain some advantages but it has also brought them into confrontation with the upper castes whose members are not always in a mood to accept them as equals. The situation of the Harijans in contemporary India, like that of the Negroes in the United States, reveals a paradox. The lessening of cultural distance has in both cases been accompanied not by a decrease but by an increase in tension and conflict.

India has not only a Harijan problem, there is also an Adivasi or tribal problem. Harijans and Adivasis are officially grouped together

as the Backward Classes and their separate identity is given constitutional recognition.[69] The tribal people numbered about 30 million at
the 1961 census and they constituted over 6 per cent of the Indian
population. They are divided into a large number of separate tribes,
differing in race, language, and culture. They are concentrated in
particular areas in the country which tend to be geographically isolated but there is no policy of keeping them in reservations.

The tribal population of India does not belong to any single racial
or physical type. The differences between the 'Veddoid' type common among certain tribes in central and south India and the 'Palaeo-
Mongoloid' type found in the north-east hill areas might be greater
than the differences between the tribal people and their non-tribal
neighbours in any particular area. Fürer-Haimendorf has however
rightly pointed out that differences of the latter kind also exist[70] and
Majumdar's anthropometric data seem to point in the same direction.[71]

After drawing attention to differences in physical type between
the tribal and the non-tribal population, Fürer-Haimendorf says:

It is all the more remarkable that despite racial differences no less fundamental than those found in countries with acute race problems, there have never
been any cases of racial tension in India.[72]

One important factor is the very great variety of physical types which
has prevented polarization of the population along racial lines. This
does not mean that differences do not exist or are not socially recognized. Indeed, tribal solidarity is perhaps being given a new lease of
life by democratic politics. However, the conflict is transferred on to a
different plane where the cleavage between tribals and non-tribals
becomes one among a number of politically relevant ethnic
distinctions.

We have so far considered ethnic differentiation among groups
that are hierarchically arranged, for, although the Adivasis are in the
strict sense outside the caste system, they are almost everywhere
ranked below caste Hindus. We may now turn to ethnic differentiation between groups that are not hierarchically arranged, such as
those based on religion or on language. In some sense these provide
the most fundamental cleavages in contemporary Indian society.
When one talks about 'national integration' in India one has primarily in mind the problem of holding together the different religious
and linguistic communities. While one can distinguish analytically
between ethnic identities of different kinds, hierarchical and non-
hierarchical, in reality these often tend to become confused.

India has been described as a multi-religious nation. Hindus are in an overwhelming majority, accounting for around 80 per cent of the population: Muslims constitute a significant minority with a little more than 10 per cent of the population. There are other religious groups that are of significance in particular regions, such as Sikhs in the Punjab and Christians in Kerala. However for the country as a whole the cleavage that has greatest significance is that between Hindus and Muslims. If there is a 'communal' problem in the country its prototype is that which grows out of the relations between these two communities.[73]

Hindus and Muslims in India do not belong to separate races. In actuality they are both racially very mixed. This is only be expressed as the majority of Indian Muslims are the descendants of converts from Hinduism.

Spear argues that there were two principal types of conversion: clan or group conversion as a consequence of which castes such as Rajputs, Jats, and Gujjars in north India have Hindu as well as Muslim sections; and mass conversions through which low caste Hindu, particularly in Bengal, embraced Islam.[74] The last point finds confirmation in Majumdar's anthropometric data referred to above; the low caste Namasudras are closer in physical appearance to the Muslims than they are to the upper caste Hindus.[75]

Hindus and Muslims have coexisted as communities in different parts of India for a millennium. Religious differences have been associated with a host of other differences in ways of life. These differences have not always been the same, but the fact of difference has remained, heightened at times and subdued at others. Hindus and Muslims might not differ in physical type but religious ideology has provided each community with a basis for consciously organizing its identity in opposition to the other. Over the centuries the two communities have borrowed much from each other and during the past few decades they have been exposed to similar forces of change. This however, has not erased the boundaries between them. Indeed, the pattern of Hindu-Muslim relations in recent Indian history would seem to show that groups might become more conscious of their opposed identities precisely at a time when external differences between them are being reduced.

The population of India is also divided on the basis of language. The divisions of language and religion generally cut across and do not reinforce each other as they do to a large extent in countries like Malaysia and Sri Lanka. This, in addition to the fact that both linguistic and religious groups are many and not two, tends to make the conflict between communities diffused rather than polarized.

Over a dozen major languages are spoken in India but there is none which is the mother tongue of a majority of the people. The speakers of the different languages are not randomly distributed throughout the country. Each language has its 'homeland' so linguistic differences largely coincide with regional differences. The different states that constitute the Union of India are in effect linguistic units. This means that the ethnic identity provided by language has both a cultural basis and a political organization.

Differences between linguistic groups can give rise to two kinds of tensions. At one level are the disputes between the different linguistic states over particular issues, for instance the question of boundaries or the distribution of river water.[76] At another level one encounters the problem of linguistic minorities in virtually every state; these problems are likely to be particularly acute in large metropolitan cities like Bombay or Calcutta which attract people from all over the country. Ethnic boundaries based on language are in a way crucial; they restrict communication between people in the literal sense of the term. Differences of language have in reality very little to do with differences of race, although in one important case linguistic differences have been represented in a racial idiom. The different languages of India belong to two major families, the Indo-Aryan languages spoken in the north by about three-quarter of the population and the Dravidian languages spoken in the four southern states by about a quarter of population. People in the southern state have particularly since Independence, sometimes expressed a fear of domination by the north[77] and a separatist political movement developed there although its influence has been confined almost wholly to one state, Tamil Nadu.[78] One of the arguments advanced by leaders of this movement was that southern Indians, being Dravidians, had a separate identity in race, language, and culture, and should free themselves from the domination of the Aryan northern Indians.[79] Tamil separatism has now become subdued and we no longer hear the racial argument very frequently but language barriers are, in other respects, no less significant than they were before.

We have moved a long distance from a consideration of racial differences to differences of quite another kind which are at times expressed in a racial idiom. Ethnic identity must not be thought of as something which defines the character of one group in opposition to another for all time. In India the same individual has a number of different identities according to caste, religion, and language, and anyone of these might become more important than the others, depending upon context and situation. It is not enough to know that boundaries exist between groups, one must also examine the situations under which some boundaries are ignored and others become significant. Thus, in one context, Tamil-speaking Hindus and Muslims might unite to defend themselves against 'Aryan' domination; in another context Hindus from both north and south India might regard Muslims as aliens among them.

Although ethnic differences have a bearing on social conflict, a knowledge of the former is not sufficient to predict the pattern of the latter. In order to understand the scale and intensity of conflicts between ethnic groups we have to take a number of factors into account. These are the objective differences between them, the social awareness of these differences, and the political organization of this awareness.

As we have seen, the objective differences themselves are of many kinds. They may be roughly grouped together as physical or cultural. Cultural differences in turn can be based on religion, language, or region. There is no direct relationship between the degree of these differences and the extent to which people are aware of them. Differences of colour might exist to the same degree in two societies and yet people might be acutely aware of them in one society and not in the other. Cultural differences are more difficult to measure. Also, in any case, there are no satisfactory criteria by which one can compare the awareness of, say, religious differences with that of linguistic differences.

People might be highly conscious of their differences, whether physical or cultural, without their consciousness acquiring a political form. In traditional Indian society there were not only differences between castes; but people were universally aware of these differences. Yet castes were not always organized into mutually antagonistic groups. They began to organize themselves into associations at a time when people were beginning to feel that caste consciousness would fade away. The course of political conflict remains unpredictable. There is no general theory which can enable us to delineate in exact terms the relationship between cultural differences and their organization into mutually antagonistic groups.

Notes

1. I am grateful to my colleagues A. Sharma and S.C. Tiwari of the Department of Anthropology and M.S.A. Rao of the Department of Sociology, University of Delhi for much help in the preparation of this article.

2. For an interesting discussion , see Anthony de Reuck and Julie Knight (eds), *Caste and Race, Comparative Approaches*, London, 1967.

3. Among the more notable community studies going back to this period are John Dollerd *Caste and Class in a Southern Town*, New Delhi, 1937 and Allison Davis, Burleigh B. Gardner and Mary R. Gardner, *Deep South, A Social Anthropological Study of Caste and Class*, Chicago, 1941.

4. Gunnar Myrdal, *An American Dilemma: The Negro Problem in Modern Democracy*, p. 667, 688, New York, 1944

5. Pierre L. van den Berghe, *Race and Racism: A Comparative Perspective*, New York, 1967, speaks of whites, Africans, Asians, and coloureds as constituting the four 'castes' or 'colour-caste' of South African society.

6. Myrdal, op cit.

7. André Béteille, *Castes: Old and New: Essays in Social Structure and Social Stratification*, p. 3, Bombay, 1969.

8. Irawati Karve, *Hindu Society: An Interpretation*, p. 10, Poona, 1961.

9. For American examples, see the case studies by Dollard and by Davis, Gardner and Gardener cited above; for an Indian case study, see Kathleen Gough, 'Caste in a Tanjore Village', in E.R. Leach (ed.), *Aspects of Caste in North India, Ceylon and North-West Pakistan*, p. 49, Cambridge, 1960.

10. Gerald D. Berreman, *Hindus of the Himalayas*, p. 241, Berkeley, 1963.

11. See de Reuck and Knight (eds), op cit.

12. Louis Dumont, 'Caste, Racism and "Stratification": Reflections of a Social Anthropologists', *Contributions to Indian Sociology*, no. 5, 1961, pp. 20–43.

13. E.R. Leach, 'Introduction: What Should We Mean by Caste?', in Leach (ed.), op cit.

14. S.J. Tambiah presents this opposition as a 'gross simplification' in a discussion reported in de Reuck and Knight (eds), op cit., pp. 328–9.

15. W. Lloyd Warner, 'Introduction: Deep South—A Social Anthropological Study of Caste and Class', in Davis, Gardner and Gardner, op cit., pp. 3–14.

16. Myrdal, op cit.

17. Warner, op cit.

18. Myrdal, op cit., p. 113.

19. Kingsley Davis, 'Intermarriage in Caste Society', *American Anthropologist*, vol. 43, 1941, pp. 386–7.

20. Louis Dumont, 'Caste: A Phenomenon of Social Structure or an Aspect of Indian Culture?', in de Reuck and Knight (eds), op cit., pp. 28–38.

21. Louis Dumont, *Homo Hierarchicus: Essai sur le Systeme des Castes,* Paris, 1966.

22. Karve, op cit.

23. Leach, op cit.

24. Berreman, op cit.

25. André Béteille, 'The Politics of "Non-antagonistic Strata"', *Contributions to Indian Sociology,* New Series, no. III, 1969, p. 17–31. One way in which conflicts between castes were structured in the past was through the opposition between the 'right-hand' and the 'left-hand' castes prevalent in many parts of South India; see J.H. Hutton, *Caste in India: Its Nature, Function, and Origins,* Bombay, 1961.

26. Herald D. Berreman, 'Caste in Cross-cultural Perspective', in G. DeVos and H. Wagatsuma (eds), *Japan's Invisible Race, Caste in Culture and Personality,* p. 297, Berkeley, 1966.

27. Ibid.

28. van den Berghe, op cit.

29. For typical village studies, see Adrian C. Mayer, *Caste and Kinship in Central India: A Village and its Region,* London, 1960; and André Béteille, *Caste, Class and Power: Changing Patterns of Stratification in a Tanjore Village,* Berkeley, 1995.

30. Béteille, *Caste, Class and Power ...* op cit.

31. Ibid.

32. McKim Marriott, 'Caste Ranking and Food Traditions: A Matrix Analysis', in Milton Singer and Bernard S. Cohn (eds), *Structure and Change in Indian Society,* pp. 111–71, Chicago, 1969.

33. Ralf Dahrendorf, *Class and Class Conflict in an Industrial Society,* London, 1959.

34. M.N. Srinivas, 'Varna and Caste', in M.N. Srinivas (ed.), *Caste in Modern India and Other Essays,* Bombay, 1962.

35. Karve, op cit.

36. G.S. Ghurye, *Caste and Race in India,* London, 1932.

37. Karve, op. cit.

38. I. Karve and K.C. Malhotra, 'A Biological Comparison of Eight Endogamous Groups of the Same Rank', *Current Anthropology,* vol. 9, 1968, pp. 109–16.

39. Béteille, *Caste, Class and Power ...* op cit.

40. Ibid.

41. H.H. Risley, *The People of India,* Calcutta, 1908.

42. Risley, op. cit., p. 29.

43. P.C. Mahalanobis, 'A Revision of Risley's Anthropometric Data', *Samkhya,* vol. 1, 1933, pp. 70–105; Ghurye, op cit.

44. Ghurye, op cit., p. 111.

45. Ghurye, op cit., p. 107.

46. D.N. Majumdar and C.R. Rao, *Race Elements in Bengal: Quantitative Study*, Calcutta, 1960.

47. Majumdar and Rao, op cit., p. 102.

48. Majumdar and Rao, op cit., p. 103.

49. Karve and Malhotra, op cit.

50. Ibid.

51. L.D. Sanghvi and V.R. Khanolkar, 'Data Relating to Seven Genetical Characters in Six Endogamous Groups in Bombay', *Annals of Eugenics*, vol. 15, 1990, p. 16.

52. Sanghvi and Khanolkar, op cit., p. 62.

53. André Béteille, 'Race and Descent as Social Categories in India', Daedalus, vol. 96, 1967, p. 444–61.

54. In a discussion reported in de Reuck and Knight (eds), op cit., pp. 110–11.

55. Béteille, 'Race and Descent as Social Categories in India', op cit.

56. H.S. Morris, 'Ethnic Groups', in David I. Sills (ed.), *International Encyclopedia of the Social Science*, vol. 5, 1968, p. 167.

57. Nathan Glazer and Daniel Patrick Moynihan, *Beyond the Melting Pot: The Negroes, Puerto Ricans, Jews, Italians, and Irish of New York City*, Cambridge, Mass., 1964.

58. J.S. Furnivall, *Colonial Policy and Practice: A Comparative Study of Burma and Netherlands India*, New York, 1956.

59. Fredrik Barth, 'Introduction', in Fredrik Barth (ed.), *Ethnic Conflicts and Boundaries: The Social Organization of Culture Difference*, p. 14, London, 1962.

60. Harald Eidheim, 'When Ethnic Identity is a Social Stigma', in Barth (ed.), op cit., pp. 39–57.

61. Barth, op cit.

62. I am indebted for the information to Jonathan P. Parry who has made an intensive study of the hill Rajputs in Kangra district.

63. Lloyd I. Rudolph and Susanne Hoeber Rudolph, *The Modernity of Tradition: Political Development in India*, Chicago, 1967; André Béteille, 'Caste and Politics in Tamilnad', in Béteille, *Caste: Old and New ...*, op cit.

64. Glazer and Moynihan, op cit.

65. Rajni Kothari (ed.), *Caste in Indian Politics*, New Delhi, 1970.

66. Lloyd I Rudolph and Susanne Hoeber Rudolph, 'The Political Role of India's Caste Associations', *Pacific Affairs*, vol. xxxiii, 1960, pp. 5–22.

67. Selig S. Harrison, 'Caste and the Andhra Communists', American Political Science Review, vol. I, 1956.

68. Owen M. Lynch, *The Politics of Untouchability*, New York, 1969.

69. André Béteille, 'The Future of the Backward Classes: The Compelling Demands of Status and Power', *Perspectives*, Supplement to the *Indian Journal of Public Administration*, vol. XI, 1965, pp. 1–39.

70. Christoph von Furer-Haimendorf, 'The Position of the Tribal Population in Modern India', in Philip Mason (ed.), *India and Ceylon: Unity and Diversity*, p. 183, London, 1967.

71. Majumdar and Rao, op cit.

72. Fürer-Haimendorf, op cit., p. 188.

73. See, for instance, the issue of *Seminar* no. 24, Aug. 1961, devoted to communalism.

74. Percival Spear, 'The Position of the Muslims, Before and After Partiton', in Mason (ed.), op cit. pp. 33–4.

75. Majumdar and Rao, op cit., p. 102.

76. Selig S. Harrison, '*India: The Most Dangerous Decade*, Bombay, 1960.

77. See, for instance, the issue of *Seminar*, no. 23 July 1961, devoted to north and south.

78. Robert L. Hardgrave Jr., *The Dravidian Movement*, Bombay, 1965.

79. Béteille, 'Race and Descent as Social Categories in India', op cit.

7

Ethno-Linguistic Issues in the Indian Federal Context*

A.R. Kamat

Ethno-Lingual Situation

According to the 1971 Census, India has over 1000 languages and mothertongues. Fifteen languages (recognized presumably as the principal or possible official state languages) are recorded in the Eighth Schedule of the Constitution. They are: Assamese (A), Bengali (B), Gujarati (G), Hindi (H), Kannada (Kn), Kashmiri (Ks), Malayalam (Ml), Marathi (Mr), Oriya (Or), Punjabi (P), Sanskrit (Sk), Sindhi (S), Tamil (TM), Telugu (Tl), and Urdu (U). The mention of Sanskrit is obviously for sentimental-cum-cultural reasons and has little operational signature, Sindhi, which was added to the Schedule later, in 1966, recognizes the presence of the sizeable ethnic-linguistic group that was forced out of its former homeland of Sind at the time of Partition and which has now no distinct contiguous territorial basis of its own in India. These languages, apart from Sanskrit, will often be referred to as Schedule VIII languages in what follows and the

* *Economic and Political Weekly*, vol. xv, nos 24 and 25, 14–21 June 1980.

This is a revised version of a paper prepared for the All-India Social Sciences Conference held in January 1978 at Calcutta. The author is grateful to A.R. Kelkar of the University of Poona and L.M. Khubchandani, Pune, both distinguished linguistic scholars, for their suggestions. However, the author alone is responsible for the shortcomings of facts and argument.

abbreviations indicated after them in parenthesis used to refer to them in tables and elsewhere.

According to the 1971 Census the Schedule VIII languages (and the mother tongues (MT) falling under them) covered 95.37 per cent of the total population of India (Table 7.1). Another set of 16 languages (and mother tongues grouped under them), each having over

Table 7.1
Distribution of Speakers of Schedule VIII Language

Language	Speakers	Percentage (to total population in India)	Percentage of speakers in home state to total speakers
Assamese (A)	8960	1.65	99.4
Bengali (B)	44,792	8.17	84.4
Gujarati (G)	25,865	4.72	92.3
Kannada (Kn)	21,711	3.96	89.0
Kashmiri (Ks)	2495	0.46	98.3
Malayalam (Ml)	21,939	4.00	93.4
Marathi (Mr)	41,765	7.62	92.5
Oriya (Or)	19,863	3.62	93.0
Punjabi(P)	14,108	2.57	76.3
Sanskrit	2	N	–
Sindhi	1677	0.31	–*
Tamil (Tm)	37,690	6.8	92.4
Telugu (Tl)	44,757	8.17	83.0
Hindi (H)	208,514	38.04	94.2 (92.7)**
Urdu (U)	28,621	5.22	–***
India	548,160	95.37	

Notes:
* Sindhi has no home state; the speakers are largely concentrated in Gujarat, Maharashtra, Madhya Pradesh, and Rajasthan.
** There are six home states for Hindi (Uttar Pradesh, Bihar, Madhya Pradesh, Rajasthan, Haryana, and Himachal Pradesh, and Delhi), The percentage given is to the total population of these areas; the bracketed figure is the percentage for the six states (without Delhi).
*** There is no home state for Urdu. The percentage is to the total population of four states: UP, Bihar, MP, and Rajasthan, (and the union territory of Delhi).
Source: Census of India 1971.

10,000 speakers, accounts for the bulk of the remaining population. These languages (and mother tongues) number 100. The remaining mother tongues, which have very few speakers each, make up the total of 1000 language/mother tongues said to be prevalent in India.[1]

After Independence, many of the Indian states were reorganized, not of course without widespread struggles of the people, along linguistic lines. Thus, almost every major state has what may be called a 'home' language, of which it is a 'home' state. Column 4 in Table 1 gives the percentage of speakers of Schedule VIII languages (except Sanskrit) which are concentrated in their 'home' states. This shows how far the linguistic reorganization has succeeded in bringing together in a state (or states) the speakers of the major languages. It is clear that large swathes of speakers of Bengali, Kannada, Punjabi, and Telugu remain outside the corresponding states and very often live in neighbouring areas, where the language of the majority is different.

The case of Sindhi and Urdu is, however, quite different. They have no contiguous territory that can be called their home states and are dispersed over several states. For instance, the Sindhi-speaking population of 16.77 lakhs is largely spread across Gujarat (6.08 lakhs), Maharashtra (4.32 lakhs), Madhya Pradesh (2.42 lakhs), and Rajasthan 12.40 lakhs), making up 90.76 per cent of the Sindhi-speaking population in India. Although these states are contiguous, that is not at all true of the Sindhi-speaking localities. One can clearly see the Partition–migration effect on the geographical distribution pattern of the Sindhis.

In the case of Urdu with 286.21 lakh speakers and over five per cent of the total Indian population, the major concentrations are even more widely dispersed: Uttar Pradesh (92.73 lakhs), Bihar (49.93 lakhs), Maharashtra (36.62 lakhs), Andhra Pradesh (33.00 lakhs), Karnataka (26.37 lakhs), Madhya Pradesh (10.01 lakhs), West Bengal (9.50 lakhs), Tamil Nadu (7.60 lakhs), Rajasthan (6.51 lakhs), and Gujarat (5.82 lakhs). Here too one can clearly see the effect of Partition (in the reverse) together with the historical situation.

On the other hand, Hindi has six home states unlike the rest of the Schedule VIII languages which have one each. They are UP, Bihar, MP, Haryana, Himachal Pradesh, and Delhi. They cover 94.2 (92.7) per cent of the Hindi speaking population.

Linguistic–Geographical Mapping

Table 7.2 is constructed from the relevant 1971 Census tables to study the language distributions over states and union territories. The states

and territories are sequenced here differently from the usual alpha-
betical order. The seventeen larger states are grouped in geographical and linguistic configurations. Group I includes (a) Jammu and
Kashmir which has Kashmiri as the principal language, a language of
Dardic origin; and (b) Punjab, with the principal language Punjabi,
which along with the languages of states in Groups II, III, IV is an
Indo-Aryan language. (Dardic and Indo-Aryan are both branches of
the Indo-Aryan family of which Iranian is the third branch). This
group (Group I) focuses the north-west zone. Group II comprises the
six heartland states of the north-central zone with Hindi as the home-
language: Haryana, HP, Rajasthan, UP, MP and Bihar. The eastern
states of West Bengal, Assam, and Orissa make Group III, while
Gujarat and Maharashtra constitute the west zone (Group IV). Finally Group V comprises the four south zone states of AP, Karnataka,
Tamil Nadu, and Kerala with their four principal languages of
Dravidian origin. The sixth group includes the remaining five states,
with relatively much smaller population, arranged in order of their
population strengths. Finally the seventh group comprises the Union
Territories arranged by population.

There are some notable features of this linguistic-geographical
mapping. The Hindi-belt states (Group II) constitute 41.16 per cent of
Indian population; if Punjab, with its allied language, Punjabi, is
added, this contiguous region accounts for 42.99 (or 43) per cent of
the population. The remaining principal groups III, IV, and V, the
eastern, western and southern zones respectively, have 14.82, 14.07,
and 26.66 per cent of the Indian population. The Indo-Aryan linguistic groups of states thus constitute 71.88 per cent, and the Dravidian
language group covers 26.66 per cent of the population. Moreover if
one includes Tripura, Delhi, Goa, Pondicherry, and Chandigarh, all
of which mostly speak Schedule VIII languages, the total area dominated by them covers most of the Indian population. In the other
smaller states and Union Territories the languages spoken are not
close to the Schedule VIII ones and/ or are not covered by them. They
are spoken mostly in the border areas in the north-east and north-
west. This does not mean however that the areas covered by the states
and territories where the schedule VIII languages predominate do
not have people speaking languages that are not linguistically close
to or not covered by them. However, as indicated by Tables 7.1 and
7.2, and also in the beginning, they do not add to more than about 4
per cent of the population.

Having considered the principal features of the linguistic–

Table 7.2
Language Distributions Over States

	Total population (in '000)	Percentage of speakers of Schedule VIII languages	Percentage of speakers of the home languages	Percentage of Hindi speakers	Percentage of Urdu speakers	Percentage of speakers of other important languages of Schedule VIII
I. Jammu and Kashmir	4617	72.06	(Ks)53.14	15.06	0.28	P 3.45
Punjab	13,551	99.81	(P) 79.49	20.01	0.21	
II. Haryana	10,037	99.83	(H) 89.42	–	1.95	P 8.34
Himachal Pradesh	3460	92.98	(H) 86.87	–	0.29	P 4.75, Ks 0.90
Rajasthan	25,766	96.70	(H) 91.13	–	2.53	Sindhi 0.93
Uttar Pradesh	88,341	99.91	(H) 88.54	–	10.50	P 0.58
Madhya Pradesh	41,654	91.65	(H) 83.30	–	2.40	Mr2.49,Or1.16
Bihar	56,353	93.03	(H) 79.77	–	8.86	B 3.47
III. West Bengal	44,312	94.47	(B) 85.32	6.13	2.14	B 19.44, Or 1.00
Assam	14,958	85.66	(A) 59.54	5.34	0.04	T12.28, B1.51
Orissa	21,945	91.06	(Or) 84.15	1.56	1.31	
IV. Gujarat	26,697	96.78	(G) 89.40	1.61	2.18	Sindhi 2.28, Mr 0.97
Maharashtra	50,412	96.91	(Mr)76.61	5.02	7.26	G 2.76, Kn 1.54, Tl 1.52, Sindhi 0.86
V. Andhra Pradesh	54,816	99.07	(Tl) 85.37	2.28	7.59	Tm 1.27, Mr 0.82 Tl 8.18, Mr 4.05.
Karnataka	29,299	94.02	(Kn) 65.97	1.80	9.00	Tm 3.38, Ml 1.45

(contd.)

(Table 7.2 contd.)

	Total population (in '000)	Percentage of speakers of Schedule viii languages	Percentage of speakers of the home languages	Percentage of Hindi speakers	Percentage of Urdu speakers	Percentage of speakers of other important languages of Schedule VIII
Tamil Nadu	41,199	99.87	(Tm)84.51	0.19	1.84	Tl 8.74, Kn 2.56, Ml 1.36, G 0.48
Kerala	21,347	99.20	(Ml)96.02	0.05	0.05	Tm 2.37
VI. Tripura	1556	71.36	(B) 68.79	1.48	–	Or 0.89
Manipur	1073	3.03		1.08	0.03	B 1.40
Meghalaya	1012	13.88		1.70	0.14	B 9.29, A 2.31
Nagaland	516	7.32		3.37	0.05	B 1.66, A 1.27
Sikkim	210	3.61		2.94	0.10	
VII. Delhi	4066	99.32	(H) 75.97	–	5.68	P 13.40, B 1.00; Tm 0.92, Sindhi 0.85
Goa, Daman and Diu	858	34.12		1.37	2.24	Mr 19.71, G 7.08, Kn 193
Pondicherry	472	99.68	(Tm) 89.01	0.23	0.71	Ml 5.43, Tl 3.69
Arunachal Pradesh	468	12.99		3.28	0.07	B 5.10, A 3.06
Chandigarh	257	99.49	(H) 55.96	–	0.66	P 40.67
Andaman and Nicobar Islands	115	77.06		16.07	2.16	B 24.42 Tm 12.61 Ml 12.12, Tl 8.13
Dadra and Nagar Haveli	74	16.24		1.58	0.18	G 12.07, Mr 2.29
Lakshadweep	32	84.67	(Ml) 83.90	0.19	0.10	

Source: Census of India, 1971.

geographical mapping of India, let us now take up the primarily linguistic issues (although some of them will inevitably have geographical and other significance). First, let us consider Hindi which claims 2085.14 lakh speakers. Of these, 1964.17 lakhs or 94.20 per cent live in the Hindi belt proper including Delhi (and 1991.28 lakh or 95.50 per cent if one includes Punjab). Incidentally, the eastern, western, and southern groups of states have respectively 38.55. 29.58, and 16.10 lakhs of Hindi speakers, that is, 1.85 per cent, 1.42 per cent, and 0.70 per cent respectively. If one adds the speakers of Urdu (which has in common with Hindi a *khari boli* base but which uses the Perso–Arabic script and draws on classical Persian in contrast to Hindi which draws on Sanskrit), the Hindi–Urdu, or 'Hirdu'[2] speaking population, amounts to 2237.35 lakhs or 43.26 per cent of the total Indian population. In the Hindi belt (Group II plus Delhi) the Urdu speakers are 161.24 lakhs (or 56.34 per cent of the total Urdu speakers in India). If they are added to Hindi speakers, the 'Hirdu' speaking fraternity in the Hindi belt amounts to 2125.41 lakhs or 95.00 per cent of the total 'Hirdu' speaking population in India. This is clearly indicative of the geographical concentration in the central zone of Hindi (and 'Hirdu') speaking population.

Linguistic Minorities

Let us now consider the minority language groups. Column 4 in Table 7.1 indicates that substantial numbers of speakers of Bengali, Kannada, Punjabi, and Telugu are spread outside their home states. This is also confirmed from the percentage of the corresponding home language speakers given in column 4 of Table 7.2. For instance, Punjabi speakers form 3.45, 8.34, 4.75, and 13.40 per cent of the populations of J&K, Haryana, HP and Delhi respectively. Similarly, there is a substantial number of Bengalis in Assam, Bihar, and Orissa; Gujaratis in Maharashtra; Marathas in MP and Karanataka; Oriyas in West Bengal and Assam; Telugus in Orissa, Maharashtra, Karnataka, and Tamil Nadu; Tamilians in AP, Karnataka, and Kerala; Kannadigas in Maharashtra and Tamil Nadu; and Malayalis in Karnataka and Tamil Nadu. (Sindhi speakers' dispersed distribution has already been mentioned above). It is clear there are sizeable minority language groups related to Schedule VIII languages in almost all the 17 larger states. Many of them live in the border areas between the concerned states and in the large cities, and reflect influences of old historic migrations principally due to political factors, the newer migrations after the country's industrialization and urbanization during the pre- and post-Independence periods, and the residual effects of the linguistic reorganization of states.

Apart from these and overlapping them are two other important minority language groups: the Hindi and Urdu speakers. Hindi speakers have a substantial weightage in J&K (15.06 per cent) and Punjab (20.01 per cent) to a lesser extent in West Bengal, Assam, Maharashtra, and to a still lesser extent in AP, Orissa, Gujarat, and Karnataka. In the other two southern states they negligible. The Urdu speaking population, as we have seen above, is to be found in the wider Hindi belt excluding Punjab and HP; then in Karnataka, AP, and Maharashtra, and to a lesser extent in West Bengal, Orissa, Gujarat and Tamil Nadu. They are negligible in Assam and Kerala. Here again, one can see the working of the earlier and recent historical processes including Partition (which in particular seriously affected the composition in Punjab, Haryana, HP, and Assam).

Ethno-lingual changes in population groups are subject to socio-cultural influences which are themselves, directly or indirectly the product of economic and political (including its administrative aspects) influences. With the growth of education, and economic, political, and social developments of the regions there ensue two apparently contradictory processes: (i) an attempt to discover one's separate identity and at self-assertion; and (ii) an attempt to seek affinity and affiliation to a larger or more powerful group.[3] In the period immediately before Independence, three principal variants of 'Hirdu' (apart from other numerous regional variants) came to the fore: Hindi, Urdu and Hindustani, the last due to a powerful plea from Gandhi that a common national language be adopted based on the first two. From the Censuses of 1951 and 1961 it appears that there was what Ashish Bose has described as 'displacement' of these variants during the first decade after Independence.[4] (It is my belief that the way in which the Census apparatus operates and the political forces working at the time, considerably influence the census statistics.) For instance, in UP, the Hindustani variant disappeared as mother tongue and the proportion of Urdu speakers increased very considerably. The latter happened not only in urban areas but even (and to a much greater extent) in rural areas. This is significant because Urdu is perhaps the 'most urban' of the Indian languages. Almost two-fifths of its speakers live in urban areas. This tendency of self-assertion on the part of Urdu aspirants appears to have somewhat slowed down in the next decade (1961–71).

Another illustration of this process is the proliferation and diminution of the number and numerical strength of the various mother tongues (MT) falling under the Schedule VIII languages and particularly under the Hindi group, (Note for instances that there are over 40 such languages/MT cited under Hindi in the 1971 Census volume.) It appears that during 1951–61 these variants proliferated and sought to crystallize in Bihar. The population claiming Bhojpuri, Magadhi, and Maithili (together) increased during this period from about one lakh to 156 lakhs.[5] This tendency brought down the proportion of Hindi speakers in the state from 81.0 per cent in 1951 to 44.3 per cent in 1961. In the 1971 Census, however, the proportion of Hindi speakers was 79.8 per cent. In the absence of a more detailed Census volume (like that of 1961) published so far it is difficult to determine whether it is the Bhojpuri, Magadhi, or Maithili speakers who have chosen to merge themselves into the Hindi speakers' stream or whether it is the Census authorities who forced this merger on them. It is, however, quite likely that the political and educational processes mentioned so far, together with economic development may have induced a large number of the speakers of these variants to opt for Hindi and thus reduce their social isolation. A similar process may be observed for Rajasthani which accounted for 56.4 per cent of the population in Rajasthan in 1961.[6] (In this connection, it may be worth noting that Khubchandani[7] described states in Groups I and II of Table 7.2 as a 'fluid' zone where language identities had not then (by 1961) crystallized. It is my contention that by 1971 they are beginning to crystalize the merger process, swamping the self-assertion process in most states, except in the case of Urdu.) Another marked tendency, undoubtedly for political reasons, is that many Punjabi Hindus are suspected to have returned Hindi as their mother tongue in the 1971 Census.

Other Smaller Language Groups

A third issue in the linguistic process of consolidation and assimilation is the case of languages that are not (or cannot be) included as mother tongue variants of Schedule VIII languages. Take Konkani and Santali, for instance, figures for which (in thousands) for 1961 and 1971 are given in Table 7.4.

Now it is well known that the Konkani speakers, although concentrated in contiguous units, are not concentrated in contiguous geographical territories. The future of their development is an open question except perhaps in Goa which has a compact population (along with the adjoining region in Karnataka). One however finds

Table 7.3
Second Language Speakers in Selected States

('000)

State	Population	Second languages speakers of				Speakers per thousand	
		Hindi	Urdu	H+U	English	Hirdu	English
J&K	3561	62	244	306	17	86	5
West Bengal	34,926	434	77	5111	1468	15	42
Assam (old)	11,003	275	0	275	288	25	26
Orissa	17,549	139	N	139	235	8	13
Gujarat	20,633	525	60	585	285	28	14
Maharashtra	39,554	2436	90	2526	965	64	24
Andhra Pradesh	35,983	301	333	6344	870	18	24
Karnataka	23,587	219	99	318	473	133	20
Tamil Nadu	33,687	30	36	66	1224	2	36
Kerala	16,954	35	2	37	679	2	40

Source: Census of India, 1971.

Table 7.4
Second Language Speakers by Schedule VIII Languages

Language	Total	Second languages speakers of				Speakers per thousand	
		H	U	H+U	E	H+U	E
All India							
A	6803	150	–	150	158	22	23
B	33,754	615	69	684	1563	20	46
G	20,106	7744	78	852	4244	42	21
Kn	17,306	177	82	259	326	15	19
Ks	1914	15	158	173	88	90	4
Ml	16,995	81	7	88	762	5	45
Mr	32,767	2018	65	2083	527	64	16
Or	15,611	252	–	252	209	16	13
P	9808	726	240	966	407	98	41
S	977	219	6	225	87	230	889
Tm	30,465	99	43	142	1258	5	41
Tl	370,641	328	292	620	855	16	22
'Home'-state							
A	6784	147	–	147	156	22	23

(contd.)

(Table 7.4 contd.)

Language	Total	Second languages speakers of				Speakers per thousand	
		H	U	H+U	E	H+U	E
B	29,408	237	60	297	1299	10	44
G	188,672	470	56	526	243	28	13
Kn	15,361	143	77	220	2883	14	1
Ml	9896	13	157	170	6	90	3
Mr	30,233	1623	51	1674	453	55	15
Or	14,415	106	–	196	7	14	15
P(Old)	8337	400	173	573	69	292	43
Tm	28,011	17	33	50	1075	2	38
Tl	30,932	232	284	516	726	17	23

Source: Census of India, 1971.

that in Goa itself the Konkani concentration has fallen, from 88.8 per cent in 1961 to 64.8 per cent in 1971 and also in absolute numbers. Not dissimilar is the case of Santals. The difference is that they are not to be found in as concentrated a mass in any district-size region as the Konkanis in Goa and its periphery. Here again, the near-stabilization of Santal numbers in Orissa poses questions that need to be answered. The cases of other tribal languages like Bhili (33.99 lakhs), Gondi (16.88 lakhs) is no different. The dispersal of Sindhi speakers has already been mentioned.

However, languages such as Dogri (12.99 lakhs, of which 11.39 lakhs or 87.7 per cent live in J&K) and Tulu (11.58 lakhs of which 10.43 lakhs or 90.1 per cent live in Karnataka) have perhaps a better prospect of preservation and even consolidation. That however will greatly depend on their present linguistic development, the development potential, affinity or a clear separate identity from the ruling language in the state or at the Centre, and the numerical weight it carries in the state. The last two seem to be in favour of Dogri, but not of Tulu. One also wonders about the fate of Coorgi with a population of just 70,000, of whom 98.5 per cent are concentrated in Coorg district alone.

Inter-Regional Communication

Finally, we consider the question of a language of all-India inter-linguistic communication (referred to hereafter as AIILC or AIILCL). I am deliberately avoiding calling it the official language at this stage. In the ensuing discussion we do not propose to enter much into normative consideration or examine the potentiality of a language for AIILC which has been done by individuals with diverse views, sometimes quite acrimoniously; nor do deal with the indecisive and procrastinating policies relating to them of almost all parties, as also the developments leading to and following the Hindi–English conflicts and confrontations of the mid-sixties. I will rather present the issue as the most important aspect of bilingualism that is manifesting itself now and in the recent past.

At the outset it should be remembered that much of the bilingualism in India today (in line with many other multilingual countries) is due to the linguistic accommodation that speakers of other languages try to arrive at in a region where the home language is different. This is particularly necessary in the border areas where chunks of linguistic minority groups live, and also in the urban areas to which they have migrated for employment. Here, and particularly in the former, they adopt or manage to acquire at least a working knowledge of the local regional languages as a contact language or a second language. This is not however, the same as learning a language for AIILC. For the latter purpose the languages that need to be considered in the Indian context at the present time are 'Hirdu' and English. It should be observed in passing that the two may serve the AIILC purpose at different levels; but this point, although important, will be ignored for the present.

Now 'Hirdu' or Hirdu–Punjabi speakers (I include Punjabi speakers amongst them as they can acquire it without much difficulty) in their large north-central zone (consisting of Group I (b) and Group II states of Table 7.2) seen to opt for English as the AIILC language. So do speakers of these languages who have migrated to other regions, if they are able to learn English in addition to acquiring a working knowledge of the local language (except perhaps in big cities). The crux of the problem is therefore to examine the preference status of speakers of non-'Hirdu' languages in their own states and when they are migrants to the 'Hirdu'–Punjabi zone.

The 1961 Census returns reveal that for India as a whole the following are the numbers of persons who reported the respective languages as second languages: English 112.38 lakhs; 'Hirdu-Punjabi 118.34 lakhs (Hindi 93.96 lakhs, Urdu 20.06 lakhs and Punjabi 4.65 lakhs). So in overall terms 'Hirdu' seems to have an edge over English. But if an analysis by states shows a different pattern (Table 7.3). Hindi 'home' states and Punjab are omitted for obvious reasons. Table 7.3 clearly shows that those who know 'Hirdu' besides their non-'Hirdu' mother tongue are much fewer in all non-'Hirdu' states (except in J&K, Gujarat, and Maharashtra) than those who know English, even accounting for the small number of those among the latter who may have 'Hirdu' as their mother tongue, the English-knowing sections have a decisive edge over 'Hirdu'-knowing sections in these states, and overwhelmingly so in West Bengal, Kerala, and Tamil Nadu. The sheer size of these sections in West Bengal and Tamil Nadu explains the more acute opposition to Hindi in these states as well as the more vocal support for the continuation of English as the AIILC. If one considers the four southern states the numbers are 10.55 lakhs ('Hirdu') against 32.46 (English); and if we add West Bengal, the five states have 15.66 lakhs ('Hirdu') against 47.14 lakhs (English). The preference trends observed above are confirmed in and alternative way by Table 7.4 prepared on the basis of the 1961 Census figures for bilingualism.

Table 7.5

Religion Distribution Over States

Unit	Total population	Hindus	Muslims	Christians	Sikhs, Buddhists, Jains where significant	Other religions and persuasions	Religion not stated
India	5488,160	82.72	11.20	2.59	Sikhs 1.89, Buddhists 0.71, Jains 0.48	0.40	0.01
Jammu and Kashmir	4617	30.42	65.85	0.16	Sikhs 2.29, Buddhists 1.26	N	N
Punjab	13,551	37.54	0.84	1.20	Sikhs 60.22	N	0.03
Haryana	10,037	89.23	4.04	0.10	Sikhs	6.29	0.02
Himachal Pradesh	3460	96.08	1.45	0.10	Sikhs 1.30, Buddhists 1.04	0.01	N
Rajasthan	25,766	89.63	6.90	0.12	Sikhs 1.33, Jains 1.99	0.02	N
Uttar Pradesh	88,341	83.76	15.48	0.15	Sikhs 0.42	N	N
Madhya Pradesh	41,654	93.68	4.36	0.69	Jains O0.83	N	N
Bihar	56,353	83.46	13.48	1.17		1.73	N
West Bengal	44,312	78.11	20.46	0.57		0.44	N
Assam	14,625	72.51	24.56	2.61		N	N
Orissa	21,945	96.25	1.49	1.73		0.42	N
Gujarat	26,697	89.28	8.42	0.41	Jains 1.69	0.07	0.04
Maharashtra	50,412	81.94	8.40	1.42	Buddhists 6.47, Jains 1.40	0.16	0.01
Andhra Pradesh	54,816	87.63	8.09	4.19		N	N

(contd.)

(Table 7.5 contd.)

Unit	Total population	Hindus	Muslims	Christians	Sikhs, Buddhists, Jains where significant	Other religions and persuasions	Religion not stated
Karnataka	29,299	86.46	10.63	2.09	Jains 0.75	N	N
Tamil Nadu	41,199	89.02	5.11	5.75		0.01	N
Kerala	21,347	59.41	19.50	21.05		N	0.01
Tripura	1556	89.55	6.68	1.01	Buddhists 2.72	–	–
Manipur	1073	58.97	6.61	26.03		7.75	0.36
Meghalaya	1012	18.50	2.60	46.98		31.45	0.13
Nagaland	516	11.43	0.58	66.76		20.94	N
Sikkim	210	68.88	0.16	0.79	Buddhists 29.84	0.19	N
Delhi	4066	83.82	6.47	1.08	Sikhs 7.16, Jains 1.24	0.01	0.01
Goa Daman and Diu	858	64.18	3.76	31.77		0.03	0.07
Pondicherry	472	84.97	6.18	8.76		0.02	0.01
Arunachal Pradesh	468	21.99	0.18	0.79	Sikhs 0.27, Buddhists 13.13	63.46	0.17
Chandigarh	257	71.68	1.45	0.97	Sikhs 25.45, Jains 0.39	0.02	N
Andaman and Nicobar Islands	115	60.92	10.12	26.35	Sikhs 0.75	1.10	0.66
Dadra and Nagar Haveli	74	95.83	1.00	2.58	Jains 0.41	0.03	0.05
Lakshadweep	32	4.86	94.37	0.75		0.61	–
Mizoram	332	6.39	0.57	86.09	Buddhists	0.01	–

Source: Census of India, 1971.

We have seen earlier that those using English as a communication or contact language are comparable in number to those who know 'Hirdu' as a second language: 112,38 lakhs as against 115.38 lakhs, of which the hard core of purely Hindi-knowers is 9366 lakhs. (The two categories may have some people knowing both. This does not much affect the argument). That however, is taking India as a whole. The distributions are uneven over different regions.

It is also not difficult to imagine the strata to which the Hindi and English-knowing bilinguals belong. Considering the status that English currently has, status that English currently has, it is clear that the English bilinguals will on the average belong to the upper strata of society and will have much greater mobility, both vertical and horizontal, while the Hindi bilinguals will generally belong to a much lower economic and social status and have less mobility. Educationally, the English bilinguals can be more or less taken as synonymous with those who have passed the matriculation or SSC examination (although in a few states one can do so without offering English). If this is a reasonable assumption, it provides a way projecting the estimation of English bilinguals to the 1971 data. According to the 1971 data, there were 217,48 lakh matriculates and (among them) 42.50 lakh graduates in India.[8] If we divide them between the 'Hirdu' and non-'Hirdu' zones in the ratio 40:60 (a more realistic division would be 35:65 or even 30:70 considering much higher literacy and therefore, more education in the non-'Hirdu' zone), the 'English lobby' in the latter would comprise roughly 130 lakh and the hard core (the graduates) roughly 25 lakhs. On the other hand, the 'Hirdu' knowing bilinguals must not have appreciably increased in the southern states in some of which at least Hindi is not a compulsory subject in secondary education. Thus actually the growth of education (during 1961–71), in particular and in the post-Independence period in general) may have considerably strengthened the English lobby in the relevant part of the country both absolutely and relatively. Moreover, this is, as observed above, the most influential, the most vocal section of society. The prospect of Hindi being acceptable as the AIILC language in place of English seem to have become even less during the last decade. (The educational growth during the last six years, after 1971, has probably tilted this position still further, as it is well known that secondary and higher education have been growing considerably faster than literacy during post-Independence period, and particularly after 1961).

Ethno-Religious Situation

Table 5 gives the distribution of population by the main religions (Hinduism, Islam, and Christianity); the relatively smaller religions (Sikh, Buddhist, Jain) are mentioned where proportionately significant. The Table also indicates the strength of 'other religions and persuasions', mostly of tribal origin. In all the 17 larger states all except J&K and Punjab have a large Hindu majority; J&K has a Muslim majority (65.85 per cent), and Punjab a Sikh majority (60.22 per cent). The two have substantial Hindu minorities: 30.42 and 37.54 per cent respectively. Kerala has its own unique composition: Hindus 59.41 per cent, Muslims 19.50 per cent, Christians 21.05 per cent. Muslims are numerically sizeable in all the 17 states except in Haryana, HP, Punjab, and Orissa, clearly reflective of Partition emigration in the first three. Besides Kerala, they are also proportionately quite weighty in Asssam, West Bengal, UP, Bihar, and Karnataka, and to a lesser extent in Gujarat, Maharashtra, and AP. Christians are more in evidence in AP and Tamil Nadu besides Kerala; Sikhs in Haryana and MP besides Punjab; Buddhists in Maharashtra (clearly a consequence of the conversions following Ambedkar's in 1956); and the community of Jains is to be found mainly in Maharashtra, Rajasthan, Gujarat, Karanataka, and MP. Among the five smaller states, while Hindus predominate in Tripura and Manipur (which has a sizeable Christian component, 26.03 per cent), Christians are in a majority in Nagaland (66.76 per cent). The influence of Christianity in some of these border states is due to missionary activities amongst the tribals before and after Independence. Besides, tribal beliefs and persuasions persist in some of them, particularly in Meghalaya and Nagaland. In the Union Territories on the border, Mizoram has a large Christian majority (80.09 per cent) and tribal beliefs predominate (63.46 per cent) in Arunachal Pradesh.

In the Indian context, language has an association with religion in certain respects. For instances, Hindus in all states are usually speakers of Schedule VIII languages except Punjabi and Urdu; Sikhs mostly speak Punjabi and a large proportion of Muslims in many states (the major exceptions being, J&K, Kerala, Bengal and Assam, and also Gujarat and Tamil Nadu to a large extent) seek affiliation to Urdu. (Actually, Urdu used to be the language of both Hindus and Muslims in many parts in the north, in the period prior to Independence.) This affiliation can be measured by what Ashish Bose calls Language–Religion (LR) Index = Speakers of Urdu/Muslims, multiplied by 100.[9]

This involves a not unreasonable assumption that there are only a small number of non-Muslims who speak Urdu. He compiled the LR Index for 1951 and 1961, and I have extended it to 1971. The figures for some states are given below.

State	LR Index		
	1951	1961	1971
AP	66	94	94
Bihar	61	72	66
Gujarat	25	34	26
MP	35	56	55
Tamil Nadu	30	39	36
Maharashtra	85	90	86
Karnataka	45	87	85
Orissa	90	99	105
Rajasthan	16	39	37
UP	48	73	68
West Bengal	11	12	12

It appears that the big spurt in the index during the first decades has perhaps reached its peak and there is an incipient tendency of its coming down. This indicates that the frantic effort to establish self-identity through a declared adoption of Urdu in preference to the regional language has exhausted itself and there is perhaps a beginning on the part of some Muslims to seek their natural affinity to the regional languages. (Actually, to draw a firmer conclusion, cross-Tables of language by religion and schooling language by religion need to be constructed.)

Another consequence, where perhaps religion has influenced a cultural-political decision, is the decision about state (or official) language in some of the recently-born, smaller border states in the north-east. They have chosen English as the state language (unlike most other states which have chosen the regional language, that is, the 'home' language). The reasons are to be sought in the multiplicity of tribal languages that prevail in the region, absence of a decisive influence of any of the Schedule VIII languages, and also the missionary effort that has been responsible for the spread of education (in English) as well as of Christianity.

Nations, Nationalities, National Minorities

It is helpful to consider the ethno–linguistic issues in the framework of the categories of nations, nationalities, national minorities, etc. that relate to political science. One should also remember in this context that an understanding and solution of the ethno-linguistic problems lie in the last analysis in the realm of politics and not in that of linguistics alone.

Take Stalin's definition of a nation as 'a historically evolved, stable community of language, territory, economic life, and psychological make-up [manifested in community of culture];[10] or Don Luigi Sturzo's analysis of the concept where, 'the nexus of a national community' consists of 'tradition, customs, language, territory, social rights and economic interests;[11] or E.H. Carr's exposition that although 'the nation is not a definable and clearly recognisable entity', it has 'such natural and universal elements as attachments to one's native land and speech and a sense of wider kinship';[12] and similar other definitions. A common language and a contiguous common territory are understood to be the two absolutely essential elements in the formation of a nation. They are also more easily identifiable than the other two commonalities—common economic interests and a common tradition of culture—which are more vulnerable to (external) political, economic and social pressures, including subjugation.

A nationality may be defined as a people having some characteristics that go towards the making of a nation, and who are striving for a measure of political, economic, and cultural autonomy.[13] It may (or may not) develop an alternative centre of allegiance among the people, strive for recognition as a nation, and struggle to form its own distinct nation–state. It should also be recognized that mere cultural autonomy is meaningless unless accompanied by a corresponding share in economic and political power, that is, along with corresponding economic and political rights.

First, it should be recognized that modern nation and nation-state are categories pertaining to the era of capitalism. Consequently, the issues pertaining to nations, nationalists, and national minorities in their modern contexts, including the right of self-determination of nations, are the products of capitalist development, first in the west and then spreading to the rest of the world. Secondly, the issues concerning them need to be considered in their historical socio-economic and cultural contexts and cannot be universalized like mathematical propositions. Marxists of earlier vintage (both Indian and non-Indian) were greatly influenced by Stalin's formulations, and perhaps rightly so. The weakness in their understanding was that they treated them as cut-and-dried geometrical theorems (including a QED), without bothering to see that 'economic life', and more so 'psychological make-up' and a 'community of culture' are not amenable to 'geometrical' thinking. They also ignored the fact that Stalin's formulations were made specifically in the context of the contemporary national problems of Europe in general and the Russian Empire in particular. In contemporary times when there are over 150 nation–states in the United Nations, the old formulations, although valid as far as the basic content of the concepts of nation, nation–state, nationality, etc., will need considerable modifications with regard to issue pertaining to them, including the right of self-determination and its actual exercise.

Let me briefly review the Indian situation in this light both in its historical and present context. A study of the history of national political thought in India shows that in the earlier period, until almost the twenties of this century, many leaders considered India as consisting of *several* nations (mostly along linguistic lines). A parallel trend was to project India, on the basis of its broad (Hindu) cultural unity, as *one* nation, dating from ancient times. This was, firstly, an effort to enter the mainstream of bourgeois world thought on their own terms, and secondly, to counter the imperialist argument that India was only a conglomeration of disparate peoples and therefore did not and could not aspire to be a modern nation–state like the west European nations. The second trend in the national movement strengthened considerably after it assumed a militant, country-wide character in the 1920s and 1930s. The one-nation theory was the consequence of the economic and administrative unification of India under the aegis of British imperialism, the rise of the national bourgeoisie which had developed an all India linkage, and its hegemony over the national movement. A third trend, that of 'nationalism based on religion' giving rise to the theory of the Hindu nation (Hindu Rashtra Vad) also made an appearance. Along with it was soon born its counterpart, the two-nation theory, of the Muslim political and intellectual leaders. While the Hindu Rashtra Vad could be contained by the Indian bourgeoisie—both had operatively the same goal of one nation—the Muslim leadership, entrenched in the feudal–bourgeoisie classes, with the active support of the imperialist rulers, pressed hard its claim for a separate 'home-land' and succeeded in partitioning the country at the time of the transfer of power in 1947.

What was the Marxist and Communist position? The CPI, it appears, had hardly any authoritative position in the 1920s, and in the early and mid-1930s on this question. During the period of the Second World War the party did take the position that India consisted of a number of nations and that the future independent Indian state should be a multinational federal state, which implied the recognition for each distinct constituent nationality of the right of self-determination (and its exercise). Here the CPI drew heavily on the analogy of the USSR and Stalin's formulations of the national question, ignoring their specific historical context and the socialist revolution. Having a small base, the already not very commendable exposition and practice of the 'people war' policy and an even lesser understanding of the dynamics of the national question in India, the CPI took an easy way out by trying to explain away the Muslim League's demand for Pakistan as the authentic expression of a democratic urge of the nationalities in the north-west and north-east of the Indian subcontinent. While this unsound (and therefore untenable) analysis of the national question of India at that juncture brought some theoretical support to the pro-Partition political forces, it cannot be said that the communist position was in any sense operationally effective in shaping the events that actually took place. They would have taken place irrespective of whatever the ideological position of the CPI, whose power of intervention in the march of events in those days was extremely limited. All that it did was to burden the CPI with another unenviable legacy for the post-Independent period.

What is the Marxist position now? There is the general impression that the whole question has been pushed under the carpet. I must confess that I have not been able to keep track of the latest positions of the two (or more) communist parties on the national question. However, whatever the stand or stands of the two (or more) communist parties, I think it is necessary for the Marxist intellectuals to take a position. They should unhesitatingly maintain that India is a multinational country, the major nations among them broadly coinciding with the linguistically reorganized states. They have therefore the implied inherent right of self-determination but at the same time it is in their own interests not to exercise it, nor to harp on it. The principal reason for this self-abnegation is that none of these 'nations' or 'nationalities' is oppressed by the ruling classes belonging to another specific nationality. The oppressor or ruling classes in India have an all-India multinational composition. That is why, except at the peak moment of the movements for linguistic states there was no attempt to tag a specific communal or linguistic label to the oppressors, nor was there a movement resembling a national movement for freedom. (This has to be contrasted with the authentic national movement for liberation in Bangladesh a few years ago which led to the break-up of Pakistan.)

While this is true of all the major ethno–linguistic regional groups (that is the linguistic states of the Indian union), the situation as regards the much smaller ethno-linguistic tribal groups in the border areas is different. Here there undoubtedly exists a feeling of an alien oppression and exploitation. It is not however in the larger interests of these peoples themselves to ask for the exercise of self-determination as that will make them helpless pawns in the international political game. On the other hand, the Indian federal state has to strive and convince them, by adopting far-reaching political and economic measures in the overall democratic framework, that their real interests lie in joining the national distinct cultural identities. The only solution of this vexatious problem therefore lies in quickly developing these regions economically, scrupulously keeping out external exploiters, and extending and deepening the political economic, and cultural democratic process amongst the indigenous population.

In short, the Marxists have one again to think clearly on these issues concerning the existence of nations, nationalities, and national minorities in this vast and populous land. There is no need to fight shy of this when a person of the eminence of Suniti Kumar Chatterjee has described this country as 'united nations' of India.[14] At the same time, they must abandon the temptation of drawing easy parallels with the other vast multinational states like the USSR and China. The proper approach is to analyse the actual situation about the interrelationships between the various ethno–linguistic groups and their problems, in the context of a federal structure. Some of these issues without doubt mixed up with other factors (religion; non-Indian language like English, etc). An attempt is made in the next two parts to deal with the more important amongst them.

The Language (Intra-state) Problem

Thus we are back to the consideration of the language problems in India, a factual analytical basis for which has been laid in Part I. What are these problems? They are principally concerned with: (i) the official language(s) in states (that is, the languages of government and administration), (ii) the official language at the Centre, (iii) a 'link' language or language for inter-langual communication, (iv) the 'national' language (*rashtra bhasha*), and (v) the media of instruction at different stages of education.

In devising solutions for these problems the main (and perhaps the only) principle that should guide us in the widening and deepening of the democratic framework. That is, the policies and practices must be such as will help greater and greater participation of larger and larger number of people at all levels in all departments of life. It is rue that for this, a correct language policy is not the only, nor even the principal determinant, but it is sufficiently important and an incorrect policy can certainly prove a formidable hindrance in the development of the democratic process.

Viewed thus, questions (i) and (v) suggest their own solution. As the overwhelming majority of people in all larger states of the union speaks the regional language (the Schedule VIII languages), it follows that the principal official language in a state and the medium of instruction at all stages of education has to be the regional language. It was for this reason and with this aim that the states were linguistically reorganized. If we have not succeeded in achieving this so far, the blame has to be squarely laid at the door of the ruling classes including the bureaucracy because, for the upper layers of the educated, the difficulties of transition will be considerable. They have nonetheless to be faced and overcome. It is apparent that the ruling classes including the educated élite have been following a policy of self-imposed, selfish linguistic rule: in the face of the slightest difficulty continue with English.

It is true there are, and will always be, sizeable linguistic minorities in the state. Wherever they are in large numbers, educational facility in their mother tongue will have to be provided for primary and secondary education (and even for higher education whereever they are concentrated in large enough numbers). Simultaneously provision has also to be made for them to acquire greater and greater proficiency in the regional (state) languages. In some parts of the state, and even in its administration at the seat of the government, the language of a large enough minority group will have to be adopted as the second official language.

Even so, after adopting this policy, there will remain the questions of: (a) the use of 'standard' language against the use of dialects, (b) the cases of languages like Konkani, Tulu, and other submerged or dispersed languages, (c) the development of tribal languages like Santali and (d) Urdu. As the democratic solutions for (a) through (c) have been indicated a number of times earlier, I shall only focus on the question of Urdu.

As observed in Part I, Urdu speakers are much more dispersed over India than any other Schedule VIII language. Moreover, they are more urbanized than others. It is therefore necessary (and not difficult) to make provisions for their education wherever they exist in sizeable numbers at all stages of education. However, like the other linguistic minorities, it is desirable for Urdu speakers in their own interest to acquire a thorough command of regional language.

Currently Urdu is the only state language in J&K and recognized as a subsidiary state language in AP. (Curiously, Kashmiri has no official status in J&K). Urdu was for some time recognized as the second official language (the first official language being the principal regional language) in some other states after Independence. However, under the majori'y pressure or otherwise this was discontinued giving rise to considerable discontent. There is no reason why Urdu cannot be recognized again as the second official language in the districts where there are sizeable concentrations of Urdu speakers.

Let us however frankly recognize the other dimension of the problem: its association with religion because of its script and its connections with Persian and Arabic as a principal source of vocabulary, its origin as the language of the former Muslim rulers, and its consistent avowal (not entirely altruistic) by the British rulers and by Muslim leaders (even after Independence) as the language of religion and culture of the Indian Muslims. Therefore, the roots of the problem are partly historic–political, partly religio–cultural, and, as happens in the case of feudal bourgeoisie and rising middle class interests, they are partly real and justifiable and partly unreal (and even fallacious) and therefore unjustifiable.

In the case of religion, for instance, while Muslims account for 11.2 per cent of the total Indian population, Urdu speakers account for only 5.22 per cent. It will be observed that in Assam, Bengal, Kerala, and Kashmir, where the concentration of Muslims is proportionately most substantial, their mother tongue is the regional language, not Urdu. Many of them, are accomplished creative writers in their own right in these languages.

The crux of the problem is politico–psychological and the vested interests on both sides of the barrier are exploiting this for their own narrow upper class ends. While Hindu revivalism is not to humiliate and even battle with the Muslim minority for their so-called 'sin' of Partition, the Muslim minority in its sense of helplessness and insecurity is being drawn back into isolation by their narrow-minded, selfish religious interests with frequent loud cries of 'Islam in danger'. The reflection of the latter is to be found in the tendency on the part of some of the middle and upper class Muslims to opt for Urdu for educational (and Census) purposes even though their mother tongue is actually the regional language. This is an unwise and alienating step, and suicidal to their own socio-economic interests. With the advance of democracy and education, more and more of the governmental as well as private business is bound to be carried through the medium of the regional language in each state. Educated Muslims, who do not see this sign of the times are doing a grievous disservice to their own community.

On the other hand, it is incumbent on the majority community to be generous in providing facilities for education in Urdu at all levels wherever there is a real demand backed by adequate numbers. Nothing should be done to cut off the Urdu-speaking Muslims from their legitimate cultural roots. This is the only way of helping them to emerge from isolation and the grip of the reactionary section of their leadership, and join the mainstream of Indian society as a free and equal community.

The Language (Inter-state) Problem

So far we have been discussing the language question at the state level. A much more difficult problem is with respect to the so-called official language, or the language of administration at the Centre and of communication with and between states as well as the 'link' language for inter-people communication at various levels. I shall skip the constitutional position on English and Hindi, including the conflicts and confrontations on the question of adoption of Hindi to replace English as the official language as everyone is aware of them.

What is the social reality today? English still rules in practice as the official language, at the Centre and for inter-state communication, and it is also in a dominant position in the higher reaches of intra-state administration. It is also the language of higher learning and (more so) of science and technology, or industry, business, and trade at the all-India level, of the more influential national press, and the 'link' language for the intelligentsia. Along with industrial development and educational and technological advances, including research, together with their international inter linkages, the status of English in India has been raised, not lowered, in the post-47 period. (Even in

Bihar, the centre of Angrezi-*hatao* movement, the number of English-medium schools has risen sharply in recent years.) This has considerably expanded and strengthened the élitist channel of education and has produced an influential 'super élite' which is a close ally of the ruling classes.[15] However, as has been observed in Part I, English literacy encompasses not more than about 3.5 to 4 per cent of the total and literates in English constitute only about one-eighth to one-tenth of the total literates in the country. Although it is doubtful whether a large part of them (matriculates and even graduates) have adequate knowledge of the English language, our socio-economic structure has placed them at the top of the pyramid. Thus English too reigns as the 'link' language of the educated.

At the lower levels of literacy what is the 'link' language of India ? Whenever and wherever there is mobility at these levels, communication usually takes place in a mixture of Hindi, the local language, and the language of the speaker: a sort of a 'bazar' Hindustani that varies from place to place. A factor that promotes this process is the Hindi film and radio broadcast of film music ubiquitous throughout India. It is also true that most political leaders who address common audiences in states other than their own often do so in some sort of Hindi.

Hindi or rather 'Hirdu' has also an advantage in overall numbers in the sense that encompasses 43.26 per cent of the Indian population; together with Punjabi the percentage rises to 45.83. As is well known, the Gujarati and Marathi speaking peoples have no aversion to Hindi; indeed, the three-language formula in education is fully operational in these two states. Thus, the number of 'Hindiphils' rises to 58.17 per cent in the population. The hardcore resistance to Hindi is in the north-east and south, that is, among 36 to 37 per cent of the population. (This counting of numbers is not intended to advocate 'Hirdu' being forced as the official language on the unwilling who, though technically in a minority, are formidable in terms of numbers: about 20 crores.)

Notwithstanding the several factors in their favour mentioned earlier, together with the general fervour for a 'national' language at the time of Independence, the Hindiwallahs frittered away these advantages during the immediate Independence period. This was due to: (i) their greater and greater stress on Sanskritic Hindi at the expense of simple Hindustani; (ii) the deliberate discouragement of Urdu; (iii) a big-brother chauvinistic attitude towards other languages, some of which are claimed to be as well (if not better) developed as vehicles of modern thought and great literature as Hindi; (iv) cheating on the three-language formula and eagerness to cash in on Hindi as the official language;[16] (v) their selfish attempt to corner resources and positions created for the spread of Hindi at the cost of the many devoted non-Hindi speaking workers for Hindi; and finally (vi) their insistence on making it the *rashtra bhasha*, rather than a 'link' language for inter-lingual communication and formal administration, and the consequent fear of the non-'Hirdu' speakers in terms of jobs and service. Had the constituent assembly retained the loose federal structure that had been proposed in pre-Partition days some of the factors mentioned earlier worked against Hindi or 'Hirdu' would not have hardened.

Thus Hindi or 'Hirdu' suffered a decisive setback because of the selfishness of its Hindi protagonists. On the other hand, the cause of the regional languages has also languished. The reorganization of states on linguistic lines did release considerable new social forces resulting in the rise of a new (middle-caste, rural) political élite in the states. The limited political democratizition of the post-Independence period together with the formation of linguistic states did give an impetus to the regional languages. This initial advance however, was soon ground to a halt because of the continuation and inordinate influence of English on education, economic life and administration. The new strata that have risen and are rising to positions of power and prestige in social and political life are understandably not willing to be satisfied with anything less that an English education. They have seen the rich harvest garnered by those who have become the present 'super élite' through their 'mastery' over English. Therefore, in spite of the ever-increasing numbers of youth getting educated largely through the regional language, the language democratization of the state administration and the higher level private, non-governmental sector has slowed down considerably.

What, then, do the Marxist and progressives, do to deal with these linguistic issues? On two things there can be scarcely any doubts or reservations. First, they must insist that all the Indian languages must come into their own and rise to their full potential as the democratic vehicles of government and administration, of economy and politics, of education and culture of the people concerned. Second, this cannot be done unless the alienating, constricting, and subjugating influence of English is purposefully and consciously eliminated, relegating it to its proper place: that of a second language, useful as a window on the world and in the intermediate stages as a 'link' language for higher academic, scientific, and technological purposes. This has to be attempted in a large measure at the state level.

It seems, however, the elimination and replacement of English from its present status as the official language of the federal centre will take quite a long time considering the politico–economic and socio-cultural strength of the English-knowing sections in this country and their regional and strategic concentrations (strategic in the Indian socio–economic and political structure). It should be remembered that although continuation of English in this role is largely in the interests of the ruling classes, including the 'super élite', a large number of youths from the deprived sections coming to the education for the first time will be alienated from the progressive movement if it insists on the immediate replacement of English at the present juncture; (which in effect means depriving them of their only prospect of social and economic upliftment). One has to recognize that the elimination of English and the real flowering of Indian languages cannot be fully accomplished before the next stage of people's democratic advance.[17]

It will however, be opportunism on the part of the progressive movement not to spell out the long-term perspective of the language issue, even as regards the possible principal Indian 'link' language that will eventually replace English in the kind of federal polity which one visualizes for India. That language, by the very logic of circumstances, will be 'Hirdu', democratically, restructured and bereft of its present élitist, highly Sanskritic overtones.

In the meanwhile, that is, in the short run, there are several urgent democratic tasks as regards the widespread use and development of Indian languages in their own regions, and solution of the difficulties of the linguistic minorities. The progressive movement must insist, and at whichever level they have influence and power, promote the use of regional language(s) and a drive to banish English except where it is absolutely essential. More and more democracy means greater and greater mobility and participation by the common people at all levels. This implies an insistence on the use of the peoples' languages at all levels. Simultaneously, they must themselves vigorously pursue the development of the language. I think in this important task, the progressives have, thus far totally failed. Even their effort in the writing and publication of party-political material and supporting literature is meagre and nothing to be proud about, except perhaps in Kerala and West Bengal.

Indian languages have not benefited from even a consistent

bourgeois effort for their development. There is no or very little worthwhile, serious, intellectual effort made through utilization of languages. Scholars and popularizers, barring a few honourable exceptions, are busy with their writings in English to win all-India and international acclaim and recognition. The result is a complete lopsidedness in the development of Indian languages. In the present time this overdue task, neglected by the bourgeois scholars, becomes a historic responsibility of the progressives which they must effectively discharge. Whatever our criticisms of Stalin on his theory and practice of Marxism, he was absolutely right when, after the end of the Second World War, he exhorted the communists and patriots to pick up and hold high the banner of democracy and national liberation which the bourgeoisie had dropped so unceremoniously. It is their task, their duty, to complete these unfinished tasks in the democratic development of our languages.

Notes

1. *Census of India 1971*, Series I, Part II–C(i); Social and Cultural Tables, Government of India, New Delhi.

2. For coinage of this word, see Ashok R. Kelkar, 'Studies in Hindi–Urdu'. I, Deccan College, Poona, 1968.

3. This point is further developed in my forthcoming work on Education and Social Change.

4. Ashish Bose, 'Some Aspects of the Linguistic Demography of India', *in* 'Language and Society in India', Proceedings of a Seminar held in 1967, Indian Institute of Advanced Study, Simla, 1969, pp. 37–51.

5. Ibid. Also see, I.V. Sakharov, 'Ethno-linguistic' Geography of India— Facts and Figures', in *Economic and Socio-Cultural Dimensions of Regionalization*, Office of the Registrar General, Ministry of Home Affairs, New Delhi, 1972, pp. 387–426.

6. Sakharov, op cit., p. 418; The 1971 Census seems to have become a victim of a political game to manipulate numbers in order to boost the strength of Hindi speakers. See L.M. Khubchandani, 'Language Factor in Census: A Socio-linguistic Perspective', in Albert Verdoodt and Kjolseth (eds) *'Language in Sociology*, E. Peeters, Leuven (Belgium), 1976, para 3.3 and fn 12.

7. Ibid., L.M. Khubchandani, 'Mother Tongue in Multilingual Societies', pp. 427–50.

8. *Census of India, 1971*, Tables B–III–Parts A and B (mimeo). Registrar General, Ministry of Home Affairs, New Delhi. According to these figures, literates constitute 29.4 per cent, 'English literates' or SSC holders 3.97 per

cent and among them graduates or degree holders comprise 0.78 per cent of the population. This means that 'English literates' constitute approximately 13 per cent of the total literates.

9. Ashish Bose, op cit., fn 4.

10. Joseph Stalin, *Marxism and the National and Colonial Question,* Lawrence & Wishart, London, 1942, p. 8.

11. Don Luigi Sturzo, *Nationalism and Internationalism,* New York, 1946, pp. 16–7.

12. E.H. Carr, *Nationalism and After,* Macmillan, New York, 1945, p. 40.

13. Karl W. Deutch, *Nationalism and Social Communication,* John Wiley, New York, 1953, pp. 78–80.

14. Suniti Kumar Chatterjee, 'Language and Society in India', Proceedings of a Seminar of Advanced Study, Simla, 1969 (inaugural address).

15. See A.R. Kamat, (i), *The Educational Situation and Other Essays on Education,* People's Publishing House, New Delhi, 1973: (ii) 'Education After Independence: A Social Analysis, Lala Lajpatrai Memorial Lectures, Lala Lajpatrai Institute, Bombay, 1977; this is further corroborated by a recent study by Y.C. Bhatnagar, 'Two Faces of Bilingualism', *Mainstream,* 28 April 1979, pp. 15–19, which investigates bilingualism in Maharashtra (1971 census).

16. The three language formula for secondary schools was intended to teach (i) the regional language, English, and Hindi in non-Hindi areas, and (ii) Hindi, English, and a non-Hindi regional language in Hindi areas. The Hindi areas did not carry out this programme in its intended spirit, often offering Sanskrit as the third language. It should be observed, however, that there is not motivation for Hindi speaking students to learn a non-Hindi regional languages; nor is there much enthusiasm (in fact, as mentioned above, there is acute opposition) to learning Hindi in the eastern and southern states.

17. The point is further elaborated in A.R. Kamat, The Place of English (unpublished manuscript). The Marathi version forms a chapter in *Bharateeya Shikshanachi Vatchal,* Lok Vangmaya Griha, Bombay, 1979.

8

Politics of Diversity
Religious Communities and Multiple Patriarchies[*]

Kumkum Sangari

This chapter is part of an essay that was published in the Economic
and Political Weekly. *Here the author reviews the current debate
between maintaining religion-based personal laws and instituting a
uniform civil code in the context of gender inequality and Hindu
majoritarianism. Challenging the assumptions on which positions
that advocate legal pluralism and defend personal laws have based
their case, the author seeks to demonstrate that prevailing notions of
community are bureaucratic, reductive, static and essentialist, and
defeat their own declared objective of maintaining social pluralism,
critiques the enmeshment of religious community with personal laws
as a form of new orientalism that is both patriarchal and ideologically
laden, and argues against positions advocating reform of personal
laws by state and community. The author critiques ideologies of
cultural diversity that rest on assumptions of discrete homogeneous
communities on religion as the singular axis of diversity, on a
conflation of religion, culture and patriarchies, and on a confusion of
social disparity with diversity, as all being incapable of reckoning
with existing cultural diversity.*

[*] *Economic and Political Weekly,* vol. 30, no. 51, December 1995.

Communities, Patriarchies And Religious Identity

The broad ideological conception of religious communities has uncomfortable implications as religious 'communities' are not only inegalitarian or class differentiated but also specifically undemocratic regarding women. Community identities can be as much punitive as protective for women and that too, protective on patriarchal and proprietorial assumptions. If, as the more extreme arguments for reform of personal laws from 'within' appear to desire,[1] communities were to legally govern, reform, and adjudicate themselves, taking full responsibility for being either agents of change or protectors of the status quo, what will prevent them from trying to be self-legislating patriarchies; from strengthening local, interpersonal patriarchal control; and from continuing to hand power over to mullahs, priests, pandits or other chosen interpreters? There is little evidence to show that communities are committed to internal democratization of gender differences. Also, if such democratization remains as pressing an issue (if not more so), even after communities have retained or achieved some measure of legal autonomy, then why not simply struggle for a thorough going democratization process on wider non-denominational basis of collectivity, in the first place?

Women's own religious beliefs, consent to a religious identity and community as well as their agency in maintaining these, are often presented as a rationale for maintaining personal laws and reforming them only from within. This is a complex issue, partly because it can be argued for women from beleaguered minorities as well as from the chauvinistic majority.

In certain kinds of contemporary analysis, overly anxious to establish that religion is not false consciousness, religion is simply turned into a matter of faith or belief alone, thus eliding the issue that religion prevails as an *institution* more than consciousness, true or false. This formulation not only serves as a catchall but irons out the complexity of the relations between gender and religion; it is then followed by the proposition that religious belief is giving agency to women. More often than not the implication is that the presence of such an agency for women makes secular feminism questionable or even redundant. Thus a pernicious continuum is made between primordial denomination, women's belief, and women's agency.

Consequently, some serious questions are never asked. What is the nature of women's consent? When they consent to the punitive aspects of religious identity or community are they in fact consenting to the patriarchies with which these are meshed, or vice versa, or both? Alternatively, is their consent effectively consent to the host of other social factors in which both religions and patriarchies are enmeshed? Thus women's consent to religious definition may go beyond questions of individual faith and reflect the ways to which religions and patriarchies are articulating with other social structures. Should we confuse women consent to patriarchal assertions of community, their inability or fear to step out of these, in this particular political, conjuncture with the sum of their needs and aspirations? For instance, women's consent to the Muslim community and to Hindutva enacts very different and antagonist relations of power; while women's active investment in Hindutva (a complex historical, political, economic, class/caste differentiated and conjunctural phenomena), may have little to do with religious belief per se. Instead of conflating such consent with 'feminist agency' (a current preoccupation with some anti-communal feminists), a different type of analysis could be undertaken. Women's consent to a patriarchy has in the past and still does empower them for *selected* forms of social agency; further, this consent works through appropriating available hegemonic and/or legitimating languages, thereby forcing these languages into new ideological locales and pushing their previous proponents into more stringent, political self-definition or at worst into apology and retraction.[2] Alternatively, to give another instance, many Muslim women may be caught in a double impasse: first, because a uniform civil code is seen to endanger the identity of physically endangered Muslims, the very claim to gender equality now implies disloyalty for antagonism towards the community;[3] second, belief in Islam now appears to entail being prepared to accept patriarchal personal laws.

It is argued, in discussions and in writing, that opposing minority personal laws denigrates the laudable efforts as well as subsumes the initiatives of women involved in reforming personal laws from within. Undoubtedly, some Muslim and Christian women have religious yet reformist standpoints, oppose a uniform civil code, and, as believers, struggle to eradicate some gender inequalities or 'corruptions' from their personal law. I believe that the issue needs to be posed differently: it should be disentangled from belief and concentrate instead on the nature and pitfalls of reform from within. Second, we have to determine if the strategies of religious reformism from within also have space for those other women who may or may not be believers, but find consent punitive, or who find primordial belonging an impediment to choice, if not an imposition, or who do not consent,[4] or more to the point, who *need alternative* in order to dissent in an effective way. This is important for two reasons. A feminist politics must account for women's consent to patriarchies, but it can scarcely afford to give political or theoretical primacy to women's will to consent to forms of social oppression *over and above* their will to contest these; as such primacy is already on offer by a standard form of male conservatism.[5] Nor can feminist politics take on board a divisive (or for that matter, a unifying) politics based on essentialist identities whether primordial or biological.[6]

The Question of Representing 'Other Women'

In this context, confining women to community identity and personal laws becomes a way of dismantling and pre-empting cross-denominational or extra-religious feminist collectivities. Against the potential dangers of representing 'other' women, that is women of other denominations, we must place the dangers of refusing to represent each other. Refusal of a common ground of struggle is also a form of othering. Particularism can be, segregationist in its logic. Unless, universality is granted in principle (though not necessarily as a strategic mode of organization) as the possibility of mutual representation, feminist groups run the danger of replicating the structures of communalism.

The right to scrutinize and interrogate our entire social milieu is a democratic right for all, and one that is particularly crucial for feminists, and this cannot be a right confined to or reserved for one's own primordial denomination: If it is suspended in the name of religious community,[7] then it will prevent women from critiqueing a significant determinant of patriarchal oppression in India, namely religion. Indeed, it may altogether silence women, some in the name of belonging and loyalty to their religious group, and others because they have no 'right' to speak of any religion but their 'own'. It is ironic too that inhabitants of a subcontinent, rich in irreverence, in both *comparison* and *critique* of religious philosophies, hierarchies, institutions, and practices that were not limited by personal belonging, as well as rife with oppressions in the name of religions, should now be asked to piously desist from criticism of any but their 'own' religion, within the rubric of a postmodernist politics of (self)-representation. Not only does this version of postmodernism, when transposed to the question of Indian personal laws, become unfaithful to its basic tenets of deconstructing the demarcation between withins and withouts, but ignores the material evidence of the fluidity of religions that I have discussed earlier. More significantly for feminists, this proposition of self-representation rests on a proprietorial view of religions (and as a corollary even separate 'life-worlds'), as the exclusive property of particular groups, and, as I will discuss later, one in which assumptions about owning religions 'naturally' extend to ownership of women.[8]

The women who are (or are sought to be) united on the basis of systemic, overlapping patriarchies are nevertheless simultaneously divided along other lines. Three such divisions are pertinent to my argument: first, by class, overdetermined by caste, and the accompanying power to oppress other women and men; second, by consent to patriarchies and their compensatory structures and an accompanying delegated power to oppress other women; and third, by the choice of a right-wing politics that gives them a political armoury for 'othering' men and women from other religions.[9] And here, the way in which feminists take up particular issues determines whether they are or are not classist, casteist, undemocratic, or compromising with patriarchal arrangements. If they are, then, and only then, do these turn effectively into divisions among women, instead of being, as they should be, divisions that must be *challenged* by feminism.

I do not think, however, that differences in religious faith can by themselves produce equally significant divisions between women. The particularity of religious belief need not by itself either constitute a division along lines of power or alter the distribution of social power. To the extent that all religions are implicated in and enter into the broad process of social legitimation of patriarchies, a challenge to patriarchies constitutes a threat to specific forms of religious legitimation. In this regard, religious affiliation makes a difference *to* women but need not produce a conflict *between* them; especially if women are willing to question the casteist or communal discriminations that inhere in some religious practices and are ready to consider that aspects of religions may be working to reconcile them to patriarchal oppression.

It is only when religious affiliation is translated into a politics and is aligned with institutions that maintain forms of power and privilege that it has the capacity to divide women. Thus, the institutionalization and communalization of religions have acted as a powerful divisive force aggravated by the involvement of some women in entwining religion with the politics of the Hindu right. The right wing appropriation of feminists' agenda or the language of citizenship and democracy is not unique to India and its function here, as elsewhere, is to divide and derail left, democratic, feminist agendas.

If this is an acceptable line of reasoning then the question arises as to why we should recede from a secular democratic agenda and from a commitment to common struggles? The divisions among women along lines of class, consent, and political choice have to be fought through persuasion and/or political confrontation, not through a capitulative politics of differnce, exclusivism, or hyper-particularism.

One issue posed by feminists in the light of the recent riot-torn communal situation is whether gender unity can withstand communal hostility. Feminist groups, Flavia Agnes argues, are already over-inflected with 'Hindu' assumptions, an evidence of which is their past failure to mount a thoroughgoing critique of Hindu personal law, and cannot be isolated from the wider political contradictions; moreover, she argues that in the aftermath of the riots, women do not have a separate existence away from their communal identity where legal issues can be discussed on a common platform.[10] Her argument may fit well with another claiming that currently religious identities have acquired a pre-eminence and the only way to break out is by working within them or by 'negotiating' them. In practice, this could mean that the patriarchal systems operating in the country may henceforth have to be separately opposed by women from within different denominational groupings, while the range of these groupings could now be expanded beyond designated minorities and stretch to women opposing patriarchal practices from within the fold of Hindu communal organizations. If so, we will be unable to address the fact that the political play of denominational 'communities' with its logic of aggression and defence impedes women's individuation, and now being added on to inequalities in wage and non-wage work as well as in inheritance, is driving women further back.

I think the question of why women consent to religious definition and the answer to this question, as well as the path to a common politics, hinge on our understanding of patriarchies: on the way patriarchies are embedded in or articulating with class structures, caste–class inequality, religious practices, wider dialectics of social legitimation, and other political formations. It is only if we see patriarchies as self-sufficient, unrelated to one another, isolated from wider social processes, and determined by religion alone that we can support singular, separate struggles against them along denominational lines. If we see them as intrinsically part of the wider social formation then we have to devise modes of organizations and struggle that can encompass all the social inequalities that patriarchies are related to, embedded in, and structured or enabled by. Attacking patriarchal oppressions is not a sectoral issue confined to women but central to any agenda for social change. Can we afford yet again to separate the 'women question' from a wider struggle, and this time as victims of the divisions enforced by communalization? If feminism is to be an egalitarian, democratic, and secular force allied with other such forces, then this, along with the very nature of patriarchies (to which I will return), requires a common politics.

Community, State, Religion, Patriarchy

It is untenable to draw a sharp line between community and state on either the question of religions or of patriarchies as there are structural, ideological, political, and administrative linkages between the two. Indeed, the kind of religious communities discussed here have been constituted precisely in relation to the state.

The separation between state and civil society rests on an *analytic* distinction. At a structural level, they can and often do interpenetrate; state structures can be replicated *in* family or community. The family's patriarchal arrangements, like those of a community, though in somewhat different ways, can be complicit with the state and its juridical institutions.[11] The relation of the state to women is patriarchal, undemocratic, and class differentiated; the state has persistently defined women in relation to men, used and made labour grids, perpetuated the invisibility of domestic labour, governed both land relations and distribution of resources, enforced the rule of property in ways specially unjust to women, created class and gender inequalities through 'development', reproduced women's economic dependence, co-opted many women's initiatives, and is now (with the new economic liberalization) withdrawing from its welfare functions (which could have mitigated the patriarchies operating in family, community, and workplace).

At the political and administrative levels, it colludes with 'local' and 'community' patriarchies. A triangular relation has obtained between personal laws 'representatives' of a community and the state.[12] It is possible to trace a history of both conflict and cooperation between the community and the state's control at different times. Effectively, however, though a demand for separate Shariat courts has recently been made, it is the state that administers all the personal laws. Further, the state itself has built loopholes in laws and has sustained discriminatory laws, including personal laws, in order to water down the constitutional horizon of gender equality. Its own collusions frequently contradict its stated reformist aims. It has tolerated patriarchies in the state apparatus (e.g. police and judiciary), and barely implemented the better laws that do exist.

Similarly, the state has supported patriarchal interests on religious grounds both ideologically and in practice. There is a long history not only of representing the defence of patriarchal arrangements, privileges and/or the sexual regulation of women as the *defence* of religion but also of the interested representation of patriarchal arrangements as religious *rights* by 'community' spokesmen. Virulent instances, from every denomination, whether minority or majority, can be found in the debates surrounding the Special Marriages Act, the Hindu Code Bill, and the Uniform Civil Code.[13] The coding of patriarchy as religion by community spokesmen has been and is by and large shared by the state which selected *denomination* above differential class, caste, and regional practices and, above an uncompromising secularism as the primary basis for defining family laws. Insofar as personal laws curtail women's rights, they define and defend male privileges; only the constitution of women's rights can dismantle them. Thus male privilege is preserved in personal laws through coparcenary provisions, male testamentary rights, unilateral divorce, bigamy, restitution of conjugal rights, inadequate maintenance, lack of residence, and guardianship and custodial rights for women.

Another major dilution of the line between state and community has occurred in the way the state has been called upon to maintain religious boundaries, and has often done so even though it had successfully established itself as the authority that could 'allow' people to opt for laws (such as provisions in the CrPc) other than their personal laws.[14]

The state has been asked to *protect* religious boundaries in two different ways: through demands for exemption by minority religious spokesmen, and through demands for a uniform civil code by Hindu communalists. I will argue that despite differences, *both* have de facto functioned as demands to close boundaries, deny possibilities of individual exit, and ensure the internal cohesion of a religious 'community' through appropriate laws. (This also raises a question about whether so-called religious communities are indeed internally cohesive, as asking the state to ensure community cohesion through laws suggests that they may in fact be tenuous or precarious.)

In a mode similar to earlier Hindu protests at the introduction of an optional civil law on marriage and divorce, which lasted from the 1860s, to the 1950s, Muslim religious spokesmen have also persistently perceived the very institution of enabling, optional civil laws as threatening. Their objection to the Special Marriages Act (1954) rested on the belief that its existence would encourage Muslims to circumvent their religious laws and obligations, and sought exemptions that were not conceded. A similar demand for exemption was made (along with tribals, and later with a section of Parsis) regarding the proposed Adoption of Children Bill (1972). With the notorious Muslim Women's Act, the government helped Muslim religious leaders by blocking off the access of divorced Muslim women to the minimal yet relatively more liberal provisions for maintenance in the CrPc.[15]

The Hindu communal demand for a uniform civil code, as for instance following on the recent conversion/bigamy judgment, is an attempt to abolish personal law so that Hindus cannot convert and thereby gain access to Muslim personal law. It is not as if Hindu communalists are seriously interested in eradicating bigamy as a patriarchal practice prevalent among Hindus. Rather, they object to Hindus gaining legal access to polygamy through conversion. That is, they object first and foremost to Hindus choosing to become Muslims. (There is a particular ideological embarrassment here: how will the Hindu right pose as the liberator of Muslim women from a patriarchal personal law if Hindu men are converting to Islam to endulge in polygamy?) Secondly, they wish to equalize male privileges.

Hindu male opposition to Muslim personal laws has most frequently been made (in the past as well as now by the BJP) on the competitive patriarchal ground of equivalence of male 'rights': either the state should encroach on the patriarchal privileges or 'religious rights' of all men or of none, and is suffused with male jealousy.[16] The prehistory of current Hindu male opposition to Muslim personal law lies in their failed attempts to fully protect male privileges in the 1950s. In the debates on the Hindu Code Bill, Hindus had not only defended polygamy as having shastric sanction; as being a means for fulfilling the ritual necessity for sons and thus of ensuring spiritual benefit, but had also warned that if polygamy became illegal Hindu men would have to convert to Islam to marry more than one woman or would be forced to keep concubines.[17] The confusion between spiritual benefit and male promiscuity must have been amazing. If men could be willing to renounce Hinduism and convert in order to have more wives then surely male privilege must be stronger than primordial loyalty, as presumably all spiritual benefits would be lost on conversion!

In recent judgments, the judiciary has also assisted in closing routes of exit from personal law. In the nineteenth century, and even up to the 1930s, conversion of an individual, family, caste group, or community to either Sikhism, Islam, or Christianity did not always lead to a change of personal law which was in part retained and engrafted on personal law as a custom.[18] Since 1887, personal law had applied only in disputes between two people of the *same* religion, whether by birth or by conversion, and ceased to do so if one party converted; subsequently, if a personal law was still applied to such a dispute it was for discretionary and contextual reasons, that is, because it was more conducive to justice and relevant in specific cases. This principle of arbitration has been gradually eroded. A tendentious 1983 judgment gave an unprecedented, formulaic, virtually religious sanctity to Hindu personal law by insisting on a supreme and unchangeable regime of primordiality. Justice Leila Seth of Delhi High Court ruled in *Vilayat Raj* v *Sunila* not only that if a Hindu spouse converts to Islam the marriage could only be dissolved under the Hindu personal law in which it was solemnized, but further that 'even if *both* the parties to a Hindu marriage get converted to a religion other than Hindu, their earlier Hindu marriage can only be dissolved under the provisions of the Hindu Marriage Act (1955)'. An indefensible and dubious extension of the Special Marriage Act (which was meant for inter-religious marriages and justifiably allowed dissolution of marriage, conversion notwithstanding, only under the same Act), was made to Hindu personal law.[19]

The consequences of such precedents are visible in the Supreme Court judgment on *Sarla Mudgal and Ors* v *Union of India* (1995, 3 SCC 635). This being a dispute between a husband converted to Islam and his Hindu wife, the court could have used earlier precedents in which neither Hindu nor Muslim personal law was applied and sought the remedy in secular laws governing divorce and bigamy under which the offence was already punishable. Instead, Justice Kuldip Singh invalidated the application of Muslim personal law through an argument of claims and counterclaims, sought a practical remedy in an application of *both* Hindu personal law and section 494 IPC but rested his statement on an ideologically loaded reinforcement of religio–legal boundaries, in which the very existence of Muslim personal law was represented as an encouragement for Hindu bigamy.

till the time we achieve the goal—Uniform Civil Code for all the citizens of India—there is an open *inducement* to a Hindu husband, who wants to enter into a second marriage while the first marriage is subsisting, to become a Muslim. Since monogamy is the law for Hindus and the Muslim law permits as many as four wives in India, an *errant* Hindu embraces Islam to circumvent the provisions of Hindu law and to escape from penal consequences [my emphasis].

He seems to forget that the major inducement to bigamy is not legal pluralism but male privilege, and that most instances of Hindu bigamy occur without conversion.[20] The judgment invokes a familiar comparative schema between men of different communities; legal change is advocated to suppress Muslim polygamy and Hindu conversion, but bigamy is scarcely an issue in its own right. Instead, the rhetoric of the judgment makes absolute the rule of Hindu personal law, overdramatizes conversion,[21] and in what is obviously a complementary move, demands a uniform civil code. A principled attack on bigamy would have distanced itself from Hindu communal rhetoric, confronted gender inequality and all-prevailing patriarchies, sought to improve secular laws on bigamy, divorce, and intra-community marriages, and critiqued the ambiguities of Hindu personal law that assist bigamy.[22]

Muslim religious spokesmen want to close all routes from Muslim personal law to common laws through exemptions. Hindu communalists want to block any route from Hindu personal law to Muslim personal law by abolishing personal law. In each case, the very existence of other laws seems to undermine 'community'. Though from apparently contradictory positions—the former from a position upholding existing legal pluralism and continuation of Muslim personal law but opposing any further pluralization by way of either optional or common non-religious, gender-just laws; the latter by demanding legal uniformity and abolition of personal laws—both want to foster exclusivity, foreclose choice and movement from personal to non-religious laws (for Muslims) or traffic between denominations (for Hindus). Both want to harden and freeze boundaries. Hindu communalists are, in addition, committed to attacking Muslim legal particularity, even if it is at the cost of a uniform civil code. That is precisely why they express little concern about losing their personal law is that they assume that Hindu personal law will be the model for a uniform civil code, so that *only* Muslim legal particularity will be eroded.

Evidently, the acts of defining as well as the definitions of religion and community are predicated on patriarchal privileges, and the state has more often than not been complicit in these because it is itself implicated in patriarchies, in the exploitation of religious identities, and in encashing denomination for electoral purposes. For instance, though the state did not accede to a continuation of polygamy in the Hindu Code Bill in the 1950s, it did introduce some new clauses with no textual religious sanction that made conversion legally punitive for Hindus. These are based on the non-secular assumption that different religions cannot co-exist within a family: conversion is a ground for immediate divorce in the Hindu Marriage Act; the Hindu Adoption and Maintenance Act decrees that only Hindus can adopt Hindus, a widow cannot adopt a Hindu child if she has converted, and a wife is not entitled to maintenance if she ceases to be a Hindu; the Hindu Minority and Guardianship Act rules that ceasing to be Hindu will deprive either spouse of their claim to guardianship of their children, while children and descendants of a convert lose their claim to the property of a Hindu relative unless they are Hindu when succession opens.[23] It appears that religious primordiality was more important than primordial ties based on kinship, family, and nurture; further, conversion is assumed to produce grave incompatibility or repugnance while a change in belief is equated with vicious misdeeds. The state also communalized the Special Marriage Act in 1976 along similar lines.[24]

As communities have themselves become a device that helps the state to mitigate class polarizations and co-opt groups, it is doubtful if consolidating religious communities can 'challenge' the state. In this sense, a multiplication of 'community rights' over and above those that already exist (freedom to worship, to open schools, and to practise personal laws) may well assist the state but are not likely to guarantee full protection of the civic and democratic rights of minorities. Also the maintenance and institution of 'community rights' over, above, or opposed to the rights of individual women, who form half of every community, is likely to intensify male privilege. As defense of community rights has been an undemocratic way of enhancing individual male patriarchal privileges, it is unethical to support them, especially in the name of democracy.

Community Versus State: Problems of Reform from Within or Above

The absolute and binary opposition between state and community on the question of personal law is false; it needs to be dismantled and reconstructed as an argument for the rights of all women. For that matter, the opposition between community and nation on the question of personal law is equally misleading: if a uniform civil code has sought legitimacy from a concept of nation as a homogenous entity, the personal laws have also sought legitimacy from another concept of the nation as a conglomerate of discrete 'major' religions defined through equivalent reductions and homogenization. However, as the issue has been frequently posed in this way, it has acquired a contentious resonance that first needs to be addressed on its own terms.

Beneath the opposition between a state-imposed uniform civil code and personal laws that are sought to be reformed from 'within' a community (and the related opposition between reform of personal laws, from within and from above by the state) lies an unresolved but entirely patriarchal concern; who will control and regulate women and in whom will the agency for reform be vested? Is patriarchal control and/or reform to be excercised by the state and its institutions or by the community? Will community control act in tandem with the state or independently of it, as in the recent demand for separate Shariat courts?

The choice between personal laws and a so-called uniform civil code at one level appears to hinge on a choice of patriarchal jurisdictions. Does this choice have any meaning for women? Will the jurisdiction of 'community' representatives, usually male, functioning either independently or through a surrogate state be preferable to that of an impersonal state? Significantly, the experience of reform of personal law from within has, in the case of Christians, met only with procrastination from the state,[25] while for Muslims it has been one of entrenchment of religious, elites and a 'community' patriarchy complicit with the state. The reform of Hindu personal law from above by the state did challenge religious elites[26] but culminated instead in the promulgation of patriarchal laws by the state.[27] The legitimacy of the state is dubious, whether in supporting reforms from within or in reforming from above. In both, reform of personal laws is a bargaining counter for the state which retains the power to decide whether or not to reform the personal law of any community.[28]

Posing the question of laws in binary terms of community versus state is thus pre-feminist and carries the patriarchal legacy of male reformism. Nineteenth-century male reformism, it must be remembered, was invested less in eliminating patriarchies than in reformulating them. It is pre-feminist in the way it elides feminists[29] as agents of choice, decision and makes the state and community the major actors. Indeed it is only if feminist agency is omitted or denied (or restricted to the primordial religious group), that the question can be turned into the male-reformist one of whose patriarchal jurisdiction women should come under, or posed as one of whose patriarchal jurisdiction will be, a *better* option: that of community or of the state.

Till now, feminist initiatives to reform personal laws have been baulked as often by the state as by the pandits, mullahs, or priests who supposedly represent the 'community'. In my view, *any attempt to either reform personal laws or to make new common laws with a feminist agenda* will come up against both the state and religious 'community' patriarchal arrangements.

For women, community jurisdiction is as problematic as that of the state; the patriarchies of neither are acceptable. The former is grinding because it intensifies the difficulty of daily, local, interpersonal relationships, making it difficult to claim democratic rights contravened by personal law. The latter involves problems of implementation, functions through a self-contradicting, increasing delegitimized, often coercive and patriarchal state machinery.

A major difference, however, between state and community is that of a theoretical horizon. In personal law, women claim as wives, mothers, or daughters, and have a schizophrenic relation with citizenship, upholding a pernicious opposition between private and public, between being members of a community and having full rights as citizens. Unlike communities, the state is theoretically committed to ensuring the rights of citizens as citizens. In striving for new common laws (formulated differently from existing laws by feminists) ratified by the state, women can define and claim a direct relation to the state, unmediated by community, as citizens with fundamental democratic rights; only as citizens can women potentially challenge divisions based on denomination, on public and private, on legal categorizations, and seek, if they wish, secular collectivities. If elements of contestation and struggle are fundamental determinants on construction and implementation of legislation, then the history of state intervention is also itself partly a history of struggles *against* patriarchal relations institutionalized through the state.[30]

Finally, the implicit recognition in the Constitution that religions have sustained and legitimized caste and gender discrimination[31] led the state to be at once a 'protector' of religious freedom and a reformer of injustices based on religion: this contradiction too can be purposively and subversively used by feminists.

Apart from the risks of isolation and failure, a struggle to reform personal laws from within, places the onus on a small number of persons.[32] While making a bid for new common laws, the complicities of the state in encashing religious differences, drawing on and using particular sets of patriarchal relations, should be opposed; at the same time, it should be asked to provide juridical spaces, live up to its arbitrating functions, and be held systematically accountable as an agency of change and implementation. Such a strategy would have the added advantage of being a struggle in which feminist, left and democratic forces could join.

Religion, Law, and the Private Domain

The orientalisms that flourished in imperialized formations turned religion, which they saw as immutable, into a primary axis of social classification. One longstanding orientalist axiom was that India in its past and present yields no distinction between religion and law. This ascribed fusion of religion and law, accompanied by a corollary characterization of the Indian masses as desiring and enacting a cosmic, holistic life, is now employed by the contemporary successors of orientalists to defend traditions,[33] of which personal laws are assumed to be a part, on the ground that all attempts towards secular laws are intrusive, violent, and 'Western' devices.

The early orientalist identification of religion and law now survives primarily as the identification of religion with *personal* laws and with *religious* community. The present discourse on religious community seeks to make it fully determining in the social, legal, and political arena. In a characteristic combination of Eurocentric theory and indigenist sentiment, this theoretical tendency continues, implicitly, to deny to Indians the dignity of choice and political affiliation while subsuming the question of rights, especially those of women, under primordial denomination.

I doubt if the Indian past or present would bear out the orientalists. The undeniably wide sprawl of religion in social life is not identical with the so-called indivisibility of religion and law. From ancient times (as in the *Arthashastra* and the Smritis) to the Mughal period it is possible to see religion as a mode for legitimating law, kingship, and extraction of surplus; that is, to see the very indivisibility of religion and law as an aspect of a working and workable ideology. Manipulation of the 'sources' of laws and customs dates back to ancient India.[34] Plural systems of legal arbitration, the legal force of local non-religious customs, and the lack of coincidence between any single religion and any one legal system, also challenge a simplistic conflation of religion and law. It is thus possible to approach the question contextually and contingently, to see how the lines between religion and law were drawn differently at different times, along lines of region, caste, and strata, delimiting or extending the purview of religion as the case may be.

I will argue that the present legal purview of religion, confined to personal laws, that is, to matters related to family, marriage, and certain types of inheritance, and impinging most heavily on the lives of women, certainly puts the orientalist axiom and its modern mutants themselves into the realm of ideology.

From the nineteenth century the legal purview of religion has steadily narrowed, coming increasingly into conflict with the exigencies of capitalism and its legal structures which seek to promote both individuation and class reproduction. Ambedkar's impatience with the spread of religion in social life and his argument for its legal delimitation came from the viewpoint that management of class relations and distribution of resources could not be tied to religion.[35] Since the colonial era there have been successive and cumulative attempts to split off religion from most areas. Male inheritance was one of these; male individuation was sought even within coparcenary systems but female individuation was blocked off in the name of preserving the family and the personal affairs of religious communities.[36]

Religion no longer determines the laws relating to the ownership of agricultural land, tenancy, crime, commerce, international relations, and the like but is largely confined to laws relating to family, marriage, and some forms of inheritance,[37] thereby producing an uneasy and unreal division between public and private. Unreal, because in practice the areas in which personal laws operate are interdependent with and related to all the other areas in law and in women's lives: women are governed not by family laws alone but by most other laws; inheritance, in different regional and legal combinations,[38] straddles the public and private domain; while the legal compartmentalization of public and private, of work and family life, is at once 'illusory as women's family lives and work capacities are completely intertwined and mutually determining as well as utterly prejudicial for women.[39] Uneasy, because this division simultaneously esconces religion as a means for the public regulation of 'private' family affairs on the one hand, and on the other effectively places religion in the domain of the 'private' in the sense that its legal purview is restricted to family matters.

Several definitional questions arise from such division. The peculiar bracketing of laws related to marriage and family as 'personal' laws produces, a gendered definition of religion that falls more heavily on women. Does not this display the collective interests of men from different religions in maintaining gendered power hierarchies? The location of religion in the 'private' domain has repercussions too. It serves to transpose the liberal rationale of the family as a private sanctuary ideally beyond state intervention (which has proved so detrimental for women)[40] on to the religious community and its personal laws. It also shifts the onus of maintaining community identity onto women in marriage and women *in* familial relations. Finally, this notion of religion assists in the replay of a classic logic, honed by colonial administrators and middle class Indians in the early nineteenth century, in which patriarchies had to be 'at once preserved and reformed',[41] but this time, on the ground of personal laws. Is this demarcation of private and public consolingly pre-modern or eminently 'modern'? In other words, is in actuality an instantiation of the cliched liberal division of public and private, with the public as the sphere of universality, nationality, impartiality, equality in the eyes of the law, built on consent, and the private as the sphere of particularism built on the 'natural' subjugation of women?

It is important to discuss the ideological rationales implicit in several types of conflations of law, religion, community, belief, and women that are being made in defence of personal laws and the social diversity they are presumed to represent.

In arguments resting on the conflation of religion, law community, and belief, any critique of the bases of personal laws is seen as an attack on community rights, on religion, and on matters of belief. Yet why should group rights or a sense of community not be rebuilt and claimed on lines other than the patriarchal? If the educational and cultural rights of minorities deserve to be protected, why should their, or anyone else's, 'patriarchal rights' be protected? Are we to define patriarchies sometimes as religion and sometimes as culture? Are patriarchies the sole determinants or 'guarantors' of religion?

Are patriarchies to be treated as an essential or an alterable part of religion, that is, does the solution lie in atheism or in reform? Why should a separation of law and religion per se undermine either the sense of belonging to a community, or professing and practicing a religion? If that was the case, how come the presence of common laws in most areas other than the family as well as of some secular laws governing the family have not already destroyed religion and belief?

In my view, there can only be three implicit rationales for a conflation of religion, law, community, and belief, and the corollary fear of any critique of the principles or bases of personal laws. The first is that religion should be ratified by the state as family law. This is fairly dubious and could simply amount to a means for maintaining patriarchies. The second is that once family law is split off from religion, the triad of religion, community, and faith will be weakened. This amounts to saying that religion, community, and belief depend on the continuation of patriarchies, or worse, that group rights cannot but be based on a supersession of women's individual rights. In either case this is scarcely feminist. There is a third implicit rationale, which is, that while all other laws can be shared by different denominations and by believers and non-believers alike, family laws must be singled out for religious legitimation, and can only be changed, even on lines of gender justice, if their religious legitimation is not challenged. This third implication also has serious consequences for women: it is tantamount to saying that women in their family relations, must both signify and be kept forcibly in an ideologically pre-capitalist and pre-contractual realm, never mind whether the world is changing. Even if women acquire further rights through reform of personal laws, these *rights must be seen to fall under the rule of religion,* be ratified by it, and must not contradict it. Also, as all three rationales come into play *only* in the domain of family law, the conclusion is inescapable that the covert conflation is in fact one of women with religion and belief and community identity. That is, women are uniquely required to be guarantors and preservers of a pre-capitalist enclave produced by modern political and economic procedures. This is such a conservative position, so rehashed over 200 years, and so obsessed with creating cultural spectacles geared to neocolonialism and global consumption,[42] that it does not even deserve to be entertained, least of all from a feminist standpoint.

It is also possible to outline another slightly different conflation in which the legitimacy of personal laws is derived from identifying them with social plurality while social plurality hinges on a conflation of law, religion, and women's rights. Would the delinking of law from religion destroy cultural plurality and diversity of beliefs and religious practices? Surely it would only curtail sanctification of patriarchies through religion and its further ratification by law. (Indeed, it might partly *free* religions from the tyranny of legal definition.) It need not stop the practice of religion in non-patriarchal ways. Alternatively, is it that the introduction of the *same* rights for all women will destroy plurality, that is, is it that *unevenness* of rights makes for social plurality? This latter is both anti-modernist and anti-feminist. Otherwise, is it that the nominal existence of personal laws is crucial regardless of how much their content is altered through reform? If that, however, is the position of the upholders of social difference, then surely theirs is a tokenist, non-substantive particularism alone.

Personal Laws and Homogenization

A major sticking point in these positions is a fear of homogenization. However, the belief that personal laws express religious plurality, and the expectation that they will continue to do so if reformed with a view to gender equality, is borne out neither by the history of their formation nor by their contents.

The pluralism that personal laws supposedly represent is in actuality premised on an enormous reduction while the very notion of religion which underlies personal laws is one formed through a process of homogenization. The British homogenized personal laws through codification and further codified custom through the accumulation of case law, scarcely incorporating the enormous diversity or variations of belief, sect, and practice in different regions and classes that existed even within the rubric of the major denominations. Subsequent reforms of personal law have shown no respect for or commitment to this substantial diversity. Indeed, the reformed Hindu law and the Shariat Application Act helped to create newly unified versions of Hindu and Muslim. This did not happen by default; the reformers of personal laws first directly confronted and then sought to erase the diversity of customs in order to homogenize the various Hindu and Muslim 'communities' across the subcontinent. Even now, reform of personal laws from within, 'without' or above is likely to continue this process and intensify the conception of sharply defined, bounded, and exclusive religions on which such laws are based. What is worse, it resembles a specific logic of communalization on which much of the present politics of electoral blocs rests.

The reforms of Hindu and Muslim personal laws have so far produced two different models of homogenization, though both are in part, facets or extensions of a common history of nineteenth-century reformism. The colonial regime had already introduced a degree of anglicization, privileging textual over customary law in what have been called processes of Islamicization and Brahmin-ization,[43] and codified customary law, piecemeal. As the realm of common statutory law expanded, creating the still extant division between the public and the private, the personal laws governing the private domain came to be labelled religious laws, though they were either actually state enactments or the contents of their rules had substantively changed.[44] Subsequent reforms of these personal laws[45] made similar attempts to homogenize the variety of regional custom-ary laws, though only with partial success.

The reform of Hindu personal law after Independence displays certain notable characteristics. Firstly, the state veered between secu-lar and religious legitimation. The first proposals for the reform of Hindu law used a religious basis but the final proposals (e.g. for divorce) could not be traced to religious texts, and the claim of pandits to be legislators was disallowed; at the same time, some rules were allowed to continue because they were religious, even though they contravened constitutional principles of gender equality.[46] Conse-quently the Hindu Code Bill was both Hinduizing and de-Hinduizing; in an arbitrary way it made the law both less and more religious.

Secondly, it produced a tendentious legal description of a 'Hindu'. It purposively included the Buddhist, Jain, and Sikh despite protests. The plea of Sikhs and some Buddhists to be governed by their own laws was rejected. So too was that of Jains on the ground that their few differences from Hinduism were not fundamental! It further included anyone who was *not* a Muslim, Christian, Parsi, or Jew; and it also mentions that this code would apply to any Hindu, Buddhist, Jain, or Sikh, who has merely deviated from the orthodox practices of his religion but has not embraced the Muslim, Zoroastrian, Jewish religion. Next, it was extended to cover even those who did not 'profess' Hinduism and were not 'active followers'. Finally, it was reluctant to make or continue regional exemptions.[47]

The bill thus attacked most principles of religious plurality and choice; it first recognized the existence and claims of in-between and unclassifiable areas, discrete belief systems, overlapping religions, non-believers, regional specificity, and then proceeded to deny them any legal provenance. The negative description of a Hindu, as one who was not a member of the four excluded religions, produced a Hindu so tightly manacled to his/her birth that even non-belief could not provide an exit. Even though the constitution provided for the right of non-belief and atheism,[48] the reformed Hindu law *took away the freedom of legal self-definition and self-designation* from individuals born in 'Hindu' families. Thus, despite its crass assimilationism, it instituted a new primordialism; even as it described more people as 'Hindu' than had ever been done before and included people who had no stake in being so defined, it drew a new boundary. What was worse, this description of Hinduism solely in relation to four excluded religions, meant that these religions inevitably became its legal 'others'. This could be partly related to the punitive laws on conversion discussed earlier: once non-belief had been de-recognized as a mode of exit from personal law, it remained only to try and seal the remaining possibility of exit through conversion. As the legal definition of Hinduism had been artificially so enlarged, presumably all that a 'Hindu' could now convert to was to the four excluded religions. Thus, even the social meanings of conversion were narrowed as much mobility that would have amounted to conversion in the past would now look like movement *within* the spacious ambit of this Hinduism. With the Hindu Mahasabha's *'shuddhi'* campaigns from the 1920s and the accompanying fear they whipped up about Hindus converting to Islam, conversion had become a volatile issue entangled in communal violence, and remained so in the aftermath of Partition. Though the attack on religious fluidity also had other antecedents in the colonial period which had made Christianity and Islam the principal opponents of Hinduism, and even this 'negative' definition of Hinduism can be seen taking shape in the 1891 Census,[49] the state now virtually handed a completed agenda to the Hindu communalists. Ironically, all this was subsequently defined in the name of Hinduism being at once a culture and cultural synthesis. When the reform proposals were discussed in the Lok Sabha it was claimed that Hinduism was not a religion but a culture; a synthesis of the varied beliefs, customs and practices of different people![50] The Hindu as legal entity became difficult to distinguish from that desired by the Hindu Mahasabha.[51]

Thirdly, the erratic homogenization of diverse schools of Hindu law, premised on a northern upper caste model,[52] at one level attempted to create a homogenized 'Hindu' patriarchy through forms of levelling. Even women who had more rights in some areas of inheritance were now to make do with less under the Hindu Code Bill.[53] It preserved and universalized coparcenary law, derived from the *mitakshara*, that is prejudicial for women. However, there was no uniformity in some clauses (such as inheritance or adoption), while some unexplained exceptions were made with the result that many customs and practices of Hindu laws continued to operate.[54]

Finally, the uneasy and inconsistent break from its upper caste, shastric origins and models, made it difficult for the Hindu Code Bill to either fully absorb lower caste and class practices into homogeneous laws or to consider them separately. These were carelessly overridden,[55] with the exception of the customary divorces which were saved as 80 per cent of 'lower caste Hindus' already followed various customs of divorce.[56] The state sought to act as an agent of unification, at certain levels, of different castes and patriarchies but with uneven results. Ironically, attempting to iron out the inconsistencies and remaining diversities in Hindu law may amount to another round of homogenizing the 'Hindu'.

The reform of the 1930s homogenized Muslim personal law on somewhat different lines. It involved an onslaught on customary law and customary variations as well as on the way customary law constituted contiguous, syncretic collectivities that were not 'Muslim' communities; it introduced legal homogeneity among Muslims as a basis for common religious identity, entrenched religious elites, and achieved a predominance of scriptural law *through legislation.* Many of these features make the homogenization of personal law appeared to be a facet of the those nineteenth-century reformist movements that had set out to Islamize by purging syncriticism. Like the reforms of Hindu law, it had also set out to fasten Muslims to their personal law.

Till the 1937 codification of Shariati Application Act, Muslims had followed Islamic law in certain matters and customary usage in others while regional laws and usages had been continually engrafted as customs.[57] Haryana Muslim landowners preferred customary law (more consonant with class and patriarchal interest) over and above the Shariat law. The objectives of this bill were legal reform, 'securing uniformity among Muslims in all their social and personal relations', to thereby 'do justice to the claims of women for inheriting family property, who, under customary law are debarred from succeeding to the same'.[58] More specifically, it was initiated by the ulema to bring the Muslims of Punjab, North West Frontier, and

Central Provinces, hitherto under customary law, under a central personal law that would apply to all Muslims in the country. The Act improved women's property rights, but by representing the customary domain as one of corruption and deprivation alone and its own task as that a 'restoration', Mulsim women, governed by a range of customary laws, now came under a more textual regime.[59] The ulema wanted to establish principle that Muslim personal law and not custom should be applied to Muslims. The bill attacked local customs and usages as too 'changeable', sought to ensure certainty and definitiveness in laws by divesting them of all custom and usages as well as 'obedience' of Muslims to their own laws. As a compromise with Jinnah who wanted an option between the Shariat and customary law, benefiting property rights of traders and landholders, options were allowed for adoption, wills, and legacies.[60]

This process of homogenization continued with the passing of the Dissolution of Muslim Marriages Act 1939. This was an amalgam of liberal features from four schools of jurisprudence, giving Muslim women limited rights to seek divorce.[61] The 1937 Act tackled the discrepancy between women's Shariat rights to property and customary practice in such a way that attacking custom became a means of homogenization. The 1939 Act, using the same rhetoric of restoration made a notable departure from classical Islamic law in ruling that apostasy of women would no longer be a ground for dissolution of marriage. Whereas this could have been a provision encouraging intra-religious marriages, tolerance and individual choice, the fact that it was restricted to women (male apostasy remained a ground for dissolution of marriage), gave it a different ideological location. It curtailed the opportunity for women to get out of a difficult marriage by apostasy;[62] and was initiated by the ulema when they discovered that a number of Muslim women were renouncing Islam or claiming conversion to qualify as divorcee under Hanafi law, and their fear that women would continue to do so.[63] Women could simply have been granted better rights to divorce, while prevailing judicial practice of either not using or employing discretion in the application of a personal law to cases of the conversion of married women seeking to dissolve the marriage, could have continued.[64] Muslim fears of *shuddhi* and of the abduction and conversion of women may have played a role alongside the notion of women as 'community' property. If the 1937 Act asserted the rule of personal law over a singular Muslim community, the 1939 Act asserted the rule of personal law and community over Muslim women, but in doing so it reversed the methods of the earlier Act; now men were more fully governed by classical Islamic law than women. Boundaries were tightened to keep women in. Conversion would not affect the marital status of a woman but neither could it any longer free her from conjugal bonds or from her husband's personal law.

Significantly, conversion functioned as a customary loophole for seeking divorce not only for Muslim but also Hindu, Christian, and Parsi women. In some cases where the courts declared their marriages not dissolved by conversion, the reasoning seems patriarchal.[65] For instance, in Robasa Khanum, a Parsi woman converted to Islam and claimed her marriage was dissolved, the judgment praised the exemplary modernity of the 1939 Act, interpreted her action as a unilateral repudiation of marriage, and upheld the sanctity of the Zoroastrian vow![66] Male unilateral divorce, both legally and extra-judicially, was a norm, but women moving from one religion to another to seek a divorce threatened *everyone*, Hindu, Muslim, Parsi, Christian, as it challenged religious boundaries, male proprietorship, and patriarchal laws.

If patriarchies, like violence, have to be legitimated, and on the same ground, as representing the 'whole' community, then community spokesmen have as much interest in suppressing difference as communalists, and as I have tried to show, the state itself has invested in tendentious ways of suppressing difference. In this context, reform of personal law has been homogenizing, whether it was carried out from within or without. Ironically, all these reforms claimed to be working on behalf of improving the status of women.

The belief that reform of personal laws will at once uphold gender justice and guarantee social diversity[67] is groundless. Indeed, reform of personal laws from within or above is, in our context, itself an issue of the reduction of diversity, the suppression of cultural difference, and the negation of space for choosing, changing, or disavowing religions. Personal laws have been a principle of homogenization on religious lines; from the colonial to the contemporary period, they have selectively and arbitrarily universalized high textuality, regional or upper caste practices, and reformulated patriarchies both in their initial codification and in successive reforms. Further, they failed to sift the customary domain and incorporate more egalitarian aspects, oscillated between bourgeois patriarchy and non-interference in 'native' religions, or capitulated to upper caste/class patriarchal interests.

My further questions is: How much of the 'religious character' and 'diversity' of personal laws will remain after a further reform on the lines of gender justice? Even if we were to differentiate our feminist perspective and our sensitivity to social plurality from these earlier attempts, would reform of personal laws from the point of view of gender justice be less homogenizing? Gender justice can only push all the different personal laws into a *similar* direction as there are not at the moment an infinite number of ways to bring it about.

The question then needs to be posed not as one of homogenization per se but of its nature, principles, and limits. New common laws for women would also be homogenizing; however, while personal laws sought to unify denominational groups, such laws would seek common rights on a nonreligious, egalitarian, and emancipatory principle. Fully developed precedence for an unoppressive form of homogenization, based in an intelligent relation with social diversity, that adds to existing legal and customary rights and eliminates existing legal and customary disabilities, are unlikely to be found in colonial India or in contemporary laws.

Notes

1. For instance, Partha Chatterjee recommends self-governing religious communities. His concern is to find 'a defensible argument' and a 'strategic politics' for minority cultural rights in the present situation. He bases these rights in the self-justificatory potentials of a minority, and these are in turn based on the 'consent' that each 'religious group' will seek from its members through some forms of internal elective democracy and representative institutions (such as the Gurudwara Prabhandak Committee) thrown up from political processes within each minority group ('Secularism and Toleration', *Economic and Political Weekly (EPW)* 9 July, 1994, pp. 1775–77). There are several evident difficulties in his formulation. The somewhat voluntarist assumptions that religious groups can generate internal political processes separate from the wider polity and that these will be 'democratic', are fairly problematic. His idea that an 'elective' process will throw up 'true' representatives of each religious group does not take operative power structures into account while the belief that 'community' representation will be just in its own terms (to women?) seems ungrounded. The conception of community consent does not tackle consent to render inequality; where and how women will become agents in the internal transformation of religious groups or challenge their 'regulative powers' is left undiscussed; nor does the essay consider the likelihood that the democratic aspirations of many women may not or cannot be tied to communitarian or, denominational identities.

2. For a discussion of the question of consent and that of women committed to Hindutva, see Kumkum Sangari, 'Consent, Agency and Rhetorics of Incitement', *EPW*, 28: 18, 1 May, 1993.

3. On this point, see also Archana Prasher, *Women and Family Law Reform in India,* Sage, New Delhi, 1992, p. 184.

4. For instance Muslim and non-Muslim women protested against the Muslim Women's Bill in 1986, while Shahbano was made to withdraw her case by religious leaders (Prashar, pp. 311–13).

5. It is worth recalling that after the Deorala widow-immolation the imagination of metropolitan ideologues, overdetermined by a nativist anti-colonialism, was gripped by the idea of a 'voluntary sati' as an expression of the widows own 'free will', and that their notions coincided with the views of those locally involved in this and similar episodes. See Kumkum Sangari, 'Perpetuating the Myth', seminar, 342, February 1988.

6. Lovibond's attempt to describe an anti-essentialist universalist politics may be useful. She points out that 'the ultimate goal of liberation movements is not to invent new 'identities' along the lines laid down by existing structures of domination, but to dismantle these structures and so release the energies of each individual for the work of active (as opposed to reactive) self-definition. In this sense a universalist politics, far from leading to 'essentialism', calls into question every 'essence' arising from social arrangements which could be amended through collective choice.' See Sabina Lovibond, 'Feminism and Pragmatism: A Reply to Richard Rorty', *New Left Review,* 193, 1992, 74.

7. Chatterjee argues through a Foucauldian notion of 'governmentality' for an acceptance in the present political context of a situation 'where a group could insist on its right not to give reasons for doing things differently provided it explains itself adequately in its own chosen forum' (p. 1775). He does not explain the principles by which such inscrutability will be withheld from or denied to majority religious communities or to 'minorities' within majorities. For instance one ground for defence of widow-immolation after the Deorala episode was that 'westernized' women were strangers to the niceties of Hindu belief and therefore had no right to oppose it!

8. In our context, self-representation may give communalism and proprietary patriarchies a new lease of life.

9. For an elaboration of these, see Sangari, 'Consent, Agency'.

10. Flavia Agnes, 'Women's Movement within a Secular Framework', *EPW,* 29:19, 7 May, 1994, pp. 1123–27.

11. Madhu Kishwar has pointed out that exploitative family structures which keep women subjected receive crucial support from the state through laws and rules of behaviour which legitimate the authority of the male members over the lives of members or the family ('some Aspects of Bondage: the Denial of Fundamental Rights to Women', Manushi 31, Jan.–Feb. 1983).

12. Not only did the government accept religio–political leaders as sole spokesmen for the entire 'community' but the state has been party to the construction of the Shariat as immutable (Prasher, p. 172). Hasan has also

emphasized the mutual complementarity of government and religious leadership in reinforcing community identity and the narrow construction of this identity in terms of personal law; Congress ideology and political practice reduced minority rights to personal law and reduced this in turn to religious rights. The protests of Muslim women against the Muslim Women's Bill involved confrontation of both state and community, but liberal and progressive opinion was ignored. See Zoya Hasan, 'Communalism, State Policy, and the Question of Women's Right, in Contemporary India'. *Bulletin of Concerned Asian Scholars*, 25:4, 1993, 11, 14; 'Minority Identity in *Foreign Identities: Gender Communities and the State*, Zoya Hasan (ed.), Kali, Delhi, 1994, pp. 63, 68.

13. Hindus initiated this style of defence in their opposition to the proposed Special Marriages Act from 1868 to 1872 and to its later amendments in the 1920s and 1950s. This among other things, was made on the ground that the Act challenged the notion of marriage as sacramental and indissoluble, threatened to constrict the unrestricted polygamy of Hindu men, undermined the ways in which religion prevented the free choice of spouse and regulated sexuality, undercut the patriarchal authority of the family and the social authority of caste. Muslim opposition, which first appeared in the 1930s and 1950s, was focused on the way it sanctioned intercommunity marriages. (I owe this information to Amrita Chhachhi's excellent and as yet unpublished paper entitled 'Of Blood and Race: the Special Marriages Act Debates, 1862–1976'). In the arguments against the Uniform Civil Code and Hindu Code bill patriarchal arrangements continued to be defended as religious rights. Hindus were vocal in defending polygamy and opposing property rights for women on religious grounds. An identical conception of patriarchal arrangements has underwritten the defence of minority personal laws by community spokesmen. The underlying assumptions of these interested representations were so well understood in the 1940s–1950s that Raj Kumari Amrit Kaur, Hansa Mehta, Ambedkar, and Ayyar argued against freedom of religion *and* religious practices in the constituent assembly debates on the ground that inclusion of the word. 'practice' would be used to prevent reform (Prasher, pp. 223–5).

14. On this latter point also see Prasher, p. 274,

15. Prasher, pp. 161–2, 169–72, 309–10, Muslims, objected to the Uniform Civil Code clause in the constitution. The Minorities Commission to whom the Adoption bill was later referred recommended that religious groups should not be excluded because 'minorities within a religious minority have the freedom to believe, profess and practice their own version of their religion' (ibid. pp. 17, 231). Regarding the Muslim Women's Bill, it has been pointed out that rather than opposing state intervention in the internal affairs of the Muslim community, Muslim fundamentalists in fact secured state backing to enforce control over women (Amrita Chhachhi, 'Forced Identities:

the State, Communalism, Fundamentalism and women in India' in *Women, Islam and the State.* Deniz Kandiyoti (ed.), Temple University Press, Philadelphia, 1993, p. 167).

16. The desire for an equivalence of male 'rights' was evident in the common argument in the 1950s (one still being made), that by not enacting a uniform civil code the government was encroaching only upon the religious rights of Hindus but was afraid to encroach similarly on the rights of others (Parasher, p. 237). The most vociferous opposition to the Hindu Code bill in the 1940s came from the Hindu Mahasabha; Shyama Prasad Mukherjee argued for a uniform civil code instead of reform of Hindu laws, but even that code had to be optional! So even at that lime the opponents of the Hindu Code bill, that is defender, of patriarchal privileges, were also proponents of a uniform civil code! (See Reba Som, 'Jawaharlal Nehru and the Hindu Code: A Victory of Symbol over Substance', NMML Occasional Papers, April 1992, PP. 15–18).

17. Prasher, P. 114, Shahida Lateef, 'Defining Women through Legislation' in *Foreign Identities,* p. 50. In fact some argued that Hindus would accept monogamy only when Muslims did (ibid. p. 52)! Others compared compulsory monogamy to 'racial suicide'; it would destroy India the way it had destroyed the Roman empire (Som. pp. 20–1).

18. A.M. Bhattacharjee *Muslim law and the Constitution,* 2nd edn, Eastern Law House, Calcutta, 1994, pp. 33–4: John Malcolm, *Sketch of the Sikhs,* London, np. 1812, p.133.

19. Bhattacharji, *Muslim Law,* pp. 89–91, 99–104.

20. The learned judge seems unaware of the figures for bigamy and polygamy presented by the Census Commission of India, 1961: tribals 15.2 per cent, Buddhists 7.9 per cent, Jains 6.72 per cent, Hindus 5.8 per cent, and Muslims 5.7 per cent. See also *Report of Committee on the Status of Women,* Government of India, 1975.

21. The judgment even suggests framing a Conversion of Religion Act to check abuse of religion! This would be somewhat farcical if it did not fuel communal organizations seeking to whip up hysteria over conversions; the VHP announced soon after the judgment that it was working towards setting up 9000 Hindu missionaries to meet the challenge of Islamicization and Christianization and the consequent demographic decline of Hindus (Hindu, 3 July 1995).

22. Hindu personal law assisted polygamy by validating customary rituals and ceremonies; if *saptapadi* and *vivahahoma* cannot be proved then the marriage becomes invalid (Agnes, p. 1125; and Flavia Agnes, *State, Gender and the Rhetoric of Law Reform.* SNDT University, Bombay, 1995, pp. 199–200.

23. For a discussion of these and other clauses and their creation of new anti-secular biases in some areas see A.M. Bhattacharji who points out that many of these clauses violate Article 15 of the Constitution (*Hindu Law and*

the Constitution, Eastern Law House, Calcutta, 1994, pp. 130–42; see also J. Duncan Derrett, *Religion, Law and the State in India*, Faber 1968, London, pp. 332–3, 342; K.G. Kannabiran, 'Outlawing Oral Divorce: Reform through Court Decree', *EPW*, 29:25, 18 June, 1994, p. 1510; Bhattacharjee, *Muslim Law*, pp. 112–13; Prasher, p. 100; Madhu Kishwar, 'Codified Hindu Law: Myth and Reality', *EPW*, 29:33, 13 August 1994, p. 2156. While the laws do not altogether preclude inheritance on conversion, they do make it more difficult and arbitrary.

24. See Prasher for details, p. 272. Since 1976, for instance, Hindus who marry under the Special Marriage Act inherit under Hindu personal law and not under the Indian Succession Act. This amendment under which Hindus would continue to be governed by Hindu Succession Act could deter a Hindu from marrying a non-Hindu woman because then he would forfeit his rights to ancestral property (Agnes, *State, Gender*, p. 200). The Act also has loopholes that can be used to prevent intercommunity marriages (Chhachhi in Foreign identities, p. 82).

25. Christian women seeking reforms have produced a draft bill of Christian Marriage Act with the unanimous assent of heads of churches which is in abeyance since early 1994.

26. Prasher, p. 139.

27. For instance the new testamentary provisions introduced in the Hindu Succession Act with regard to ancestral property rendered property more mobile in the hand of individual male owners, prevented fragmentation of urban family business or family agricultural holding, and assisted fathers to obviate the newly given right of property to daughters, thereby taking away women's limited customary rights and making the man's will paramount (Som, pp. 45–6: Kishwar, p. 2156). In fact the testamentary provisions were explicitly offered as a loophole through which to avoid giving women property (Prasher, p. 128). For a detailed discussion of gender inequalities in this Act, see Bina Agarwal, 'Gender and Legal Rights in Agricultural Land in India', *EPW*, Review of Agriculture, 30:12 March 1995, A-43.

28. On this point, see Prasher, pp. 271–3.

29. For me, feminist agency is not merely women's agency but the organized initiatives of women and men committed to distributive justice and women's equality within a democratic and egalitarian framework; it does not include women committed to right-wing politics.

30. Rachel Harrison and Frank Mort, 'Patriarchal Aspects of Nineteenth Century State Formation', in *Capitalism, State Formation and Marxist Theory*, Philip Corrigan (ed.), Quartet, London, 1980, pp. 81–2.

31. The clause on social reform was added due to the stated fears of Ambedkar and others that freedom to propagate and practice would perpetuate these injustices.

32. It also carries the inflections of voluntarism. The historical coordinates of reforms during the colonial period were predicated on struggles within

denominations, class formation, degrees of embourgeoisement: effectively part of a historical process in which public male agencies were formative and preceded those of women. The same historical process cannot mechanically repeat itself, and more creative, broad-based strategies need to be evolved.

33. For a discussion of new orientalizing discourses, see Kumkum Sangari, 'Introduction: Representations in History', *Journal of Arts and Ideas*, nos 17–18, June 1989.

34. Indeed, brahminical law had a regionally variant status and was often reduced to a useful embellishment for Kshatriya hegemony.

35. In the debates on the Hindu Code bill, Ambedkar, noting the consequences of a conflation of religion and law, complained: 'The religious conceptions in this country are so vast that they cover every aspect of life, from birth to death. There is nothing which is not religion and if personal law is to be saved I am sure about it that in social matters we will come to a standstill ... There is nothing extraordinary in saying that we ought to strive hereafter to limit the definition of religion in such a manner that we shall not extend it beyond beliefs and such rituals as may be connected with ceremonials which are essentially religious. It is not necessary, that the sort of laws, for instance, laws relating to tenancy or laws relating to succession should be governed by religion ... I personally do not understand why religion should be given this vast expansive jurisdiction so as to cover the whole of life and to prevent legislature from encroaching upon that field.' (*Constituent Assembly Debates*, vol. 7, p. 781).

(K.M. Munshi too wanted to split religious imperatives from class reproduction. He argued against the protection of personal law from state intervention in 'secular' areas of religion or those that fell within the purview of social welfare or reform; he said if succession or inheritance related personal laws were believed to be a part of religion it would contradict the constitutional promise of sex equality (Prasher, p. 227).

36. Male individuation did not conflict with the family or 'religion' in the way that female individuation did and still does. The Hindu Gains of Learning Act (1930) provided for individual ownership of the income a person earned by virtue of his 'learning', it no longer had to be part of the coparcenary. This trend continued after Independence, and with the Hindu Code bill men were allowed to keep their own earnings giving them the double benefit of male individuation as well as continued share in the coparcenary. As Agnes points out, while a space was carved for men's individual property rights within the joint family, *'stridhan'* for women was rolled back (*State, Gender*, p. 191). For a discussion of some of the gaps between male and female individuation, see Kumkum Sangari, 'The Amenities of Domestic Life: Questions on Labour', *Social Scientist*, 21:9–11 Sept.–Nov. 1993, p. 20.

37. Prasher, p. 249.

38. For discriminatory and patrilineal forms in devolution and tenancy

rights in agricultural land, as well the variations in these in each state and in specific personal laws, see Agarwal, pp. A39, 43–5, 51–2.

39. Legal compartmentalization simultaneously reflects and assists a wider process of class differentiation by devaluing or excluding certain categories of women's labour from 'work'. See Sangari, 'The Amenities', pp. 2–3, 11–20.

40. The conception of the family as private and beyond the appropriate intervention of the law has been an important dimension of legal reinforcement of women's subordination; it has been used to insulate from legal review the discrimination women face within the family (Ratna Kapur and Brenda Cossman, 'On Women, Equality and the Constitution: Through the Looking Glass of Feminism', *National Law School Journal*, I, 1993, p. 56).

41. See Kumkum Sangari, 'Relating Histories: Definitions of Literacy, Literature, Gender in Early Nineteenth Century Calcutta and England', in *Rethinking English*, Svati Joshi (ed.), Trianka, Delhi, 1991, pp. 39, 50–8.

42. Sangari, 'Perpetuating the Myth', p. 30.

43. Prasher, pp. 72–3.

44. Prasher, p. 76.

45. Personal laws were a compound of custom, statute, usage, and case law (Bhattacharji, p. 68). For the transformatory effects of case law, see Bernard S. Cohn, 'Law and the Colonial State in India' in History and Power in the Study of Law: New Directions in Legal Anthropology, June Starr and Jane F. Collier (ed.), Cornell University Press, Ithaca, 1989.

46. Prasher, pp. 272, 99–100. The Anti-Hindu Code Committee headed by Swami Karpatri was claiming that only pandits could sanction change (Latif in *Foreign Identities*, p. 49).

47. For instance of Punjab, which had till then been under customary law. For details of these provisions, see Prasher, pp. 102–3, 108.

48. Article 25 says that the right to freedom of religion must include the right not to believe in any religion and even to be entirely atheistic.

49. The 1891 Census of the North-Western Provinces, faced with the amorphousness or syncretism of lower caste and class popular religions, eventually classified 'Hindus' by 'striking out the members of fairly recognizable religions' such as Islam and Christianity and calling 'everyone else a Hindu' (Crooke, pp. 240–2). The further expansion of the term Hinduism, both backwards in time and by assimilating more and more sects occurred in the early twentieth century and bestowed a spurious unity (Heinrich von Stietencron, 'Hinduism: On the Proper Use of a Deceptive Term', in *Hinduism Reconsidered*, Gunther D. Sontheimer and Hermann Kulke (eds), Manohar, Delhi, 1991, pp. 13–16. Even Gandhi, who believed in communal harmony had opposed conversion to non-Hindu faiths (Forrester, p. 82).

50. Prasher, p. 104, In fact this legal definition of the Hindu was further extended, in order to protect *male* coparcenary rights, to those Hindus not married under Hindu personal law by the 1976 amendment of the Special Marriages Act.

51. Veer Savarkar of the Hindu Mahasabha, who hated conversions of Hindus, wanted national definition of a Hindu that could embrace Sanatani, Sikh, Brahmo, and Arya Samaji and argued for a 'racial and cultural unity' (Dhananjay Keer), *Savarkar and His Times*, A.V. Keer, Bombay, 1950, pp. 130, 230.

52. Prasher, p. 109; Kishwar, p. 2163.

53. The Hindu Code bill imposed patrilineal inheritance on many groups that did not practice it. As it was designed to bring about a unity of Hindus through legal uniformity, it overrode textual and customary laws of practices even when they were beneficial to women (Kishwar, p. 2152, 2158, 2163). The rights of Jain women to hold property absolutely (Prasher, p. 120) would now get watered down by the testamentary provision. For its other gender injustices see Prasher, pp. 118–19, 128–9.

54. Customs relating to ceremonies of marriage, to prohibited relationships, and to customary divorces were saved and could continue to be operative, but no explanation was provided (Prasher, pp. 109, 111).

55. The coparcenary clauses of the Hindu Code bill would chiefly be applicable only to upper caste/class Hindus, since as Jack Goody points out, the prolonged association of upper groups was with 'joint undivided families' and of the poor with stem households (*The Ancient, the Oriental and the Primitive*, Cambridge University Press, Cambridge, 1990, p. 475).

56. Prasher, p. 109; Derrett, *Religion, Law*, pp. 357–8.

57. Bhattacharji, p. 32.

58. Bhattacharji, p. 26; Lateef in *Forging Identities* p. 43, 45; Chhachhi in ibid. p. 82; Maitrayee Mukhopadhyay, 'Between Community and State: the Question of Women's Rights and Personal Laws', in ibid., p. 111; Prasher, pp. 147–8: it did not apply to agricultural land, 99 per cent of all property (ibid., p. 148).

59. The Act had adverse effect on women in matrilineal communities (Agarwal. P. A52). Significantly, M.S. Aney opposed the bill on the ground that it would constitute a barrier between Hindus and Muslims who interacted at many levels (Lateef in *Forging Identities*, p. 44).

60. Such an option existed in Cutchi Memons Act of 1920. See Prasher, pp. 146–8, 150; Bhattacharji, p. 26; Shahida Lateef, *Muslim Women in India: Political and Private Realities*, Kali, Delhi, 1990, pp. 70–1.

61. Lateef; *Muslim Women*, p. 71.

62. Prashar, p. 155.

63. John L. Esposito, *Women in Muslim Family Law*, Syracuse, New York, Syracuse University Press, 1982, p. 81; Prasher, p. 151; Chhachhi in *Forging Identities*, p. 82.

64. Judges had used Muslim personal law in the event of conversion by a non-Muslim wife to Islam to release her from a bad marriage as well as to release a Muslim woman from a marriage she loathed by converting *from* Islam (Bhattacharji, pp. 86–7, 90–1).

65. *Ram Kumari*, 1991, Calcutta, 244; *Budansa* vs *Fatima* 1914 IC 697 MHC; *Nandi Zainab* vs *the Crown* ILR 1920 Lahore 440; *Robasa Khanum* vs *Khodadad Bomaji Irani* 1946 BLR 864 and AIR 1947 Bom. 272.

66. Significantly, Muslim personal law was not applied to this case because both parties were not Muslims, but the same reasoning was not extended to Parsi personal law, in effect, the husband's personal law predominated. They entered into a solemn pact that the marriage could be monogamous and could only be dissolved according to the tenets of the Zoroastrian religion. It would be patently contrary to justice and right that one party to solemn pact should be allowed to repudiate it as a unilateral act. It would be tantamount to permitting the wife to force a divorce upon her husband although he may not want it and although the marriage vows which both of them have taken, would not permit it. (Bhattacharji, p. 88).

67. Most recently expressed by S.P. Sathe who argues for a reform of different laws for different communities from the standpoint of uniform principles of gender justice, equality of sexes, and liberty of the individual: 'such uniformity can sustain the diversity of the laws', 'Uniform Civil Code: Implications of Supreme Court Intervention', *EPW*, 30: 35, 2 Sept. 1995.

9

Community Formation and Communal Conflict
Namasudra–Muslim Riot in Jessore–Khulna*

Sekhar Bandyopadhyay

Introduction

Community-consciousness eventually leading to communal conflicts in India has so far been explained either in terms of class–community continuum or of the inherent religiosity of the people in a traditional society, élite manipulation or the lack of it adding another dimension to such interpretative models. This chapter only seeks to emphasize that there were also some other important social imperatives behind such community formation and communal violence. I argue that for the submerged groups collective action was often necessary to establish their self-image or to assert their self-respect, and in so doing, to defy the accepted norms of reverence that had hitherto subjected

* *Economic and Political Weekly*, vol. xxv, no. 46, 17 Nov. 1990.

This is an enlarged version of a paper presented at the 50th Session of the Indian History Congress at Gorakhpur University. I am indebted to Professor Barun De for his valuable comments on the earlier draft of the essay.

them to social humiliation. Such attempts at self-affirmation required the breaking of the barriers of defence that involved them in frictions, both violent and non-violent, with those who were used to being revered. Such conflicts further strengthened the exclusivist ethos of a community by identifying and distinguishing its members from the others. The lines of demarcation between the communities were thus more sharply drawn, separating 'we' from 'they' in definite numerical terms. Religious or caste identities certainly provided the primary basis for such community formation, as these were the most important elements of peasant culture, and were for them the most convenient reference categories. This process however had other dimensions too: religion was not the be all and end all of community consciousness or communal conflict, nor did such communal alignments always run along class lines. Community consciousness, even if temporarily or in moments of conflict, both divided the classes and also cut across the class barriers.

The riot reviewed here is an excellent illustration of these various aspects of this particular social process. It occurred in May 1911 in the interior villages of the districts of Jessore and Khulna in the then presidency division of Bengal (now in Bangladesh) and involved the two most articulate peasant communities of rural east Bengal, Muslims and Namasudras. The story has been reconstructed primarily from a police file that contains a very perceptive report by the famous Gurusaday Dutta, who was then the magistrate of Khulna. Though it essentially reflects an official perspective, it also provides valuable insights into the 'feelings' of the people involved in the afray. In addition, the events of the riot narrated in other relevant police file, when placed in proper context, also reveal some important social dimensions of the process of community-formation in the Bengal countryside.

Background

The shaping of the Bengali Muslim community during the nineteenth and the early twentieth centuries is by now a well known story.[1] Alongside them, another community was also gradually defining itself almost in the same way and during the same period, the Namasudras, an *antyaja* (low-born) peasant caste of eastern Bengal. Known as Chandals till the late nineteenth century, they constituted the largest segment of the Hindu agricultural population in the region. They resided largely in the marshy tracts of Faridpur, Bakarganj, and the adjacent parts of Jessore and Khulna districts. From an amphibious existence as boatmen and fishermen, they emerged as a settled peasant community by taking advantage of the land reclamations of the nineteenth century. However, these areas where they tilled the soil together with Muslims, the land was owned by high caste Hindus and higher class Muslims. Consequently, in their case, their low ritual rank by and large coincided with their subordinate class position. The community was not however economically homogeneous; a tiny minority among them had bettered their economic conditions at the turn of the century through landholding, education and professions, but due to their lack of numerical strength and low ritual status they were unable to evolve a separate social identity for themselves and effectively remained tied to the peasant community. They did however now feel all the more bitterly about the social humiliation associated with their low ritual rank. This led to the beginning, in the late nineteenth century, of an articulate caste movement with a demand for better social treatment and eradication of the existing disabilities. Later, the emergence of a protestant Vaishnava relgious sect called Matwa, with its headquarters at Orakhandi in Faridpur, lent further cohesion to the community. Both its preceptors and followers belonged to the same community and as the high caste Vaishnavas refused to have any social interaction with them, the latter acquired a greater sense of group solidarity. '*Jar dal nei tar bal nei*' (those who do not form a group do not have power) was one of the principal teachings of its guru to his disciples. This essentially conveyed the message of community-formation for collective action. The process was apparently completed by 1905, when the Namasudras emerged as a well-knit community in east Bengal, opposing almost in a body the *swadeshi* movement, which they considered to be an exclusive concern of the high caste Hindu gentry who denied them social rights.[2]

Thus, in course of the nineteenth and the early twentieth centuries an articulate community consciousness had developed both among the Bengali Muslims and the Namasudras. Two large compact bodies of people, both zealous about the honour of their communities, were thus living side by side. Each considered themselves to be superior and the slightest offence to any member was regarded as an affront to the entire community demanding immediate redress. Consequently, a series of riots occurred between the two communities over apparently petty issues from 1889 in widely scattered locations in the districts of Faridpur, Bakarganj, Mymensingh, Sylhet, Jessore, and

Khulna. On virtually every occasion huge rioting mobs were mobilized at shortest possible notice and their number on each side ranged
up to 5000 to 10,000.[3] This notwithstanding the occasional alliances
between their leaders on political issues, such as opposition to the
nationalist movement which both these communities considered to
be against their community-centric interests.

Riot of May 1911

The worst riots between the Muslims and the Namsudras of east
Bengal took place in May 1911 in the border areas of the districts of
Jessore and Khulna. The region was notorious for land disputes
leading to violent riots[4] and the immediate occasion of that under
discussion too was a dispute over the possession of a piece of land.
There was however a long background of complicated antecedents,
leading to mounting excitement, that eventually poured forth into a
fierce riot over a petty land dispute between two individuals from the
two communities.

Indeed first half of the year 1911 witnessed a series of riots in a
contiguous region around the Jessore–Khulna border, where the
Muslims and Namasudras lived side by side. The first of these riots
took place in village Nalichar (or Nalerchak) in Khulna in January
1911, when a Muslim seized some cattle belonging to a Namasudra,
for damaging his crops. Although the cattle were rescued, this was
considered by the Namasudras to be an insult, and to avenge it, about
400 to 500 Namasudras attacked this Muslim village. The Muslims in
panic set fire to a small hut, believing that the fear of being accused of
arson would cause the Namasudras to desist. The latter however
saw through the ruse and set fire to the other houses and looted them
as well. Specific complaints were received against 45 Namasudras,
of whom 12 were committed to the sessions. During March–April
that year, three more cases of riot between the two communities were
reported from Mallahat, Paikgacha, and Magura police stations of
Khulna, and all of these related to similar petty issues,[5] but none
appears to have had any far-reaching impact except the Nalichar
case.

In that case, the 12 accused Namasudras were defended by 'a
barrister from Calcutta', and the contradictions in the evidence of the
prosecution witnesses had led to their acquittal by a jury which
included two Muslims. The judgment was announced on 13 May
1911 and the news spread rapidly through the Muslim villages in the

area. The sense of resentment and revenge deepened, but no immediate action was taken by the Muslims until the matter once again came to a head brought about by the Namasudras themselves in a village called Barnal (also called Chandinagar) in Kalia police station in Jessor, about eight or nine miles away from Nalichar.[6]

A Namasudra of Barnal, Kutiswar Mandal, had been in possession of a considerable tract of land, measuring about 170 bighas in that village, rented from the Hatberia Kayastha zamindar. In Bhadra vs 1314 (August–September 1907) the land was sold in auction for arrears of rent and was settled in 1908 by some Muslims of the same village. Abdur Sardar and Krishna Mandal Tikadar, Kutiswar went to court to have the sale set aside but in April or May 1910, Abdur was finally given possession of the land. Nothing further happened till the time came to harvest the *boro* paddy (winter crop) in May 1911. It appears that the wholesale acquittal of the Namasudras in Nalichar's riot case on 13 May had given rise to a spirit of jubilation and hauteur among the Namasudras in Khulna and Jessore villages. On 6 May Kutiswar, with the help of a number of Namasudras, harvested the paddy of one portion of the disputed land. On 18 May Abdur in turn, collected some Muslims, recovered the paddy from Kutiswar's possession, and looted his house. This enraged the Namasudras who began to gather a force from Sachidah, Kamarul, and Patla, the three Namasudra villages near Nalichar, while Abdur also sent word to the Muslims in the neighbouring villages to join him. That afternoon, the Muslims looted about 17 Namasudra houses in Chandinagar and the following morning the Namasudras had their revenge by looting 34 Muslim houses including Abdur Sardar's in Chandinagar and 24 houses in the neighbouring villages of Bildhuria, Pilpanagar, and Kunjapur in Jessore.[7]

Rumours about these Namasudra rampages spread like wildfire through the Muslim villages, as Muslim messengers on horseback were sent to the north and east to spread the alarm 'the Namasudras were coming'. An influential local Muslim, Dudu Mia, the panchayat president of Kalabaria, also lent his support in mobilizing Muslims, who gathered with surprising rapidity, not only from the neighbouring villages of Jessore and Khulna, but also from two or three villages across the river Madhumati in other Faridpur district. By the afternoon of the 19th, the Muslims had gathered in overwhelming numbers, estimated from 2000 to 5000, and from this time onward they had it all their own way. From about 2 p.m. they started looting Namasudra houses: 17 in Porekhali, 19 in Khamar, and seven in

Ghanashyampur. The attack was specially fierce at Khamar where some resistance was offered by Nabakrishna Biswas, the headman and the wealthiest of the Namasudras in the region. The looting spree continued into the next day and the Namasudras in panic started leaving their villages with their women, children, and valuables.[8]

The rioting mob was, however, continuously chased by the sub-inspector of Kalia and the deputy collector, Sukesh Chandra Deb Roy. The appearance of the latter on horseback and in a sola topi (the prerogative of sahibs) gave rise to the impression that the superintendent of police had arrived, and this probably prevented the Muslims from advancing further north to Kalia. Meanwhile the magistrate of Jessore and the two superintendents of police of Khulna and Jessore arrived with the armed police, putting a stop to rioting in the afternoon of 20 May.[9]

The disturbances had thus lasted for three days and 13 villages in Jessore and five in Khulna were attacked. There were two confirmed and three unconfirmed deaths; six Namasudras and seven Muslims were injured more or less seriously. The loss of property in terms of its monetary value was not that significant as the Namasudra villagers did not own much valuable property to be looted.[10] In most cases, the damage was confined to the destruction of huts and broken household utensils such as earthen pots and pans. There were a few cases of arson and only in one instance was a Namasudra girl carried off and raped by a Muslim.[11]

The situation, however, remained tense for a few more days and as a precautionary measure, the government mobilized a contingent of military police,[12] alerting too the military authorities at Fort William.[13] Finally a punitive police force was posted in the disturbed areas for a period of a year.[16] Chandra Sekhar Kar, deputy magistrate of Nadia, was appointed as special magistrate to 'give his undivided attention to the cases' relating to this riot.[15] Later, B.N. Mukherjee replaced him in this position and as a result of their exertions, by December 1911, 17 cases (out of 20) were disposed of, in which 201 persons were convicted, 22 persons were acquitted, and 15 were discharged out of the 270 sent for trial.[16]

Some Special Features

The location of the riot of May 1911 had some special features. The area that had been directly affected comprised the southern part of the jurisdiction of the Kalia police station in Jessore and the adjoining northern part of the area falling under Sadar police station in Khulna district. The rioters assembled, however, from wider region of about 100 square miles in Jessore and five square miles in Khulna district.[17] There were a number of purely Namasudra villages both to the extreme east and to the extreme west of this region. Between these two Namasudra centres and to the north and south, there were a large number of villages inhabited by a mixed population of Namasudras and Muslims. Being conscious of their superior number in their own localities, the Namasudras took the offensive and turned a petty personal quarrel into a communal issue.[18] However, in the region as a whole particularly the jurisdiction of Kalia police station, Muslims outnumbered them by about 50 per cent.[19] Hence the situation soon got out of their control and they found themselves on the defensive.

More significantly, however, there were some other villages in the region which were inhabited by other Hindu castes and these people neither participated in, nor were affected by, the disturbances. This particular feature distinguished this riot of May 1911 from the ordinary genre of Hindu-Muslim riots and gave it the character of a Namasudras–Muslim riot per se. The members of various other Hindu castes, living in the area, being concerned about the safety of their homes consulted the local Muslims and were instructed by the latter to put up flags to distinguish them. Different castes adopted more or less distinctive flags or articles readily available. The Jalias or fishermen tied pieces of nets to sticks in front of their houses. The Kapalis or gunnybag-makers hung pieces of jute. The Kayasthas and Kaibartas hoisted white rags, the Baisnabs saffron flags which they used in worship, and the Muchis (cobblers) put up pieces of skin.[20] All these distinctive flags were erected by the non-Namasudra Hindus either on 19 or 20 May as news began to spread of the advance of the Muslims, and none of these houses, barring that of only one Brahman, was attacked by the rioters and that too by mistake.[21]

Organization

All this speaks of a premediated plan. The sudden mobilization of a Muslim mob of about 4000 strong, marching 'in a regular file of four in each row',[22] is difficult to explain otherwise. Indeed, after the Nalichar occurrence, the Muslims held meetings in Kalabaria and Bowishana (Kalia police station) in Jessore, and in Atlia in Khulna police station. At these meetings the Nalichar outrage was described as a gross insult to their community and a decision was taken to form village committees to enable well-orchestrated action when the next contingency arose. All others, apart from the Muslims, were rigidly excluded from these meetings and hence, local inhabitants remained absolutely ignorant of this organization. Some leading Muslims of the area, like Dudu Mia, the panchayat president of Kalabaria and Hatem Moulavi, the panchayat president of Atlia, were actively involved in such organizational drives. When the police received information about these meetings and enquired about them, they were assured by Dudu Mia that they were merely for discussion of religious and educational matters. No further precaution was, therefore, taken against any possible disturbance.[23] Jitendranath Ray, the Hatberia zamindar, and his men also failed to take prompt action to control the Muslim rioters who had assembled in their villages. It might have been possible, as some of the local people suspected, that they were themselves interested in such a riot to put a stop to the refractory nature of their Namasudra raiyats who had fought with them so long over the possession of the disputed *ganthi*.[24] There was also a rumour that the *naib* of the Hatberia zamindar, Kalibar Ghose, had himself brought the Muslims to punish Kuteswar Mandal. This because, while there was still a case pending between the latter and the Hatberia zamindar to set aside the sale of the land in dispute, the *naib* had settled the land with Abdur Sardar, 'a leading Muhammadan' who had 'a very bad reputation' in the neighbourhood.[25] Under the circumstances, it may seem quite possible, that the riot was contrived, though eventually it went out of control. It should however also be borne in mind, that this case alone hardly explains the rapid mobilization of so many Muslims coming from such a wide area. Furthermore later enquiries revealed, that the zamindar and his men had no inkling that such an occurrence was imminent. They provided information to the police as soon as they learnt of the riots, although this was after the police had already received information.[26] But then, no one had any prior information.[27]

Consciousness

The situation, therefore, brings us to the question of consciousness. 'The hatred', as the district magistrate of Jessore rightly comprehended, was 'due to feeling rather than to material matters'. In this part of the country, cultivation was almost entirely in the hands of Muslims and Namasudras, to the exclusion of other castes. The rise in prices and comparatively low rents made them relatively prosperous which imbued them with a spirit of independence and self-respect.[28] The waves of the new social movement started among the Namasudras at Orakandi in Faridpur had reached the Jessore–Khulna villages much earlier, to encourage the local Namasudras to claim a higher social status. Although, newspapers generally did not find their way into this affected area, a copy of a Namasudra paper of Faridpur, *Namasudra Suhrid*, which ventilated the grievances of the Namasudras, was found here.[29] It was 'an undoubted fact' that the Namasudras of this region had started regarding themselves a superior caste and were apt to adopt a contemptuous attitude towards the Muslims whom they looked down upon as an inferior community. Formerly, they used to work as servants of the other castes of Hindus and Muslims, making their ploughs and houses, thatching their huts and working for them as field labourers. Gradually, however, they gave up working for the Telis, Sundis, and other low caste Hindus. Occasionally, they combined to boycott the upper caste Hindus, like the Kayasthas. Now, they also refused to serve the Muslims, with the result that the latter had to employ immigrant and therefore, expensive labour. This naturally embittered the feelings between the two communities. This Namasudra sensitivity arising out of their newly acquired sense of pride added to this bitterness. Any supposed slight, however minor from a Muslim, to any member of their caste was taken as an insult to the caste as a whole, meriting immediate punishment. This naturally led to violent frictions particularly in centres where the Namasudras were predominant and Muslims in a minority.[30]

The Muslims for generations considered the Namasudras as an inferior people and the recent assertion of a higher status by them was naturally a cause of irritation. This lack of tolerance was amply revealed when a Khulna paper reprinted an article from a Muslim paper *Muhammadi*, violently criticizing a recent pronouncement of the Nadia pandits, that barbers might give their services to Namasudras. Although no copy of this paper was actually found in the affected area, this spirit of intolerance certainly pervaded the entire region. Moreover, during the previous two years, there had been repeated disturbances, in all of which the Namasudras were the aggressors. The Muslims retaliated with violence and were, except in the Nalichar case, successful. However, in all cases they suffered more than the Namasudras in the criminal proceedings that followed.[31] They, therefore, had ground for resentment and this was accentuated by the result of the Nalichar case in which, though greatly wronged, they failed to obtain satisfaction in the court. The Muslim sentiments were further hurt by the haughtiness of the Namasudras. While the Muslims were in a habit of using the abusive term *charal* while referring to the Namasudras, the latter also began to call them *nereys*.[32] Also, subsequent to the Nalichar judgment, the Namasudras allegedly 'gave several maunds of *batasha* (molasses candy) as *Harir-loot* (offerings to lord Hari) and fell upon any and every Muslim they met on the *hat* with repeated *Haribole* (enchantment of the name of the lord Hari)'. Consequently, when the Barnal incident took place, religious colour was deliberately lent to what was essentially a petty land dispute, by spreading exaggerated stories that a mosque had been destroyed and the Koran defiled by the Namasudra rioters. Lack of faith in the 'whimsical' court, coupled with this whipping up of religious sentiments naturally led to a violent counter-attack.[33] And the leading Muslims using their organizational networks coordinated this attack and some of them, like Hatem Modavi and Hotem Sheikh of Africa, were even seen directing the operations on horseback.[34]

Politicization

Although there is no evidence to suggest the involvement of any outside agent instigating the rioters, there was a good deal of politicization of the incident after it had already taken place. The Hindu press wasted no time in seizing this oppportunity to win over the Namasudras by supporting their causes and by condemning Muslim rowdyism. *Khulna Vasi* of 3 June 1911 reported that the Namasudras were 'robbed of all their possession by the Muslims'. The *Basumati* issue of the same day criticized the recent Muslim tendency to unite in a large body at the slightest provocation, and to oppress others.[35] The *Bengalee*, more balanced, lamented the fact that ignorant persons of both communities were so shortsighted that they forgot their obvious interests and took part in quarrels that could spell nothing but disaster for the country.[36] However, the most violent criticism of the Muslims appeared in a leading article in the *Amrita Bazaar Patrika* issue of 25 May 1911. Alleging that an inflammatory and 'filthily abusive' pamphlet entitled *The Cow and Hindu-Musalmani* had actually instigated the Muslims to attack the Namasudras and it might again cause further communal violence. Although the government sought to describe these riots as purely local in nature, and there was no evidence of this pamphlet having reached the Jessore–Khulna villages, the Hindu leaders constantly tried to tag it to the greater question of the Hindu-Muslim relationship, as Surendranath Banerjee saw in them 'further evidence of the baneful effects of the partition'.[37]

The Muslims of Jessore and Khulna, on the other hand, perturbed by such 'false' and 'exaggerated' reports in the Hindu press, appealed to the Nawab Bahadur of Dacca to represent their case to the government. In Particular, they wanted the enquiries to be conducted by 'impartial officers', 'either Mahommadan or European'.[38] Nawab Salimullah conveyed the prayer to the government, reiterating his 'implicit faith in the British administration of justice'.[39] The government however, refused to entertain it, as a special officer had already been deputed and there was no reason to suppose that he would fail to try the cases with care and scrupulous fairness.[40] However, the controversial pamphlet was forfeited in June 1911 under the Indian Press Act,[41] and subsequently the enthusiasm and interests of the politicians seemed to wane rapidly.

Conclusion

The riot under review therefore appears to have been caused by a court decision and a petty land dispute, each violating, in two different ways, the collective sense of justice of the two communities. Only subsequently was their dispute given a particular religious colour and even subsequently this purely localized conflict was politicized and made to appear to be part of a wider provincial politics. Yet, the riot was preceded and followed by an intense feeling of communal exclusivism, if not direct antipathy, on the part of the two large peasant bodies. This conflict, like many other similar conflicts before and after, was thus an important part of the process of the formation of the two communities. Hence, in order to put this riot into proper perspective, it needs to be placed within the overall history of the Namasudra–Muslim relationship in eastern Bengal.

This particular riot was in the first place not an isolated instance of confrontation between the two communities; it was indeed followed by other riots in 1923–5 and 1938, over identical issues and sentiments.[42] However, at the same time there were also instances of active cooperation between the two communities and such alliances were formed usually against the high caste Hindu gentry who were always up in the local power structure and were therefore considered by both of them to be agents of oppression, both economic and social. The two communities therefore sometimes joined hands against their landlords to press their demand for large share of the produce of the sharecroppers.[43] Often such alliances were on social issues, such as armed Muslims supporting the Namasudra's right to perform Bhawanipuja in a public rostrum erected by the Brahmans and the Kayasthas.[44] Occasionally they also combined to organize social boycott of the higher castes, sometimes refraining from accepting menial jobs and occasionally also refusing to till their lands.[45] At the political level, the alliance between the two communities on a separatist line had been formed during the days of the anti-Partition agitation and it continued till about the end of the 1930s. During this period only once were they in opposing political camps, that is, during the Khilafat movement, and this precipitated a series of violent frictions between the two communities over a large area in the districts of Faridpur and Bakarganj.[46]

The relationship between the two communities in eastern Bengal had thus taken a complex and criss-cross course. There was however one common thread that could bind all these varied situation into one composite frame, and that was the persistent urge, on the part of both the communities, including their wealthy influential leaders to affirm their newly found self-respect. In order to achieve the goal of self-affirmation they used various symbols, both verbal and non-verbal. This amounted to a violation of the existing norms of reverent behaviour and led to frictions with various groups in different situations. Thus, in order to vindicate the honour of their communities, the Muslims and the Namasudras sometimes fought among themselves, sometime combined to fight their common adversaries, and sometimes also challenged the colonial state when it sought to intervene to maintain the status quo. It is difficult to explain all these various forms of conflict either in terms of religious animosity or of economic motivation. Such factors were certainly involved, but there was also something else that we should not totally overlook.

Notes

1. For the story of the formation of the Bengali Muslim community, see Rafiuddn Ahmed, *The Bengal Muslims, 1871–1906: A Quest for Identity*, Delhi, 1981; Partha Chatterji, *Bengal 1920–1947: The Land Question*, Calcutta, 1984: Suranjan Das, *Communal Riots in Bengal 1905–1947*, Oxford University D Phil Thesis, 1987.

2. For details, see Sekhar Bandyopadhyay, 'Social Protest or Politics of Backwardness? The Namasudra Movement in Bengal, 1872–1911' in Basudeb Chattopadhyay et al (ed.), *Dissent and Consensus: Social Protest in Pre-Industrial Societies,* Calcutta, 1989, pp. 170–232; also see, *Matwa Mahasangher Laksha O Karmasuchi* (in Bengali), (2nd edn, Thakurnagar, vs 1394, p. 4.

3. District magistrate, Jessore to commissioner, presidency division, 2 June 1911,GB, Political (police), File no. P5R-1, B July 1911, Prog. nos 3268, West Bengal State Archives (hereafter WBSA).

4. Commissioner, Presidency division, to chief secretary, GB 24 January 1899, GB, Judicial (Police), April 1899, Prog. no. 25, WBSA.

5. G.S. Dutt, magistrate of Khulna, to commissioner presidency division, 5 June 1911, GB political (police), File no. PSR-1, B July 1911, Prog. nos 3268, WBSA.

6. 'Note on Musalman Namasudra disturbance on the Khulna–Jessore Border', by G.S. Dutt, officiating magistrate–collector 22 May 1911, GB, Political (Police), File no. F5R-1, B July 1911, Prog. nos 293–322, WBSA.

7. J.H. Lindsay, district magistrate, Jessore, to commissioner, presidency division 2 June 1911, GB, Political (Police), File no. P5R-1, B July 1911, Prog. nos 326–8, WBSA; G.S. Dutt, magistrate of Khulna, to commissioner, presidency division, 5 June 1911, op cit.

8. Ibid.

9. E.W. Colin, commissioner, presidency division, to chief secretary GB 9 June 1911, GB, Political (Police), File no. P5R-1, B July 1911, Prog. nos 326–8, WBSA.

10. Ibid.

11. C.J. Stevenson-Moore, chief secretary, GB to secretary, GI, home department, 29 May 1911, GB, Political (Police), File no. P5R-1, B July 1911, Prog. nos 293–322, WBSA.

12. G.S. Dutt, magistrate of Khulna, to commissioner, presidency division, 5 June 1911, op cit.; E.W. Collin, Commissioner, presidency division to chief secretary, GB, 9 June 1911, op cit.

13. E.W. Collin, commissioner, presidency division, to chief secretary, GB, 24 May 1911, GB, Political (Police), File no. PSR-1, B July 1911, Prog. nos 293–322, WBSA.

14. E.W. Collin, commissioner, presidency division, to chief secretary, GB, 9 June 1911, op cit; also E.W. Collin, commissioner, presidency division, to chief secretary, GB, 27 Nov. 1911, GB, Political (Police), File no. P5R-1, B July 1911, Prog. nos 326–8, WBSA.

15. E.W. Collin, commissioner, presidency division, to F.W. Duke, member (judicial), lieutenant governor's council 26 June 1911; also F.W. Duke to commissioner, presidency division, 1 July 1911, GB, Political (Police), File no. P5R-1, B July 1911, Prog. nos 323–5, WBSA.

16. E.W. Collin, commissioner, presidency division, to chief secretary, GB, 27 Nov. 1911, op cit; B.N. Mukherjee, special magistrate, to this district

COMMUNITY FORMATION AND COMMUNAL CONFLICT   227

magistrate, Jessore, 22 December 1911, GB, Political (Police), File no. P3P-34, B Feb. 1912, Prog. nos 43–8, WBSA.

17. E.W. Collin, commissioner, presidency division, to chief secretary, GB, 9 June 1911, op cit.

18. G.S. Dutt, magistrate of Khulna, to commissioner, presidency division, 5 June 1911, op cit.

19. E.W. Collin, commissioner, presidency division, to chief secretary, GB, 27 May 1911, GB, Political (Police), File no. P5R-1, B July 1911, Prog. nos 293–322, WBSA.

20. G.S. Dutt, magistrate of Khulna, to commissioner, presidency division, 5 June 1911, op cit.

21. L.F. Morschead, IG of Police, LP, to chief secretary, GB, Sept. 1911, GB, Political (Police), File no. P3P-34, B Feb. 1912, Prog. nos 43–8, WBSA.

22. Report by Sukesh Chandra Deb Roy, deputy magistrate, submitted to the magistrate of Jessore, GB, Political (Police), File no. P5R-1911, Prog. nos 293–322, WBSA.

23. J.H. Lindsay, magistrate of Jessore, to commissioner, presidency division 9 Sept. GB, Political (Police), File no. 3P-34, B Feb. 1912, Prog. nos 43–8, WBSA; also G.S. Dutt, magistrate of Khulna, to commissioner, presidency division, 5 June 1911, op cit.

24. Report by Sukesh Chandra Deb Roy, deputy magistrate, submitted to magistrate of Jessore, op cit.

25. J.H. Lindsay, district magistrate, Jessore, to commissioner, presidency division 2 June 1911, op cit.

26. G.S. Dutt, magistrate of Khulna, to commissioner, presidency division, 4 Sept. 1911, GB, Political (Police), File no. 3P-34, B Feb. 1912, Prog. nos 43–8.

27. J.H. Lindsay, magistrate of Jessore, to commissioner, presidency division 9 Sept. 1911, op cit.

28. J.H. Lindsay, magistrate of Jessore, to commissioner, presidency division 2 Jun 1911, op cit.

29. E.W. Collin, commissioner, presidency division, to chief secretary, GB, 9 June 1911, op cit.

30. G.S. Dutt, magistrate of Khulna, to commissioner, presidency division, 5 June 1911, op cit.

31. E.W. Collin, commissioner, presidency division, to chief secretary, GB, 9 June 1911, op cit.

32. G.S. Dutt, magistrate of Khulna, to commissioner, presidency division, 5 June 1911, op cit.

33. To the Honourable Nawab Bahadur of Dacca, the humble petition of the oppressed Muhammadans of Jessore and Khulna, 20 June 1911, GB, Political (Police), File no. P5R-34, B July 1911, Prog. nos 326–8, WBSA.

34. Third report on Khulna Namasudra–Muhomedan rioting case by J.C. Farmer, 23 May 1911, GB, Political (Police), File no. P5R-1, B July 1911, Prog. nos 326–8, WBSA.

228 COMMUNAL IDENTITY IN INDIA

35. Report on Native Papers in Bengal for the week ending 10 June 1911.

36. *Bengalee*, 26 May 1911.

37. Weekly Report of the Director of Criminal Intelligence, 30 May 1911, GI, Home (Political), B June 1911, Prog. no. 3. National Archives of India (hereafter NAI).

38. To the Honourable Nawab Bahadur of Dacca, the humble petition of the oppressed Muhammadans of Jessore and Khulna, 20 June 1911, op cit.

39. Nawab Sir Salimolla Bahadur, Dacca, to chief secretary, GB, 1 July 1911, GB, Political (Police), File no. P5R-1, B July 1911, Prog. nos 326–8, WBSA.

40. C.J. Stevenson-Moore to, chief secretary, GB, 1 July 1911, GB, Political (Police), File no. P5R-1, B July 1911, Prog. nos 326–8, WBSA.

41. Weekly Report of the Director of Criminal Intelligence, 13 June 1911, Prog. no. 2, NAI.

42. District magistrate, Faridpur, to commissioner, Dacca division, 21 May 1923, GB, Police, File no. P5R-11/23, B May 1924, Prog. nos 110–49; superintendent of police to assistant IG of police, Bengal 23 July 1925, GB Police, File no. P5R-2(4–12)/25, B March 1926, Prog. nos 95–103, Home (Confidential), File no. 248/38, WBSA.

43. Commissioner, presidency division, to chief secretary, GB 9 January 1929; magistrate of Jessore to commissioner, presidency division, 2 Jan. 1929, GB. Appointment file no. 5M–114 of 1928, Feb. 1930, Prog. nos 7–20, WBSA; also see, Tanika Sarkar, *Bengal 1928–1934: The Politics of Protest* (Delhi, 1987), pp. 38–41.

44. Magistrate to Khulna to commissioner, presidency division, 5 June 1911, GB, Political (Police), File no. P5R-1, B July 1911, Prog. nos 336–8, WBSA.

45. Weekly Report of the Director of Criminal Intelligence, 21 September 1907, GI, Home (Pol.), B Oct. 1907, Prog. no. 47 NAI; L.S.S. O'Malley, *Bengal District Gazetteers, Jessore*, Calcutta, 1912, p. 50.

46. District magistrate, Faridpur, to commissioner, Dacca division, 21 May 1923, GB, Police, File no. P5R-11/23, B May 1924, Prog. nos 110–49; superintendent of police to assistant IG of police, Bengal 23 July 1925, GB, Police, File no. P5R-2(4–12)/25, B March 1926, Prog. nos 95–103, Home (Confidential), File no. 248/38, WBSA.

Identity Politics of the 'Marginals'

10

Insiders and Outsiders in India
Primordial Collectivism and Cultural Pluralism in Nation-building*

T.K. Oommen

I

The emergence of industrial urbanism and welfare states in the First World gave birth to what is labelled 'liberal expectancy'. This implicitly presumed, if not explicitly postulated, that the ongoing process of modernization with its emphasis on meritocracy and achievement, social and spatial mobility, transport and communication revolutions facilitating interaction between socio–cultural collectivities, common system of education and mass media projecting the same set of values would eventually undermine the 'traditional' ties and values based on race, language, and religion. Similarly, the emergence of socialist states and industrial urbanism in the second world gave birth to a corresponding 'radical expectancy' hoping that the 'socialist man' would look upon class interest as the guiding principle of his social action, ignoring erstwhile identities based on religion, language and tribe. In the same vein, the ex-colonial countries of the third world latched their faith to the 'nationalist expectancy', the hope being that having fought the foreign imperial power, temporarily keeping their primordial collectivism in suspended animation,

* *International Sociology*, vol. 1, no. 1, March 1986.

the populace will work together for the realization of their common aspirations, namely, building nation-states.

It is clear, however, now that none of these expectancies have been realized and available empirical evidence suggests that the possibility of their being, in the way they were initially conceptualized, remains extremely bleak. If anything, we witness today an incessant search for 'roots' the world over, a quest that fosters primordial collectivism. It is not that the process of modernization did not leave its impact on pre-modern institutions and values but the expected displacement syndrome did not operate as was postulated. Faced with such a situation we often find that what was labelled as illegitimate or undesirable during the initial period of transition tend to get legitimized, indeed, come to be accepted as desirable at least in some contexts, as authentic expressions of popular aspirations. It is not that the same set of values and identities are accepted, acceptable, or even perceived as desirable in all nation-states; not that the strategy employed by the ruling élite or the state apparatus is the same in all the countries of the world; but a general thrust towards endorsing the primordial collectivisms as legitimate expressions of popular aspirations is clearly discernible. Which of these primordial collectivisms gets legitimized in a given nation-state depends upon its specific circumstances. One thing however is certain, and it is that no country has been successful in suppressing these tendencies or so far been indifferent to them.

If in Europe, empires dissolved into nation-states usually respecting the norm, 'one nation one state' (barring a few exceptions), the colonies by and large retained their 'multinational' character even when partitioned as in the case of India. Given this, the primary task of nation-building was to maintain and reinforce the nationalist expectancy, the content of which was threefold—political integration, economic development, and cultural pluralism. To the extent cultural pluralism is perceived to be an obstacle to the realization of the first two objectives, the situation is often described as one of national crisis, decay, and disintegration. This means that, paradoxically, it is the very nurturing of nationalities based on religion and language (the European variety) that is perceived to be the chief obstacle to nation-building in the countries of Asia and Africa. It is important to note that there is a big divide here between the cultural mainstream, the dominant nationality, which occupies the 'centre' and the dominated nationalities of the 'Periphery'. The 'communalism' of the dominant collectivity is perceived, defined, and legitimized as 'nationalism'.

It is the sole privilege of the peripheral communities to be stigmatized as 'communal'. Indeed, their assertion of primordial collectivism is stronger and visible precisely because it is more difficult to realize their 'national' aspirations. The point I want to make is this—the legitimate or the illegitimate is determined not simply by *what* is being defined, but *who* defines it.

The nationalist expectancy, it was believed, would desacralize primordial ties and partly it did, albeit temporarily. However, once the historicity of context changed, that is, with the disappearance of the alien ruler, we witness a re-sacralization of these primordial ties and the usual tendency of the mainstream is to view this with considerable alarm. I wish to suggest that this re-sacralization of primordial ties is partly an indication of the 'quest for community' and partly a response to the process of marginalization, actual or imaginary, the peripheral communities are threatened with. Why is it that primordial collectivism is more salient among those who occupy the periphery rather than the centre of the system? The quest for community is likely to crystallize more easily among the deprived, and deprivation is perceived not only in economic and political terms but also in terms of denial of one's cultural identity. Therefore, the persistent tendency to interpret the assertion of primordial collectivism exclusively in economic (class) or political (human rights) terms is naive and simplistic. The point is that the primordial collectivities located in the periphery perceive that they are denied economic and political rights precisely because of their subordination to the mainstream. To dismiss this perception as false consciousness is false.

The issues relating to primordial collectivism arise essentially in the context of cultural pluralism. Its ramifications, however, travel far beyond it, as I suggested above. Also, the two contexts in which the deprivations persist with considerable resilience are those of economy and polity. In all the three contexts, economic, politic, and cultural, the deprivations of the peripheral communities are aggravated insofar as the dominance of the mainstream is cumulative, that is, if and when it encapsulates all aspects of life. In such a situation a coercive equilibrium would exist, in which the dominated collectivities have little striking power and invariably accept their subordinate status, often pursuing a strategy of withdrawal. However, as and when the cumulative dominance, that is displaced by dispersed dominance, that is dominance in one or another context only, the tension between those at the centre and the periphery becomes visible and is articulated.

If the primordial collectivities of the periphery were only to insist on their right to practice and profess their religion or nurture and develop their language or preserve their styles of life, the problems would have remained largely manageable. When, however, they demand economic benefits and political rights on the basis of their group affiliation the situation dramatically changes. That is, the expression of primordial collectivism in instrumental terms would invariably aggravate the scope of conflicts. To complicate matters, the political parties and even the state apparatus respond to these demands, rationalizing their responses as compulsions of democratic polity and the welfare state even as they decry these demands as morally abhorrent and legally unsustainable. Thus, not only are the popular aspirations expressed in the idiom of primordial collectivism but official response is also geared to it.

It may be noted here that the expression of popular aspirations and the official responses are based on the same set of assumptions. These are: (a) that there are certain 'good things of life' which should be equitably distributed across primordial collectivities, (b) but there is differential accessibility to these among them and consequently there ensues a distributional imbalance, (c) to rectify these imbalances specific measures ought to be taken recognizing these collectivities as the beneficiaries of social policy. In this process the contradiction between the desired and desirable basis of distributive justice and the actual basis of it, namely membership in primordial collectivities, emerges. This in turn creates another problem, the hiatus between the desired basis of stratification, merit and achievement, and the operational basis of stratification: ascription. The latter often gains primacy because it provides a platform to simultaneously pursue instrumental goals *and* symbolic affinity unlike class associations which primarily promote material interests and ignore the emotional dimension. Thus, the goals pursued by primordial collectivities appear to be wholesome and are more appealing to the people. It is my contention that in independent India, primordial collectivism is pursued by the peripheral communities as a response to the twin process of expansionism and exclusivism, operated by some members of the mainstream collectively who define themselves as 'insiders' and label the collectivities of the periphery as 'outsiders'. Also, the state policy and apparatus too, by and large, perhaps unwittingly, reinforce this tendency.

Before I proceed further it is necessary to demarcate the specifics of the present discussion. It has already been hinted above that we can identify three dimensions of the mainstream—the economic, political, and cultural. If the three dimensions were coterminous, that is, the same set of social actors were present in all the three contexts, the resultant situation of cumulative domination and the consequent cumulative oppression operating through coercive equilibrium would have ensued. This, however is not the situation in India and consequently dispersed dominance and oppression come to obtain. This mismatch between the mainstreams of economy, polity, and culture produces continuing tensions in the Indian society, leading to protests and conflicts.

The real problem is that those at the 'centre' do not believe that the interests of the 'nation' are safe in the hands of those at the periphery. The hybrid economic mainstream of India, namely state-sponsored capitalism, does not trust either socialism or private capitalism. The political mainstream of India, the Congress party in its various incarnations, considers the peripheral political parties such as the National Conference of Kashmir, the CPI (M) of West Bengal, the Akali Dal of Punjub, the Telugu Desam of Andhra Pradesh, the Dravidian parties of Tamil Nadu etcetera as inauspicious omens for the nation state. Similarly, the twice-born Hindus,[2] inhabiting the Indo-Gangetic plain, the cultural mainstream, look upon the emergence of peripheral cultural nationalism with disapproval and disdain. In each of these contexts the mainstreamers are insiders and peripherals are outsiders.

Having thus specified the frame of reference I will confine my attention to the issues emanating out of cultural pluralism. The juxtaposition of insiders and outsiders and the processes of expansionism and exclusivism are all-pervasive in contemporary Indian society.[3] They operate in different contexts and levels; now they are visible and virulent, then they are subtle and submerged. Given this spread of the phenomenon, I shall rest content with discussing the issues in two contexts: religion and caste, and language and region.

II

Religious pluralism, an important ingredient of cultural pluralism in India, is well-known and ancient. Almost all the major religions of the world are professed here. One may categorize them into two—religions of Indian origin and religions of alien origin (for an elaboration, see Oommen, 1983: 92–133). Religions of Indian origin are three—Hinduism, the primal vision of the pre-Aryan indigenous people and the Hindu protestant religions. Although Hinduism is generally accepted as an indigenous Indian religion, it is well known that it came to India with the Aryan conquest and currently 83 per cent of the population is included in this category. According to the present official categorization, which I have termed the primal vision of India, the religions of the scheduled tribes (Adivasis) and the scheduled castes (Dalits), are included under the rubric Hinduism if they are not converts to other religions. It is doubtful whether both these collectivities profess Hinduism, and if given an opportunity they tend to declare that they are non-Hindus.

It may be noted here that from 1871 onwards, a religious category, designated 'primitive' appears in the Indian Census classifications. In 1901, those who belonged to this category constituted 2.92 per cent, which increased to 3.28 per cent by 1911, an increase of 20 per cent for the decade. After 1911, the term used was 'tribal' religion which accounted for 3.09 per cent in 1921 and 2.36 per cent in 1931. In 1951, free India's first census was taken and we do not come across the category of tribal religion at all. As it stands today, there are some 450 tribal communities with about fifty million members. They constitute around 7 per cent of India's total population. These people are fragmented into the 'world religions'—Hinduism, Islam, Christianity, and Buddhism. In the case of the latter three religions, it is possible for one to embrace them through 'conversion', whether real or ostensible, but no such mechanism exists in the case of Hinduism.

Ghurye (1943) argues that the scheduled tribes are just backward Hindus. N.K. Bose (1967) talks about the Hindu mode of absorbing the tribal people. Srinivas (1962) postulates that both the lower castes and tribal people attempt to move up the societal ladder by adopting the style of life, including religious rituals, of the upper castes. All these suggest that the tribal people are permanently relegated to the receiving end, constantly trying to enter or being inducted into the mainstream. It has been further argued that Hinduism is a way of life, and in order to be a Hindu one need not be a believer in Hindu doctrines. All religions have their ritual practices and postulate a style of life, but along with this one also has to believe in certain cardinal principles. To say that one need not believe in such principles of Hinduism and yet be a Hindu is just intellectual legerdemain. It facilitates the inclusion of a vast humanity which is actually non-Hindu into the Hindu fold. Small wonder then that no sociologist or social anthropologist has yet questioned the official definition of Adivasis and Dalits as Hindu. Indeed, mainstream social science in India has been in the service of mainstream society in India.

If Hindu expansionism is direct and obvious in the case of the primal vision of the pre-Aryan natives, it is circumspect and subtle in the case of Hindu protestant religions. Starting with the sixth century B.C., there have been numerous anti-Hindu (i.e. anti-Brahmanic) protest movements but only very few emerged as distinct religions while others finally led to the formation of Hindu 'sects'. The more distinct of these religions are Jainism, Buddhism and Sikhism. However, Hindu militants of all hues claim that these are mere extensions of Hinduism and they trace the rationale of their argument to the Hindu Code Bill and the Indian constitution, which treat the believers of all these religions as 'Hindus', The responses of the 'victims' vary—the Jains appear to be pursuing a strategy of reconciliation, the Buddhists one of indifference (except the neo-Buddhists, whose identity lies more in caste rather than in religious terms) and the Sikhs that of aggressive resistance. Not that all those who belong to these religious collectivities, Hindus, Jains, Buddhists, and Sikhs, behave or react in the same way but the response pattern noted above is clearly visible. On the one hand, it reveals the Hindu inclination to consider non-Hindus as Hindus and, on the other, the tendency of some to give up their identity (e.g. Jains) or to aggressively assert or over-emphasize it (e.g. Sikhs). None of the response patterns fosters authentic religious, and hence cultural, pluralism.

If Hinduism pursues the policy of expansionism in the case of Indian religions, its policy is one of exclusivism in the case of 'foreign' ones. There are two types of alien religions, Islam and Christianity, which are perceived as products of conquest and colonization, and the migrant religions, Jews, Zoroastrians and Bahais. The latter three religious collectivities are relatively small in size and the first two never attempted conversion in India and maintain their social insulation and 'ethnic' purity. This fits in well with the Hindu ethos, tolerance of alien faiths so that they do not indulge in proselytization. The Bahais did launch a conversion movement in the 1960s but quickly withdrew when the Arya Samaj intervened to frustrate it (Garlington, 1977: 101–18). Thus the two problem cases of foreign religions are Islam and Christianity.

Although pre-conquest Islam and pre-colonial Christianity existed in India, hardly anybody seems to acknowledge it, not even the intellectuals. This is not to deny that the bulk of Muslim and Christian conversions took place after conquest and colonization.

Nonetheless, to spotlight attention only on this is to castigate and stigmatize these religious collectivities and to thwart the authentic nature of Indian religious pluralism. More importantly, an over-whelming majority are converts from local castes and tribes, and hence natives of this country; only their religion is 'foreign'.

The people who belong to religions of foreign origin are perceived as lesser Indians. While this is publicly articulated only by a minority among Hindus, this appears to be the overall ethos. Beginning with the Arya Samaj and its *shuddhi* movement and ending with Vishwa Hindu Parishad and its recently concluded Hindu Ekatmata Yajna, this ethos has persisted for the past one century.[4] Two factors con-stantly invoked to stigmatize these religious collectivities are their propensity for conversion, and foreign missionary connections. As the first is a constitutionally guaranteed right, the usual tendency is to accuse them of using fraudulent means in conversion. While ad-equate administrative steps should be taken to prevent any action by these and other religious collectivities which go against the interest of the public at large, to stigmatize them as 'outsiders' goes against the very spirit of a plural society. That this is so in reality can be illus-trated by differential Hindu response to conversion depending upon the religion to which the conversion takes place.

Among the religions of Indian origin, Buddhism is missionary in nature and hence attempts proselytization. On 14 October 1956, Dr B.R. Ambedkar embraced Buddhism along with an estimated crowd of 300,000 to 600,000.[5] On 6 October 1981 the neo-Buddhists cel-ebrated the 25th anniversary of Ambedkar's *Diksha* and a crowd of 150,000 to 300,000 took to Buddhism on that day.[6] However, neither of these massive conversions disturbed the collective conscience of the nation. By contrast, when a few hundred persons converted to Islam in Meenakshipuram or to Christianity in Nagercoil (both in Tamil Nadu) not only did the Arya Samaj and/or the Vishwa Hindu Parishad immediately intervene with the *shuddhi* ceremony, but the collective conscience of the nation too seemed to be profusely bleed-ing. It is clear then that in the cognitive map and in the behavioural orientation of the Hindu majority the great divide between religions of Indian and alien origins persists.

From what I have said so far, it is clear that Hinduism simulta-neously practises expansionism in regard to other religions of Indian origin and exclusivism in the case of religions of alien origin. Para-doxically, however, the collectivities that are victims of these pro-cesses get marginalized in either case. If expansionism is assimilationist in its tenor, thereby denying specificity to the collectivities concerned, exclusivism systematically questions the very rootedness in Indian soil of the collectivities concerned.

For any discussion on Hinduism to be adequate, we have no option but to refer to the caste system. While, on the one hand, Hinduism is characterized by metaphysical tolerance, on the other, it is socially frozen through the institution of caste. Presently we are concerned with the process through which some of the caste collectivities are reckoned as constituting the 'centre' and others are consigned to the periphery of society. The Hindu theory of the origin of man clearly postulates a hierarchy in this context—the twice-born varna constituted the core with the Brahmin at the apex, the vast humanity of peasantry and artisans (the Shudras) in the middle, and those of the fifth order (the *panchamas*) were not even accounted for in the four-fold division and were thus obviously pushed to the lowest position. The theory and practice of ritual purity perfected to the finest detail constitute an immortal testimony to the Hindu genius for inclusion and exclusion.

The prevalent theories conceptualize the caste system as the product of Aryan conquest eventually pushing the indigenous Dravidian elements to the south, thereby leading to their localization. Pursuantly, it is suggested that the existing 'all-India' elements are derived from the Aryan–Brahmanic–Sanskritic sources, the Great Tradition. The 'little traditions' are mere localized cultural elements with scarcely any spatial spread, placed in a vertical relationship constantly emulating the élite norms and continually absorbing Brahmanic values. There is an enormous amount of writings of all hues reinforcing this view. Not only Hindu militants such as Bankim Chandra but incurable nationalists such as Mahatma Gandhi, perhaps unwittingly, reinforced this perspective. Social science writings are replete with rationalizations of this perspective; the concepts of little and great traditions, sanskritization etc., are only the more conspicuous and well known among these.[7] Perhaps what is evident in these efforts is to locate collectivities in vertical terms rather than placing them horizontally.

It could be argued, for instance, contrary to the current theorizations that there were two competing, parallel traditions, present throughout India as two live, interacting or counter traditions, one of the Aryan upper caste sanskritic and the other of Dravidian peasant non-sanskritic. If one were to accept it, the mainstream constituted by the twice-born caste-Hindus will not have primacy and cannot easily take over the 'burden' of protecting the national interests and be the precursor of India's collective conscience. To take over this burden, a vast humanity, comprising the peasantry, the artisans, the Dalits, the Adivasis and the Dravidians, not to speak of the religious minorities, will have to be marginalized. The efforts of the Dravidian movement to desacralize Rama and de-demonize Ravana should be seen as a protest against Vedic-Hinduism and Brahmin dominance. It is an effort to re-live the old parallel tradition and rehabilitate it to the centre from its present position in the periphery to which it was relegated.

In its eagerness to claim the *panchamas* into its fold, partly as a social reform measure and partly to stop the wave of conversions to alien religions, the Hindu orthodoxy has been showing some flexibility and adaptation. Latterly, there were instances of the Shankaracharyas of such orthodox temples as that at Puri, occasionally participating in public dining which untouchables also attend.[8] These overtures notwithstanding, it is doubtful if the Dalits actually consider themselves Hindus. Those who have done fieldwork in village India often report that the Dalits do not subscribe to the doctrine of Karma and reincarnation, an important tenet of Hinduism. Ambedkar's resolve to die a Buddhist should be seen in this context. The fact that the Dalits are treated as 'outsiders' is evident not only in the lowly status outside the fourfold varna scheme assigned to them and in the practice of untouchability but also in their residential segregation in Indian villages and, to an extent, in urban areas.

If the insider–outsider dichotomy were simply a matter of religious myth and folk-perception, perhaps it could have been gradually muted through social reforms and legislative measures. Unfortunately, however this dichotomy persists even in the policy measures adopted by the state. If an 'untouchable' converts into one of the religions of Indian origin he can by and large avail himself of the special benefits available to him under the policy of protective discrimination. Both Buddhism and Sikhism were revolts against the caste system and disapprove of untouchability. Yet, if a Dalit becomes a Sikh and lives in Punjab, he is eligible to claim all the benefits under the policy of protective discrimination. Similarly, Dalits from Maharashtra and Uttar Pradesh, even if they convert to Buddhism, can still claim some of the benefits. It is important to note that an overwhelming majority of Dalit converts to Sikhism and Buddhism live in the three states—Punjab, Maharashtra and Uttar Pradesh. In contrast, if a Dalit converts to any of the religions of alien origin, he forfeits all claims to special protection and even basic human rights (e.g. protection against the practice of untouchability). The state policy thus operates as a great obstacle against the constitutionally guaranteed right of professing any religion of one's choice. It has been argued that religions such as Christianity and Islam do not endorse the caste system and therefore converts to these religions cannot claim special protection from the state on the basis of caste. However, this argument is equally applicable to Sikhism and Buddhism. Therefore, the basis of application of the policy of protective discrimination is not what the concerned religions claim their doctrines are but the fact that some religions are of Indian and others of foreign origin.

It is clear then that both exclusivism (namely the Hindu theory of the origin of man, the practice of untouchability, etc., practised by Hindu orthodoxy) and expansionism (namely, social reform by Hindu 'progressives' and state policy) are practised in the case of the Dalits. If the former utterly alienates them, the latter denies their identity and also marginalizes them. If Hindu exclusivism questions their authenticity, expansionism endangers their autonomy. Undoubtedly such a situation does not augur well for nation-building. If Ambedkar's demand for Achutstan (which he quickly withdrew) is occasionally revived these days to claim a separate untouchable state, Dalitstan; it should be viewed as a manifestation of the extreme alienation of Dalits, a population of 100 million, from India's mainstream society. To dub this as separatist, casteist, or anti-national is to pervert the very spirit and meaning of authentic nationhood.

III

Of the two competing bases of nationalism, religion and language, the latter always had and still has, a high degree of legitimacy. However, given the extremely complex socio–linguistic situation and the nationalist expectancy, one finds substantial ambivalance in this regard in India. Beginning with the British period, an important strand of thinking was to regard 'India' as a conglomeration of distinct nations, mostly coterminous with major linguistic regions, and this was used by the British to buttress their argument that India cannot aspire to the status of an independent united nation state.[9] Two distinct sets of forces crystallized to counter the British argument by the 1930s—the religious and the secular. The religious forces gradually asserted themselves and led to the development of Hindu,

Muslim, and Sikh nationalisms,[10] and the partition of India. That religion is still invoked as the basis of nationalism is evident not only from the persistence of Hindu Rashtra Vad variously articulated by Rashtriya Swayam Sevak Sangh, Vishwa Hindu Parishad, and Virat Hindu Samaj but also from the activities of Sikh communal organizations.

The secular forces of Indian nationalism anchor to language as its basis. Although the Indian National Congress did endorse this position after Independence it did show considerable resistance to the reorganization of Indian states on a linguistic basis, arguing that it would lead to the balkanization of India. The rationale for this pattern of response should at least be partly traced to the assertion of Muslim nationalism and the division of India. However, the popular uprising of several linguistic nationalities finally led to the reorganization of Indian states in 1956 which perhaps created as many problems as it solved.

The Indian Marxists too have not so far provided a viable alternative. A mechanical application of Stalin's definition of nationality prompts them to argue that India is not a nation in view of the absence of a common language.[11] They hold the view that India is a multinational country constituted by different nationalities such as Maharashtrians, Tamils, Bengalis, etc. Irfan Habib asks and answers the question thus: 'Is India then a nation? Marxists must without hesitation answer this question in the negative. India ... is not a nation, because it meets the requirement of neither a common language nor a common culture'. (Habib, 1975: 16). This line of reasoning sees 'Indian national unity' as the function of a united struggle against imperialism. Logically, once the external enemy disappeared India should have split up into different nationalities. The fact that this did not happen and is not likely to, although there are and will be stresses and strains, even conflicts, between the different linguistic nationalities, provides adequate authenticity to Indian nationhood.

The Marxist perspective also cannot identify a 'secular' basis for Indianhood in the absence of an external enemy, the British colonizer or the Muslim conqueror. Therefore, it is not surprising that Marxist intellectuals fall back upon the mainstream Hindu culture as the basis of Indian unity. Thus Dange (1955) considers vedic Aryans as the dominant collectivity that piloted Indian development. Namboodiripad (1975 and 1980) identifies the Aryan Sanskritic stream as the dominant one, although he concedes the existence of two early centres of Indian civilization (Aryan and Tamil prior to the colonial conquest. Given this understanding, the Communists' support to Muslim 'nationalities' in the North-West and North-East in their struggle for 'self-determination' was but a logical extension. That is, the endorsement of Muslim 'nationalism' at the time of Partition was the logical corollary to the acceptance of the Hindu 'nationalism' of the pre-colonial era.

The problem of independent India is not that it is not a nation, but that it is a different type of nation vis-à-vis other nations of the world. The dictum 'one-language, one-nation' is not a workable proposition in the Indian context. A realization of this appears to have prompted the liberal–democratic leadership of independent India to pursue a policy of multi-linguism but without abandoning the notion that a nation should have one dominant or link language. This is articulated in state policy of fostering Hindi as the 'national' language.

In the territory of the Indian Union, consisting of 22 states and 9 Union Territories[12] 4 language families are found: Indo–Aryan languages spoken by nearly 73 per cent, Dravidian languages spoken by about 25 per cent, Austro–Asiatic languages spoken by about 1.5 per cent, and Tibeto–Chinese languages spoken by little over 0.5 per cent of the population. While over 1500 languages are recorded as mother tongues in Indian Censuses, only 15 of these are accorded official recognition by enlisting them in the Eighth Schedule of the Indian Constitution, under articles 344(I) and 351. These 15 languages belong to two language families: (a) Indo–Aryan: Assamese, Bengali, Gujarati, Hindi, Kashmiri, Marathi, Oriya, Punjabi, Sanskrit, Urdu, and Sindhi; (b) Dravidian: Kannada, Malayalam, Tamil, and Telugu.

A few important points may be noted here. First, the languages from the Austro–Asiatic and Tibeto–Chinese families are excluded from the Eighth Schedule not only because they are numerically small but also because they do not have scripts. It may, however, be noted that some of the languages from these groups are spoken by a substantial number of people. For example, Santali is spoken by about three million persons. It may further be noted that the majority of the Austro–Asian and Tibeto–Chinese languages are spoken by tribal communities inhabiting the hilly tracts, principally in South-Central and North-East India.

Second, not all the official languages have a 'home territory', but two have official status in more than one territorial unit—Hindi in six states and two Union Territories and Bengali in two states. Of the remaining languages recognized by the Constitution all except three (Urdu, Sindhi, and Sanskrit) have a specific state identified with them.

Third, Sindhi, spoken by less than two million people, was not accorded constitutional recognition initially but got it subsequently in 1967, after this community brought to bear influence on the Union government. Fourth, Sanskrit, on which constitutional recognition is bestowed, albeit an ancient literary and religious language, is not a living language and today it is spoken only by a handful of people. Fifth, while Kashmiri is recognized by the constitution in its homeland, Jammu and Kashmir, it is not Kashmiri but Urdu which is the official language of the state. Sixth, although English is the mother tongue of a distinct community (Anglo–Indians) and is perhaps the most widely used language in inter-regional communication as well as in administration and academy, it is not accorded any constitutional status. Finally, there are two types of states in terms of language–territory linkage; those in which the mother tongue of the majority is the official language (e.g. Tamil in Tamil Nadu, Oriya in Orissa) and those in which this is not so. For example, Urdu in Jammu and Kashmir, Hindi in Himachal Pradesh, English in Nagaland, are official languages but they are not the mother tongues of the people of these states.

Hindi has already been recognized as the language for inter-state communication, that is link language. In our Constitution, Article 343 provides that the official language of the Union shall be Hindi in Devanagri script. However, it is with reference to the acceptance of Hindi as the link language initially and as the national language eventually that we are likely to face the principal difficulty. Article 351 of the Indian Constitution reads: 'It shall be the duty of the Union to promote the spread of the Hindi language, to develop it so that it may serve as a medium of expression for all the elements of the composite culture of India and to secure its enrichment by assimilating without interfering with its genius, the forms, style and expressions, used in Hindustani and in the other languages of India specified in the Eighth Schedule, and by drawing, wherever necessary or desirable, for its vocabulary, primarily on Sanskrit and secondarily on other languages.'

It is important to note that, Hindustani is not included in the Eighth Schedule, and one is not certain about the connotations of this expression. Secondly, the eventual transformation of the official language of the Union as its national language is linked up with the assimilation by Hindi of the forms, style, and expressions used in Hindustani and other languages specified in the Eighth Schedule. However, not only are there numerous languages belonging to the four different linguistic families spoken in India, but even the Hindi spoken in the different regions within the Hindi belt vary substantially. For instance, Khari Boli, Western Hindi, and Eastern Hindi are different speech forms and are not mutually intelligible. This being the situation, if Hindi is to be transformed into the national language in each of the states where it is currently the official language, we are likely to develop different styles of Hindi. Again, it is significant to note that the article insists on relying primarily on Sanskrit for the development of Hindi. If Hindustani is the language to be developed as the national language, Persian may be as much, if not more, relevant. Admittedly, we encounter the distinction between Sanskrit, a 'native' language, and Persian, an 'alien' language.

To complicate matters, the literary languages in India, and this is true not only of Hindi and other Indo–Aryan languages but also of Dravidian languages, have never really been the vernaculars, there is a considerable gap between the two. The lexicons of modern Indian languages catalogue many expressions that are rarely found in ordinary speech forms, while the largely unrecorded dialectal words still remain a mere object of research by the linguist. An authentic enrichment of literary languages would involve a process of two-way borrowing—from a superstructure (as from Sanskrit or Persian) and from a substratum (as from dialects). While the former receives ready recognition because of its élite linkage, the latter rarely does because it is associated and identified with the folk. The Official Language Commission wrote: 'The variety of Indian linguistic media is not a national skeleton to be ashamed of and to be somehow hidden away. It is a wealth of inheritance in keeping with the continental size, ancient history and distinctive tradition of assimilating and harmonizing diverse cultural and racial elements, of which this country can be justly proud.' Instead of following this sane advice, we seem to be following a policy of *culturocide.*[13] In pursuing the policy of promoting Hindi as the national language the processes of exclusivism and expansionism are at work, in the process manufacturing outsiders and insiders in the socio–cultural context. Once again, the effort is to create a cultural mainstream constituted by the Hindi speaking populace. To be sure, the twin processes of expansionism and exclusivism are at work in the case of the dominant regional languages too.

It is thus clear that a large number of factors have contributed towards according constitutional recognition to 15 languages. The more important of these are: the size of the speech community, the level of its development as indicated by graphemical status, the political clout the speech community wields, historical and religious associations of the language, and the geopolitical importance of the speech community. The policy of political expedience creates and perpetuates a cultural threat to the less developed, numerically weak and politically docile speech communities; they even face the threat of extinction. Thus a substantial number of Indians lose their linguistic–cultural identity, while others whose mother tongue belongs to one of the official languages, define and reinforce their identity in linguistic–cultural terms. This applies not only to the numerous tribal languages, many of which have several million speakers, but also to several languages that are the mother tongues of a vast peasantry. Thus, Bhojpuri, Brij Bhasha, Magadhi, Maithili, Rajasthani, and Chattisgarhi, to mention but a few, are treated as mere dialects of Hindi, in order to projct Hindi speakers as the largest speech community and to legitimize it as the national language. In the process, nothing short of a culturocide has taken place. Hindi expansionism marginalizes and even threatens the very existence of numerous languages that are defined as its dialects.

The case of Maithili provides an interesting illustration as to how, through an aggressive official policy, a language can be marginalized.[14] First, the very process of official enumeration is used as an instrument of oppression. According to the 1971 *Census of India* Maithili speakers count a mere 4,984,811. Maithili enthusiasts however claim that there are 25 million speakers of the language. Paul Brass, who systematically studied the Maithili movement, estimates that there are at least 16 million speakers of this language (1974: 66). Second, the 1971 *Census* describes Maithili as follows: 'One of the dominant speeches in Bihar spoken by a large section of the population ... Although grammatically nearer to Bengali or Oriya, Maithili speakers have cultivated Hindi as their language of education and instruction. For strength of speakers and for currently appearing literature in Maithili it will perhaps be more practical to consider it as an important language of Eastern group of Indo–Aryan family' (Nigam, 1971: 154).

It should also be noted here that two outstanding linguists have unambiguously stated that Maithili is a distinct language. 'Maithili is a language and not a dialect ... It differs from Hindi and Bengali both in vocabulary and in grammar, and is as much a distinct language from either of them as Marathi and Oriya' (Grierson, 1909: 2). Suniti Kumar Chatterji, the national professor wrote: 'Maithili is a language by itself, with its own special characteristics ... By any stretch of imagination it cannot be described as dialect of Hindi' (Chatterjee, 1962: 213).

Given the official policy of labeling Maithili as an Indo-Aryan dialect and absorbing it into Hindi, it is not surprising that Maithili speakers have 'cultivated' Hindi as their language of education. It is however extremely doubtful that they have done so voluntarily; in all probability, the situational exigencies have compelled them to do so. This is then the result of what I have called Hindi expansionism. Indeed, Maithili is only an illustrative case and there are numerous language in India that are defined and treated as dialects of one or another 'developed' language.

Although the reorganization of Indian states was effected in 1956 based on languages, no state was formed on the basis of tribal languages. However, several tribal states/Union Territories (Nagaland, Mizoram, Arunachal Pradesh, Manipur etc.) were formed subsequently in north-east India, but tribal and not linguistic identity was the basis. In the case of tribals in other parts, particularly those of south-central India, linguistic reorganization led to the vivisection of several tribal groups between different states. For example, there are about eleven lakh Oraons whose language is Kurux. The reorganization of states left the Kurux speech community divided between four states, fragmenting it politically, culturally, and linguistically. As a corollary to this, the Oraons came to be linguistically dominated by Hindi in Bihar and Madhya Pradesh, Bengali in West Bengal, and Oriya in Orissa.

The tribal languages do not have a uniform pattern as far as scripts are concerned. Most of them have no scripts. Some have a script of their own while others have multiple scripts. The last situation, a particularly vexing one, is the product of the reorganization of Indian states. For example, the Santals got distributed into several states and Santali is written in Roman, Bengali, Oriya and Devanagri scripts. There is an influential section of Santals that advocates the adoption of regional scripts, that is, the script of the dominant language of the-state to which they belong. There is another equally influential section which insists on Santali having the same script in all the states to facilitate cultural consolidation. Finally, sectarianism also influences the choice of scripts; the Christian Santals advocating the Roman script and the Hindu Santals preferring Devanagari script.

There are several 'developed' languages other than Hindi in the Indo–Aryan family. Prominent examples are Bengali, Marathi, Gujarati etc., and these are enlisted as official languages. The degree of resistance stemming from other Indo–Aryan languages to Hindi vary considerably depending upon the definition of cultural distance from it and the degree of development, actual or imaginary, the speech community concerned attributes to its language. Thus, after Tamil, a Dravidian language, Bengali, an Indo–Aryan language, resists the 'imposition' of Hindi (Nayyar, 1969). Therefore, the acceptance or rejection of Hindi as the national language by a speech community is not a matter of linguistic proximity to the former but the latter's sense of importance or of impotence, perceived advantage or disadvantage, capacity to confront or accommodate, and so on. Those who are determined to preserve their cultural identities have to pay a price, that of foregoing many instrumental advantages. On the other hand, the speakers of Maithili, Rajasthani, Magadhi, Brij Bhasha, and numerous other 'dialects' acquire enormous instrumental payoffs by merging with the Hindi mainstream. In the process however they are committing nothing less than a cultural harakiri.

The relationship between the Hindi mainstream and the speech communities of the Austro–Asiatic, Sino–Tibetan, and Dravidian languages has always been one of domination–submission. While the speech communities of the first two language families have not yet exhibited any aggressive 'nationalistic' tendencies, the Dravidian speech communities, particularly the Tamils, did and continue to articulate their anti-Hindi resistance. The point to be noted here is that it is not simply the objective cultural distance per se that moulds this tendency, but a variety of factors in combination.

Tamil, along with Sanskrit, is an ancient language of India. To complicate matters, Sanskrit, although not a living language, is perceived as the language of Aryan Hindus. In contrast, the cultural ethos of Dravidians is expressed through a vibrant and living Tamil language. Today, in the Dravidian perception, Hindi has replaced Sanskrit and is used as an instrument of cultural oppression. Thus, to the Tamil, the anti-Hindi struggle is not simply linguistic mobilization but also anti-Aryan, which is directed against Brahmin dominance. It is this combination of language and religion that gave Tamil nationalism such strength in the initial phase, the Dravidian movement did show secessionist tendencies, but once the Dravidian parties were successful in capturing political power through legally prescribed means, the movement and the parties that emerged out of it came to be perceived as 'legitimate' entities. Thus, the Tamils have moved from the periphery of the Indo–Aryan mainstream, creating a counter-centre, thereby perceiving the demand for secession as redundant. Although, from the perspective of the Hindi–Aryan mainstream, Tamil, Telugu or such other nationalisms are 'parochial', 'regional', 'anti-national', for the latter these are but expressions of their authentic nationalist aspirations for justice and freedom *within* the framework of the Indian nation state. To my mind, the recognition of this fact is of the utmost importance for the process of nation-building in India.

I have suggested above that when a language is associated with religion, the nationalist aspirations crystallize almost spontaneously. However, in order that this should actually materialize two other conditions should also exist. First, the language concerned should not only be a 'sacred' language but also one that is used by people in their day-to-day interactions in non-religious contexts. Second, the speech community should be concentrated in substantial numbers in specific territorial units. If these conditions are not fulfilled, the identification of a language with a religion will not lead to the formation of a nationality sentiment. Thus, notwithstanding the identification of Sanskrit with twice-born Hindus, particularly Brahmins, we do not have a 'nationality' evolved around it.

In the case of Urdu, the popular perception is that it is closely linked with Indian Muslims and is strongly supported by a section of Muslim intellectuals.[15] The language of a majority of Muslims in India is not Urdu; it is only in Uttar Pradesh and Bihar that we come across Muslims who are also Urdu speakers. These two states account for nearly one-third or the Muslim population and one-half of the Urdu speakers of the country. In Jammu and Kashmir, a Muslim majority state, though the official language is Urdu, the Urdu speakers of the state constitute a mere 0.27 per cent. On the other hand, the majority of Urdu speakers are from states where the proportion of Muslims is very low.[16] This disjuncture between Urdu and Islam, and the dispersal of Urdu speakers muted the possibility of Urdu nationalism emerging in independent India. In contrast, the close association between Sikhism and Punjabi written in the Gurmukhi script and the concentration of the Punjabi speaking Sikh population within Punjab led to the crystallization of Sikh–Punjabi nationalism. The tendency on the part of Punjabi Hindus to claim Hindi as their language is an attempt to resist Sikh nationalism and not an indication of their rejection of Punjabi nationalism.

There are thus three distinct tendencies in the socio–linguistic context of India which are not conducive to nation-building in our socio–cultural context. First, the tendency to enlist numerous languages as dialects of Hindi both by Hindi enthusiasts and official policy-makers so as to annihilate these languages as cultural entities. Second, to identify some speech communities as religious collectivities, thereby fostering religion-based nationalism and obstructing the development of linguistic nationalism of all the people who belong to the speech community irrespective of their religious background.

Third, by insisting on the introduction of Hindi as the national language, creating an estrangement between the Hindi-speaking mainstream and other speech communities.[16] This estrangement exists not only between the Indo–Aryan, Dravidian, Austro-Asiatic and Sino–Tibetan languages but also between the different Indo–Aryan languages.

It has been rightly argued that colonial rule blocked the growth of nationalities in India by creating artificial administrative units. Except perhaps Bengali, Marathi, and Tamil, the cultural nationalisms of numerous collectivities were mutilated by the British, while the same policy thrust is more or less continued by free India's state, we are apt to ignore it in our patriotic fervour. The reorganization of Indian states was a leap forward in effecting a co-terminality between administrative units and cultural regions, but the task remains largely unfinished. I have already indicated that a large number of languages, have been reduced to the status of mere dialects. Associated with this is another process: many cultural regions have been denied autonomy and personality. The disjuncture between officially created administrative units such as Uttar Pradesh, Madhya Pradesh, Maharashtra, Bihar, and Andhra Pradesh, on the one hand, and the folk-regions, which are invariably cultural entities, such as Bhojpur, Chattisgarh, Magadh, Mithila, Jharkhand, Vidarbha, and Telengana, on the other should be recognized here. The tensions that exist and mobilizations that persist in many Indian states based on regional–cultural identities should be seen in this perspective. Many administrative units as they exist are artificial in people's perception. The natural regions of their cognition are either divided between several units or when undivided are tagged on to other regions not allowing them to retain and nurture their specificity.

IV

The thesis I have formulated in this chapter is that the central issues of nation-building in India revolve around the persistent tension between the Hindi speaking twice-born Hindus, who define themselves as the norm-setters and value-givers, the cultural main-stream, and a multiplicity of other primordial collectivities occupying the periphery of the system, who face either the threat of expansionism or exclusivism, depending upon their positioning in the socio–cultural space of India. The two salient elements that define collective identity and which have been the bases of nationality formation the world over are religion and language. Also, in the Indian context, these elements are strong and at least occasionally co-exist, aggravating an already complex situation characterized by a wide variety of communities with a deep sense of historicity and distinct traditions.

In their eagerness to project themselves as 'nationalistic', 'progressive', and 'secular', many social scientists have been vocal in condemning the loyalties to such entities as religion, caste, language and region somewhat indiscriminately. It is useful however to bear in mind two points here. First, the human need is not only for impersonal ties with entities such as political parties and the bureaucratic state, on the one hand, and for privatized ties, provided by primary groups such as family and kin-group, on the other, but also for intermediate structures and processes that blend and balance the two. In a country like India such ties are often provided by caste, religion, language, and region which are often labelled as communal, parochial, and anti-national. These loyalties and ties however need no be so dismissed. Second, there is a qualitative difference in the loyalties and ties between different levels and contexts. These can co-exist and one need not displace the other.

The thrust of my argument, then, is that India cannot build an authentic nation-state by building a cultural mainstream reducing the numerous collectivities of the periphery to the status of marginals. We can only have a nation-state with multiple cultural 'entities'. In pursuing this task the different cultural collectivities should be encouraged to nurture and foster their specific identities. This should not however in any way deny them equal economic opportunities and political rights. That is, while there can be and should be economic and political mainstreams in India to which all the citizens should have equal access, there cannot and should not be a cultural mainstream, precisely because the principles of recruitment to these mainstreams radically differ. The Indian nation-state will have to be built on economic justice and political democracy, firmly anchored to the principle of secularism, that is, treating all the cultural collectivities as 'insiders'. The policy of expansionism currently pursued by the cultural mainstream and the state cannot be extended from a humanistic perspective because it will eventually lead to cultural assimilation which denies identity. On the other hand, the policy of exclusivism alienates and marginalizes those collectivities that are treated as 'outsiders'. The very notion of the cultural mainstream implies both the process of expansionism and exclusivism and therefore the only viable alternative for India is to build authentic cultural pluralism reinforcing our multiple cultural streams.

Notes

1. Although the term 'ethnicity' is in wide currency and used to describe a variety of collectivities, there is near-universal agreement that it connotes a combination of biological (racial) and cultural characteristics. Thus viewed, most of the primordial collectivities in India do not fit this description. Secondly, the term 'ethnics' is invariably used to refer to minorities of various types and rarely used to identify the dominant collectivity. For these reasons I prefer the term primordial collectivities which refer to all varieties of collectivities formed on the basis of ascription: race, caste, language, religion, territory. While occasionally biological and cultural characteristics may co-exist in the case of a primordial collectivity, this is not a necessary condition.

2. It is frequently argued that the term Hindus does not denote a religious collectivity, but is a label imposed on them by Arabs or Christian missionaries (see for example, Madan, 1977: 261–78). Be that as it may, today, not only non-Hindus but Hindus too identify and define themselves as such. Therefore, the origin of the words Hindu and Hinduism apart, they are socio–culturally meaningful terms in contemporary India.

3. The prevalence of insider–outsider tension is widespread and not confined to primordial collectivities. A recent committee appointed by the University Grants Commission to inquire into the working of central universities, organizations expected to follow universal norms in student and faculty recruitments, observed: 'They give weightage to their own students for admission to subsequent courses which leads to inbreeding. The Committee found strong evidence of such inbreeding continuing in recruitment at all levels, which vitiates pursuit of excellence' (see, U.G.C., 1984).

4. I will only refer to two statements, one made some forty-five years ago and another thirty months ago. M.S. Golwalkar (1939: 55–6) wrote: 'The non-Hindu people in Hindustan must either adopt the Hindu culture and language, must learn to respect and hold in reverence Hindu religion, must entertain no idea but those of glorification of the Hindu race and culture ... may stay in the country, wholly subordinated to the Hindu nation, claiming nothing, deserving no privileges ... not even citizen's right's'. In November

1983, the Secretary General of the Vishwa Hindu Parishad said: 'Only the Hindus call this land Bharat Mata. The others do not accept this land as their Mata' (see, *Times of India,* 10.11.83).

5. The figures are taken from Zelliot (1960: 191–212).

6. The figures are taken from Anandan (1982: 34–6).

7. This is not to argue that the interaction and interdependence between great and little traditions are denied, indeed it is conceded (see Marriott, 1961: 171–222), but the relationship between the two traditions is viewed as 'vertical'.

8. It may be recalled here that neither Babu Jagjivan Ram, a former cabinet minister but a Dalit by birth, nor Mrs Indira Gandhi, a Zoroastrian by marriage (although a Brahmin by birth and prime minister of the country), were allowed to enter the temple at Puri.

9. The colonial administrators clearly denied the existence of Indian nationalism. '... there is not and never was an India, ... no Indian nation, no people of India' (Strachy, 1888: 5). 'India is only a geographical expression like Europe or Africa. It does not mark the territory of a nation and a language, but the territory of many nations and many languages' (Seeley, 1884, 255).

10. It is not true that the Sikhs never demanded a separate sovereign nation-state during the pre-Independence struggle. The demand for Sikhistan was first formally made on 22 March, 1946. The sense of a separate Sikh nationhood persisted in independent India. Master Tara Singh, who, represented his strand rhetorically, asked: 'The Hindus got Hindustan, the Muslims got Pakistan, what did the Sikhs get?' (see Schermerhorn, 1978: 141–2).

11. The four criteria Stalin (1970) used to define nationality are 'common language, common territory, common economic life and psychological make-up manifested in a common culture'. In India's case the single most important mismatch between this definition and social reality is the absence of a common language.

12. At present there are 28 states and 7 Union Territories in India.

13. The terms usually invoked to describe a situation of cultural annihilation are cultural genocide, but perhaps the term culturocide is more appropriate.

14. I have often heard the argument that the Maithili movement is the creation of a 'feudal élite' centred around the erstwhile princely family of Darbhanga and hence its inability to take off. As against this, a social scientist from the Maithila region recounted to me an interesting episode, which is perhaps indicative of the attitude of the Maithili speech community to Hindi. In a Conference of Maithili intellectuals, one of the speakers started speaking in Hindi and the instantaneous question put to him was: 'Why are you speaking in a foreign language?' The term 'foreigner' is often used in India to refer to people who do not belong to one's cultural milieu, although they are fellow citizens (see Oommen, 1982: 41–64).

15. The argument that Urdu is a common language of Hindus, Muslims, and Sikhs has been forcefully rebutted (see for instance, Azeeme, 1915: 260–76).

16. For details, see Mohammed Peer (1983: 138–49).

17. The debate on Hindi in the Constituent Assembly clearly points to this. Ambedkar (1955: 14), wrote: 'there was no article which proved more controversial than Article 115, which deals with the (Hindi) question ... Hindi won its place as national language by one vote'. Nehru conceded, after hearing the Constituent Assembly debate on Hindi: 'In some of the speeches I have listened to here and elsewhere, there is very much a tone of authoritarianism, very much a tone of Hindi speaking area being the centre of things in India, the centre of gravity and others being just the fringes of India' (Constituent Assembly Debates, 1949: 1420). Besides, primacy has been claimed for Hindi, but as a logical extension of this Uttar Pradesh is claimed to be the centre of the Hindi region. K.M. Pannicker, the Chairman of the State Reorganization Commission, in his note of dissent noted 'that the leaders from U.P. claimed that the existence of a large, powerful and well-organized state in the Gangetic valley was a guarantee for India's unity ... The same idea has been put to us in many other forms, such as U.P. is the backbone of India, the centre from which all other states derive their ideas and culture' (see the Report of the State Reorganization Commission 1956: 246).

References

Ambedkar, B.R., 1955, *Thoughts on Linguistic States*, Ramkrishna Press, Bombay.

Azeem, A. 1975, 'Urdu—A Victim of Cultural Genocide' in Imam, Z. (ed.), *Muslims in India*, Orient Longman, New Delhi.

Bose, N.K., 1967, *Culture and Society in India*, Asia Publishing House, Bombay.

Brass, P., 1974, *Language Religion and Politics in North India*, Cambridge University Press, Cambridge.

Chatterjee, S.K., 1962, *Language and Literature in Modern India*, Prakash Bhavan, Calcutta.

Dange, S.A., 1955, *India From Primitive Communism to Slavery*, People's Publishing House, New Delhi.

Garlington, W., 1977, 'The Bahai faith in Malwa' in G.A. Oddie (ed.), *Religion in South Asia*, Manohar, New Delhi.

Ghurye, G.S., 1948, *The Aborigines—So called—and their Future*, Gokhale Institute of Politics and Economics, Poona.

Golwalkar, M.S., 1919, *We or Our Nationhood Defined*, Bharat Prakashan, Nagpur.

Government Of India, 1949, *Constituent Assembly Debates*, vol. IX, no. 33, New Delhi.

Government Of India, 1956, *State Reorganization Commission—Report*, New Delhi.

Grierson, G.A., 1909, *Introduction to the Maithili Dialect of the Bihari Language as Spoken in Bihar*, 2nd edn., Baptist Mission Press, Calcutta.

Habib, I., 1975, 'Emergence of nationalities', *Social Scientist*, Aug.

Madan, T.N., 1977, 'The Quest for Hinduism', *International Social Science Journal* 19(2).

Marriott, McKim, 1961, 'Changing Channels of Cultural Transmission in India', in L.P., Vidyarthy, *'Aspects of Religion in Indian Society*, Meenakshi Prakashan, Meerut. Namboodiripad, E.M.S., 1975, 'Class Character of the Nationalist Movement', *Social Scientist*, Aug. Namboodiripad, E.M.S., 1980, 'Evolution of Society, Language and literature', *Social Scientist*, April.

Nayyar, B.R., 1969, *National Communication and language Policy in India*, Frederick A. Prager, New York.

Nigam, R.C., 1971, *Language Handbook of Mother Tongues in Census*, Census of India, Calcutta.

Oommen, T.K., 1982, 'Foreigners, Refugees and Outsiders in the Indian Context', *Sociological Bulletin*, 31(1).

Oommen, T.K., 1983, 'Religious Pluralism in India: A Sociological Perspective', in R. Singh (ed.), *Christian Perspectives on Contemporary Indian Issues*, The Institute for Development Education, Madras; M. Peer, 1983, 'Urdu language and Indian Muslims', *Guru Nanak Journal of Sociology*, IV(2).

Schermerhorn, R.A., 1978, *Ethnic Plurality in India*, University of Arizona, Press, Tuscon.

Seeley, R. Sir John, 1883, *The expansion of England*, The Macmillan Press, London.

Srinivas, M.N., 1962, *Caste in Modern India and Other Essays*, Asia Publishing House, London.

Stalin J.V., 1970, 'Critical Remarks on the National Question', first published 1913, rpt. in *'Selections from V.I. Lenin and J.V. Stalin on National/Colonial Question*, Book House, Calcutta.

Strachey, Sir John, 1888, *India: Its Administration and Progress*, Macmillan Press, London.

Sujata, A., 1982, 'Has Neo-Buddhism Lost Relevance?', *The Illustrated Weekly of India*, 22, Aug.

University Grants Commission, 1984, *Report of the Committee to Enquire Into to the Working of the Central Universities*, New Delhi.

Zelliot, E., 1960, 'Buddhism and Politics in Maharashtra', in D.E. Smith (ed.), *South Asian Politics and Religion*, University Press, Princeton.

11

Hinduism as Delhi Rule
Periyar and the National Question[*]

Gail Omvedt

As the colonial period drew to an end the surface waves of Indian politics were dominated by the issue of Muslim separatism and Hindu identity. Hinduism came to be a taken-for-granted identity, whether it was the moderate and liberal version most Congressmen subscribed to, or the increasingly virulent form of Hindu nationalism. The latter, growing throughout the 1920s and 1930s, began to increasingly emphasize not only blood and territory (race, religion and nation) but also language, projecting Sanskrit/Hindi as the quintessentially 'Indian' languages. This had a significant north Indian bias. *Hindi–Hindu–Hindustan* the emotive slogan of north Indian fundamentalism, had a powerful negative side: the equation of language, religion, and nation encouraged not only those with a different religious identity but also those with a separate linguistic identity to see themselves as a different 'nation'. Thus the other side of the powerful centralizing tendency of Hindu fundamentalism was that many anti-caste movements turned to a regional and anti-northern, as well as anti-brahmin identification.

Caste is not ethnicity, and Ambedkar above all had insisted on this distinction and taken a resolutely all-Indian, even centralist attitude. However, caste, community, and ethnicity have common features,

* Gail Omvedt, *Dalit Vision*, Orient Longman, New Delhi, 1995.

also seen in the vernacular meanings of jati and quaum, which are often overlapping. From the time of Phule a broad stream in the anti-caste movement had stressed these, seeing the brahminic élites as Aryan and themselves as non-Aryan, of a different ethnic community and even a different race. Given the diversity of India, reflected especially in the diversity of the non-brahmin and Dalit communities, it is not surprising that these mass ethnic identities got expressed in different forms in different regions. The opposition to ' brahmin' and 'Hindu' then got reflected in varying non-Hindi and sometimes anti-north Indian nationality identifications.

By the 1930s, for example, Sikh and Muslim religious identities were also taking on regional/nationalist aspects and in the process opposed Congress domination as Hindu domination and 'brahmin–bania rule'. The caste discourse of the opposition helped to link them to the non-brahmin and Dalit movements, and perhaps provided a ground for the alliances that were taking place. In the 1930s for instance, Mangoo Ram of the Punjab allied with the Unionist Party and the Namashudras with the Krishak Praja Party in Bengal. At the same time the strong Hindu–Muslim antagonisms which were developing especially in north India were, in many other regions getting diversified into demands for regional separation and autonomy. By the late 1940s the movement for Pakistan was feeding that for Dravidistan and similar trends could be seen elsewhere. Anti-Hinduism was taking on a rather complex, anti-northern, anti-centralist character.

Developments in Tamil Nadu provide an insight into the process. Here was a strongly independent Dravidian linguistic identity and a long history of being the southern centre of the subcontinent, not only unconquered by northerners but a centre of empires of its own, stretching sometimes overseas and oriented in many ways more towards south-east Asia in contrast to the northern west Asian linkages. Here, since the late nineteenth century, anti-brahminism had the built-in claim of being the non-Aryan original inhabitants of the land. This led to an idealization of ancient Tamil society; Saivaism, or the Saiva Siddhanta philosophy, was posed as an indigenous, even non-Hindu religion. This was to form the basis for claiming an identity as Dravidians and, by the 1940s and 1950s, for Tamil nationalism.

The early non-brahmin movement in Tamil Nadu was more élite-based than in Maharashtra with the relatively high-caste Vellalas and other non-brahmin landlords and professionals from the Telugu, and Malayalam speaking regions able to confront the brahmins on their own footing, increasingly without having to build much of a mass movement.[1] However, by the 1920s a new, militant, mass-oriented movement arose. Its leader was E.V. Ramaswami, 'Periyar' (1879–1973), from a merchant family of Erode. He had joined the Congress in 1919, then gradually became disillusioned with what he saw as its brahminic leadership. In the early 1920s he took part in the Vaikom temple satyagraha, reportedly clashing with Gandhi while taking a militant position. He later argued that Gandhi had pushed him out of the satyagraha when he engineered a compromise. Nonetheless, Periyar returned to Tamil Nadu as the 'hero of Vaikom'. He subsequently clashed with Congress leaders over a proposed resolution for reservations in legislatures for non-brahmins and untouchables, In 1925 Periyar left the Congress. In 1927, during a tour of south India, Gandhi defended *varnashrama* dharma and Periyar contested this hotly, in personal meetings and in articles in his journal *Kudi Arasu*. He now claimed that three conditions were necessary for India to gain its freedom: destruction of the Congress, of the so-called Hindu religion, and of brahmin domination.[2]

Periyar formed the Self-Respect League in 1926 and its first conference was held in 1929 making it a Tamil Nadu-wide movement. Its focus was similar to that of Phule's Satyashodhak Samaj, opposing brahmin priesthood, calling for the abolition of caste, and supporting the liberation of women. He attacked all religions more than Phule did, taking an atheistic stance that contrasted with the modified Saivaism of the non- brahmin élite:

> There is no god,
> there is no god,
> there is no god at all.
> He who invented god is a fool.
> He who propagates god is a scoundrel.
> He who worships god is a barbarian.

The dialectic between Phule's theism and Periyar's atheism was in a sense duplicated in the small state of Kerala where Narayanaswami Guru's 'one religion, one caste, one god' was opposed by his atheistic disciple Ayyapan with the slogan 'no religion, no caste and no god for mankind'. The radical nationalism of the Self-Respect Movement inspired many at the time, among them the poet Bharati Dasan who published his first collection in 1938 which invoked 'original' Tamil values not as in the sense of seeking a revivalistic return to a golden age but as an inspiration of an autonomous modernity:

Is it greatness to refuse the right of women
Or is it great to be happy with the progress of women?
Is it right that women marry out of love,
Or is it right that we kill them after performing a child marriage?
Is it right to believe in the Vedas, in God, in all this decay?
Or is it right to establish socialism on earth?
Will we live continuing the divisions which surround us?
Or will we live rising up through self-respect?[3]

Bharati Dasan's socialism reflected a new radicalism and a temporary coming together of anti-caste and class themes in the early 1930s. On the one hand, Periyar's egalitarianism, anti-caste radicalism, and atheism, all expressed in powerful Tamil speeches, were attracting a group of militant lower-caste youth, giving a new invigoration to the old non- brahmin movement and radicalizing it. On the other hand, a catalytic role was played by Singaravelu, a union leader from a fish workers' caste who is considered the 'first Communist of south India', and indeed was the first Indian to independently form a labour party, considered a forerunner of the Communist Party.[4]

In 1932, Periyar toured the Soviet Union and was impressed by the concrete accomplishments of atheistic socialism while Singaravelu wrote a series of articles in *Kudi Arasu* expounding socialism and a materialistic interpretation of history. On Periyar's return, he and Singaravelu placed a new programme before Self-Respect activists in December 1932 and it was suggested that a political party be formed, using the name Samadharma party as the closest Tamil equivalent to 'socialism'. Socialism now began to be propagated from Self-Respect platforms, while anti-landlord and anti-moneylender conferences were held by non-brahmin activists.

However, this coming together of the left and anti-caste movements seemed doomed from the beginning. On the one hand, conservatives in the non-brahmin movement opposed it, and when in 1933 Periyar was arrested and jailed, it was clear that British pressure was on. On the other hand, Communist leaders, centred in Bombay, regarded any dilution of a class line with suspicion. Singaravelu's type of indigenous socialism, identified with dangerous non-class forces such as the anti-caste movement and regional-national identities, had to be kept under a tight rein. Singaravelu (then in his seventies) began to argue by 1934 that the term samadharma should be dropped and the movement openly identify itself as socialist. The real split, though, was on a straightforward political issue: whether, in the 1934 elections, with no socialist party around, the Self-Respect movement should support the Justice Party or the Congress. Periyar saw his political future in a revival and radicalization of the Justice Party. The left could see it only in the Congress, which by 1935 they were identifying explicitly as the 'anti-imperialist united front'. In 1936, the Communist leadership ordered Singaravelu and others to dissolve their organization and instead join the Congress Socialist Party, apart of the solidly all-Indian National Congress within which the Communists were working. Dange's speech at the conference, which dissolved the movement stressed the dangers of linguistic nationalism: 'He reminded' the conference that not only Tamil Nadu but the whole of India is under British imperialist domination, and that unless the bondage of India under British imperialism is destroyed on an all-India scale it is impossible even to dream of socialism.[5]

The result of young radical communist cadres leaving the movement was to deprive it of a class thrust. As Periyar and his co-workers clashed with the 'brahminic' left, they increasingly identified with a linguistic nationalism. In the south it was easy to give a specific ethnic and national identity to non-Aryan: the people obviously had a language with a non-European origin and the original inhabitants were Dravidian or Tamil. Phule had attacked the story of Vishnu's avatars as representing an external, Aryan conquest of the subcontinent; Periyar described it as a conquest of the south by the north. Phule had taken Bali Raja, the mythological 'peasant king', as a hero; the Tamils took Ravana as the symbol of the south. In this they were only following popular *Ramayana* traditions. Ravana is seen as hero in many non-Valmiki versions of the epic in south and west India, South-East Asia and even Kashmir. The versions emphasize love and war, the heroism and tragic fate of Ravana, in contrast to the feudal, patriarchal, and hierarchical values emphasized by the Chinese and north Indian versions centred around Rama.

By the 1940s, Tamil/Dravidian nationalistic themes were coming to dominate opposition politics. In 1936, a Congress government (headed by Rajagopalachari) came to power in Madras Province as in most parts of India. As Congress began what Sumit Sarkar has described as 'a steady shift to the Right, occasionally veiled by "Left rhetoric"',[6] organizations of peasants and workers went on the offensive in many parts of the country. In Madras too strikes and campaigns took place, but the split between Periyar and the communists meant that there was no coordination of the class–caste struggle; not even a search for a common ground. Periyar himself was hardly an ideologue, and took only passing interest in economic issues. Without socialist cadres to push him on, he began to organize constant campaigns against the imposition of Hindi, stressing the theme of Dravidian/Tamil nationality. With the rise of the demand for Pakistan, the movement gained strength, and in 1939 the Dravida Nadu Conference for the Advocacy of a Separate and Independent Dravidastan, demanded a separate country along the lines of Pakistan.[7]

Regional nationalism was beginning to grow in various parts of India. The demand for Pakistan itself was from the outset conceived not simply in religious terms but in religio–territorial terms identified with the north-west; the earliest version spoke of 'Pakistan, Hindustan and Bengal', and that proposed in 1938–9 included Hyderabad to make up four independent states. By the 1940s Jinnah was willing to include Dravidastan as one of the four regions.[8] The 1938–9 proposal reflected a vigorous campaign in Hyderabad sponsored by the Nizam to promote a composite Hindu–Muslim 'Deccani' culture as a basis for identity. This could win over a few prominent Dalit leaders, though it was eventually compromised by its association with a feudal regime and could withstand neither Hindu nor Muslim fundamentalism.

Similarly, Sikh/Punjabi identity was expressing itself both in regional and religious terms, by sharing with the non-brahmins an antagonism towards brahmins and banias. In Kashmir, Muslim Kashmiris were beginning to conceptualize their identity not simply in religious but in regional/ethnic terms, as 'Kashmiriat'. Even in the far north-east, educated Assamese stressed an anti-Bengali identity while identifying with Hinduism (Vaishnavism), the tribals of the plains were questioning both Assamese high-caste identification and asserting a specific north-eastern identity. This identity carried the sense of being Mongoloid in contrast with the Aryan identities of both high-caste Assamese Hindus and Muslims. A first convention of the All-Assam Tribes and Races Federation in 1945 unanimously resolved that:

> In view of the fact that historically, Assam proper, with its hills, was never a part or province of India and that its people, particularly the Tribes and Races inhabiting it are ethnically and culturally different from the people of the rest of India, this convention is emphatically opposed to Assam proper with its hills being included into any proposed division of India, Pakistan or

Hindustan, and demands that it should be constituted into a separate Free State into which the Hill Districts bordering Assam be incorporated.[9]

'Subnational' identities were thus becoming a major undercurrent of politics in the 1940s. They did not, it should be noted, always imply a separatist nationalism; they could also lead to demands for autonomy coupled with a loose federal centre. Thus, for instance, the leader of the Unionist Party in Punjab, Sikandar Hayat Khan, rejected Pakistan as the equivalent of a 'Muslim raj' and suggested instead a three-tier structure with autonomous provinces grouped into seven regions, these joined in a loose confederation in which the centre had charge only over defence, external affairs, currency and customs.[10] This type of autonomy was to be the demand with which Sheikh Abdullah's National Conference agreed to Kashmir joining the Indian Union; and it was to be revived after Independence in both Punjab and Kashmir with intermittent movements for independent states.

Meanwhile Periyar had decided to focus on the question of India's future and succeeded in building a political organization that would become the major party in Tamil Nadu. In 1944 he revived the Justice Party, changed its name to Dravida Kazhagham (DK) and declared its goal to be a 'sovereign, independent Dravidian Republic'. The flag adopted was black with a red circle. Independence was declared a 'day of mourning' as representing the enslavement of the southerners.[11] Several strands were brought together by the DK with their focal point being Tamil nationalism:

> We want our country;
> Change the name to Tamil Nadu;
> All-India Union Government means a government
>   protecting religion;
> We must leave the Hindu Delhi.[12]

Tamil nationalism, linked with the anti-caste movement, thus became a powerful force in the south. However, it could win none of its major demands. The post-Independence Congress government succeeded in diluting the radicalism of the Dravidian forces. The DK gave birth to the Dravida Munnetra Kazhagham (DMK) which gave up the separatist demand, and then to the All-India Dravida Munnetra Kazhagham (AIADMK) which capitalized on the charisma of its superstar leader and asserted an all-India identity, allied with

Congress and eventually propped up its dead hero's film star com-
panion as a temperamental dictatorial leader. The major problem of
the Dravidian movement remained the difficulty of winning Dalit
support, which Phule had put at the centre of his strategy. In Tamil
Nadu, it was not the radical Ambedkar but the Hindu Mahasabhaite
M.C. Rajah who was the best known Dalit leader, and his alienation
from the Dravidian movement was the other side of distancing the
movement itself from Dalits. The south thus witnessed a powerful
non-brahmin movement and a strong opposition to 'Hinduism', but
more than in any other region was plagued by splits between communists and Dravidians, and Dalits and non-brahmins.

The currents of regional or subnational (linguistic national) identity were thus significant during the colonial period. They over-
lapped in complicated ways with claims to a non-Hindu religious
identity, but they nearly always shared a framework of opposition to
a brahmin–bania, Delhi-based centralized rule. The logical outcome
of these movements was not necessarily towards the establishment of
an independent nation-state; demands for independence were often
raised, but the thrust was just as much on a decentralized, federal
structure with much more autonomous regions than in the Indian
Union which came into existence. The triumph of the Congress finally represented both a triumph of a 'Hindu' identity and of a
centralized, Delhi-based state in the Indian subcontinent.

Notes

1. The classic study in Eugene Irschick, *Politics and Social Conflict in
South India*, (University of California Press, Berkeley, 1969). For a recent
discussion of the period of the Tamil non-brahmin movement and the issues
involved, see V. Geetha and S.V. Rajadurai, 'NeoBrahmanism: An Inten-
tional Fallacy?' *Economic and Political Weekly*, 16–23 Jan., 1993.

2. See K. Murugesan and C. Subramanyam, *Singaravelu, First Communist
in South India*, People's Publishing House, New Delhi, 1975, p. 64.

3. Quoted in Irschick, *Tamil Revivalism in the 1930s* (Madras, Cre-A,
1986), pp. 224–5.

4. On Singaravelu, see Murugesan and Subramanyam, op. cit.

5. Ibid., p. 83.

6. Sumit Sarkar, *Modern India, 1885–1947*, Macmillan India Ltd., New
Delhi, 1983, p. 351.

7. Anita Diehl, *Periyar E.V. Ramaswami*, B.I. Publications, Bombay, 1977,
p. 62.

8. R.J. Moore, 'Jinnah and the Pakistan Demand', in Robin Jeffrey, et al., ed., *India, Rebellion to Republic,* Sterling Publishers Pvt. Ltd., New Delhi, 1990.

9. Cited in Girin Phukon, 'Ethnic Nationalism in North-East India: A Brief Overview of its Legacy', *in* Deka, *North-East Quarterly* 2:3, 1986.

10. Sumit Sarkar, *Modern India,* pp. 378–80.

11. Anita Diehl, *Periyar,* pp. 62–3.

12. Ibid., p. 63.

12

Jat Sikhs
A Question of Identity*

Ravinder Kaur**

Introduction

This chapter studies the question of identity among Sikhs, especially among the Jat Sikhs of central rural Punjab. This area of the state is called the Doaba, the other two being Majha and Malwa. The Doaba region comprises the districts of Jullundur, Hosiarpur, Ludhiana, and Kapurthala, and includes some of the most fertile and productive tracts in the Punjab. However, small landholdings and increased pressure of population on land have led to considerable out-migration, especially to some Western countries like Canada, the UK, the US, and more recently to the Middle East.

Most writers on the Punjab have noticed broad cultural differences between the Majha, Malwa, and Doaba areas. Hence, any generalizations made in relation to Doaba Sikhs may not be applicable to the Sikhs of the other areas. As the fieldwork on which this chapter is based was conducted in the Doaba region, the validity of my argument may be restricted. A special characteristic of the Doaba area (besides the high incidence of out-migration is the high percentage of

* *Contributions to Indian Sociology*, (n.s.), vol. 2, no. 2, July–December 1986.

** I would like to thank Professor T.N. Madan for his helpful comments on an earlier draft.

the scheduled caste population. In Hoshiarpur district the proportion of the scheduled caste population is 28.82 per cent as against 24.71 per cent for the state.

My fieldwork was conducted in a typical village of Hoshiarpur district in 1981–2. The village, Piplanwala, like most others in the region, was settled by a single clan of Jat Sikhs, who are the dominant local caste. However, 17 other castes are represented in the village. The castes are divided between upper caste Hindus, Sikhs, and the scheduled caste (Harijans or Adharmis as they call themselves in the Punjab). The village has a somewhat higher proportion of Hindus than Sikhs, though the ranks of the Hindus are inflated by including Harijans who, in actuality are considered by the villagers to be separates from both Hindus and Sikhs.[1]

The principal Sikh castes in the village are Jat, Ramgarhiya (carpenter and ironsmith), Ramdasia (originally weavers), Chimba (tailor), and Kumhar (potter). Of these, Jats, Ramgarhiyas, and Ramdasias are numerically dominant. The principal Hindu castes are Brahmin and Khatri; besides, there are service castes like Sonar (goldsmith), Baniya (petty shopkeeper), Nai (barber), etc. The major scheduled caste are Chamar (tanners) and Churah (sweepers). There is thus a fair sprinkling of most castes in the population. The village however is referred to as a Jat Sikh village by the local people and others because of the economic and political dominance of the Jat Sikhs. Jats are largely and by preference agriculturists and landowners, and form the backbone of the Punjab peasantry. Some have found employment in the armed services and in the transport business. They also constitute the majority of the Sikhs generally. Here, the discussion moves between a consideration of Jats in the village and Jats as a category. Illustrations are drawn from the case study of Piplanwala, and whenever ethnographic evidence is cited in detail, it is from the village study. However, the interpretations offered relate these facts to the wider canvas of Jat history, culture, and politics. The discussion moves freely from a consideration of historical origins to modern-day relations within the national setting.

The Problem

As already stated, this chapter seeks to explore what being 'Sikh' means to the Jat Sikhs of central rural Punjab. There are two components in defining any kind of identity, in this case, ethnic identity. One is ascription by 'self' and the second is ascription by the 'other'.

Especially important to 'other'-ascription are diacritical features by which a category of people are easily distinguishable from others. According to Barth (1969) there is a general category of cultural traits that serve as diacritica or overt signals of identity which to others are criteria of classification. The Sikhs have a particularly noticeable set of diacritical features by which they are easily identified and which are embodied in the *rahatnama*. The *rahatnama* is the code of conduct believed to have been enjoined by the tenth Sikh Guru, Gobind Singh, on the followers of the faith. An important part of the *rahatnama* are the so-called 'five Ks', which every Sikh is enjoined to adopt. These are the *kara* (steel bangle or bracelet), *kangha* (comb), *kes* (unshorn hair), *kirpan* (steel sword), and *kachh* (knee length drawers). An accompaniment of the long hair is the turban covering it. Most Sikhs wear at least two of these overt symbols: the turban signifying uncut hair and the *kara* or the steel bracelet. Most non-Sikhs identify Sikhs by these symbols. There is also an injunction against smoking or chewing tobacco. Other commonly known distinguishing features of the Sikhs are: they are followers of the ten Sikh Gurus, from Guru Nanak to Guru Gobind Singh; they revere the holy book, the Guru Granth Sahib (the tenth Guru designated the holy book as the future Guru for all times, in place of living Gurus); their temples are known as Gurdwaras, and they perform marriage rites in accordance with the Anand Karaj ceremony, rather than vedic rites. This ceremony was instituted around the end of the eighteenth century. Finally, the ancestral (original) home of the Sikhs as Sikhs is Punjab and their mother tongue is Punjabi.

If the above ensemble is the 'identity kit' (see, Goffman, 1968) with which Sikhs generally present themselves to the outside world, what happens when a group of people do not use it with punctiliousness or consistency, yet claim to be Sikhs and view themselves and are viewed by others as staunch followers of Sikhism? My fieldwork in Piplanwala revealed that Jats do not always observe the injunction regarding unshorn hair and many often smoke tobacco (especially members of the older generation); very few wear the *kirpan* nor are they strict about the *kara* and the drawers. Only the baptized (those who have undergone the Sikh initiation ceremony called *pahul*) are faithful in their observance of all the five 'K's' and also of other injunctions. Although the village has four gurdwaras (two belong to the Jat caste, one to the Ramgarhiyas, and one to Ramdasias), Jat males rarely visit these, and regular attendance is extremely low among their women as opposed to women of other Sikh castes.

Thus, there are scarcely any outward symbols proclaiming a Sikh identity different from that of Hindus among this group of people. Even more significantly, Jats, who are the dominant caste in the village, do not seem to attach much importance to this 'negligence'. Other scholars have also commented on this. Thus, McLeod says:

since the migrations of 1947, the Jats of the Majha, Malwa and Doaba have virtually all been Sikhs. Not all, however, are visibly Sikh as the Jat commonly assumes a *considerable freedom* with regard to the observance of the Khalsa discipline (*rahat*). In his own eyes and those of others he remains a Sikh even if he cuts his beard or smokes tobacco [McLeod, 1976: 98, italics mine].

Similarly, Khushwant Singh remarks: 'Amongst the Sikh peasantry, the position is much worse. In the districts of Ambala, Ludhiana and Jullundur, most Sikh Jats trim their beards and smoke hookahs or cigarettes.' Contrastively, 'the only class of Sikhs to observe strictly the forms and symbols of Sikhism are the lower class from Northern Punjab' (1953: 179).

If observing the *rahatnama* is immaterial to Jat Sikhs, it becomes important to ask what constitutes Sikh identity for them; how do they define Sikhism and in what way do they convey to themselves and to others that they are Sikhs. That symbolism is important in identity projection and maintenance is not left in doubt by a statement made by Khushwant Singh: 'the dividing line between Sikhs and Hindus is the external appearance of the Sikh' (1953: 180). How then can a flagrant violation of the norms of Sikh ethnic identity on the part of Jat Sikhs be explained? What further complicates the problem is that, unlike Jat Sikhs in the village, the other Sikh castes do maintain the external symbols of Sikhism. Why this discrepancy between the behaviour models of different castes occupying the same ecological and cultural–religious niche? McLeod shows that Jats are affected by their lax attitude to religious symbols while in the case of other castes it can result in a loss of religious identity. Thus, he says, 'If a Khatri shaves he is regarded as a Hindu by others and soon comes to regard himself as one' (1976: 98). An explanation of the above problem is attempted in what follows:

In order to understand what Sikh identity means to the Jat, a number of theoretical and practical questions have to be explored. First, how is ethnic identity defined? Second, are there any specific features which constitute ethnic identity: for example, is religion a critical component in Sikh ethnic identity? How do non-practicing

Sikhs define or understand their allegiance to Sikhism? Is a common language or a common geographic region by itself the basis of shared ethnic identity?

It is important to remember that ethnic identities develop and shift over time (see Madan, 1974 on Bengali Muslims), and if religious consciousness is in the first instance responsible for separating one group of people from others, it need not be the sole reason for their subsequently being separate. Although Sikhism developed as a result of separation from Hinduism, it is now the way of life for a large number of people and cannot be absorbed into or dismissed as a mere sect of Hinduism. Thus, Sikh identity does not seem to be primarily a question of religious denomination, though that is the basis on which a Sikh will first distinguish himself from a Hindu or a Muslim.

The methodology used here to unravel this problem, is partly borrowed from Barth's discussion of ethnic groups and boundaries. According to him, ethnic groups are categories of ascription and identification by the actors themselves and thus have the characteristic of organizing interaction between people (see Barth 1969: 9). By this definition Jats are certainly an ethnic group both as Jats and Sikhs. There are two perspectives from which one can attempt to understand the nature of such a group. One is the internal constitution and history of separate ethnic groups and the other, which Barth advocated, is understanding the processes involved in generating and maintaining ethnic groups. The latter involves an analysis of ethnic boundaries and boundary maintenance. For Barth, the critical focus of investigation is the ethnic boundary that defines the group, not the 'cultural stuff' that it encloses. A group identifies itself as separate in the very articulation of relations with other groups. Barth allows for redrawing or redefining of boundaries due to changes within the group, which may take place as a result of economic or political reasons. As Fox (1985) shows in the case of the Sikhs, differentiation can take place within a single identity, that is, the specification of 'Singh' identity from the more generalized 'Sikh' identity. This would lead one to argue that what is happening within the boundaries of an ethnic identity is not unproblematic either.

Pursuantly, one may ask how the Jat Sikh maintains his boundary vis-à-vis Hindu castes of the village. Further, how does he maintain his identity *outside* the village? Also, why is it that the Jat may not need diacritical marks to communicate his identity while other Sikh castes of the village clearly need to do so? Finally, at a substantive level, what are the important components of Jat Sikh identity?

The plan of the rest of the chapter is as follows. It first discusses the emergence of the Jat's 'Sikh' identity against the background of Sikh history and the evolution of Sikhism as a religious faith. It then examines the nature of Jat Sikh communities today and shows how processes of identity maintenance operate within the village community and outside it. The contrasts that are drawn are between Sikhs and non-Sikhs; Jat Sikhs and non-Jat Sikhs, and rural and urban Sikhs (the last two sets essentially coincide). It is shown how Jat idenity is articulated in opposition to and through non-Jat urban Sikhs. Finally, the substantive nature of Jat Sikh identity is explored.

Historical Background

Although the Sikh religion owes its beginnings to Khatri Hindu (Guru Nanak), and the following nine Gurus also belonged to the Khatri caste, the principal body of the followers belong to the Jat caste. There was a massive influx of Jats into the Sikh fold at the time of the fifth Guru, Arjun Dev, in the mid-sixteenth to the early seventeenth centuries. According to the 1881 census, 66 per cent of the Sikh following was constituted by Jats, while Khatris were sixth with a following of 2.2 per cent. Tarkhans and Chamars followed the Jats with 6.5 per cent and 5.6 per cent respectively (McLeod, 1976: 84). The 1931 Census also recorded Jats as constituting over 50 per cent of the total Sikh population. Jats seem to have had the longest tradition of consistent adherence to the Sikh faith, which seems to have been unaffected by it changing political fortunes. The changing composition of the Sikh population, both in terms of numbers and the kind of people, has implications for the development of Sikh identity. From the institution of Sikhism, and until the tenth Guru, and even today, Sikh identity has been in a process of crystallization and in the act of separating itself from Hindu identity. To this day, there are in Punjab villages survival of customs and rituals shared by almost all castes and which are basically defined as belonging to the Hindu religious and cultural tradition.

Over a period of time, the different degrees of separation from the Hindus, and conformity to an emergent Sikhism, has led scholars like Fox to conclude that:

A single religious community, in the sense of a shared set of traditions, cultural meanings, and social practices, was absent among those who called themselves Sikhs in the late 19th century [and that] by the second half of the

19th century, the boundary separating Singhs from other Sikhs and Hindus was ill-defined [Fox 1985: 108].

Further, there was movement in and out of their respective religions on the part of both Hindus and Muslims. As a result, the social customs and culture of the Sikhs did not crystallize as a body of purely Sikh customs. The five symbols of Sikhism, or the five 'Ks', came only with the introduction of baptism by Guru Gobind Singh in 1699. How did Sikhism develop between the first and the last Gurus to impart a distinct identity to its followers? Before the tenth Guru, was it possible for rural Sikhs to differentiate themselves from non-Sikhs?

It was during the period of the fifth and sixth Gurus, Arjun Dev and Hargobind, that the first major influx of Jats into the Sikh ranks took place. Hargobind's father Arjun Dev's martyrdom at the hands of the Mughal rulers strengthened the 'this-worldly' tendencies of the religion, diverting the weight away from quietism and mysticism to political affairs, and it also brought about the first militarization of the Sikhs. It began a series of conflicts with the Muslim officialdom which lasted far into the future, in striking contrast to the religious and theological rapproachement with Islam that had characterized the teachings of Nanak.

However, during the tenure of the next two Gurus, power fell into the hands of informal leaders called *masands* who began to use religious funds for their own personal gratification. Bereft of strong leadership, many of the more nominal Sikhs reverted into the surrounding Hindu community, a process that has never wholly discontinued. In the tenth Guru's time, recruitment to the religion, especially from among Jats, again rose. Guru Gobind Singh consolidated the process of militarization of the Sikhs and continued the opposition to Mughal tyranny. He did so by creating a community of baptized Sikhs, called the Khalsa (literally, the pure). The members of the Khalsa had to undergo an initiation ceremony *(pahul)*, and to adopt the five 'Ks'. With this, Guru Gobind Singh created a new brand of Sikhs, the 'soldier–saints', who were to be guardians of the faith that had originated with Guru Nanak. He was also responsible for initiating many of the rituals, symbols and ceremonies that are distinctive of the Sikhs today. Thus, he gave Sikh men the surname of the Singh and Sikh women the surname of Kaur. He was also instrumental in defining the rules of the *rahat,* including the injunction against tobacco and meat obtained by the halal method (which is similar to the Jewish kosher). This latter feature set the Sikhs off from the Muslims who consumed halal meat. In opposition to this, the Sikhs were to adopt the *jhatka* method.[2] The creation of the Keshdhari Sikhs occurred at this time. Few Khatris accepted conversion to the new faith. They remained Sahajdhari Sikhs (those who follow the slow path to adoption and do not necessarily observe the five 'Ks') as opposed to Gobind Singh's Keshdhari Sikhs. The bulk of the converts were Jat peasants of the central districts of the Punjab. They took over the leadership from the Khatris. The rise of militant Sikhism meant the growth of Jat power in the Punjab.

Given the large numbers of Jats joining the Panth (meaning the Sikh brotherhood, sometimes with undertones of nationalism), a substantial portion of what *now* constitutes Sikh identity might have been and probably is what *formerly* constituted Jat identity. McLeod says that, typically, many of the features so commonly regarded as *Sikh* should properly be regarded as characteristically *Jat* (see McLeod, 1976: 103).

The numbers of the Sikhs fluctuated again during the period of the *misls*[3] and during the reign of Ranjit Singh. While the increase in numbers up to then had been largely due to an influx of Jats during the reign of Ranjit Singh, that continued through the first years of British dominance, many Khatris and Aroras were converted to Sikhism. In spite of the numerical strength of Jats, the Sikhs personnel of all the higher services, civil or military, were predominantly non-Jat (Khushwant Singh 1963: 181). Yet, overall, the last decade of the nineteenth century and the first decade of the twentieth saw a phenomenal rise in the numbers of the Sikhs. According to Khushwant Singh, the economic advantages of being Sikh checked the disintegration of Sikhism and its lapse into Hinduism (1966, vol. 2: 119).

A preference for Jats among various ruling classes stabilized their position at the top of the caste hierarchy among the Sikhs. This upward mobility of Jat Sikhs had begun in the time of Guru Gobind Singh, when a large number of those baptized were Jats. It was the baptized Keshdhari Jats who had been the chief instruments of the Sikh rise to power and consequently became the landowning aristocracy during the rule of Maharaja Ranjit Singh. It was at the same time that Hindus with an inclination towards Sikhism started bringing up at least one son in the family as a Keshdhari Sikh (these Hindus largely belonged to the Khatri, Arora, and Baniya jatis).

During this period there were the Keshdhari or baptized Sikhs;

those who adopted some of the five symbols but were not baptized; sahajdharis or Nanakpanthis (those who believed in Sikhism but did not adopt the 'five Ks'), mixed families which were partly Hindu and partly Sikh, and intermarrying Hindu and Sikh families. Commenting on this situation, Fox says that in the late nineteenth century, in the Punjab, there were several populations calling themselves 'Sikh', and they had separate images of what the religious identity meant, who was included within it, and which cultural meanings and practices marked them as distinctive. 'There was a conglomerate of practices and beliefs between baptized and unbaptized professor of Sikhism, and the various labels did not index identities that were unequivocally defined in terms of religious beliefs and social practices' (Fox, 1985: 111). The next section elaborates this point.

Sikhism in Rural Communities Today

The Sikh community as one knows it today came into being over a period of time during which its character remained in flux and the differentiation of religion from Hinduism fuzzy. Today, a Sikh supposedly knows what is expected of him and the values of which he is expected to conform to as a member of community. The sense of Sikh identity has sharpened with the various movements launched by urban Sikhs during the nineteenth and twentieth centuries for the control of Sikh gurdwaras and for a Punjabi Suba. The Sikh's political party, Akali Dal, the Chief Khalsa Diwan (an organization for promotion of education and Sikh culture), and the Shiromani Gurdwara Prabhandak Committee (SGPC) (the body entrusted with the management of the Gurdwara) have played significant roles in defining the identity of Sikhs as a separate religious community. As Paul Brass says:

Three sets of symbols have been especially prominent in the development of communal consciousness among the Sikhs—historical symbols derived from the history of the Sikh Kingdoms before the British conquest of the Punjab; religious symbols which have been used to define the boundaries between Sikhs and Hindus in modern time; and linguistic symbols which have associated the Sikhs with a particular form of the Punjab's language written in the Gurumukhi script [1974: 278].

He goes on to say: 'There is no doubt that the sense of Sikh separateness is strongest among a particular social class of Sikhs—that is, the Jat Sikh peasantry ... [ibid.: 285]. Against this background, it is necessary to explain the apparently paradoxical and errant behaviour of Sikh Jats alluded to at the beginning of the chapter.

The majority of Jat Sikhs belong to the rural areas of Punjab as opposed to Khatri Sikhs who are to be found largely in urban areas. Most Jats are agriculturists, but also with a later tradition of service in the military. They are an enterprising people who do not hesitate to migrate in search of work and therefore Jat settlements are to be found in the UK, Canada, parts of the USA, Malaysia and more recently, in the countries of the Middle East. They were favoured by the British as agriculturists which led to their recruitment as settlers for the canal colonies. They were also recruited into the Indian army by the British who strengthened the militant 'Singh' image in the process (see Fox, 1985 on the formation of 'Singh' identity).

In the Punjab, Jats coexist with Hindus and Harijans and also with non-Jat and Mazhabi Sikhs (the latter are low-caste converts to Sikhism), and prior to Partition, they coexisted with Muslims too. The rural scene is not only chatacterized by followers of different religions, but also by numerous caste groups. Although the caste system was never as strong in Punjab as in most other parts of the country, and Sikhism weakened it further, it still continues to exist. Caste as an occupational division of labour was, and is, an intrinsic part of village life. Thus Jats are landowners and agriculturists, Khatris and Baniyas, moneylenders and shopkeepers. Until recently Brahmin priest also retained his role at rites of passage. There are water-carrier, barber, sweeper, potter, carpenter, ironsmith, and goldsmith castes, besides Chamars who are leatherworkers and agricultural labourers. Prior to 1947, the village population was distributed over three major religions (Hinduism, Sikhism, and Islam) and numerous castes. Thus, the Jat Sikh had to define himself within a community of Hindu castes and other non-Jat Sikh castes.

Community studies reveal that, besides observing Hindu marriage rites, Jats, who are ostensibly Sikhs, until very recently practised Hindu funeral customs, including immersion of the post-cremation remains in sacred rivers. Thus Hershman says:

the process of conversion from Hinduism to Sikhism was begun by the Jats of the Jullundur Doaba in the second half of the 19th century, but even by 1946 the Jats were still not unambiguously Sikh and retained many Hindu customs including the employment of Brahmans as family priests [1981: 23].

The Anand Marriage Act was passed into law as late as 1901, and was only then that a non-Brahmanical ceremony became legal for Sikhs.

Today many Sikhs immerse the remains of their dead in rivers holy to
the Sikh tradition rather than in the Ganges. It is however true that
not all Sikhs have adopted the suffix Singh and this is not restricted to
Sahajdhari Sikhs alone. My own fieldwork revealed that there were
many Jat Sikhs in the village who had names such as Ram Lal, or Ram
Saran, or Ram Das (rather than Ram Singh), though their children
now bear the 'Singh' suffix. The significance of the nature of these
'survivals' will be highlighted later.

I.P. Singh (1959: 277) dates the decline of the importance of
Brahmanical ceremonies in Sikh Rural life to as late as 1922–3, and
links it to the Sikh reform movement. He argues that the Hinduization
of the Sikh masses occurred after the fall of Ranjit Singh's empire. The
Singh sabha and the Akali movements led to a progressive purging
of Hindu customs and Brahmanical influences and the institutionalization of Sikh traditions and rituals.

Thus, in the village today, during *shraadh* (ancestor propitiation
rites), instead of feeding Brahmans, five Sikhs (the symbolic representatives of the *panj pyaras*)[4] are fed; instead of Brahman priests,
Sikh *granthis* or *bhais* are employed at all life-cycle ceremonies and
the latter can belong to any group. These changes led Singh to assert
that 'the part played by Brahman in the religious life of the Sikhs has
been completely wiped out' (I.P. Singh 1959: 289).

The Rural–Rural Contrast

In the village of Piplanwala, most Jat men cut their hair and maintain
only a trimmed beard or none at all. Within the village they rarely
wear turbans. A piece of cloth might be wound carelessly round the
head as protection againts the afternoon sun while a man is at work in
the fields. With hair cut short of shorn, no *kangha* (comb) may be
worn in it. Most of them do not carry the *kirpan* either and are
unbaptized Sikhs. Jat men rarely visit the gurudwaras (there are four
in the village) and it is not a part of the daily routine of Jat women. By
contrast, the other Sikh castes of Piplanwala, especially Ramgarhiyas
(Tarkhans and Lohars) and Ramdasias (weavers), are 'visible' Sikhs.
They are very conscientious in their observances, devout in their
allegiance to the faith and actively involved in keeping it alive. Both
men and women participate in religious worship and *sewa* (service)
and children are socialized into the faith through activities centred
around the gurdwara which reinforce religious and ethnic identity.

Within the village the Jat is confident of his identify as a Sikh; he does not need demonstrate it by sporting unshorn hair and beard or by participating in gurdwara activities. What is it that accounts for his successes in conveying Sikh identity without the diacritical marks, and without his behaviour conforming to Sikh values, while other castes like Ramgarhiyas and Ramdasias are unable to do so? There are two principal reasons for this. First, the village community is usually a small unit where most people still know each other at a personal, dyadic level, and the caste, religious, and economic status of most members is well known. Thus, Jat peasants do not have to inform their fellow villagers that they belong to such and such religion by a display of external symbols. However, by the same logic, other Sikh castes should not need to do so either. The explanation for this contradiction lies in the fact that both Ramgarhiyas and Ramdasias need to distinguish themselves from Hindu caste members who live in the same village. Corresponding to both these castes there are Hindu Tarkhans (Ramgarhiyas) and non-Sikh or Hindu weavers and Chamars to whom they must demonstrate their identity and devoutness. The Jats, on the other hand, have no such problem of identity-maintenance because all of them in the village are Sikhs. Hershman's comment that 'it is perhaps best to make explicit that in Punjab the word Sikh is primarily associated with the Jats while the word Hindu is associated with Brahmans' makes sense in this context (1981: 23).

However, whenever the Jat farmer goes outside the village, he dons his turban. When he is visiting relatives or meeting village or local district officials, applying for a loan, or conducting any official business, he goes dressed as a proper 'Sikh'. When celebrating Baisakhi or a wedding, he wears his turban. Thus on ritual occasions he conforms to the identity prescribed by his religious tenets.

Within the village community, there are certain categories of Jats who do maintain the prescribed symbols of Sikhism. These are the ·important or 'big' men of the community: big landlords, political leaders, panchayat heads, religious heads etc. Some of them undergo the initiation *(pahul)* ceremony and most are quite successful in projecting a 'five Ks' image of Sikhism to the other villagers. Thus the leaders of the community, secular and others, metonymically serve to display its religious status and affiliation. A remark by S.S. Barnala, the then Chief Minister of Punjab, throws light on the significance of this device of identity-maintenance. He said: 'As a leader of the party, it is proper for me to have a flowing beard. I am an *amritdhari* Sikh' (quoted in *India Today*, Voices, 31 January 1986). From a tied beard during the Janata Party phase, when he was a minister at the Centre,

he has gone on to sport a flowing one in his Akali Dal phase, affirm-
ing his religious identity over the political, or perhaps signifying the
inseparability of religion and politics.

In pointing out that Sikh customs and observances in the villages
are still marked by Hindu residues, many scholars overlook the fact
that most of these can be classified as rural or village customs which
belong to the folk tradition rather than to any particular religious
community or tradition. Thus, pre-wedding rites are common for all
Punjabis whether they are Hindus, Muslims, or Sikhs. For example,
the *maiyan* ceremony performed before marriage as well as ancestor
rites and birth rituals are common to all villagers. Similarly, the
village joins together in the celebration of many feasts and festivals
which have more to do with communal well-being than religion as
such. The majority of village observances belong to the non-
Brahmanical folk tradition rather than to any particular Great Tradition, whether Hindu, Muslim, or Sikh.

The Jat's pragmatic attitude to religions is also a part of the explanation for his lax attitude towards Sikh symbolism. As was mentioned earlier, Jat men and women rarely visit the gurdwara and are
not overly concerned with theological debate and exposition or understanding. There is not even a daily routine of prayer in the home,
unlike that followed by women of other Sikh castes. The Jat male is
more concerned with tending his fields early in the morning than
starting the day by invoking God's blessing in the gurdwara. Pettigrew
quotes a former Jat president of the SGPC as saying:

Master Tara Singh (a non-Jat Sikh political leader) never raised any slogan for
the benefit of the rural people. The general opinions is that his activities are
confined solely to gurdwaras. He does not fight for the small farmer—*and for
the Jats the gurdwara does not have an important place in rural social life.*
[Pettigrew n.d.:2 italics mine.]

In the fieldwork village of Piplanwala, the two popular gurdwaras
(out of four) were those of the Ramdasias and Ramgarhiyas; these
were active all year round, especially in terms of daily attendance.
The Ramgarhiya gurdwara, which was built by a wealthy and devout Tarkhan Sikh, was attended by most castes and also patronized
by the Jat caste who did not then have a gurdwara of their own. It was
only when the Tarkhan founder, Sher Singh, objected to the sloppiness
of Jat religious observances by calling the former 'sirkate' (headless)
referring to their shorn hair, that the Jats decided to build a gurdwara.
He also antagonized the lower caste Sikhs by remaining mindful of

their origins. Having built their own place of worship, the Jats lapsed into their easy ways.

Although the gurdwara and the so-called Great Tradition religion does not hold the Jat Sikh in its grip, there are various ritual observances that the Jat does follow. Most of these relate to the well-being of agriculture, for example, propitiation of the water deity *khwaja*, performed at wells and tubewells every Thursday, propitiation of and rituals involving the wellbeing of farm and milch animals, consecration of new grain, and the like. In short, the Jats have a practical or pragmatic attitude to religion.

At the level of belief, most villagers believe in a vatriety of magico–religious spirits and influences. Thus they do not hesitate to visit the grave sites of Muslim *pirs* they believe in a number of local deities and their relationship with these is also very practical concerning the granting of wishes, curing of illnesses, and other everyday concerns. These practices show that villagers follow a certain set of beliefs irrespective of whether they belong to the Hindu, Sikh, or Muslim religious traditions.

However, that is not to say that Sikhism as a religion does not hold an important position in the village or in the Jat world-view. Indeed, in Punjab, village life is coloured by the Sikh raith in general; community life is organized around the gurdwara and by the institution of *langar* (community kitchen) and performance *akhand path* (an uninterrupted reading of the Sikh holy book). Most castes, including Hindus, visit gurdwaras at one time or another and hold the *akhand path* during important family celebrations. Festivals like Baisakhi and Basant Panchmi, although largely of seasonal significance, have a distinct Sikh flavour in the Punjab. They are associated with important events in Sikh history, for example, the creation of the Khalsa on Baisakhi day. In Piplanwala, Basant Panchmi is associated with a visit to the area by Guru Hargobind. I.P. Singh (1959: 283), in his description of a Sikh village, also notes this trend in which most Hindu festivals have been 'Sikhized'.

What kinds of sanctions, if any, are there against infringements of Sikh taboos in the village? A case in point is the consumption of tobacco. Most elderly Jats in the village smoke, although the trend is becoming less common. Most medium-sized and small landholders grow a small patch of tobacco in their fields for domestic consumption. When directly confronted, they shamefacedly admit that they smoke occasionally. Others tease the smokers by calling them 'Chamars', thereby referring to a fall in caste status rather than a loss of religious identity. In another instance, I confronted a wealthy Jat landlord (who is atypical of village landlords in terms of having broken most village and social conventions; he leads a very feudal lifestyle), while he was smoking a cigarette, with a question from the household census which enquired about his religion. Caught off-guard, he replied that he was both a Hindu and a Sikh. Being an educated villager, he plunged into a explanation of how the Sikhs were the guardians and protectors of the Hindus. He would not deny that he was a Sikh, but to explain the cigarette in his hand, he claimed that the Hindu identity was subsumed within the Sikh identity, both having been one people originally. This is an inversion of the usual assumption that Sikhism is subsumed within Hinduism, but can be explained by the fact that the Doaba is a Jat Sikh-dominated area.

A question that arises out of the above discussion is: what constitutes primary identity in the village? Is caste, occupation, or religion the primary defining aspect of identity? It was interesting to find that different sections of the village population answered the household census questions differently, indicating by their answers what they considered to be the most defining aspect of their identity or the identity they wished to project (see Berreman 1975: 71–105 from multiple identities). The Jat response was that they were Jat-zamindar. When asked about religious affiliation they answered that they were Sikh or Sikh Jat. Khatris first identified themselves as Khatris (by caste) and only then by occupation. Tarkhans identified themselves as Ramgarhiyas, the honorific title used by the carpenter and ironsmith castes, and Chamars replied that they were Adharmis (followers of their original religion). Thus, to some, caste was most important, to others religion, to yet others occupation, and so on.

For the Jats, it appears, there is an equal emphasis on the Jat (caste) part of the identity and also on the zamindar part of it. The latter emphasizes both occupation and ownership of land. The Jat might be employed as a schoolteacher, or serve in the military but he sees his primary role as that of an agriculturist; his connection with land is what he holds most dear and what identifies him.

The Jat's devotion to agriculture, to husbanding the land, colours his outlook on life. Owning land and earning money to accquire more is of paramount importance to him. Generally the Jat will not let anything interfere with his agricultural activities. Pettigrew remarks, while explaining the Jat involvement in the Akali movement for the Punjabi Suba: 'The sporadic support that the Jats did give was conditioned by the harvesting and sowing seasons as also by a lack of appreciation of the cultural stance taken by their urban coreligionists' (Pettigrew n.d.: 2). This is also proven by the fact that Punjab has produced bumper harvests even in the most politically troubled times.

A vibrant memory and knowledge of their history is an important element in Sikh identity. This knowledge is disseminated through the many historic gurdwaras in the countryside. There is a tradition of visiting historic gurdwaras located close to one's village. Most of these gurdwaras have special celebrations on their important days. Also, most of these gurdwaras celebrate important events in Sikh history. Traditional singing groups called *dhadi jathas* relate deeds of bravery in Sikh history. *Ragis* (professional singers) relate events from the lives of the Sikh Gurus and other important figures. Thus history is orally related and recalled at festivals and fairs that are patronized by the Jats as much as other villagers. As Paul Brass says, 'the symbolic memory of rule is more important in the growth of a modern sense of community and not necessarily the visible embodiment of such rule in the present' (1974: 281).

The *ardas*, which is the end-of-the-day prayer, relates various events in Sikh history. The prayer is extended to include recent and even contemporary events. Reference is made to Sikhs killed during the partition of the Punjab, and contemporary problems of the community are summarized and put before the people.

The Rural–Urban Contrast

The position of Jats vis-à-vis Sikhism becomes clearer when they are contrasted with urban, mainly Khatri Sikhs. The contrast between these two Sikh castes has always been important, because of the role of the former in the origin of the faith and in providing the intellectual leadership to the community and of the latter in providing majority support and in defending the faith. Over time, Khatris have come to be identified with the pacifist ideal of Guru Nanak while Jats proclaim the militant ideal of guru Gobind Singh. Paradoxically, it is the non-Jats who have found it necessary to adopt the five 'Ks' identity while the Jats have done so only in spirit rather than form. Further, the two groups have always been opposed in terms of being largely urban or rural Sikhs. The other contrast is that, while Khatris have largely been non-agriculturists (mostly moneylenders, small businessmen, and administrators), Jats have been landowners and cultivators. Most non-Jat Sikhs in urban areas are also known to be quite strict in following religious prescriptions. Thus, they maintain long hair and uncut beards and wear the turban and the *kara.* Most of them are likely to be *amritdharis* (initiated Sikhs) and they almost never smoke. They are more regular in gurdwara attendance, better informed about the religious scriptures (partly because of higher literacy levels), and are conscious about bringing up their children as Sikhs. Why the urban Khatri Sikh needs to maintain the 'Singh' image may be explained by the following comment made in another context by De Vos and Romanucci-Ross:

In identity-maintenance one has to assess the nature of the possible threat which close with an alien group implies. In a modern pluralistic society, where contact is intense and unavoidable, certain minor symbolic 'emblematic' measures remain vitally necessary to maintain psychological distance from those outside one's group. [1975: 369].

In the early twentieth century Khatri Sikhs strongly felt the threat of assimilation from a majority population of non-Sikh Khatris and other urban Hindus. Pettigrew quotes a prominent Sikh industrialist in Amristar as saying that, because of the social resemblance and economic integration between themselves and Hindus, there was a positive need for Sikhs to keep their turban (Pettigrew n.d.: 7).3

Fox (1985) shows how the urban Sikhs have organized themselves repeatedly to maintain boundaries vis-à-vis Hindus perhaps due to a fear of losing out in the market of urban jobs and administrative posts, first under the British and then the Congress governments. During both periods, however, they had to organize themselves on the basis of religion to mobilize rural support, because religion was what they had in common with the rural Sikhs. The urban Sikhs were the worst sufferers in the post-Partition years, when they received no land in compensation for the assets they lost in Pakistan and were forced to compete with Hindus well-entrenched in business in East Punjab. The economic differential at this point led to a salience of the ethnic separateness of Sikhs and Hindus. Later, a perceived threat of assimilation and a desire to share in or capture political power led to the demand for a Punjabi Suba by the urban Sikhs. The demand was also a direct result of the division of the Punjab on a communal basis, when independence for the peoples of the subcontinent to two separate states being formed, and also as a result of the linguistic redrawing of the boundaries of the Indian states. In both instances, the Sikhs were not given an opportunity to define themselves either on the basis of religion or language and thus felt a threat to their separate identity (see Brass, 1974). Caught between the two majority communities, urban Sikh and politicians felt it necessary to systematically elaborate those features of their own cultural tradition unique to themselves as a community. Their marginal position in urban society, unlike the secure majority position of the Jat Sikhs in rural areas, led them to find a cultural niche by adopting the 'five Ks' identity both in form and spirit.

A consideration of the role of Jats in the movements initiated by urban Sikhs will throw further light on the substance of a Jat's Sikh identity. As Fox (1985) shows, the Jat peasantry was drawn into the movement only after it had become a battle for control of Sikh temples. This was a direct attack on Hinduized *mahants* (temple functionaries) and an indirect attack on British colonial authority which was considered to be at the back of the high-handedness of the *mahants*. Fox also argues that the condition of the central Punjab peasantry had worsened considerably under British colonialism and this led them to join what he calls the third Sikh war. He further argues that militant Sikh or Singh identity crystallized as a result of the dialectic between British and Sikh interests. The British moulded the Sikhs in an image conducive to their own military and economic interests. For example, they introduced army regulations requiring the observance of Sikh religious symbols. By doing so, they wished to promote an image of the Sikhs as a martial race, separate from other recruits. At a later stage, the Sikhs used the very symbols that the British had encouraged them to adopt to reinforce the so-called martial identity when they themselves fought the British. As Fox says, the 'lion' that the British created roared back at them (Fox 1985)!

During the Punjabi Suba movement too the Jats joined in a later stage. Pettigrew's reasoning, which fits our theory of Jat Sikh identity, is that as the Jats felt secure in their ethnic identity, confident and even arrogant, for them the issue of having it politically defined and crystallized in a Punjabi-speaking state did not arise (Pettigrew n.d.: 4). Yet the Jats eventually supported the movement in large numbers. The resolution of this paradox lies in a comment by a president of the Akali Dal who was a close associate of Master Tara Singh (the leader of the Punjabi Suba movement): 'The Jats have deep faith. Their work is such that they cannot perform rituals. But once a *morcha* (movement) begins the spark is ignited to that deep faith' (quoted in Pettigrew n.d.: 18). This reinforces our earlier point that rituals are secondary in a Jat's life. In part, the relative lack of rituals in Sikhism might have attracted Jats in large numbers to the religion. Also, its egalitarian character appealed to them, as social distinctions hold much less sway than among other castes. One finds little distinction of social classes among Jats. Jat household possessions are more or less the same whether a family has fifty or five acres of land. The diet and apparel of higher and lower class Jats too does not vary much.

Religion is the common platform that unites rural and urban Sikhs whose interests otherwise are quite dissimilar. It provides the common identity for both sections of the Sikh population, and the urban Sikh clearly utilizes religious identity and the separation it signifies both for cultural reasons and material advantage; it therefore becomes important to determine what element of this religious identity appeals to the rural Jat. It is true that Jat sentiment rarely crystallizes as a result of ethnic conflict or competition. Historically, Jats did not mobilize against Hindu moneylenders or Muslim landlords. It would appear that what they have always mobilized against has been the perceived tyranny of the state, whether against Muslim persecution on British colonialism or later, in support of their urban co-religionists' demand for a Punjabi Suba. Each time, in doing so, the Jats have answered the 'call of the Khalsa'.

Periodically Jats have utilized the militant Sikh identity to fight for a 'worthy' cause. Historically, it is seen that the numbers of Jats joining the Sikh faith rose in times of trouble or militancy and fell during peaceful times. Thus, in the seventeenth century, they joined Guru Hargobind's army in large numbers to fight against growing Muslim repression. This intensified during Guru Gobind Singh's time when they received the five symbols of Sikhism. In contrast, during Maharaja Ranjit Singh's time, there were more conversions from among the Khatri castes. Khatris and even some Brahmins converted to Sikhism during this period and the early years of British occupation when the fortunes of the Sikhs were in ascendance. Marenco confirms this in the following statement: 'during the Sikh rule and early years of the British occupation, large numbers of Hindus living in northern Punjab, mainly Khatris and Aroras, were converted to Sikhism' (1976: 43). Ranjit Singh's rule had brought political stability and prosperity to the Punjab, and during the early years of British rule, Sikhs were a favoured people, both as servicemen and as agriculturists.

During British colonial rule, Jats fought many wars for the British both at home and abroad. They were also relocated by the British to the newly founded canal colonies. Finally, they mobilized against the British themselves when their Sikh brethren from the cities roused them. During Partition, Jat Sikhs were instrumental in avenging attacks on both Sikhs and Hindus in West Punjab. Later, they were mobilized by urban Sikhs in the support of a Punjabi Suba. Although initially disinterested (for reasons discussed earlier), they participated in a mass uprising against the Congress government under Pratap Singh Kairon, and went to jail in thousands.

In this last instance, it was the status of being a minority which constantly had to fight for its own interests and against it own disintegration that brought together rural and urban Sikhs. In a sense, the Jats' Sikh identity, beyond the village level is articulated through the agency of urban non-Jat Sikhs. This also testifies that once the Jat Sikh is outside the village community, and has to act at a regional or national level, the need to emphasize and retain boundaries forces itself upon him.

Conclusion

This chapter argues that the rural Punjabi Jat is secure in his Sikh identity. Process of boundary maintenance are reinforced or facilitated by his numerical and socio-economic dominance in Punjab villages, where he is the landowner and at the head of the caste hierarchy. Other castes and classes in the village define themselves in relation to the Jat.

Because, within the village, the Jat does not have to fight to maintain, preserve, or project his Sikh identity, he has not been assertive at a religious level. Non-Jat Sikhs, who are not in a dominant position, and who have to differentiate themselves from Hindus of the same caste (for example, Khatris and Ramgarhiyas), have to display the overt symbols of their religion. The identity crisis has, however, been felt more strongly by the Untouchable castes. The latter have variously tried to adopt a Hindu or Sikh identity or, when rejecting both, asserted an independent one. This explains the Adharm movement among the Chamars of Punjab and the politicization of Churahs (sweepers) in organizing themselves as followers of Balmiki (the Untouchable sage who is believed to have written the epic poem *Ramayana*).

At the village level, Jats have never felt a threat to their identity; beyond the village, especially at the regional and the national level, their concerns become the same as those of urban Sikhs. Once outside his village, the Jat merges with other Sikhs and is no longer in a majority in relation to Hindus. Also, the need to have an impact at the state and national levels leads Jat Sikhs to define themselves as a politically-oriented minority: hence the militant Sikh identity where politics is concerned. It is a way of convincing themselves that they hold their cultural and political destiny in their own hands. It is at this level that they uphold the principle of the inseparability of politics and religion.

Notes

1. Although Harijans are counted as Hindus in census classifications, they are a fairly distinct group with their own set of beliefs and practices. Hence, for the present purpose they are considered as being separate from both Hindus and Sikhs.

2. In the *jhatka* method, the animal is slaughtered by severing the head with a single blow of instrument as opposed to the *halal* method, in which the jugular is severed.

3. After the death of the tenth Guru, Gobind Singh, the Sikhs were organized in small groups of confederalists called *misls* after Ranjit Singh, the ruler of the Punjab, belonging to the Sukerchakie *misl* (see Smith 196).

4. The first five men initiated as Sikhs by Guru Gobind Singh were called the *panj pyaras* the five beloved ones. Since then, five initiated Sikhs are present at ritual ceremonies, symbolically representing the pristine purity of the community.

References

Barth, Fredrik, *Ethnic Groups and Boundaries*, Little, Brown and Company, Boston, 1969.

Berreman, Gerald, 'Bazar Behaviour: Social Identity and Social Interaction in Urban India', in G. De Vos and Romanucci-Ross (eds), *Ethnic Identity*, Mayfield Publishing Co., California, 1973.

Brass, Paul, *Language, Religion and Politics in North India*, Cambridge University Press, London, 1974.

De Vos, G. and L. Romanucci-Ross, *Ethnic Identity: Cultural Continuities and Change*, Mayfield Publishing Co., California, 1975.

Fox, Richard, *Lions of the Punjab: Culture in the Making*, University of California Press, Berkeley, Los Angeles, 1985.

Goffman, Erving, *Asylums*, Penguin, Harmondsworth, 1968.

Madan, T.N., The Dialectic of Ethnic and National Boundaries in the Evolution of Bangladesh', in Suren Navlakhas (ed.), *Studies in Asian Social Development*, Vikas Publishing House, Delhi, 1974.

Marenco, Ethne K., *The Evolution of Sikh Society*, Heritage Publishers, New Delhi, 1976.

McLeod, W.H., *The Evolution of Sikh Community*, Clarendon Press, Oxford, 1976.

Pettigrew, Joyce, 'The Influence of Urban Sikhs on the Development of the Movement for a Punjabi-speaking State', mimeo, n.d.

Singh, I.P., 'A Sikh Village', in Milton Singer (ed.), *Traditional India Structure and Change*, The American Folklore Society, Biographical and Special Series, vol. X, Philadelpia, 1989.

Singh, K., *The Sikhs*, George Allen & Unwin, London, 1953.

——, (ed.) *A History of the Sikhs*, vol. I, Oxford University Press, Delhi, 1963, 1977.

——, (ed.) *A History of the Sikhs*, vol. II, Oxford University Press, Delhi, 1963, 1977.

Smith, M.W., 'The Misal: A Structural Village Group of India and Pakistan', *American Anthropologist*, 1952, 54:1, 41–56.

13

Fluid Boundaries
Christian 'Communities' in India

Rowena Robinson

Introduction

When we talk of communal and community identity, we need to ask ourselves which levels we are talking about: are we speaking of internal understandings of community identity, the ways in which other communities look at a particular group, or the ways in which the state or political authorities define and label groups within a particular territory? In other words, context defines the way in which community boundaries get drawn.

Moreover, one needs to look at the specificities of communities as they were historically formed and the ways in which they constructed themselves. In this chapter this is what I look at in a comparative perspective: moments or conjunctures in the development and negotiation of community boundaries of different regional Christian groups. This is not to give a sense of permanence or to suggest that boundaries thus congeal, but to give a feel of difference on a comparative basis, and this is something that has not so far been attempted. The location of a group in a particular socio–cultural and material matrix is germane to understanding how boundaries are drawn and how groups thus differently located relate themselves to, for instance Hinduism, in varying ways. I also look briefly at the contemporary politics of Christian identity, particularly in relation to the creation of the 'Dalit Christian'.

Today to speak of identities and communities is to bring up an issue, a problem. It is also to get involved in a raging political debate. The waters I traverse in this paper are somewhat calmer, though they take off from political, legal, indeed even constitutional definitions and have, in turn, implications for these.

As such, the sociology of group identities in India is written off right at the very outset. Does it even have the legitimacy to exist, one might ask, when the preamble to the Indian Constitution defines us as a 'secular' republic, where equality is promoted among all citizens regardless of belief, faith, or patterns of worship. It certainly appears here that caste or religion is not perceived as in any way impinging on the relationship of the 'individual' with the state. On the other hand, the Constitution itself recognizes and defines particular social groups—Scheduled Castes, Scheduled Tribes, Other Backward Classes, and the like. It is one of its categories that gets implicated in the concerns of this chapter: minority community (Article 29 and 30).

To use the notion of minority community (or majority, for that matter) is to operate at only one level of the socio–political reality. Clearly the phrases conjure up notions that exist in the political imagination and can redefine the terms of political association. However, when viewed as groups at the level of sustained social action and interaction, lifestyle, custom or mores, a different picture emerges. The 'communities' show themselves as fractured, if not, indeed, sequestered entities, each with a different history and social trajectory.

When talking of Christians, I will argue here, we need really to talk of communities, rather than community. Conversion, in different areas, brought into being different Christian communities, belonging to various denominations. Each arose out of a particular social milieu and finds itself located within this, drawing on it in the construction of its own identity. Thus, there are regional variations and the identity of groups is produced in different ways. Though there is a greater sense of association between separate groups today due to their formation into larger bodies, distinctness marks the level of everyday living.

Different groups, when drawing on regional traditions and patterns, constituted their identity in unique and complex ways. Everywhere, I will argue, processes of continuity and discontinuity with regional Hinduism, or in some cases, tribal culture are perceived, and these are constructed out of several different components. I will not here be discussing negotiations with Muslim, Sikh, and other cultural patterns, though these may be relevant in some regions.

What are the ingredients that enter into the construction of group boundaries and how are negotiations made with regional cultural patterns? In different communities, there are differences in the manner and to the extent that continuity and discontinuity implicate some of these elements: the relationship of the missionaries or converters to their own culture and to the state or other colonial authorities; the relationship of the converts with the mission, their expectations of it, both social and material, their own location within the particular regional socio–cultural order; and the character of their association, economic, social and political, with other social groups within that order.

For instance, Catholic and Protestant missionaries had differing attitudes towards caste. In general, Catholic missionaries were more tolerant of the social distinctions of caste and of encouraging mass conversions in which entire caste groups changed their faith. This led to the perpetuation of caste differences even after conversion. Catholicism, which came to the Indian shores from sixteenth century Europe, for instance, was itself imbued with a spirit of hierarchy that was based on estate.

It is not surprising, therefore, that the Portuguese should have no difficulty in bringing about group conversion, whether in south or western India. Protestant evangelists, on the other hand, because of their much greater emphasis on individualism, found it more difficult to come to terms with group conversions, though their view too did not remain the same consistently. Thus, the degree of embeddedness of a group in regional idioms of caste varies from place to place.

Again, it is important to look at the relationship between missionaries and the state. In sixteenth century Goa, trade, conquest and Christianization went hand in hand for the Portuguese, the sword accompanying the cross in the quest for spices. The king and the Papacy were allied in what was termed the Padroado form of jurisdiction. In Goa, missionaries could use state forces to destroy temples, quell resistance to conversion, and punish the rebellious. The regime made possible mass conversions of both high and low castes. What identified it was an intolerance of the substance, if not the form of indigenous culture and religion. This was typified by the Inquisition established in 1560 to prevent recourse by the converts to non-Christian customs—its range of prohibitions covered a number of socio–cultural practices.

Conversions took place between 1527 and 1549 among castes with fishing and boat handling skills such as the Mukkuvars and the Paravas along the southern coast, where trade and mission were conducted within the shelter of the forts. For both these groups, Christianity became a means of strengthening their jati identity. Involved as they were in occupations considered low and ritually defiling, conversion served not as a means of climbing up the status ladder but of sharpening their distinctiveness from the world of the agrarian caste system.

During the British period the missionaries had no access to state forces to bring about conversions. Where mass conversions took place, converts appear to have had some aspirations for social or economic mobility, dignity, and in some instances educational benefits or as an escape from varying forms of oppression. Protestant missionaries fought caste and the retention of Hindu or tribal ritual, kinship or cultural practices, viewing these as 'idolatry', but groups often found ways of retaining or reconfiguring these. Again, particular expectations can lead to change and the drawing of distinctions: for instance expectations of mobility or the desire to resist subjugation to the dropping of some caste markers. Among high caste Goans, the anticipation of the retention of privilege may have had some influence in the adoption of Portuguese norms and habits: for instance, dress and food codes. Thus, one has to look at the relationship of the convert group to the mission as well as to the other social groups in the area.

Mapping Christian Communities

The Indian census merges Christians into a single group, but they belong to different denominations. Catholics form the largest group constituting nearly 50 per cent of the total population. Another 40 per cent are Protestants, 7 per cent Orthodox Christians and 6 per cent belong to indigenous sects. Catholics consider the Pope as the supreme head in all religious affairs and are organized according to a well-defined hierarchy. Protestantism includes many distinct persuasions and churches. Orthodox groups, such as the Syrian Christians, are affiliated to one of the Orthodox churches of eastern Europe or west Asia or to churches dependent on these. Most Indian indigenous sects arose through separation from mother churches in the

West, though some have broken away from Orthodox churches (D'Souza, 1993).

According to the 1991 census there are 19,640,284 Christians in India, who constitute 2.34 per cent of the population. The Christian population in the country has an uneven spread. 28.62 per cent belong to Kerala, 16.18 per cent to Tamil Nadu 4.37 per cent to Karnataka, and 6.19 per cent to Andhra Pradesh. These four states account for 55.36 per cent of the total Christian population. Another area of concentration is in the north-east, where Assam, Nagaland, Meghalaya, Mizoram, and Manipur together have 21.41 per cent of the Christians. Elsewhere Christians are more scattered, though in Goa they constitute 29.86 per cent of the population.

Intertwined with demographic distinctions are those of denominational and temporal significance. The south and west were early home to Christian traditions: the Syrian Christians of Kerala trace their origin to A.D. 1 while Catholicism in Goa is four hundred years old. It was however only at the end of the eighteenth century that the north witnessed a significant growth in Christian mission activity. A few efforts predated that period and there were small, scattered groups of converts. The mid-eighteenth century conversions to Catholicism in Bettiah where the local ruler patronized the mission, is an interesting case (Sahay, 1986). In the north-east, where Protestantism dominates, Christianity is largely the product of nineteenth and twentieth-century conversions.

While the popular image of Christians as descendants of low-caste, low-status converts stretches the reality, it is true that over 50 per cent of all Christians are from the Untouchable castes, 15 to 20 per cent are tribal in origin, while the upper caste Christians, largely from Kerala and the Konkan coast, constitute a quarter of the total (Tharamangalam, 1996). In the south we find the sixteenth century converts to Catholicism from boat-handling and fishing communities, the Paravas and Mukkuvars. Again, in Tamil Nadu, as in other areas in the south, there are upper-caste converts in some places and also converts from scheduled caste communities. In Goa, the pattern of conversion was such that it changed the complexion of entire villages—thus, groups across the caste hierarchy got converted.

Christianity is often associated with British rule and the process of Westernization, but its appearance in India preceded the British by several hundred years. Indeed, one might say that Christianity in India is as old as the faith itself. Historians agree that there was a Christian community in Kerala in first century A.D. Though it maintained links with Chaldea or Persia, it remained relatively isolated from Western Christianity at least till the sixteenth century. Kerala Christianity was linked to west Asia not western Europe.

Mediating Difference: Christian Communities in Regional Cultures

In this section I shall speak a little about the constitution of community identity for different regional groups in relation to the cultural patterns within which they are embedded. These cultural patterns include idioms of caste, ritual and symbolic codes, ideas of kinship, patrimony, or marriage. As I will also try to show, despite the best efforts of missionaries to eradicate caste, often privileged groups themselves refused to give up their caste entitlements, carrying these, so to say, across the 'religious' divide.

Among Christian Mukkuvars and Paravas, jati boundaries operated as the limits of the community. In other cases, as in Goa, the Christian community was forged out of the conversion of different castes. One is, therefore, interested both in inter-caste relations within particular communities and in the construction and mediation of boundaries between Christians in different regions and their largely Hindu neighbours.

To address the second first. The Syrian Christians were incorporated into Kerala society as a high status group or jati. Their identity hinged on their religious autonomy: the group was enabled across the centuries to reproduce its distinct religious practices. Some of the community's practices, however, revealed its assimilation of the dominant cultural models of the surrounding society. Its outer or public life related, at one time. To its affiliation to Hindu kings and shows even now in its adherence to Hindu norms of hierarchy and endogamy.

The Syrian Christians have a long history of prestige and privilege, enjoyed under different local rulers. Syrian holy places were incorporated into the network of shrines and temples which comprised the ruler's domains and to which he made benefactions. It is through their warrior and mercantile skills and their tradition of rendering service as pepper brokers and revenue officers in Malabar, for which they revived honour and social privileges from the regional rulers, that the patrilineal, prosperous Syrians established themselves as a high status group in relation to the indigenous hierarchy. They negotiated their position through alliance with the local rulers and maintained their status by adherence to the purity–pollution norms of regional Hindu society.

To this day there are points where the boundaries between the Kerala Syrians and Hindus are blurred, as in the rituals of house-building or astrology. The ceremonies of marriage and birth among the Syrian Christians also manifest many similarities with Hindu custom, particularly in the use of ritual substances such as sandal-wood paste, milk, flowers, arecanut and rice. Death rituals, however, express Christian canonical themes, especially in the ideas concerning life-after-death and the anticipation of the final judgement.

The inner life of the community is therefore, defined liturgically and by its Christian ethic and world-view. Hindu symbolic codes, ideas about ceremonial foods and prestations inform the domestic ceremonies in all life-affirming rituals. The boundaries do not however entirely disappear: each group maintains its individuality within Kerala society, aware of and accepting similarities as well as differences (Visvanathan, 1993, 1995; Houtart and lemercinier, 1981).

The relationship of Mukkuvar popular Christianity with Hinduism is much more problematically defined, a fact no doubt linked to the Mukkuvars' degraded social position. Mukkuvar popular Christianity goes beyond the doctrinal limits set by the church. It takes particular strands from Tamil non-Sanskritic Hinduism, in turn reconfiguring and subverting these. This tension is most clearly elaborated in the conceptualization of the feminine divine—the disjunction between her benign and evil forms (Ram, 1991).

While the image of Mary is dominant in Mukkuvar popular Christianity, all reference to her virginity, a motif so critical in Catholic theological discourse, is suppressed and she is revered simply and unequivocally in her maternal aspect as Maataa, The Mukkuvar Christian Maataa has some qualities akin to the Tamil village goddess, particularly in her power to heal through possession. Mukkuvar religion also has a place for Hindu female divinities, such as the non-Sanskritic female village deity Eseki and her companions SuDalai MaaDan and Vannara MaaDan.

Within Tamil Hinduism, Eseki has both harmful and redemptive powers in her capacity as village goddess, and she is more conspicuously worshipped by the lower castes. In this form and in her power to inflict wrath and destruction, the goddess inverts the Sanskritic image of the female divine as the submissive consort of a male deity. By opening its boundaries to the entry of Eseki, Mukkuvar popular Christianity both sets itself at a distance from Sanskritic imaginings and establishes a close but contentious relationship with Tamil lower Hinduism (Ram, 1991).

In Mukkuvar popular Catholicism, Eseki is stripped of her redemptive capacities: it is the Maataa alone who has the benign healing powers, while Eseki and her companions are purely evil and destructive. The Mukkuvar fisherfolk are despised by the culturally ascendant upper-caste Hindus but, as they make their living outside the framework of agrarian society, they are not dependent on the latter for material sustenance. The relationship between Eseki and Mary, thus, condenses in itself the ambivalent, indeed even hostile, attitude of the Mukkuvars to caste society.

It is finally an expression of the autonomy of the Mukkuvars' religious identity that they can incorporate Hindu divinities while defining them, in opposition to the benevolent Maataa, as unrelentingly evil (Ram, 1991). Thus, even while sacred boundaries are fluid, the relationship with Hindu deities may be contested rather than simply syncretic. The working of the goddess tradition into Mukkuvar popular Christianity, and its redefinitions on this terrain, simultaneously enables engagement with particular strands of Tamil culture as well as representation, by the Christians, of their separate religious affiliation.

As a function of their location within a Hindu milieu and their separation from it through their distinct religious identity, many Catholic groups in south India developed ideas about a complex pantheon of Christian divine beings and the ritual modes through which their power could be accessed parallel to those existing about deities within Hinduism. Catholicism in the region had its feast days, processions and cults, and its forms worship incorporated many aspects of Hindu devotion (Mosse, 1994).

It would appear that higher in the divine hierarchies, the purity and separation of traditions is more strictly maintained. Ritual conducted by the Brahman priest for the superior deities such as Shiva, Parvati, or Vishnu is regarded as constituting an entirety separate realm from the worship of the Trinity conducted by the Christian priest. Both are acceptable but distinct forms of association with the divine. At this level, mutual participation in ceremonies is uncommon and generally forbidden.

In rural Tamil Nadu, just as Hindus participate in cults to saints, Catholics interact with particular categories of Hindu village gods and goddesses for preservation from attack at moments and sites of vulnerability. At the lowest level of the divine hierarchy the realm of ghosts, demons, and other agents of ill fortune, the interaction between Hinduism and Catholicism is greatest (Mosse, 1994). Indeed, for various reasons one often finds that it is not just at the lower reaches of the *divine* pantheon that the intermingling of traditions is greater, but also among the more inferior ranks of the social order.

In the multi-caste, class stratified Protestant community in Madras, for instance, one discovers greater interaction with Hinduism at the lower levels of the social hierarchy. At this level are encountered beliefs in the intervention of *pey* (ghosts of persons who die untimely or inauspicious deaths), demons, or other evil spirits in everyday life. Such syncretism is officially denied by those who belong to the higher social strata. Constituting the élite of the community and participating in the framing of its dominant theological discourse, they dismiss the views and observances of the more lowly groups as superstition (Caplan, 1987).

In Goa, too, it is predominantly the higher castes who are represented in the priesthood, and it is they who retain greater control over the organization of feasts in different village churches. They tend to regard beliefs in spirits or *bhut* with disparagement and a certain degree of ridicule. However, the lower social groups openly espouse such beliefs and visit Hindu religious specialists to deal with the *bhut*, the spirits of persons who died premature or violent deaths, which may have been the cause of some illness or misfortune in their lives. In these cases they participate and cooperate with the religious specialist or *gaddhi* in a number of different ways in the process of identification of the harmful spirit and in making decisions regarding the action to be taken in case of suspected spirit affliction.

It is possible, therefore, that the vitality of ideas and practices about spirit affliction among the lower social groups may be related in part to the fact that this is an area, outside the setting of the church, in which they appear to exercise a degree of control over the ritual activity involved. On the other hand, given their relatively larger clerical representation and domination in church-centred activities and rituals, there is an overt and more close identification by the higher social groups or the élite with the church's stance that practices concerned with spirit affliction and healing are to be condemned as pagan and that belief in them is unworthy of the true Christian.

The negotiation of caste differences within Christian groups constitutes an area of considerable historical and sociological interest. Wherever group conversions took place the converts carried their caste identities with them even as they shed their religious affiliation.

In contradiction to the popular understanding, which is unable to come to terms with how an egalitarian religion condones inequality, it may be pointed out that Christian missionaries have not always and everywhere unequivocally opposed caste, or all its implied distinctions.

Indeed, the Christianity that entered western and southern India in the sixteenth century incorporated within itself a hierarchical vision of society. According to notions extant in Catholic Europe at the time, the clergy, knights, and labourers constituted the three principal orders of the hierarchical social whole. Common worship and the sharing in the Eucharistic body of Christ brought the different groups together but they remained in a relationship of inequality.

It is not surprising, therefore, that status differences expressed in the idiom of caste were maintained among Christians in the Konkan region. In Tamil Nadu, ideas of servitude and respect, purity and impurity continued to inform the relations between castes among converts. Here, as in Goa, Christianity embedded itself in the indigenous socio–ritual order. Analogous to the pattern existing in Hindu temples, a structure of rights, and honours in the celebration of feasts developed around village churches, which articulated local systems of caste rank and precedence (Bayly, 1989; Mosse, 1986).

In Goa, as in areas of Tamil Nadu, rights and honours centred around temple festivals were replaced by those around church feasts, over which the superior social groups retained control. Village churches played a role in articulating and maintaining local patterns of hierarchy. Their rituals and celebrations were occasions for the demonstration of rank. Alternatively, rank could be contested through conflicts over control of church ritual. Upwardly mobile groups in Goa and Tamil Nadu are known to have engaged in such disputes (Robinson, 1994; Mosse, 1986)

It appears that missionaries came to terms with the existence of caste under certain conditions. However, it should be recognized that the attitudes of different denominations diverged, and the position of a particular denomination could itself change. Catholic missionaries, by not discouraging group conversions, quite frequently ended up working within the framework of caste, though many condemned its most exploitative expressions. Protestants seem to have, much more consistently, regarded the caste system as an obstacle to evangelization and attempted to foster individual conversions, but the mass movements of the late nineteenth century caused them to reassess their attitudes (Forrester, 1980).

Converts themselves often resisted any missionary efforts to establish egalitarian relations, the high castes defending the maintenance of status distinctions. Groups that converted in the mass movements may have hoped to gain a measure of freedom from the oppressive structures of caste. Whether due to lack of serious missionary initiative or high-caste opposition within the community, this hope was not fully realized.

In Kerala, the converts from Untouchable groups such as the Pulayas and Parayas are largely landless labourers and work for Syrian Christians and other landed upper castes. There is no question of interdining or intermarriage between the Syrians and the Untouchable converts. In many cases, the latter worship in their own churches. If they worship with the Syrian Christians, they have separate places to sit. In general, they receive less pastoral care and are very poorly represented in positions of power in the church.

In rural Tamil Nadu untouchable converts often remain residentially segregated from the higher castes. Ideas of purity and impurity persist. For instance, the Malaiman Udayan Christians of a North Arcot village do not enter the *cheris* (village residential areas for untouchables) of the Adi Dravidas for fear of being polluted (Tharamangalam, 1996). Again, other caste rankings are also maintained. The relationship between Christian Vellalas and Nadars in Tamil Nadu has been particularly contentious. Neither in Karnataka nor in Andhra Pradesh did Untouchables find significant improvement in their economic or social conditions after conversion (Japhet, 1988). In the north, too, marriage and social intercourse between converts from the high castes and those with outcaste backgrounds appears to have been rare (Webster, 1976).

It seems to be a characteristic of many Indian Christian groups that while there may be considerable variability in the pattern of interaction between the high and middle ranking sections there is a much more radical divide between caste Christians as a whole and converts from amongst Untouchables (D'Costa, 1977; Tharamangalam, 1996). There is difference again in the degree to which ideas and practices of pollution persist. The idea of blood purity maintained by endogamy appears to be quite widespread, though certain other notions of bodily pollution exist to varying degrees.

Practices relating to birth, menstrual, and death pollution have been recorded this century among the Syrian Christians of Kerala, but they are much rarer today. Tamil Nadu Christians, both rural and urban, also appear to have retained such ideas, if with modifications.

Among Madras Protestants, for instance, many women are still reluctant to enter a church or, in particular, to receive communion when they are menstruating (Caplan, 1980). However, they are not segregated during menstruation and do not avoid cooking. Some traces of pollution practices appear to exist among Christians in central India (Sahay, 1986).

A final point needs to be made. Christian missionaries, we have noted, did not have a single attitude towards caste. When they opposed it, they often took up cudgels on behalf of their lower-caste converts. In south India, missionaries were active in fighting for the rights of pariahs and converts to use public paths and to withdraw from providing inferior and degrading services to the high castes. They fought for the right of Nadar women to cover the upper part of their bodies and, both in north and south India. They struggled to establish the rights of Christian converts to use public wells.

Missionary efforts were involved in bringing into operation the Caste Disabilities Removal Act (Act xxi of 1850). Interestingly, such missionary activity also stimulated particular Hindu movements for the reform of the caste system. Again, to counter the spread of Christianity, Hindus found they had to change their attitude towards those expelled from caste due to conversion and to reframe the rules for their re-entry. It was acknowledged that traditional modes of expiation needed to be modified to make them simpler and less painful, thus facilitating, more and more reconversions (Oddie, 1969). Clearly, negotiation with the norms of the wider society entails more than the situation of a Christian community in relation to regional Hinduism. It also implicates the configuration of relationships within these communities themselves.

The drawing of boundaries between Christian groups and their neighbours involved more than the negotiation of differences of faith, such as ideas about kinship and marriage, about gender valuation and inheritance. Missionaries condemned many indigenous socio–cultural practices, seeking to prohibit the converts from maintaining these. In many cases, however, the call of shared regional cultural norms, of the imperatives of a shared universe, shared social and material concerns, shared values of inheritance proved stronger.

Among the matrilineal Khasi, a woman's youngest daughter lived in the ancestral house, was custodian of the property and responsible for the performance of particular rituals. A number of households genealogically related, worshipping common deities and having a common ancestral cult constituted the *ing*. Occasions of birth, marriage, and death were celebrated in the *ing*.

Conversion led to a decline in the *ing*'s religious functions and consequently, to the mother's brother's hold over the household. Paternal authority increased. The church regarded the father as the head of the family: he played certain ritual roles such as leading the daughter to the altar at her wedding and handing over the child for baptism. With conversion came the possibility of a change in the role of the youngest daughter. As she is no longer responsible for the ritual cult, the supervision of the mother's brother over her decreases. While she usually inherits the bulk of property, her siblings can also now be bequeathed a part of the assets. Hence, she is possibly freer to do with hers as she wishes without being called to account (Nongbri, 1980).

Sanctified monogamous marriage is the Christian ideal. Therefore, cohabitation among the Khasi was checked by the missionaries: the couple was suspended from participation in Christian rituals until the marriage rite had been performed (Nongbri, 1980). Similarly, Toda polyandry and Santhal customs of polygyny, divorce, and marriage by purchase of a husband for an unmarried mother were all opposed (Troisi, 1979).

Converted Tamil Nadu Paravas found they had to follow the rules of consanguinity framed by the church to regulate marriages between cousins and other blood relations, which prohibit marriage in the direct line of descent between all ancestors and descendants and in the collateral line up to the third degree of relationship. These rules conflicted with the preferred Parava system of alliance in which a man marries his mother's brother's daughter. However, interestingly, the right of the sister's sons appears to be acknowledged ritually in the course of the marriage ceremonies as the bridegroom is called upon to present them with a part of the dowry he obtains. In turn, perhaps as a sign of acceptance of the marriage, he is presented with a suit of clothes (Bayly, 1989).

In Goa, the Portuguese instituted both the church's rules on consanguineous marriages and the legal right of a daughter to inherit. The first would, for instance, prohibit a man without a natural heir from marrying his daughter to a close kinsman in order to retain property in the patriline. The law giving the daughter inheritance rights also clashed with the indigenous cultural norm of patriliny. Dispensations from church rules of consanguinity may be obtained in certain cases, though compensation in the form of land or money has to be paid.

It is not surprising that Christians, particularly the landed upper castes, often seek such dispensations to protect the fragmentation of property. Again, daughters customarily release their shares in immovable property in favour of their brothers. At marriage, they take from their natal homes a dowry of jewellery and other movable items. Clearly, despite the introduction of new inheritance patterns, the local normative order is abided by. The significance Christians accord to indigenous modes may perhaps be understood against the backdrop of the importance of land as a resource and a source of status, control, and stability in this patrilineal, caste society.

Among most Christian groups, with some variations, celebrations of life-cycle rituals are informed by regional ritual and symbolic codes. In certain areas, indigenous practices of gift-giving, the use of certain ritual materials and melodies, and ideas regarding auspicious and inauspicious times, spaces, and directions enter Christian life-cycle celebrations. In many places, calendrical feasts of the church, though centred around Christian divinities, also draw on patterns and motifs from regional traditions. In Tamil Nadu, for instance, feasts often involve flag-hoisting ceremonies, elaborate processions, and rules of rank and precedence ordering the participation of different castes on the model of Hindu temple festivals (Bayly, 1989; Mosse, 1986).

Christianity also introduced novel dietary habits that sometimes clashed with indigenous food codes. Among tribal communities such as the Santhal, Naga, or Paite, certain Christian flesh-eating habits may not have disagreed with the prevailing custom. In Goa, the eating of pork and beef was imposed during conversion and conflicted sharply with upper-caste norms. Paradoxically, in aligning themselves with the rulers, the converted upper castes took on their dietary habits and re-conceived them, especially the eating of pork which involves too the capacity to purchase it, as marks of superior status.

The case of the Syrian Christians is interesting. Their diet includes beef, pork, and fish yet they are regarded as a high-ranking jati within Kerala society. Moreover, in the past they appear to have acted as pollution-neutralizers in certain contexts. For example, provisions purchased for a Hindu temple could be purified before use by the touch of a Syrian (Fuller, 1976). Christian groups in Tamil Nadu, though, in consonance with prevailing cultural values, regard beef and pork as polluting and unclean and refrain from their consumption (Caplan, 1980).

Clearly, different groups, while drawing on regional traditions and patterns, constituted their identity in unique and complex ways. Processes of continuity and discontinuity are discernible everywhere and appear to be constructed out of several elements. Partly implicated are the relationship of the missionaries to their own culture and to the state and colonial authorities. Implicated too are the converts' relationship to the church or mission, their material and social expectations, their location within the regional socio–cultural order, the nature of their interaction with other regional social groups, and their negotiation with changing socio–political circumstances.

Contemporary Movements

I do not wish to give the impression that group identities remain immutable and unchanging. I will therefore focus, though very briefly, on the radical new ways in which the identity of Christian groups is being reconstituted today in the complex social and political environment. For instance, one may point to the greater association of the different denominations today and their coming together in bodies such as the Church of South India or the Church of North India. Here, however, I focus more on the constitution of the Christian Dalit identity because that is the most visible politically, though other movements and shifts also receive mention.

Disprivileged Christian groups have begun to challenge their position in new and radical ways today. One of the modes is through the construction of the category of 'Dalit' Christians. The term, meaning 'broken' or 'ground down', has been drawn from the Maharashtrian experience for use by and for Christians from Untouchable castes. Bodies such as the Christian Dalit Liberation Movement and the National Coordination Committee for scheduled caste Christians have emerged to promote Dalit struggles against casteism within and outside the church and to demand the extension of the benefits of positive discrimination aimed at the scheduled castes to Dalit Christians.

Dalit Christian movements are backed by a number of church intellectuals and aim to construct a Dalit theology. It is recognized that the upper castes are over-represented at all levels or theological education. The broad endeavour is to reform Indian theology, which had its support and roots among the upper castes, so that it reflects the experiences and concerns of the lowliest. Accordingly, Dalit theology must be a product of Dalits themselves (Prabhakar, 1988).

There are some complexities to be noted here in the constitution of this identity. Though this is the most visible Christian movement today and certainly the most politically focused, it is by no means the only attempt to come to terms with prejudice and inequality. The Liberation Theology movement, millennial Pentecostal cults and movements towards the indigenization of church architecture and ritual are all efforts to de-hierarchize the church or churches and to harmonize their celebrations and rituals with wider cultural patterns.

Discomfort with the dominance of the upper social groups in the church finds its expression among theologians and priests, apart from the disprivileged lay people. Liberation theology and the role played by religion in radical political movements in south America influenced sections of the Catholic order of the Society of Jesus in particular to deliberately opt to serve the poor. While providing formal education remains the Society's primary aim, liberation theologians within the order lay stress on educating the poorest sections of society in order to enable them to find their political voice and thence fight against oppression by the higher castes and classes.

At a different level, one finds in contemporary India the aspiration for equality being articulated through chiliastic movements or shamanistic cults drawing their support principally from disprivileged groups. Millennial Pentecostal movements attract those among Madras Protestants who are socially deprived and, in the modern urban environment, find themselves among the lower classes. Pentecostal groups draw on the power of the Holy Ghost to effect cures and miracles and counteract the influence of malignant spirits (Caplan, 1987). Such groups provide succour and a sense of power through the warding off of evil for those on the margins or at the lower ends of the socio–political and economic orders.

The Christ Ashram in the Goan village of Nuvem was founded by Miguel Colaco, of lower caste and class background. The problems of clients, usually believed to be the result of evil magic, brought to work against them, are dealt with through exorcism, healing, prayer, and penance. Again, it is principally the lowest section, caught in the rapidly changing society and economy of Goa and unable to find anchor or stability, who patronize the Ashram (Newman, 1981).

Another trend within contemporary Catholicism may be mentioned when speaking about change. While a degree of syncretism has always characterized popular Christianity, in recent decades the church has *officially* begun to promote the indigenization of its modes of worship in certain specific respects. Encouraging seating arrangements on the floor in churches, the harmonization of the architecture of new churches with indigenous forms, the *aarti* and the use of ritual items such as garlands or *agarbatti* are some expressions of the shift.

Thus, there are a number of movements within contemporary Indian Christianity, which appears to be characterized by considerable fluidity. It is in a process of transformation and negotiation with a rapidly changing post-colonial society. There is greater diversification as sectarian and charismatic movements draw believers from the Church's fold. Across India, rural and urban communities are witnessing change. It is of substantial sociological relevance, therefore, to analyse the manner in which different groups make sense of the shifts, using ritual and religion in novel and often radical ways, to crystallize and articulate social experience.

The Dalit movement, to return, has two complex aspects. One is the outer political aspect. Various bodies have emerged, as said earlier, coordinating the struggle. In this struggle, the Dalit Christians from all over the country attempt to come together on the basis of shared experiences of inequality and with varying degrees of success, to forge linkages with Dalits from other religious communities drawing, again, on common social and material backgrounds of subjugation. In the process, the motif of religious difference is suppressed. Dalits from other communities, however, are sometimes wary of this association because it might lessen the share of privileges and benefits available to them and, even if this did not happen, their prospects of getting reserved seats in employment might lessen given that Christian Dalits with their greater access to education would supersede them.

Today, the Church as a whole has decided to back the political struggles of the Dalits for reservations. This does not, however, mean that the structures of inequality within the Church or Churches themselves get addressed. Within the different Churches, Dalits wage another struggle. This one brings them in opposition with the upper caste and upper class, largely urban-based élites and in an attempted association with other oppressed groups, notably the tribal Christians.

The internal struggle of the Dalits is aimed at fighting caste/class inequalities within the different Churches and at constructing a Dalit theology. While it is believed that Dalit theology should be produced by Dalits themselves, some elites—theologians and priests—are also involved in this process of redefinition.

Finally, the Liberation Theology movement which has attracted and influenced sections among the priesthood and particularly the Society of Jesus in India is a movement not initiated by the Dalits but seeking to empower them as well as other oppressed sections both within and without the Churches.

So, clearly the different aspects of the Dalit struggle involve the forging of dissimilar identities and alliances in the varying contexts. On the one hand, is the attempt at unity with other scheduled castes, on the other, the striving for association with tribal and oppressed groups within Christianity itself. Dalits are sometimes joined, even led, by higher groups in their political and social struggles. However, their vocalization of a need for a Dalit theology written by *them* simultaneously articulates their continuing sense of remoteness from the élites. Perhaps even greater complexity in the enunciation of identities may be anticipated: if, for instance, women's struggles and the demand for a gender-sensitive theology enter the arena.

References

Bayly, Susan, *Saints, Goddesses and Kings*, Cambridge University Press, Cambridge, 1989.

Caplan, Lionel, 'Caste and Castelessness among South Indian Christians', *Contributions to Indian Sociology*, 14(2), 1980.

——, *Class and Culture in Urban India: Fundamentalism in a Christian Community*, Clarendon Press, Oxford, 1987.

D'Costa, Adelyne, 'Caste Stratification among the Roman Catholics of Goa', *Man in India*, 57(4), 1977.

D'Souza, A.B., 'Popular Christianity: A Case Study among the Catholics of Mangalore', PhD thesis, University of Delhi, 1993.

Forrester, Duncan B., *Caste and Christianity*, Curzon Press Ltd., London and Dublin and Humanities Press Inc., Atlantic Highlands, New Jersey, 1980.

Fuller, C.J., 'Kerala Christians and the Caste System', *Man*, 11, 1976.

Houtart, F. and G. Lemercinier, *Genesis and Institutionalization of the Indian Catholicism*, Université Catholique de Louvain, Louvain, 1981.

Japhet, S., 'Caste Oppression in the Catholic Church', *in* M.E. Prabhakar (ed.), *Towards a Dalit Theology*, ISPCK, Delhi, 1988.

Mosse, C.D.F., Caste, Christianity and Hinduism: A Study of Social Organization and Religion in Rural Ramnad, PhD thesis, University of Oxford, 1986.

——, 'Catholic Saints and the Hindu Village Pantheon in Rural Tamil Nadu, India', *Man*, (n.s.), 29(2), 1994.

Newman, R., 'Faith is All: Emotion and Devotion in a Goan Sect', *Numen*, 28(2), 1981.

Nongbri, Tiplut, 'Religion and Social Change among the Khasi', PhD thesis, University of Delhi, 1980.

Oddie, G.A., 'Protestant Missions, Caste and Social Change in India, 1850–1914', *The Indian Economic and Social History Review*, 6(3), 1969.

Prabhakar, M.E., (ed.), *Towards a Dalit Theology*, ISPCK, Delhi, 1988.

Ram, Kalpana, *Mukkuvar Women*, Zed Books Limited, London and New Jersey, 1991.

Bibliography

Ahmad, Imtiaz (ed.), *Caste and Social Stratification Among Muslims in India*, Manohar, New Delhi, 1978.
——, 'Caste Mobility Movements in North India', *Indian Economic and Social History Review*, VIII, 2, 1971.
Ahmed, Rafiuddin, *The Bengal Muslims: The Quest for Idenitity*, Oxford University Press (OUP), Delhi, 1981.
——, *Understanding Bengal Muslims: Interpretative Essays*, OUP, Delhi, 2001.
Ahmed, Syed Nesar, *Origins of Muslim Consciousness in India: A World System Perspective*, Greenwood Press, New York, 1991.
Alam, Javeed, *India: Living with Modernity*, OUP, New Delhi, 1999.
Allen, D., *Religion and Political Conflict in South Asia*, OUP, New Delhi, 1992.
Aloysius, G., *Nationalism without a Nation in India*, OUP, New Delhi, 1997.
Anderson, Benedict, *Imagined Communities: Reflections on the Origin and Spread of Nationalism*, Verso, London, 1991 (rpt).
Appadorai, Arjun, 'Number in the Colonial Imagination', in C.A. Breckenridge and P. Van der Veer (eds), *Orientalism and Postcolonial Predicament*, University of Pensylvania Press, Philadelphia, 1993.
Aurobindo, Sri, *On Nationalism*, Sri Aurobindo Ashram, Pondichery, 1965.
Austin, Granville, *The Indian Constitution: The Cornerstone of a Nation*, OUP, New Delhi, 1999 (rpt).
Bandyopadhyay, Sekhar, 'From Alienation to Integration: Changes in the Politics of Caste in Bengal, 1937–47', *Indian Economic and Social History Review*, 31 March 1994.
Banerjee, S.N. *A Nation in the Making*, OUP, Bombay, 1925.

Barnett, M.R., *The Politics of Cultural Nationalism in South India*, Princeton University Press, New Jersey, 1976.

Baruah, Sanjib, '"Ethnic" Conflict as State–Society Struggle: The Poetics and Politics of Assamese Micro-nationalism', *Modern Asian Studies*, 28, 3, 1994.

Basu, Sajal, *Regional Movments: Politics of Language, Ethnicity–Identity*, Manohar, New Delhi, 1992.

Basu, Tapan et al., *Khaki Shorts and Saffron Flags: A Critique of the Hindu Right*, Orient Longman, New Delhi, 1993.

Bayly, Chris, 'The Pre-history of Communalism? Religious Conflict in India, 1700–1860', *Modern Asian Studies*, 19, 2, 1985.

Béteille, André, *Society and Politics in India: Essays in a Comparative Perspective*, OUP, New Delhi, 1991, pp. 89–21.

———, *The Backward Classes in Contemporary India*, OUP, New Delhi, 1992 (rpt).

Bhargava, Rajeev, Amiya Kumar Bagchi, and S. Sudarshan (eds), *Multiculturalism, Liberalism and Democracy*, OUP, New Delhi, 1999.

Bhattacharyya Sabyasachi (comp. and ed.), *The Mahatma and the Poet: Letters and Debates Between Gandhi and Tagore*, 1915–41, National Book Trust, New Delhi, 1997.

Bose, Sugata, 'Nation, Reason and Religion: India's Independence in International Perspective, *EPW*, 17 Aug. 1998.

Bose, Sumantra, '"Hindu Nationalism" and the Crisis of the Indian State: A Theoretical Perspective', in Sugata Bose and Ayesha Jalal (eds) *Nationalism, Democracy and Development: State and Politics in India*, OUP, New Delhi, 1997.

Brass, Paul, *Ethnicity and Nationalism: Theory and Comparison*, Sage New Delhi, 1991.

———, *Language, Religion and Politics*, University of California Press, Berkeley, 1974.

Broomfield, John H., *Élite Conflict in a Plural Society*, University of California Press, Berkeley, 1968.

Cascardi, A.J., *The Subject of Modernity*, Cambridge University Press, New York, 1992.

Castells, Manuel, *The Power of Identity*, Basil Blackwell, Oxford, 1997.

Chakrabarty, Bidyut, 'Nationalism and National Identity: An Unresolved Agenda', *Social Science Probings*, March 1994–December 1995.

Chakravarty Papia, *Hindu Response to Nationalist Ferment: Bengal, 1909–1935*, Subaranarekha, Calcutta, 1992.

Chandhoke, Neera, *Beyond Secularism: The Rights of Religious Minorities*, OUP, New Delhi, 1999.

Chatterjee, P.C. (ed.), *Self-Images, Identity and Nationality*, Indian Institute of Advanced Studies, Shimla, 1989.

Chatterjee, Partha, 'The Politics of Appropriation', *Frontier*, 19, 8–10, 1986.
——, 'Agrarian Relations and Communalism in Bengal, 1926–35', in Ranajit Guha (ed.), *Subaltern Studies*, vol. 1, OUP, New Delhi, 1982.
——, 'Bengal: Rise and Growth of a Nationality', *Social Scientist*, 14, 1, 1975.
——, *The Nation and Its Fragments: Colonial and Post-colonial Histories*, OUP, New Delhi, 1994.
Chaube, S.K. 'Tribal Societies and Nation Building in North East India', in B. Pakem (ed.), *Nationality, Ethnicity and Cultural Identity in North East India*, Omsons, Guwahati, 1990.
Cohen, A.P., *The Symbolic Construction of Community*, Tavistock, London, 1985.
Cohn, Bernard S., *An Anthropologist Among the Historians and Other Essays*, OUP, New Delhi, 1990.
——, *Colonialism and its Forms of Knowledge: The Birth in India*, OUP, New Delhi, 1997.
Das, Ujjwalkanti, 'The Bengal Hindu–Muslim Pact', *Bengal Past and Present*, 99, 188 (Jan.–June, 1980).
Das, Veena (ed.), *Mirror of Violence: Communities, Riots and Survivors in South Asia*, OUP, New Delhi, 1990.
Dasgupta, Joytrindra, *Language Conflict and National Development*, University of California Press, Berkeley, 1970.
Datta, Nonica, *Forming an Identity: A Social History of the Jats*, OUP, New Delhi, 1999.
Datta, P.K., *Carving Blocs: Communal Ideology in Early Twentieth Century Bengal*, OUP, New Delhi, 1999.
Devalle, Susana B.C., *Discourses of Ethnicity: Cultures and Protest in Jharkhand*, Sage, New Delhi, 1992.
Dhanagare, D.H., 'Three Constraints of Hinduism', *Seminar*, no. 411, Nov. 1993.
Engineer, Asghar Ali, 'Democracy and Politics of Identity', *EPW*, 28 March 1998.
Freitag, Sandra B., *Collective Action and Community: Public Arenas and the Emergence of Communalism in North India*, University of California Press, Berkeley, 1989.
Gellner, Ernest, *Culture, Identity and Politics*, Cambridge University Press, Cambridge, 1987.
——, *Nation and Nationalism*, Basil Blackwell, Oxford, 1983.
Golwalkar, M.S., *Bunch of Thoughts*, Jagarana Prakashan, Bangalore, 1980 (rpt).
Greenfield, Liah, *Nationalism: Five Roads to Modernity*, Harvard University Press, Cambridge, 1991.
Guha, Amalendu, 'The Indian Nation Question: A Conceptual Frame', *Nationality Question in India: Unity in Diversity, Self-determination, Confederation and Destabilization*, TDSS, Pune, 1987.

Guha, Amalendu, 'Great Nationalism and the Problem of Integration: A Tentative View', *EPW*, Annual Number, Feb. 1979.

——, 'Little Nationalism Turned Chauvinist: Assam's Anti-foreigners' Upsurge, 1979–80, *EPW*, Special issue, 1980.

Gupta, Dipankar, *The Politics of Ethnicity: Sikh Identity in a Comparative Perspective*, OUP, New Delhi, 1996.

——, *Nativism in a Metropolis: The Shiva Sena in Bombay*, Manohar, Delhi, 1982.

Gupta, Partha Sarathi, 'Identity-formation and Nation–States: Some Reflections', *Presidential Address*, 59th session, Patiala, India, 1998.

Habib, Irfan, 'Emergence of Nationalities in India', *Nationality Question in India: Unity in Diversity, Self-Determination, Confederation and Destabilization*, TDSS, Pune, 1987.

Hansen, Thomas Blom, *The Saffron Wave: Democracy and Hindu Nationalism in Modern India*, OUP, Delhi, 1999.

Hardgrave, Robert L., *The Dravidian Movement*, Popular Prakashan, Bombay, 1965.

Hasan, Mushirul, 'Minority Identity and its Discontents: Response and Representation', *EPW*, 19 Feb. 1994.

——, 'Religion and Politics: The Ulama and Khilafat Movement', *EPW*, 16, 20, 1981.

——, *Legacy of a Divided Nation: India's Muslims Since Independence*, OUP, New Delhi, 1997.

Hobsbawm, E. and T. Ranger (eds), *The Invention of Tradition*, Cambridge University Press, Cambridge, 1983.

Inden, Ronald, *Imagining India*, Basil Blackwell, Oxoford, 1990.

Irschick, Eugene P., *Politics and Social Conflict in South India: The non-Brahmin Movement and Tamil Separatism, 1916–29*, OUP, New Delhi, 1997.

Jaffrelot, Christophe, *The Hindu Nationalist Movement in India*, Viking, New Delhi, 1996.

Jalal, Ayesha and Anil Seal, 'Alternative to Partition: Muslim Politics Between the Wars', *Modern Asian Studies*, Cambridge, 15, 3, 1984.

Jalal, Ayesha, 'Exploding Communalism: The Politics of Muslim Identity in South Asia', in Sugata Bose and Ayesha Jalal (eds), *Nationalism, Democracy and Development: State and Politics in India*, OUP, New Delhi, 1997.

——, 'Nation, Reason and Religion: Punjab's Role in the Partition of India', *EPW*, 8–14 Aug. 1998.

Joseph, Sarah, 'Politics of Contemporary Communitarianism', *EPW*, 4 Oct. 1997.

Kanungo, Pralaya Ranjan, *RSS's Tryst with Politics: From Hedgewar to Sudarshan*, Manohar, New Delhi, 2002.

Karat, Prakash, *Language and Nationality Politics in India*, Orient Longman, New Delhi, 1973.

Kaviraj, Sudipta, 'Crisis of the Nation-state in India', *Political Studies*, XLII, Blackwell, Oxford, 1994.

——, 'The Imaginary Institutions of India', in Partha Chatterjee and Gyanendra Pandey (ed.), *Subaltern Studies*, vol. VII, OUP, New Delhi, 1992.

King, Robert D., *Nehru and the Language Politics of India*, OUP, New Delhi, 1997.

Kumar, Ravindar, 'The Past as a Mirror of the Present', in Ravinder Kumar (ed.), *The Making of a Nation: Essays in Indian History and Politics*, Manohar, New Delhi, 1989.

——, 'Class, Community or Nation: Gandhi's Quest for a Popular Consensus in India', *Modern Asian Studies*, 3, 4, 1969.

——, 'India: A "Nation-State" or a "Civilization-State"?, *Occasional Paper on Perspectives in Indian Development*, Nehru Memorial Museum and Library, no. VIII, New Delhi, 1989.

Kymlicka, Will, *Liberalism, Community and Culture*, OUP, Oxford, 1989.

Liddle, Joana and Roma Joshi, *Daughters of Independence: Gender, Caste and Class in India*, Kali for Women, New Delhi, 1986.

Ludden, David (ed.), *Making India Hindu: Religion, Community and the Politics of Democracy in India*, OUP, New Delhi, 1996.

Mahajan, Gurpreet, *Identities and Rights: Aspects of Liberal Democracy in India*, OUP, New Delhi, 1998.

Mahar, Michael J., *The Untouchables in Contemporary India*, University of Arizona Press, Tucson, 1972.

Marriot, MacKim, 'Changing Channels of Cultural Transmission in India', in L.P. Vidharthy (ed.), *Aspects of Religion in Indian Society*, Meenakshi Prakashan, Meerut, 1961.

——, (ed.), *India Through Hindu Categories*, Sage, New Delhi, 1990.

Mawdudi, Abula'la, *Towards Understanding Islam*, The Islamic Foundation, London, 1980.

Menon, Nivedita, 'Women and Citizenship', in Partha Chaterjee (ed.), *Wages of Freedom*, OUP, New Delhi, 1998.

Minault, Gail, *The Khilafat Movement: Religious Symbolism and Political Mobilization in India*, OUP, New Delhi, 1999 (rpt).

Moon, Penderel, *Divide and Quit: An Eyewitness Account of the Partition of India*, OUP, New Delhi, 1998.

Nandy, Ashis, Shikha Trivedy, Shail Mayaram and Achyut Yagnik, *Creating Nationality: The Ramajanmabhumi Movement and Fear of the Self*, OUP, New Delhi, 1995.

——, *The Illegitimacy of Nationalism*, OUP, New Delhi, 1994.

——, *The Intimate Enemy: Loss and Recovery of Self under Colonialism*, OUP, New Delhi, 1983.

Nandy, Ashis, 'The Fantastic India–Pakistan Battle', *Future*, 29.10.1997.

Nayer, Baldev Raj, *Minority Politics in the Punjab*, Princeton University Press, New Jersey, 1966.

Oberoi, Harjot, *The Construction of Religious Boundaries: Culture, Identity, and Diversity in the Sikh Tradition*, OUP, New Delhi, 1994.

Omvedt, Gail, *Dalits and the Democratic Revolution*, Sage, New Delhi, 1994.

Oommen, T.K., 'Citizenship and National Identity: Towards a Feasible Linkage', in T.K. Oomen (ed.), *Citizenship and National Identity: From Colonialism to Globalization*, Sage, New Delhi, 1997.

——, *Pluralism, Equality and Identity: Comparative Studies*, OUP, New Delhi, 2002.

——, 'Foreigners, Refugees and Outsiders in the Indian Context', *Sociological Bulletin*, 31.1.1982

——, 'Religious Pluralism in India: A Sociological Perspective', in R. Singh (ed.), *Christian Perspective on Contemporary Indian Issues*, Institute of Development Education, Madras, 1983.

——, *Citizenship, Nationality and Ethnicity*, Polity Press, Cambridge, 1997.

——, *State and Society in India: Studies in Nation-building*, Sage, New Delhi, 1990.

Owen, Hugh, 'Negotiating the Lucknow Pact', *The Journal of Asian Studies*, XXXI, 3, May 1972.

Pal, Bipin Chandra, *Nationality and Empire*, Yugayati Prakashan, Calcutta, 1916.

Pandey, Gyanendra, 'In Defence of the Fragments: Writing about Hindu–Muslim Riots in India Today', *EPW*, Annual Numbers 11, 12, March 1991.

——, 'In Defence of the Fragments: Writing about Hindu–Muslim Riots in India Today',in Ranajit Guha (ed.), *A Subaltern Studies Reader, 1986–1995*, OUP, New Delhi, 1998.

——, *The Construction of Communalism in Colonial North India*, OUP, New Delhi, 1998.

Parekh, Bhikhu, 'Ethnocentricity of the Nationalist Discourse', *Nations and Nationalism*,1.1.1995.

——, 'National Identity in a Multicultural Society', in Mohammad Anwar and Ranjit Sanohi (eds), *From Legislative to Imagination*, Macmillan, London, 1999.

——, 'The Concept of National Identity', *New Community*, Oxford, 21.2.1995.

——, 'Nationalism in a Comparative Perspective', *Politisches Denken Jahrbuch*, Verlag J.B. Metzler, Stuttgart, Weimer, 1994.

Rao, B. Shiva, *The Framing of India's Constitution*, vol. II, Select Documents, IIPA, New Delhi, 1967.

Raz, Joseph, 'Multiculturalism: A Liberal Perspective', *Dissent*, Winter, 1994.

Roy, M.N., *India in Transition*, Nachiketa Publications, Bombay, 1971.

Saiyid, M.H., *Muhammad Ali Jinnah: A Political Study*, Ashraf, Lahore, 1953.

Sarkar, Sumit, 'The Anti-secular Critique of Hindutva: Problems of a Shared Discursive Space', *Germinal*, vol. 1, 1994.

———, 'The Fascism of the Sangh Parivar', *EPW*, 30 Jan. 1993.

———, *Writing Social History*, OUP, New Delhi, 1997.

Sarkar, Tanika, 'Pragmatics of the Hindu Right: Politics of Women's Organizations', *EPW*, 31 July 1999.

———, 'The Women as Communal Subject: Rashtrasevika Samiti and Ram Janmabhoomi Movement', *EPW*, 31 Aug. 1991.

Sathyamurthy, T.V. (ed.), *State and Nation in the Context of Social Change*, vol. 1, OUP, New Delhi, 1994.

Savarkar, V.D., *Hindu Rashtra Darshan*, Veer Savarkar Prakashan, Bombay, 1992.

———, *Who is a Hindu? Hindutva*, S.P. Gokhale, Poona, 1949.

Schermerhorn, R.A., *Ethnic Plurality in India*, Arizona University Press, Tuscon, 1978.

Seal, Anil, *The Emergence of Indian Nationalism: Competition and collaboration in the Later Nineteenth Century*, Cambridge University Press, Cambridge 1968.

Sen, Amartya, 'India's Pluralism', *India International Quarterly*, 20.3.1993.

———, *Reasons Before Identity*, OUP, New Delhi, 1999.

Sheth, D.L. and Gurpreet Mahajan, *Minority-Identities and the Nation State*, OUP, New Delhi, 1999.

Smith, Anthony, *National Identity*, University of Nevada Press, Las Vegas, 1991.

Srivastava, Sushil, 'Constructing the Hindu Identity: European Moral and Intellectual Adventurism in 18th Century India', *EPW*, 1997.

Sunder, Nandini, 'The Indian Census, Identity and Inequality', in Ramachandra Guha and Jonathan P. Parry, *Institutions and Inequalities: Essays in Honour of André Béteille*, OUP, New Delhi, 1999.

Tagore, Rabindranath, *Nationalism*, Rupa, Delhi, 1994 (rpt of collection, originally published in 1917).

Tamir, Yael, 'Enigma of Nationalism'. *World Politics*, vol. 47, no. 3, April 1995.

Taylor, Charles, 'the Dynamics of Democratic Exclusion', *Journal of Democracy*, vol. 9, 4 Oct. 1998.

———, *The Ethics of Authenticity*, Harvard University Press, Cambridge, 1991.

Thapar, Romila, 'Imagined Religious Communities? Ancient History and the Modern Search for a Hindu Identity', *Modern Asian Studies*, 23.2.1989.

———, 'The Tyranny of Labels', Zakir Hussain Memorial Lecture, Nov. 1996.

The Kelkar Commission Report, 1955.

The Mandal Commission Report, 1955.

The Report of the All Parties Conference, All India Congress Committee, Allahabad, 1928.

The Report of the Backward Classes Commission, (second part), vol. III to IV Government of India, 1980.

Vanaik, Achin, *Communalism Contested: Religion, Modernity and the Secularization*, Vistaar Publications, New Delhi, 1997.

——, *The Painful Transition: Bourgeois Democracy in India*, Verso, London, 1990.

Vivekananda, Swami, *State, Society and Socialism*, Advaita Ashrama, Calcutta, 1995 (rpt).

Weiner, Myron, *Sons of the Soil: Migration and Ethnic Conflict in India*, OUP, New Delhi, 1988.

Zaidi, A.M. and S.G. Zaidi (eds), *The Encyclopedia of the Indian National Congress*, vol. 12.

Zavos John, 'Searching for Hindu Nationalism in Modern Indian History: Analysis of Some Early Ideological Developments', *EPW*, 7 Aug. 1999.

——, *The Emergence of Hindu Nationalism in India*, OUP, Delhi, 2000.

Index

Notes on Contributors

Bidyut Chakrabarty is Professor in Political Science, University of Delhi, Delhi, India.

Bhikhu Parekh is member of the House of Lords, UK and Millennium Professor, London School of Economics, University of London, UK.

André Béteille is formerly Professor in Sociology, University of Delhi, Delhi, India.

A.R. Kamat is formerly Professor in Economics, Gokhale Institute of Politics, Pune, India.

Kumkum Sangari is Reader in English, I.P. College, University of Delhi, Delhi, India.

Sekhar Bandyopadhyay is Senior Lecturer, Department of History, Victoria University, Wellington, New Zealand.

T.K. Oommen is Professor in Sociology, School of Social Sciences, Jawaharlal Nehru University, Delhi, India.

Gail Omvedt is Senior Fellow, Nehru Memorial Museum and Library, Delhi, India.

Ravinder Kaur is Professor in Sociology, Indian Institute of Technology, Delhi, India.

Rowena Robinson is Associate Professor in Sociology, Indian Institute of Technology, Mumbai, India.